THE CHINESE CINEMA BOOK

THE CHINESE CINEMA BOOK

Edited by Song Hwee Lim and Julian Ward

A BFI book published by Palgrave Macmillan

First published in 2011 by
PALGRAVE MACMILLAN

on behalf of the

BRITISH FILM INSTITUTE
21 Stephen Street, London W1T 1LN
www.bfi.org.uk

There's more to discover about film and television through the BFI. Our world-renowned archive, cinemas, festivals, films, publications and learning resources are here to inspire you.

Palgrave Macmillan in the UK is an imprint of Macmillan Publishers Limited, registered in England, company number 785998, of 4 Crinan Street, London N1 9XW. Palgrave® and Macmillan® are registered trademarks in the United States, the United Kingdom, Europe and other countries.

Cover design: couch
Cover image: *Still Life* (Jia Zhangke, 2006), © Xstream Pictures Ltd
Text design: couch

Set by Cambrian Typesetters, Camberley, Surrey
Printed in China

This book is printed on paper suitable for recycling and made from fully managed and sustained forest sources. Logging, pulping and manufacturing processes are expected to conform to the environmental regulations of the country of origin.

British Library Cataloguing-in-Publication Data
A catalogue record for this book is available from the British Library
A catalog record for this book is available from the Library of Congress

ISBN 978–1–84457–344–8 (pbk)
ISBN 978–1–84457–345–5 (hbk)

Contents

Acknowledgments

The editors would like to thank Chris Berry and Sheldon Lu for their early support of this project; Rebecca Barden, Joy Tucker and Sophia Contento at BFI Publishing and Palgrave Macmillan for their guidance; the Confucius Institute for Scotland in the University of Edinburgh and its director, Professor Natascha Gentz, for a grant towards the preparation of the Chinese names, Chinese titles and the index, and Zou Yijie for compiling them; Louise Williams and Wan-Jui Wang for their contribution to the bibliography of book-length studies of Chinese cinemas in the English language, earlier versions of which have been published in the *Journal of Chinese Cinemas* (issues 1.1, 2.3, 3.3, 4.1 and 5.1), and Intellect Books for permission to reprint them. Gina Marchetti thanks Fanny Chan for her help with the Chinese glossary.

Notes on Contributors

CHRIS BERRY is Professor of Film and Television Studies at Goldsmiths, University of London. Primary publications include: (with Mary Farquhar) *Cinema and the National: China on Screen* (2006); *Postsocialist Cinema in Post-Mao China: The Cultural Revolution after the Cultural Revolution* (2004); (edited with Lu Xinyu and Lisa Rofel), *The New Chinese Documentary Film Movement: For the Public Record* (2010); (edited with Nicola Liscutin and Jonathan D. Mackintosh), *Cultural Studies and Cultural Industries in Northeast Asia: What a Difference a Region Makes* (2009); (edited with Ying Zhu) *TV China* (2008); and (editor) *Chinese Films in Focus II* (2008).

YOMI BRAESTER is Professor of Comparative Literature and Cinema Studies at the University of Washington in Seattle. He is the author of *Witness against History: Literature, Film and Public Discourse in Twentieth-Century China* (2003) and *Painting the City Red: Chinese Cinema and the Urban Contract* (2010).

KENNETH CHAN is Assistant Professor of Film Studies at the University of Northern Colorado. His book *Remade in Hollywood: The Global Chinese Presence in Transnational Cinemas* was published in 2009. Chan's essays have also appeared in scholarly journals such as *Cinema Journal*, *Tulsa Studies in Women's Literature*, *Discourse* and *Camera Obscura*. He is also a member of the editorial board of the *Journal of Chinese Cinemas* and volunteers as the chair of the International Advisory Board of the Asian Film Archive, Singapore.

REY CHOW is Anne Firor Scott Professor of Literature at Duke University. Since her years as a graduate student at Stanford University, she has specialised in the making of cultural forms such as literature and film, and in the discursive encounters among modernity, sexuality, postcoloniality and ethnicity. Her book, *Primitive Passions* (1995) (on contemporary Chinese cinema) was awarded the James Russell Lowell Prize by the Modern Language Association. Before Duke, Chow was Andrew W. Mellon Professor of the Humanities at Brown University. Her current work includes a co-edited special issue, 'The Sense of Sound', for the journal *differences* (forthcoming in 2011–12), and an essay collection in progress, *Entanglements: or, Transmedial Thinking about Capture*.

ANNE CIECKO is an Associate Professor of international cinema in the Department of Communication at the University of Massachusetts-Amherst, editor of *Contemporary Asian Cinema: Popular Culture in a Global Frame* (2006) and author of numerous articles on Asian and Asian diasporic cinema in journals and anthologies, including *Asian Cinema*, *Asian Journal of Communication*, *Cinema Journal*, *Cultural Studies in China* (2005), *Fandom: Identities and Communities in a Mediated World* (2007), *Global Currents: Media and Technology Now* (2004), *Jump Cut*, *Postscript*, *Tamkang Review* and *Transnational Chinese Cinemas* (1997), among others.

GUO-JUIN HONG is Andrew W. Mellon Assistant Professor of Chinese Culture in the Department of Asian and Middle Eastern Studies at Duke University. Hong's forthcoming book, *Taiwan Cinema: A Contested*

Nation on Screen (2011), is the first full-length study of Taiwan cinema in the English language that covers its entire history since the colonial period. Hong's published articles cover topics on 1930s Shanghai cinema, New Taiwan Cinema, documentary film and the queer movement. His essay on colonial modernity in 1930s Shanghai received an Honourable Mention for the 2009 Katherine Kovacs Essay Awards by the Society for Cinema and Media Studies. Hong teaches courses on Chinese-language cinemas, film historiography, melodrama, documentary and visual culture.

XUELEI HUANG is a post-doctoral research fellow at Academia Sinica in Taiwan. She received her PhD from Heidelberg University in 2009. She is currently working on a book project with the working title *Imag(in)ing the Isms: Towards a Sociological Look at the Mingxing (Star) Motion Picture Company, 1922–1938*. Her essays on early Chinese film culture and print culture have appeared in academic journals such as *Modern Chinese Literature and Culture*, among others.

LEON HUNT is a Senior Lecturer in Screen Media at Brunel University. He is the author of *British Low Culture: From Safari Suits to Sexploitation, Kung Fu Cult Masters: From Bruce Lee to Crouching Tiger* (1998, recently translated by Peking University Press) and the BFI TV Classics monograph on *The League of Gentlemen* (2008), and co-editor of *East Asian Cinemas: Exploring Transnational Connections on Film* (2008). He is currently writing a book about cult British TV comedy and co-editing a book on the undead.

WENDY LARSON is Professor of East Asian Languages and Literatures at the University of Oregon, specialising in modern Chinese literature and film. Her most recent monograph is *From Ah Q to Lei Feng: Freud and Revolutionary Spirit in 20th Century China* (2009). Her present research is on national culture on the global stage, with a focus on twentieth- and twenty-first-century China.

VIVIAN P. Y. LEE is Assistant Professor in the Department of Chinese, Translation and Linguistics, City University of Hong Kong. Her work on Chinese cinemas has appeared in the *Journal of Chinese Cinemas, Scope, Asian Cinema* and *Modern Chinese Literature and Culture*. She is the author of *Hong Kong Cinema Since*

1997: The Post-nostalgic Imagination (2009). Her edited volume, *East Asian Cinemas: Regional Flows and Global Transformations*, will be published by Palgrave Macmillan in April 2011.

SONG HWEE LIM is Senior Lecturer in Film Studies at the University of Exeter, UK. He is the author of *Celluloid Comrades: Representations of Male Homosexuality in Contemporary Chinese Cinemas* (2006), co-editor of *Remapping World Cinema: Identity, Culture and Politics in Film* (2006) and founding editor of the *Journal of Chinese Cinemas*. He is currently working on a book project entitled *Tsai Ming-liang and a Cinema of Slowness*.

TONGLIN LU is Chair Professor at Shanghai Jiaotong University and Professor at the University of Montreal. She teaches contemporary Chinese culture and cultural theory. Author of *Confronting Modernity: Chinese Cinemas in Taiwan and Mainland China* (2001), she is in the process of publishing special issues on the 'Chinese Perspective on Zizek' in *positions: East Asian Cultural Critique* (2011) and on 'Transnational Asian Cinema' in *China Review* (2010), while completing a manuscript on Chinese independent cinema.

JASON MCGRATH is Associate Professor of Chinese film and literature at the University of Minnesota – Twin Cities. He is the author of *Postsocialist Modernity: Chinese Cinema, Literature, and Criticism in the Market Age* (2008). His essays on Chinese film also have appeared in journals such as *Modern Chinese Literature and Culture* and *The Opera Quarterly*, as well anthologies including *Chinese Films in Focus* (2003, 2008), *The Urban Generation* (2007) and *China's Literary and Cultural Scenes at the Turn of the 21st Century* (2008).

GINA MARCHETTI teaches in the Department of Comparative Literature, School of Humanities, at the University of Hong Kong. Her books include *Romance and the 'Yellow Peril': Race, Sex and Discursive Strategies in Hollywood Fiction* (1993), *Andrew Lau and Alan Mak's INFERNAL AFFAIRS – The Trilogy* (2007) and *From Tian'anmen to Times Square: Transnational China and the Chinese Diaspora on Global Screens* (2006), as well as other edited volumes.

LAIKWAN PANG is Professor in the Department of Cultural and Religious Studies at the Chinese University of Hong Kong. She is the author of *Building a*

New China in Cinema: The Chinese Left-wing Cinema Movement, 1932–37 (2002), Cultural Control and Globalization in Asia: Copyright, Piracy, and Cinema (2006), as well as The Distorting Mirror: Visual Modernity in China (2007). Her latest book Creativity and Its Discontents: China's Creative Industries and International Property Rights Offenses is forthcoming at Duke University Press.

PAUL G. PICKOWICZ is Distinguished Professor of History and Chinese Studies at the University of California, San Diego, and inaugural holder of the UC San Diego Endowed Chair in Modern Chinese History. His main interest is the social and cultural history of twentieth-century China. His film-related book projects include New Chinese Cinemas (1994) and From Underground to Independent (2006). Other book projects include Marxist Literary Thought in China (1981), Chinese Village, Socialist State (1991), Revolution, Resistance and Reform in Village China (2005), The Chinese Cultural Revolution as History (2006) and Dilemmas of Victory: The Early Years of the PRC (2007). A new volume, China on the Margins, was published in 2010.

STEPHEN TEO is Associate Professor in the Wee Kim Wee School of Communication and Information, Nanyang Technological University, Singapore. Teo is a leading scholar of Hong Kong cinema and is now focusing on Chinese and other Asian cinemas in his research. He is the author of Hong Kong Cinema: The Extra Dimensions (1997), Wong Kar-wai (2005), King Hu's A Touch of Zen (2007), Director in Action: Johnnie To and the Hong Kong Action Film (2007) and Chinese Martial Arts Cinema: The Wuxia Tradition (2009). His next book will be The Asian Cinema Experience.

JAMES UDDEN is Associate Professor of Film Studies at Gettysburg College in Pennsylvania. He has published widely on Asian cinema in various publications, and has recently published the first book-length manscript on the Taiwanese film director, Hou Hsiao-hsien, entitled, No Man an Island: The

Cinema of Hou Hsiao-hsien (2009). He has also published chapters in anthologies, The Cinema of Small Nations (2007) and Cinema Taiwan: Politics, Popularity and State of the Arts (2007).

YIMAN WANG is Assistant Professor of Film and Digital Media at UC – Santa Cruz. She is completing a book on cross-Pacific film remakes. Her work on film remakes and adaptation, border-crossing stars, Chinese cinema and DV documentaries has appeared in Quarterly Review of Film and Video, Film Quarterly, Camera Obscura, Journal of Film and Video, Literature/Film Quarterly, positions: east asia cultures critique, Journal of Chinese Cinemas, Chinese Films in Focus (2003, 2008) and Idols of Modernity: Movie Stars of the 1920s (2010).

JULIAN WARD is Senior Lecturer in Chinese Studies attached to the Asian Studies department of the University of Edinburgh. He is Associate Editor of the Journal of Chinese Cinemas and has written articles on the representation in film in different eras of Communist China of the Sino-Japanese War. He is the author of Xu Xiake (1587–1641): The Art of Travel Writing (2000), a study of China's foremost travel writer of the imperial period.

ZHIWEI XIAO is Associate Professor of history at California State University, San Marcos. His research focuses on Chinese film history and he has published numerous articles on topics concerning film censorship, movie theatre etiquette reform and Hollywood in China.

YINGJIN ZHANG is Professor of Chinese and Comparative Literature at University of California, San Diego. His English books include The City in Modern Chinese Literature and Film (1996), Encyclopedia of Chinese Film (1998), China in a Polycentric World (1998), Cinema and Urban Culture in Shanghai (1999), Screening China (2002), Chinese National Cinema (2004), From Underground to Independent (2006), Cinema, Space, and Polylocality in a Globalizing China (2010) and Chinese Film Stars (2010).

Introduction

The Coming of Age of Chinese Cinema Studies

Song Hwee Lim and Julian Ward

Chinese Cinema Studies: Twenty Years On

It was in 1991 that the British Film Institute published its first collected essays on Chinese film, *Perspectives on Chinese Cinema*.[1] Planning the volume before 1989, the editor, Chris Berry, saw the book as 'marking, indeed celebrating, the emergence both of Chinese cinema on the international film scene and of Chinese film studies within academia'.[2] Writing the introduction on the eve of the first anniversary of the Tiananmen massacre, Berry noted that his earlier celebratory mood now seemed 'sadly ironic' and wondered 'what effects the current political freeze is having on film production'.[3] How times have changed or, at least, moved on. Twenty years later, with the publication of this volume, we can say with confidence that the state of Chinese cinema on the international film scene and of Chinese film studies within academia has moved from emergence towards establishment, and that Chinese films and Chinese film studies are increasingly located within or moving into the mainstream of international film culture and of Anglophone academia. What remains ironic, though, is the unexpected turn of politics and its intersection with film-making. To take an example: if the Chinese director Zhang Yimou suffered political freezing in the aftermath of the Tiananmen incident (his various films being banned or censored in the 1990s), he has also (been) transformed, in the new millennium, into the darling of the Chinese Communist Party (CCP), charged with making what was, at the time, the most expensive Chinese film ever made (*Curse of the Golden Flower*, 2006) and with staging the most extravagant Olympics Games opening ceremony in 2008. As the 'footprints' of the fireworks made their way from the stadium and across central Beijing to arrive at Tiananmen Square (as it turned out, the 'footprints' we saw on 'live' television were computer generated images rather than real fireworks in another CCP attempt at 'whitewashing'),[4] the spectre of the Tiananmen massacre remained a shadow lurking beneath the spectacle orchestrated by the Fifth Generation director previously famed for his allegorical critique, through gender representation, of the Chinese patriarchy in all its guises.[5]

Some form of political deep freezing on film production no doubt still exists in the People's Republic of China (PRC), but what we witnessed in the 'footprints' of 2008 was also the nimbleness of a beast that, with the thaw of time, defrosted a former dissenting film-maker so that he now happily bathes himself in the glory of the state. As China sails full steam into global capitalism in the twenty-first century, as film-makers who were once consigned to the margin reposition themselves in the mainstream while a new generation occupies the margin, the shadow that politics casts on film-making, in the PRC at least, will not disappear altogether, but it also perhaps will not be as long and dark as before. More importantly, if politics was the premise of most Chinese-language films (including those from Taiwan, Hong Kong and the Chinese diaspora) and of a substantial proportion of scholarship on Chinese cinema in the 1990s, it arguably does not exert the same dominance in the new millennium as a more diverse range of concerns and interests compete to usher in a more pluralistic outlook on Chinese cinema and Chinese film studies.

The blossoming of Chinese cinema studies is evident on many fronts. In terms of publication, over a hundred book-length studies on Chinese cinema have appeared between 1991 and 2010,[6] and the field of Chinese cinema studies even has, since 2007, its own dedicated journal, the *Journal of Chinese Cinemas*, to boot. There are also numerous publications in the forms of special issues and articles in academic journals, chapters in edited volumes on East Asian cinema, etc. Whereas in 1985 'scholars of Chinese cinema working outside Chinese societies could have met comfortably in the average living room',[7] panels on Chinese cinema now regularly feature in annual meetings of major scholarly organisations (for example, Association for Asian Studies, Society for Cinema and Media Studies), and dedicated workshops and conferences have been organised across many parts of the world. Moreover, not only is there a much greater interaction between scholars working within and outside Chinese societies, many scholars of Chinese cinema based in Anglophone academia now hail from these Chinese societies. Finally, in many Anglophone universities it has become equally legitimate to research on Chinese cinema as on any other academic subject, whether in the disciplines of Chinese/East Asian studies or film/media studies. All of these developments clearly demonstrate that not only is there a demand for publications on Chinese cinema but also that the state of research activities in the field is growing from strength to strength.

Twenty years on, *The Chinese Cinema Book* aims to provide a critical introduction to the study of Chinese cinema, covering historically from the birth of cinema to the present day and geographically from China, Taiwan and Hong Kong to the Chinese diaspora. By adopting a more thematic approach to each historical period rather than a general one that attempts to cover all grounds (from production and socio-cultural contexts to textual analysis), and by going beyond a chronological account and examining a range of topics from stars and genres to mainstream cinema and independent film-making, this volume aims to achieve a sharper focus and to grant more space to key issues that deserve dedicated space in their own right rather than being subsumed under a single historical narrative. It is therefore unique in providing an overview of the 'state of the field' from multiple angles: methodological, thematic and geographical.

Rewriting Film Historiography and Moving Beyond the National

For those who write about Chinese film, the major topics of debate, such as the classification of films into such categories as socialist or nationalist, soft or hard, independent or mainstream, may persist to the present day. Research on these topics has benefited from the enormous rise in the number of films available and the greater access to archival material. The conclusions reached by earlier generations of scholars may not always be rejected, but a more nuanced picture is now possible.

The history of Chinese cinema can be roughly divided into three periods: the start of the twentieth century to the end of World War II; the Cold War period; and since the New Waves from the early 1980s, with each region of China, Taiwan and Hong Kong experiencing varying (sometimes totally distinct) forms of developments in genres, production and exhibition. Each of these periods was punctuated by a succession of wars and revolutions, during which film-makers participated in a wide range of movements, whether voluntarily, in the case of the League of Left Wing Artists in the 1930s or the various New Waves of the 1980s, or under duress, in the case of the Anti-Rightist campaign (1957–8) or the Cultural Revolution (1966–76). Given this tumultuous background, the resourcefulness of individuals working under the most difficult conditions was remarkable.

While the historical chapters from Part Two to Part Four in this book place discrete physical locations, both within and outside China, in a clearly defined historical timeframe, this is not to lose sight of the fact that Chinese film-makers were not operating in a vacuum. This is abundantly clear from the early years of the twentieth century, when, as Xuelei Huang and Zhiwei Xiao note, China's weakness ensured that the finance and expertise required for the production of films could be provided only by westerners. Indeed, as Laikwan Pang's chapter shows, it was not until the 1930s that the first great wave of Chinese films and Chinese stars appeared in the cosmopolitan city of Shanghai. Following the arrival of the Japanese in the late 1930s, the film industry fragmented, the talent dispersing to locations in and outside the country, a complex process outlined by Yiman Wang. In the long run, this process resulted in a diversification and strengthening of Chinese film: Paul G. Pickowicz picks up the thread to tell the story of the enduring cinematic masterpieces produced in the midst of the devastating civil war that engulfed China shortly after the Japanese surrender. With many of those whose lives had been disrupted choosing not to return to Shanghai after 1949, the narrative then necessarily divides to cover the very different types of films that developed in the three main regions of Chinese film-making. Julian Ward catalogues the struggles of the film-makers to accommodate the demands of the new Communist government in the PRC. At the same time, the political and social importance of the Chinese language assumed centre stage outside the PRC: Guo-Juin Hong shows how the Nationalist Party in Taiwan supported the production of so-called Healthy Realism films in Mandarin, while Stephen Teo traces the first steps of the production in Hong Kong of Cantonese-language films, which attracted audiences across South-East Asia.

Political insecurity and instability became the norm in the mid-1970s following the deaths of Mao Zedong and Chiang Kai-shek, the leading figures of the old order, and there was great uncertainty surrounding the return of Hong Kong to Chinese rule. The end of the old era also paved the way for new forms of cinema to emerge. Wendy Larson looks at the crucial early stages of the Fifth Generation films in China, when a younger generation, allowed access to foreign films and anxious to move away from the limited parameters of Socialist Realism, began to stretch the boundaries of political acceptability. At the same time as these directors were being fêted at international festivals, New Wave films from Taiwan and Hong Kong were similarly garnering global attention and festival awards. Tonglin Lu and Vivian P. Y. Lee offer critical appraisals of, respectively, the Taiwan New Cinema and the Hong Kong New Wave, as well as of their legacies. Back in the PRC, the films made by Chen Kaige, Zhang Yimou and Tian Zhuangzhuang attracted domestic controversy for allegedly presenting a false image of a pre-Communist China designed to appeal to foreigners. Before long the Sixth Generation sprung up, producing films which moved away from the representation of the nation's past to show the realities of everyday life in a rapidly changing China. This is picked up in a chapter in Part Five where Jason McGrath notes that, for the first time in Communist China, films were being made outside the state system and the locus shifted from the rural to the urban.

While the categorisations of Fifth and Sixth Generations, urban or independent, were initially helpful, they soon became reductive at best or simply irrelevant, partly as the styles became formulaic and partly as film-makers had to adjust to rapidly changing economic and social realities. Many of the Fifth Generation directors, for example, responded to the huge changes affecting China by moving ever closer to the mainstream. Yomi Braester (in Part Five) looks at the work of Feng Xiaogang, who successfully made the transition from TV to cinema, establishing his reputation as director of New Year films. These films are able not only to appeal to a popular audience but also, in the case of *Aftershock* (2010), about the devastating Tangshan earthquake of 1976, to receive a favourable response from international critics.

While this book is partly organised by historical periods and geographical regions, it is clear that the production and, especially, consumption of films are rarely confined to the boundary of a single nation. This is particularly true in the case of Chinese cinema in that, barring periods of geopolitical isolation, there has always been cross-fertilisation of cast and crew among the three regions of film production. (Both the PRC independent film-making and mainstream cinema discussed above have benefited from foreign investment and co-production.) The transnational nature of Chinese cinema is most salient when we look at stars, auteurs and genres, the focus of Part Five of the book. Indeed, this transnationalism is not restricted to flows among the Chinese regions but stretches further afield to South-East Asia and the western world. One of the earliest fascinations that Chinese cinema held for a global audience was the genre of martial arts films, a subject of the chapter by Leon Hunt focusing on three pairs of martial arts stars from the 1970s to the present day: the global stars Bruce Lee and Jackie Chan, the regional favourites Wang Yu and Fu Sheng, and new kids on the block Jet Li and Zhang Ziyi. Meanwhile, another related genre, *wuxia* (swordplay film), has been given a new lease of life thanks to the phenomenal success of Ang Lee's *Crouching Tiger, Hidden Dragon* (2000). Not only has this film reinvigorated the genre, leading Fifth Generation directors like Zhang Yimou and Chen Kaige to jump on the bandwagon, its box-office breaking reception in the United States has also meant that Hollywood is now a major player in the remaking of this genre, as Kenneth Chan's chapter demonstrates.

Chinese cinema, therefore, is known not only as a collective of distinct national cinemas that address local historical and political concerns but also for its transnational stars and genres. More recently, it has been the turn of Chinese auteurs to become the centre of global cinematic attention. Following the success of various New Wave films at numerous international film festivals since the 1980s, figures such as Hou Hsiao-hsien, Edward Yang and Wong Kar-wai have become undisputed masters of their craft to gain their rightful place in the pantheon of world cinema auteurs. They are a hard act to follow, though second generation auteurs have begun to break through and are currently celebrated around the world. James Udden delineates the challenges facing some of these auteurs, including Tsai Ming-liang, Jia Zhangke and Fruit Chan, as they stand on the shoulders of giants. Finally, with a proliferation of private film clubs, easy access to pirate CDs and online downloading, viewing patterns have changed beyond recognition in the age of digital technology. The breakdown of boundaries among media platforms corresponds to a transmedia phenomenon in Chinese cinema as film stars are often also pop stars, and their celebrity status is now mediated on multiple platforms by their fans. The notion of nationhood is becoming increasingly irrelevant as the virtual world of the World Wide Web is where stars meet fans and where reputations are made or broken since scandals can immediately turn viral, as Anne Ciecko's study shows.

Last but not least, the transnational character of Chinese cinema is not only reflected in its mode of production, circulation of cast and crew, travelling of genres and auteurs, but is also important for issues covered in Part One of this volume. Partly owing to the historical fact that there have existed, for most of the twentieth century, three Chinese polities and a global diaspora going back many generations, the meaning of Chineseness has always been a contested one and to speak of Chinese cinema in the singular, as we have done in this book for the sake of consistency in style, can be contentious.[8] The three chapters by Chris Berry, Yingjin Zhang and Song Hwee Lim engage with the problematic of transnationalism in different ways, from the conceptual and historical to the ideological and political, while Gina Marchetti grants cinemas of the Chinese diaspora their due attention. As the title of Part One indicates, the territories, trajectories and historiographies traversed by Chinese cinema are multiple and flexible (to recall Aihwa Ong's argument about flexible citizenship),[9] and it is in the spirit of this 'liquidity of being', as Rey Chow so elegantly ruminates in her Afterword, that we hope this volume will contribute to a polycentric and multifaceted understanding of Chinese cinema.

Use of This Book

This book does not pretend to offer a comprehensive coverage of Chinese cinema throughout its long and complicated history and multifarious manifestations. While it strives to give space to previously neglected topics of study, it also aims to strike a balance so that films mentioned in these critical reflections on issues and contexts are either available for research or else fairly easily accessible for viewing pleasure. To this aim this volume can be used in conjunction with another BFI book, *Chinese Film in Focus II* (ed. Chris Berry, 2008). They complement each other well as this volume provides the contexts for the examination of specific case studies in the other book. We have thus, at the end of each chapter in this volume, cross-referenced relevant chapters from *Chinese Film in Focus II* as further reading items so readers can follow up on detailed analyses of related films if they wish.

Notes

1. The 1991 BFI volume was marked as the second, expanded edition on the first, published in 1985 by Cornell East Asian Papers. We take the BFI version as the starting point of *major* English-language publications on Chinese cinema because the Cornell version did not receive as wide a circulation and had a narrower coverage.
2. Chris Berry, 'Introduction', in Chris Berry (ed.), *Perspectives of Chinese Cinema* (London: BFI, 1991), pp. 1–5 (1).
3. Ibid.
4. The other infamous 'whitewashing' incident of the opening ceremony was the lip-synching performance of a song by a young girl who was standing in for the voice of the singer whose face was regarded as not pretty enough to be paraded in public under the glare of global media attention.
5. This observation is partly indebted to Ackbar Abbas, who made a connection between the Tiananmen incident and the opening ceremony of the Olympic Games in his talk, on 4 June 2010, at a conference on 'Spectacle and the City' held at the University of Amsterdam.

6. See Appendix 1 at the end of this book for a list of publications.

7. Berry, 'Introduction', p. 1.

8. For a case for a plural notion of 'Chinese cinemas', see Song Hwee Lim, 'A New Beginning: Possible Directions in Chinese Cinemas Studies', *Journal of Chinese Cinemas* vol. 1 no. 1 (2007), pp. 3–8.

9. Aihwa Ong, *Flexible Citizenship: The Cultural Logics of Transnationality* (Durham and London: Duke University Press, 1999).

PART ONE

Territories, Trajectories, Historiographies

1 Transnational Chinese Cinema Studies

Chris Berry

This chapter examines a doubled object. The term, 'transnational Chinese cinema studies', designates both a type of cinema and a field of study. The watershed moment in the emergence of the field was the publication in 1997 of Sheldon Hsiao-peng Lu's anthology, *Transnational Chinese Cinemas*.[1] Almost overnight, it went from being relatively rarely used to becoming perhaps the most commonly used term in Chinese cinema studies as a whole. Despite this wide usage, there has been limited discussion of what 'transnational Chinese cinema' means. As a result, it has been used not only widely but also loosely and sometimes in ways that are contradictory. In these circumstances, some have even called for the abandonment of the term altogether.

This chapter traces some of the main usages and key intellectual debates about 'transnational Chinese cinema'. Those debates include not only questions about what the 'transnational' actually means but also whether it represents capitulation to Hollywood or a new form of nationalistic triumphalism in the world of global trade. The chapter will argue that the term has greatest use when more closely defined against alternative terms like 'international' and 'global'. However, this is not because such a definition is straightforward. Rather, it is because, in attempting to counter conceptual sloppiness, such an effort opens the way to a more focused and critical debate that will further develop our understanding of what is at stake when we talk about the transnational in relation to Chinese cinema. In this sense, the 'transnational' becomes a method, as Yiman Wang has advocated.[2]

It is not only in relation to Chinese cinema that the idea of 'transnational cinema' remains woolly and ill-defined. In the first issue of *Transnational Cinemas*, Will Higbee and Song Hwee Lim call for a 'critical transnationalism', as opposed to the established tendency to deploy the term loosely. Analysing existing usage, they point to three main patterns. The first rejects 'national cinema' as a theoretical model that cannot accommodate the movement of films across borders, reception of foreign films and so forth. The second focuses on cultural formations that sustain cinemas that exceed the borders of individual nation-states or operate at a more local level within them; for example, Arab-language cinemas, Chinese-language cinemas, Telugu-language cinema in South India and so on. The third is the focus on diasporic, exilic and other cinemas that challenge ideas of stable national cultural identity.[3]

Although Higbee and Lim's article examines transnational cinema studies in general, it is their analysis of the discourse surrounding transnational Chinese cinema in particular that leads them to express a concern. Referring to films like Zhang Yimou's *Hero* (2002), they write, 'one of the potential weaknesses of the conceptual term "transnational cinema" … [is that] it risks celebrating the supranational flow or transnational exchange of peoples, images and cultures at the expense of the specific cultural, historical or ideological context in which these exchanges take place'.[4] In the Chinese case, this would refer to those popular (and some academic) writers who see every global box-office record for a Chinese blockbuster as a nationalistic triumph.

When scholarship has gone beyond unreflexive usage, this has not necessarily narrowed down the range of uses. Indeed, in some cases the opposite has happened. For example, a special issue of the

Hero

Journal of Chinese Cinemas was devoted to the topic of the transnational in 2008. The call for papers asked authors to interrogate the term, and the essays were chosen precisely because they not only did that but also pushed the boundaries of what 'transnational' could mean.[5] One essay belongs to Higbee and Lim's first pattern of practices that do not fit into a national cinema model by examining the archive records on censorship by the British authorities of foreign films imported into Hong Kong during the Cold War era (1950–70).[6] Also within that first pattern is Yiman Wang's aforementioned essay that proclaims the transnational as a method and traces how a Lubitsch film gets remade in Shanghai, and then the remake gets remade in Hong Kong.[7] Zakir Hussein Raju's essay fits both the second and third patterns discerned by Higbee and Lim by positioning recent Malaysian Chinese films as part of a larger transnational Chinese festival cinema shaped by other transnational Chinese films and addressed to transnational audiences.[8]

However, two essays in the same issue push the envelope even further. Rossella Ferrari proliferates the 'trans' by examining how works by Hong Kong art collective Zuni Icosahedron not only cross state borders but also the borders between media to produce transmedial and transtextual lineages.[9] Finally, Emilie Yueh-yu Yeh and Darrell William Davis articulate a vision of the transnational as 'hyper-national' by looking at the activities of the government-owned China Film Group, which they interpret as engaged in national consolidation and transnational reach.[10]

As well as referring to an array of different types of film and film-making, the essays in the special issue of *Journal of Chinese Cinemas* are historically wide-ranging. Others have gone right back to the very beginnings of the cinema. In the introductory essay to his seminal anthology, Sheldon Hsiao-peng Lu writes that 'We begin in 1896 because that was the year of the beginning of film consumption and distribution of an essentially transnational nature in China.'[11] Here a certain ambiguity can be discerned. For he also notes, 'The occasion for [*Transnational Chinese Cinemas*] is the globalization of Chinese cinemas in the international film market.'[12] In the first quotation, Lu takes the scope of the book and the 'transnational' back to the beginnings of Chinese cinema. In the second, he notes a connection between transnational cinema and the more recent phenomenon of globalisation, but with globalisation only classified as a kind of trigger ('The occasion …') for thinking about the transnational.

From this account, it is clear that the potential meanings of 'transnational cinema' are many and various. It can be traced back to the beginnings of cinema itself. Or it can be dated from the impact of globalisation in the cinema. It can refer to big-budget blockbuster cinema associated with the operations of global corporate capital. Or it can refer to small-budget diasporic and exilic cinema. It can refer to films that challenge national identity, or it can refer to the consumption of foreign films as part of the process of a discourse about what national identity is. Does this upsurge in talking about transnational cinema exist because there has really been an increase in the amount of activity in recent years, making it command our attention? Given that statistics continue to be collected largely on the basis of the territorial nation-state, this is hard to measure. Or does the surge in use of the term mean that the transnational is a conceptual framework, and now that it has been widely adopted many hitherto invisible and neglected phenomena have come into view? For an individual scholar who wishes to use the concept of 'transnational cinema' as a research tool these are urgent questions, because the existing unexamined proliferation of the transnational puts it in danger of becoming too contradictory and too similar to many other terms to be useful.

Yingjin Zhang is one of the few scholars to have interrogated the term 'transnational' more thoroughly. Facing the proliferation of sometimes conflicting meanings described above, he goes on to question whether it is useful at all:

The term 'transnational' remains unsettled primarily because of multiple interpretations of the national in transnationalism. What is emphasized in the term 'transnational'? If it is the national, then what does this 'national' encompass – national culture, language, economy, politics, ethnicity, religion, and/or regionalism? If the emphasis falls on the prefix 'trans' (i.e., on cinema's ability to cross and bring

together, if not transcend, different nations, cultures, and languages), then this aspect of transnational film studies is already subsumed by comparative film studies.[13]

Zhang's argument rightly throws down the gauntlet to transnational cinema studies. No doubt, different scholars will continue to use the term 'transnational' in a variety of different and even contradictory ways, often without even bothering to define it. But if he is correct that 'transnational' is just a fashionable word with no distinct meaning of its own – no critical leverage as a concept – then there is no reason to hang on to it.

However, can transnational film studies really be subsumed by comparative film studies? The idea of comparative film studies suggests bounded entities that can be held separate from one another for the purposes of comparison. This could take us back all too easily to the idea of cinemas distinguished according to territorial polities – nation-states – with films flowing back and forth as exports and imports. Even understood beyond the nation-state, the comparative does not easily make space for the phenomena that not only cross but straddle and defy borders analysed in the essays mentioned above. For example, how can we make sense of the film festival circuit that is the cultural field supporting Malaysian Chinese cinema within a comparative perspective? How can it accommodate Chinese blockbuster films that put together their cast and crew from different countries, shoot on location, outsource parts of their production such as music and computer-generated effects, and then go on to aim at multiplex audiences around the world?

Yet, Zhang's argument does alert us to the need to try and develop the transnational as a concept. Although the term 'transnational' has been used to refer to many different and sometimes conflicting things in film studies, these different usages all have one thing in common – they originated around the same time as the discourse on globalisation was becoming widespread towards the end of the last century. This is different from the situation in economic studies, where globalisation as a deeper level of integration follows 'internationalization (as in the increasing interwovenness of national economies through international trade) and transnationalization (as in the increasing organization of production on a cross-border basis by multi-national organizations)'.[14] But in the case of film studies, the 'transnational' tracks or even comes after 'globalisation' as a popular discourse.

Of course, the debates about what exactly the term 'globalisation' means are at least as complicated as those concerning the 'transnational'. However, it is generally thought of as a recent 'epochal transformation' characterised by a rollback in the functions and powers of the state, especially concerning the economy, both in what goes on inside its borders and over what crosses those borders. Saskia Sassen calls these changes 'processes of denationalization'.[15] Within many nation-states, as part of this rollback, state-owned enterprises have been sold to private enterprises. Those states that operate command economies have often stepped back to allow citizens and companies to take the initiative more. Regulations that block or inhibit trade between nation-states are being lowered, enabling those who wish to operate across national borders more straightforwardly and with less need for state approval, as, for example, in various free trade zones and agreements like the European Union, the North American Free Trade Agreement and the Closer Economic Partnership Agreement between Hong Kong and the mainland People's Republic. Although arguments proliferate about the reasons for and forms of change in China, the recent history of the post-Mao 'Reform' (gaige) era in the People's Republic can be seen a classic example of these developments.[16] On the cinematic front, the decreased role of direct state ownership in both Taiwan and the People's Republic are examples of the rollback of the state, and restrictions on imports and exports, as well as flows of investment capital, have all been considerably relaxed.

Taking all these factors into account, we can see that both the terms 'globalisation' and 'transnational' (as used in film studies) refer to a larger structural shift in the world order away from the old order of nation-states. For the purposes of this chapter, that organisation of the world order around nation-states can be called the 'international order'. According to the principles and presumptions that organise this system, the nation-state is understood to have complete sovereignty over the territory that it rules, and the world order is organised as transactions of various kinds between and regulated by these states. It is literally an international order. In the transnational

order, the nation-state does not disappear. Indeed, in recent years we have seen the emergence of a large number of new nation-states. But with the rollback in the absolute power of the nation-state described above, a new order emerges in which citizens and – at least as important – corporations have greater relative autonomy from the state in regard to at least the economy and can operate economically across state borders more easily. The nation-state as the ultimate power regulating the world order is no longer taken for granted.

However, we must recognise that the *conceptual* distinction between the transnational and the international does not enable a simple sorting out of phenomena into two piles of *objects* neatly labelled 'national cinema' (circulating in an international order) and 'transnational cinema'. Rather it constitutes a problematic that animates the analysis of various practices and objects. The change from an international to a transnational order is not something that happened suddenly on a particular date. Despite the fact that we can say consciousness of the phenomenon came to a head in the late 1990s, it remains difficult to draw a clear historical line that would distinguish an era of the international from the transnational.

This difficulty of distinguishing the national/international and the transnational as objects stems from the fact that the transnational develops out of rather than against the international order of nation-states. When companies were founded within the borders of individual nation-states, those territorially bounded polities provided suitable spaces for their protection and development. Yet these same companies were also able to call upon the administrative and military resources of the nation-states they were located in to support their interests beyond the borders of the individual nation-state. An example of this process would be the Opium Wars, conducted against the Qing Empire and to protect the interests of British merchants. As a result of this, some scholars have referred to the era of colonialism and imperialism as 'proto-globalisation'.[17] Viewed through this lens, Kenny Ng's analysis of the censorship activities of the British administrators of Hong Kong during the postwar era sits as an example where the international order is already stretched towards the transnational.[18] The British administration in Hong Kong cannot be seen as a national government exercising sovereignty over imports. Yet, at the same time, its insistence on monitoring what comes into the 'free port' of Hong Kong manifests a resistance to free transborder movement of cinema and the continued dominance of the national model, for it behaves *as though* it is a national government, because that it is the only political form with legitimacy.

The same drive for profit maximisation and accumulation that established the international order as the playing field – level or not – on which corporations conducted their business has now led away from the concentrated and regulated model of Fordist mass production to the post-Fordist model of flexible production and distribution. Post-Fordism seeks out the cheapest sources of labour, parts and supplies, crossing national borders and driving what we know as globalisation. Hollywood once followed a more or less Fordist model, gathering all the elements of the industry into Los Angeles to create maximum economies of scale.[19] Today, Hollywood is a hub in a network and globalised industry that operates what Toby Miller and his colleagues have called the New International Division of Cultural Labour (NICL) to seek out the cheapest locations, post-production facilities and so forth to further maximise profits.[20]

It is this process where one order grows out of the other that makes distinguishing the two historically difficult. Just when did Hollywood cease to be a nationally based industry that exported as part of an international order and become a hub in a global network that operates in a transnational order? Similarly, when did the mainland Chinese film industry cease to be a state-funded national industry producing films to educate the public within the People's Republic and become focused on producing blockbusters aimed at global markets? The predominance of globalisation means that such a move will inevitably be seen through the framework of the transnational. But Emilie Yeh and Darrell Davis's analysis of the China Film Group, referred to earlier, challenges us to consider whether this might be an enhancement of the power of the Chinese state within that transnational order, or, as they put it, a hyper-nationalism.[21]

If distinguishing the concepts of the transnational, the international and the national and the actual practices they might refer to makes visible an intellectual problematic within which to examine transnational Chinese cinema, the question of the conceptual relationship of the transnational to globalisation still requires further attention. If we

accept the transition from Fordist to post-Fordist mode of production as underpinning the logic of the move from an international to a transnational order, does this mean using the concept of the transnational runs the risk of subscribing to the values of globalising neo-liberalism? As already mentioned, Higbee and Lim see this as a particular problem in the kind of work on Chinese transnational cinema that unreflectively celebrates blockbuster culture as a nationalist triumph, a critique that runs parallel to Yeh and Davis's analysis of the China Film Group.[22]

Higbee and Lim are quite right to raise this issue. However, while the forces of capitalist accumulation may be among the primary forces driving the establishment of the international order, it would be a mistake to suggest that this order was uncontested. The same is true of the transnational order. Just because this order is driven in many cases by the fantasy of achieving what Michael Hardt and Antonio Negri have written about as the smooth space of Empire,[23] it does not mean that fantasy either has been or inevitably will be realised. In fact, the very existence of their book, written against that order, is evidence of resistance. Nor does it mean that all film-makers operating in the space opened up by the transnational order are operating according to the principles of profit maximisation and accumulation.

Anna Tsing's work on the conceptual distinction between globalisation as an ideology and the transnational as a practice (or a multiplicity of practices) is useful for grasping this distinction. Many people use the terms 'global' and 'transnational' interchangeably, and that has been the practice of this chapter so far. However, Anna Tsing has argued for a distinction between the two terms. She suggests we should use 'globalisation' as part of the ideological rhetoric of globalism, whereas we should use 'transnational' to refer to the specific 'transborder projects' that actually constitute the growth of the transnational on the ground, so to speak.[24] At first, this idea of a myriad of transborder projects can sound like Sassen's idea that 'globalization consists of an enormous variety of micro-processes that begin to denationalize'.[25] However, not only do Tsing's 'transnational projects' constitute a multiplicity of different and often micro-level practices, but also they are not necessarily unified in their promotion of globalisation, even if they operate within it. Tsing argues that the rhetoric of globalisation driven by neo-liberal transnational capitalism seeks to present it as a force of nature, a 'flow', limited by the 'barriers' put in place by the nation-state. However, she points out that, at the same time, forces opposed to neo-liberal global capitalism also operate as transnational networks, organisations and projects within the same transnational order, as do various alternative NGOs and other organisations and formations driven by values that have nothing to do with profit maximisation.

Tsing's account helps us to understand the transnational as an order that the fantasy of total globalised capitalism both helps to constitute and operates within, but which at the same time exceeds that fantasy and includes other forces antithetical to it or simply different from it. This approach is crucial if we are to avoid the dangers that Higbee and Lim have pointed to. It enables an understanding of the transnational that includes all the activities and forces that are unleashed by globalisation, including those that do not subscribe to the logic of capitalist accumulation driving it. Once the 'barriers' set up by the nation-state are 'removed' or 'lowered', or, to put it another way, once nation-states and other agents encourage transborder production practice, there is little evidence yet of any 'flow' that simply and naturally spreads out evenly across the idealised 'smooth' space of the globe. Instead, as the examples of transborder Chinese film-making indicate, flow occurs in particular channels, in particular directions and in particular ways as part of Tsing's 'transnational projects'. Plenty of Chinese film-makers are working outside the territorial states they were born in. Some have gone to Hollywood. But not many are working, say, in the Mexican film industry, or in Europe. There are reasons why they gravitate to certain places and not to others. Perhaps not surprisingly, the greatest flows of personnel and investment appear to have been among people situated in different Chinese-speaking territories.

But here again, the risk of emphasising language would be to see simply another 'natural force' at work, along with the market – cultural and ethnic affinity. Therefore, it is equally important to observe that these flows have not occurred smoothly and evenly across Chinese-speaking territories, but rather between particular networked cities, with Taipei, Hong Kong and Beijing featuring especially strongly. While there might be significant numbers of Taiwan film industry personnel leaving Taipei for the mainland, not many

are headed to rural Gansu, or even to Shanghai. Shanghai's once-strong film production industry has been in decline for some time as the move away from a command economy that distributed film production across the territory of the People's Republic has given way to a market economy where production companies have tended to gather in creative clusters in one city. In the case of the Chinese film industry, that city is Beijing, where the all-important government censors are based as well as the state-owned China Film Group discussed by Emilie Yeh and Darrell Davis and which continues to dominate distribution and exhibition. This is an instance of how the forces shaping the transnational operate *below* the national level. One set of perhaps counterintuitive questions for research on transnational cinema to undertake is precisely what the new patterns are that emerge below the transnational order, and how to account for them.

But to return to Tsing's idea of a multitude of transnational projects constituting *transborder* cinema practices, these cannot all be reduced to and accounted for wholly in terms of the logic of the market, its so-called 'imperatives', and the even larger forces such as cultural affinity that shape it in certain ways. An example would be the well-known independent film-maker Jia Zhangke, whose *Still Life* (*Sanxia Haoren*) won the Golden Lion at Venice in 2006. Until 2004, he was working as an unofficial film-maker within the People's Republic. Being unofficial meant that his films could not be released commercially in China. Of course, being unofficial did not mean he operated outside of the logic of the market altogether. His films were marketed outside China, and people invested in them. Nonetheless, the decision to start making films in a manner that excluded him from access to his own domestic market suggests a practice motivated and shaped by other concerns, as is also indicated by his continued tendency not to prioritise the box office so far.

Jia Zhangke is not alone in this experience. Similar patterns operate for those engaged in experimental film, documentary film and many more areas of cinema, and this is true not only in the mainland People's Republic but also in Hong Kong and Taiwan. Although their budgets and also their resources are very limited, the reduced cost of international communication thanks to the internet and the reduced cost of circulating and screening films that are digitised

Still Life

rather than celluloid have made such activities more and more common. All these activities or transborder projects, as Tsing would call them, are at least alternative to if not actually opposed to the ideology of neo-liberal globalisation. Yet, paradoxically, they are enabled by and even dependent upon the changes that neo-liberal globalisation has been so crucial in driving forward. Jia's early films could not have been made at all, never mind shown in international film festivals, if the command economy and tight control of the border were still in place. Here, again, we see the logic of a transnational world order at work in the shaping of even those transborder projects that do not support it or prioritise accumulation.

It is precisely because the transnational is a world order that it plays a role in shaping all Chinese film-making activities today. And because the forces producing it grow out of those that produced the international order of nation-states before it, once discovered it is not surprising that we can see its roots going back to the very beginning of Chinese cinema, as Sheldon Lu suggests in the introduction to his anthology.[26] In these circumstances, the very widespread usage of the term in the last decade and

more is completely understandable, and cannot be dismissed simply as fashion. However, by producing a more defined understanding of the transnational as a world order and as various practices under that world order, perhaps we can move from an unexamined and loose usage of the term towards the 'critical transnationalism' in transnational Chinese cinema studies that Higbee and Lim have advocated.

Notes

1. Sheldon Hsiao-peng Lu (ed.), *Transnational Chinese Cinemas: Identity, Nationhood, Gender* (Honolulu: University of Hawaii Press, 1997).
2. Yiman Wang, 'The "Transnational" as Methodology: Transnationalizing Chinese Film Studies Through the Example of *The Love Parade* and its Chinese Remakes', *Journal of Chinese Cinemas* vol. 2 no. 1 (2008), pp. 9–21.
3. Will Higbee and Song Hwee Lim, 'Concepts of Transnational Cinema: Towards a Critical Transnationalism in Film Studies', *Transnational Cinemas* vol. 1 no. 1 (2010), pp. 7–21.
4. Ibid., pp. 11–12.
5. As one of the co-editors of the issue along with Laikwan Pang, here I am speaking from experience.

6. Kenny K. K. Ng, 'Inhibition vs Exhibition: Political Censorship of Chinese and Foreign Cinemas in Postwar Hong Kong', *Journal of Chinese Cinemas* vol. 2 no. 1 (2008), pp. 23–35.

7. Wang, 'The "Transnational" as Methodology'.

8. Zakir Hossain Raju, 'Filmic Imaginations of the Malaysian Chinese: "*Mahua* cinema" as a Transnational Chinese Cinema', *Journal of Chinese Cinemas* vol. 2 no. 1 (2008), pp. 67–79.

9. Rossella Ferrari, 'Transnation/Transmedia/Transtext: Border-Crossing from Screen to Stage in Greater China', *Journal of Chinese Cinemas* vol. 2 no. 1 (2008), pp. 53–65.

10. Emilie Yueh-yu Yeh and Darrell William Davis, 'Re-nationalizing China's Film Industry: Case Study on the China Film Group and Film Marketization', *Journal of Chinese Cinemas* vol. 2 no. 1 (2008), pp. 37–51.

11. Sheldon Hsiao-peng Lu (ed.), 'Historical Introduction: Chinese Cinemas (1896–1996) and Transnational Film Studies', in Lu (ed.), *Transnational Chinese Cinemas*, p. 2.

12. Lu, 'Historical Introduction', p. 1.

13. Yingjin Zhang, 'Comparative Film Studies, Transnational Film Studies: Interdisciplinarity, Crossmediality, and Transcultural Visuality in Chinese Cinema', *Journal of Chinese Cinemas* vol. 1 no. 1 (2007), pp. 27–40 (37).

14. Ankie Hoogevelt , *Globalization and the Postcolonial World Economy: The New Political Economy of Development* (Baltimore, MD: Johns Hopkins University Press: 1997), p. 114.

15. Saskia Sassen, *Territory, Authority, Rights: From Medieval to Global Assemblages* (Princeton, NJ: Princeton University Press, 2006), p. 1.

16. See, for example, Yasheng Huang, *Capitalism with Chinese Characteristics: Entrepreneurship and the State* (New York: Cambridge University Press, 2008).

17. Tony Ballantyne, 'Empire, Knowledge, and Culture: From Proto-Globalization to Modern Globalization', in A. G. Hopkins (ed.), *Globalization in World History* (New York: Norton, 2002), pp. 116–40.

18. Ng, 'Inhibition vs Exhibition'.

19. Hoogevelt, *Globalization and the Postcolonial World Economy*, pp. 90–113.

20. Toby Miller, Nitin Govil, John McMurria and Richard Maxwell, *Global Hollywood* (London: BFI, 2001), pp. 44–82.

21. Yeh and Davis, 'Re-nationalizing China's Film Industry'.

22. Higbee and Lim, 'Concepts of Transnational Cinema', pp. 11–12.

23. Michael Hardt and Antonio Negri, *Empire* (Cambridge: Harvard University Press, 2001), p. 333.

24. Anna Tsing, 'The Global Situation', *Cultural Anthropology* vol. 15 no. 3 (2000), pp. 327–60.

25. Sassen, *Territory, Authority, Rights*, p. 1.

26. Lu, 'Historical Introduction', p. 2.

Further Reading in *Chinese Films In Focus II*

On Zhang Yimou's *Hero*, see Chapter 17, '*Hero*: The Return of a Traditional Masculine Ideal in China' by Kam Louie.

2 National Cinema as Translocal Practice

Reflections on Chinese Film Historiography

Yingjin Zhang

By situating Chinese cinema in a complex network of localities, trajectories and histories, this chapter contends that, beyond the recent tendency to debunk the myth of consensus associated with national cinema,[1] we may go further by constructing translocal practice as fundamental to Chinese film industries and film-makers from the silent era to the current age of globalisation. Many pioneers in Chinese cinema – notably Lai Manwai (Li Minwei, 1892–1953), Luo Mingyou (1902–1967) and Moon Kwan (Guan Wenqing, 1896–1995) – travelled across various geocultural localities (e.g., Hong Kong, Shanghai, San Francisco), and their trajectories formed complicated business networks and cultural associations. The craze for martial arts films in the late 1920s strengthened the translocal linkages between Shanghai and South-East Asia, and the Hong Kong and Cantonese connections were prominent in Shanghai cinema of the 1920s–30s. Lianhua's vision for 'domestic cinema' (*guopian*) was implemented through an ambitious amalgamation of industrial, cultural and human resources from regional nodes such as Beijing, North-East China, Shanghai and Hong Kong. The wartime and postwar transfer of film-makers and financial resources from Shanghai to Chongqing and Hong Kong only intensified translocal networking that further expanded the parameters of Chinese cinema, whereas the influx of Singapore money into Hong Kong in the mid-1950s established MP&GI and Shaw Brothers as two powerhouses of Chinese-language cinema around the world. By tracing the multiplicity of localities and trajectories glossed over by conventional nation-centred historiography, this chapter rethinks issues of film historiography and argues in favour of a new conception of Chinese cinema as translocal practices both below and above the scale of the nation-state.

Theoretically, my challenge to the standard history of Chinese national cinema consists of three steps. First, we stand to gain from certain insights from postmodern historiography when we re-examine Chinese cinema in terms of discontinuity and fragmentation rather than the conventional organic model of progress and decline. Second, we may re-envision Chinese film history as comprised of a multitude of temporalities, spatialities and localities, requiring a polyphonic structure of narrative with particular attention to interstitials and interplays between various nodal points. Third, we should develop a system of translocal practices that attends not so much to exclusive identity formation as to open-ended diasporic ventures. Judging from its century-long operations, Chinese cinema is as much translocal as it is national and transnational, and the translocal perspective promises to shed new light on an array of hitherto neglected issues in Chinese film history.

Film History: Discontinuity and Fragmentation

As early as 1984, Fredric Jameson reminded us of one crucial idea from postmodern scholarship: 'The principal contribution that contemporary historiography has made is to insist on history as a series of breaks rather than as a continuity.'[2] Around the same time, Roger Chartier encouraged scholars to draw on Michel Foucault's insight and treat 'the procedures of discourse in their discontinuity and their specificity'.[3] The new emphasis on discontinuity thus works against what Linda Hutcheon described as

Luo Mingyou, Lai Manwai, Sun Yu, Ruan Lingyu and other
Lianhua people in the 1930s

'the limitations of that nineteenth-century teleological
(but also linear, causal, sequential) narrative of literary
history' or history in general.[4] In other words, history
can no longer be conceived exclusively in monolithic
terms of development and progress towards a certain
telos. Instead, postmodern historiography
'acknowledges diversity, complexity, and contradiction
by making them structural principles, and it forgoes
closure as well as consensus'.[5] More specifically, in its
shift from global history to sectorial or fragmentary
history, from monumental history to diagrammatic
history, from historicist history to structural history,
and from documental history to conjectural history,
postmodern historiography seeks to abandon 'the
unilateral idea of causality', and 'the idea of totality
seems to be left aside, substituted by the ideas of
plurality, fragmentation, and absence of centre'.[6]

From the postmodern perspective of discontinuity,
fragmentation and diversity, official Chinese film
history looks incredibly homogeneous and monolithic.[7]
Nationalism is identified as the central thread running
from the 1920s through the 1940s, and nation-building
assumes continuity throughout the socialist period
from the 1950s to the 1970s. Standard Chinese film
history has adopted two strategies typical of the
national cinema paradigm, as expounded by Andrew
Higson: (1) to identify 'a select series of relatively self-
contained quality film movements to carry forward the
banner of national cinema'; (2) 'to produce a realist
national cinema which can "reflect" the contemporary
social and political realities' and 'to represent what is
imagined to be the national past, its people, its
landscape, and its cultural heritage, in a mode that can

itself be understood as national, and as traditional'.[8]
Not surprisingly, thanks to its initial association with a
team of underground Communists in Shanghai, the
leftwing film movement was singled out as the most
significant force before 1949, and its brand of realism
spawned subsequent variations and ensured the
continuity of Chinese cinema all the way to the new
millennium.[9]

However, even the term 'leftwing' (zuoyi) itself has
recently been questioned by Chinese scholars, who have
increasingly opted to discard the ideologically charged
term and embrace alternatives like 'newly emerging'
(xinxing), 'new-born' (xinsheng) or simply 'new film
movement', which are historically accurate due to their
frequent occurrences in the early 1930s.[10] What
consequences would this change of terms entail for
Chinese film history? For one thing, the movement in
question can no longer be considered homogeneous, as
film-makers like Sun Yu (1900–1990) and Wu Yonggang
(1907–1982) would change or modify their ideological
positions from one project to another, thereby resulting
in discontinuity rather continuity on an individual
basis.[11] For another, the ideologically neutral terms like
xinxing and xinsheng draw attention to the 'newness'
(xin) that would highlight the movement's departure
from the commercial production of the late 1920s
(particularly the martial arts genre) and from other
contenders of national cinema during the 1930s (like
the Nationalist-sponsored New Life Movement); as such,
the new film movement may be better understood as

Veteran Shanghai star Zhao Dan playing a beggar in *The Life of
Wu Xun*, a target of a nationwide political campaign

one of numerous ruptures or fragments – albeit a significant one – in a century of Chinese film history.

On a small scale, two films from the transition year of 1950, right after the People's Republic of China was founded, illustrate the complexity engendered by discontinuity and fragmentation. On the one hand, the humanist tradition traceable from *Orphan Rescues Grandfather* (Guer jiu zu ji, 1923) to postwar Wenhua studio productions, was fatally ruptured by the suppression of *The Life of Wu Xun* (Wu Xun zhuan, 1950): from the early 1950s, film-makers of varied ideological persuasions were no longer granted the right to express any historical vision not aligned with the one endorsed by the top Communist leader Mao Zedong. What was worse, the financial difficulties created by the nationwide campaign against the film drove private film companies

in Shanghai to the brink of bankruptcy, and all of them quickly 'volunteered' to merge into the state sector.[12]

On the other hand, *The White-Haired Girl* (Bai maonü, 1950), based on a Communist-approved village play from the Yan'an period, still contains fragments of female sexuality in its revolutionary narrative of class struggle. Sure, Xi'er's fantasy from the play that the landlord would marry her after having raped and impregnated her is removed from the film,[13] but the scene of her giving birth to a still-born child in the wildness still foregrounds the sexual violence and burdens her with an undesirable past. In the 1972 film of the revolutionary ballet version, the image of Xi'er is completely sanitised: not only has the landlord's rape failed, but no pregnancy or child is allowed to tarnish Xi'er as a wholesome female fighter.[14]

The White-Haired Girl

The Life of Wu Xun and *The White-Haired Girl* testify to the power of a totalising discourse that has plotted a singular development of Chinese cinema in official historiography. Upon closer scrutiny, however, both contain fragments of unspeakable stories on- and offscreen (the former is still denied public access), and both demonstrate the great extent to which individual voices would be suppressed and unofficial memories repressed in the socialist period.

Polyphonic Narrative: Nodes and Voices

In order to retrieve repressed voices and lost memories of the past, postmodern historiography has experimented with different narrative or presentational strategies. Although encyclopaedic literary history has received much attention,[15] I have found the theory and practice of comparative literary history most illuminating. Departing from the national model, comparative literary history 'consists of a great many *microhistories*, i.e., of localized, perspectival, and situated stories that cannot be easily read as symbols or synecdoches of an overarching organic system'.[16] Marginalised by a grand history of national development, many such microhistories or minor stories constitute fissures and fragments that refuse or exceed totalisation. Indeed, I suggest that Chinese cinema as translocal practice strives for the same goals set for comparative literary history: to capture 'multiplicity, not totality – perspectival insight, not empyrean oversight', as well as to 'construct a history without closure, one that can be entered through many points and can unfold through many coherent, informed, and focused narrative lines'.[17]

Methodologically, comparative literary history postulates concepts of *node* as 'the starting point for multiple derivations' as well as 'a point in a network at which the multiple lines of development come together'.[18] Five principal nodes – temporal (particular years), topographical (cities, border areas), institutional (censorship organisations, theatres), literary (genre, movement, period) and figurative (symbols, legends) – are deployed to organise materials in an overlapping manner, to map the simultaneity of the non-simultaneous or the non-simultaneity of the simultaneous.[19] As a result, traditional classification schemes by authors and periods have undergone 'a fragmentation', and the historians are freed from pursuing causal logic and are instead focused on 'nodal points, coincidences, returns, resurgences', so as 'to produce an effect of heterogeneity and to dispute the traditional orderliness of most histories'.[20] To evoke a musical metaphor, 'a strategy of multivocal description' would ensure that a new literary or film history 'unfolds through a polyphony of large-scale narratives' and small-scale stories at the same time.[21]

Further research is needed to develop a system of polyphonic narratives, but I would suggest that oral history has much to offer in rethinking Chinese film history, both comparatively and collaboratively.[22] One such collaborative attempt was launched in Taiwan in 1990, when the Chinese Taipei Film Archive started to rescue the materials related to 'Taiwanese-dialect films' (*Taiyu pian*), a rich local cultural tradition that had been suppressed as a taboo subject before the Nationalist government's decision to lift its thirty-eight-year-old martial law in Taiwan in July 1987. The fissure in popular memory is such that Liao Gene-fon (Liao Jinfeng), a scholar from the generation born in the 1960s, would confess that he 'never knew the existence of Taiwanese-dialect films before 1989'.[23] The confessed ignorance is shocking because Taiwanese-dialect films constituted a significant cultural force in the mid-1950s through the 1960s. Whereas only 373 'Mandarin films' (*guoyu pian*) were completed in Taiwan from 1955 to 1969, 1,052 Taiwanese-dialect films were produced during the same period, and the dialect film production continued until 1981, totalling close to two thousand titles.[24] Thanks to an oral history group under the Chinese Taipei Film Archive, we now have access to personal voices of people active in Taiwanese-dialect film production, including veteran directors Li Quanxi (b. 1926), who attended college in Xiamen (a coastal city across the Taiwan Strait) in the mid-1940s, and Liang Zhefu (1920–1992), who moved from Hong Kong to Taiwan and was involved in Cantonese, Taiwanese and Mandarin film productions.

The significance of Taiwanese-dialect films resides not merely in their status of alterity to the state-funded Mandarin production of 'policy films' (*zhengce pian*) in Cold War Taiwan, but also in the initial configuration of different nodes, in particular the topographical node of a rural–urban border network, the institutional node of itinerant *gezaixi* troupes and the figurative nodes of traditional Chinese myths and legends.[25] What this oral history project brought to public awareness is not just a long-suppressed tradition of grassroots opposition and subversion, but also a complicated process of negotiation and interplay between the dominant and the popular, between official history and personal voices, between the nationalist vision endorsed by the state and translocal networks pursued by the film-makers.

The Hong Kong Film Archive's project in oral history was launched in 1994 and interviewed over 200 film veterans over a seven-year period. To a greater extent than its Taiwan counterpart, the Hong Kong project emphasises the multiple translocal experiences of people whose contributions to Chinese film history had fallen into the cracks between the territorial focuses on mainland China or Hong Kong. While the project's first volume retrieves the voices from such wartime and postwar producers, directors and stars as Tong Yuejuan (1914–2003), Yue Feng (1909–1999) and Li Lihua (b. 1925), who traversed Shanghai and Hong Kong back and forth multiple times, the second volume refreshes the memories of people affiliated with Hong Kong 'leftist films' (zuopai dianying) in the 1950s and 60s. As she has done elsewhere,[26] Tong Yuejuan defends her husband Zhang Shankun (1907–1957) against such charges as 'traitor' or 'collaborator', which arose due to the secret ties he maintained with the Chongqing-based Nationalist groups while also dealing with Japanese occupation forces, including their sympathetic leader Kawakita Nagamasa (1903–1981). Yue Feng validates Zhang's Nationalist ties and Kawakita's protection of 'patriotic' Chinese film-makers like himself, which explains why he was chosen to co-direct the controversial Sino-Japanese coproduction, Remorse in Shanghai (Chunjiang yihen, 1944). More outspoken than others, Li Lihua claims that Remorse in Shanghai, where she co-stars with a mixed Sino-Japanese cast, was a 'patriotic feature' and that occupied Shanghai was the front line during the war. After her postwar success in a Shanghai comedy, Phony Phoenix (Jiafeng xuhuang, 1947), Li became the highest-earning female star in Hong Kong during the 1950s and 60s, had a Hollywood stint in Frank Borzage's China Doll (1958) and extended her career to Taiwan in the 1970s, working in turns with border-crossing directors like Li Hanxiang (1926–1996), King Hu (Hu Jinquan, 1931–1997) and Liang Zhefu.[27]

The Hong Kong oral history project demonstrates that wartime Shanghai and postwar Hong Kong constitute two very different topographical and institutional nodes and that film people navigated across political fault lines through translocal personnel and business networking. Such networking is prominent in the discovery and promotion of new stars for Great Wall, a stronghold of leftist film-making in Hong Kong whose productions enjoyed decent box office in Hong Kong, mainland China and South-East Asia from the late 1940s to the mid-1960s. Ideological and financial tensions complicated Great Wall's management and production, which involved a large group of Shanghai émigrés, such as producers Zhang Shankun and Yuan Yang-an (1904–1994), directors Yue Feng and Li Pingqian (1902–1984), as well as 'leftist' actors like Liu Qiong (1913–2002) and Shu Shi (b. 1916). As general manager, Yuan steered Great Wall through a crisis moment when its eight employees were expelled to mainland China in January 1952 by the Hong Kong government for their political activities, and he successfully discovered rising female stars like Xia Meng (Hsia Moon, b. 1933) and Lin Dai (Linda Lin, 1934–1964). To promote Great Wall stars, Yuan launched the Great Wall Pictorial (Changchen huabao) in 1950, a glossy popular monthly in Hong Kong and overseas modelled in part on the long-running The Young Companion (Liangyou huabao) in Shanghai, for which Yuan served as a trustee when he was a top attorney there. Before he left Great Wall due to increasing disagreements with the political manipulation by the behind-the-scenes communist connections, Yuan directed The True Story of Ah Q (A Q zhengzhuan, 1958), an adaptation of Lu Xun's famous novella that was more than twenty years ahead of its 'authorised' mainland version released in 1981.[28] Regrettably, the Hong Kong project did not secure a personal testimony from Yuan Yang-an, but many Great Wall veterans commented on an age of idealism that remains marginalised in the film histories of both mainland China and Hong Kong.

The importance of oral history is not lost to mainland scholars, although the political situation has long been so precarious that veteran film-makers may not speak as candidly as their counterparts in Hong Kong and Taiwan.[29] Nonetheless, Lu Hongshi's recent oral history project on early Chinese cinema offers interviews with the translocal, yet marginalised film-makers such as Tang Xiaodan (b. 1910) and He Feiguang (1913–1997). After spending his childhood in Indonesia, Tang had an illustrious directorial career that includes White Gold Dragon (Baijin long, 1931) and other Cantonese films in Shanghai and Hong Kong, war films and comedies in Chongqing and postwar Shanghai, as well as a number of memorable titles in socialist China.

Born in Taiwan, He Feiguang travelled to Shanghai at age sixteen and took up film acting. He directed several patriotic films during the war and was credited for the first postwar feature in Hong Kong. Ironically, simply because of his Taiwan origin, he was not allowed to direct during the socialist period even though he had joined the Communist army and fought in the Korean War.[30]

As illustrated above, oral history helps us locate lost voices and repressed memories, which serve as signposts for rethinking history. The model of nodal points in comparative film history highlights not only the richness of polyphonic narrative but also the complexity of translocal networking in Chinese cinema.

Translocal Practice: Diasporic and Polylocal

Commenting on the by-now familiar trope of the Hong Kong–Shanghai connection during the war, Wen-hsin Yeh offers an intriguing suggestion: 'Chinese cinema in its formative period was … not a national enterprise self-contained within the boundaries of the nation-state but a diasporic venture connecting the Chinese populations in Shanghai, Hong Kong, Singapore, Southeast Asia, Australia, and North America.'[31] Yeh's questioning of the national status of early Chinese cinema was based on the evidence of the local grounding of early Chinese operations, in particular in large cities like Shanghai and Hong Kong. For Laikwan Pang, even members of the leftwing film movement could be conceived of as 'specific products of the city rather than of the nation', although their 'self-avowed national profile was obvious'.[32] Given such a multilayered articulation between the city, the nation and the world, 1930s Shanghai cinema was cosmopolitan and synergetic, drawing inspiration from Hollywood and Europe as well as from regional Chinese literary and theatrical traditions.

Shanghai cinema thus foregrounds what I call the 'polylocality' of Chinese cinema, which, by the late 1930s, had transformed cosmopolitan cities like Shanghai and Hong Kong into prominent topographical nodes and had made translocal practice a common strategy for sustaining its institutional node. Not surprisingly, Hong Kong cinema had successfully launched translocal, diasporic ventures. According to Yu Muyun, forty out of sixty Cantonese directors in the 1930s had come from Shanghai, and together they directed more than 200 Cantonese features in the decade.[33] After all, the first two Cantonese talkies were

produced outside Hong Kong: *White Gold Dragon* came from Shanghai's Tianyi, and *Romance of the Songsters* (Gelü qingchao, 1931) from San Francisco's Grandview (Daguan).[34] From the opposite direction, Cantonese film-makers were highly active in Shanghai cinema, and they included producers, directors, actors, musicians, crew members, distributors and theatre owners.[35] The traffic between Hong Kong and Shanghai continued before and after the war, and the rise of Shaw Brothers, which relocated its centre of operations from Singapore to Hong Kong in the mid-1950s, further consolidated Hong Kong cinema as an outstanding example of diasporic ventures – so much so that one scholar characterises Hong Kong cinema from 1956 to 1979 as 'Chinese diasporic cinema'.[36]

Admittedly, the diasporic does not automatically rule out the national, and here I caution against the binary implication of national versus diasporic as formulated by Wen Hsin-Yeh.[37] When Grandview was relocated to Hong Kong as a diasporic venture in 1935, among its earliest releases was *Lifeline* (Shengming xian, 1935), a patriotic film that predated its Shanghai counterparts and featured a famous theme song rendered by Cho-fan Ng (Wu Chufan, 1911–1993), a Japan-born Cantonese actor.[38] Like Lai Mai-wai, who was born in Japan and was closely involved with the Nationalist Revolution of the 1910s and 20s, Cho-fan Ng would identify with China's national defence during the war and envision Hong Kong cinema as part of a regional culture in South China (hua'nan).[39] Indeed, during the 1930s, 'South China films' (Hua'nan dianying) and 'Cantonese films' (Yueyu pian) were standard terms in contemporary publications, whereas the geographically limited term 'Hong Kong cinema' was rarely used.[40]

Terms like *hua'nan* acknowledge border-crossing, translocal operations, and I argue that the translocal subsumes the diasporic in that one does not have to be in diaspora to conduct translocal networking. While deeply entrenched in the local theatre, Cantonese opera movies (Yueyu xiqu pian) from the very beginning were inventive in exploring translocal resources. *White Gold Dragon*, a Shanghai production, was adapted from Malcolm St Clair's silent film, *The Grand Duchess and the Waiter* (1926), and *My Kingdom for a Husband* (Xuangong yanshi, 1957), produced in Hong Kong, was an adaptation of Ernst Lubitsch's romantic comedy, *The Love Parade* (1929). In fact, both Cantonese features were based on the popular Cantonese operas Sit Kok-seen

(Xue Juexian, 1904–1956) had adapted from Hollywood films, and as early as 1926, Sit had moved to Shanghai to establish his own Feifei Film Company.[41] In terms of its creative synergy, Hong Kong cinema was polylocal and translocal in its formative years, and it has remained strategically so until today.

From 1926 to 1953, Sit Kok-seen starred in thirty-five films, and his star power extended beyond Hong Kong and reached *hua'nan* as well as South-East Asia. His operatic and filmic ventures demonstrate that the translocal does not have to be grounded in a fixed locale, and nor is it always articulated at the scale of the nation. The translocal tends to evade the centripetal force of homogeneity and conformity in conventional historiography and is therefore free to explore fragments and ruptures in national history.

Conclusion: The Need for Rupture

To challenge received wisdom regarding teleological progress and national representation, what Stephen Greenblatt posits as the 'need for rupture' is provocative in the context of rethinking Chinese film history as well:

> To write cultural history we need more a sharp awareness of accidental judgments than a theory of the organic; more an account of purposes mistook than a narrative of gradual emergence; more a chronicle of carnal, bloody, and unnatural acts than a story of inevitable progress from traceable origins. We need to understand colonisation, exile, emigration, wandering, contamination, and unexpected consequences, along with the fierce compulsions of greed, longing, and restlessness, for it is these disruptive forces that principally shape the history.[42]

From the perspective of rupture, we are no longer obliged to discern any hidden law of historical development. In this light, the transformation of Chen Kaige (b. 1952) and Zhang Yimou (b. 1950) from avant-garde 'auteurs' in the 1980s to blockbuster directors in the 2000s does not represent any inevitable 'progress' in film history or aesthetics but rather owes itself to ruptures created by the contingencies of market reform, international cultural politics and transnational capital flows. Multinational in production, distribution and exhibition, recent Chinese blockbuster films rely on translocal practices in a shifting landscape of global cinema.

Notes

1. For a recent critique of the national cinema paradigm, see Yingjin Zhang, *Cinema, Space, and Polylocality in a Globalizing China* (Honolulu: University of Hawaii, 2010), pp. 16–28.
2. Fredric Jameson, 'An Overview', in Tak-Wai Wong and Ackbar Abbas (eds), *Rewriting Literary History* (Hong Kong: Hong Kong University Press, 1984), p. 347.
3. Roger Chartier, *Cultural History: Between Practices and Representations*, trans. Lydia G. Cochrane (Cambridge: Polity Press, 1988), pp. 10–11.
4. Linda Hutcheon, 'Rethinking the National Model', in Linda Hutcheon and Mario J. Valdés (eds), *Rethinking Literary History: A Dialogue on Theory* (New York: Oxford University Press, 2002), p. 8.
5. Emory Elliott (ed.), *Columbia Literature History of the United States* (New York: Columbia University Press, 1988), p. xiii.
6. Jenaro Talens and Santos Zunzunegui, 'Toward a True History of Cinema: Film History as Narration', *Boundary 2* vol. 24 no. 1 (1997), pp. 28–9.
7. The classic example is Cheng Jihua, Li Shaobai, and Xing Zuwen, *Zhongguo dianying fazhan shi* [History of the Development of Chinese Cinema] (Beijing: Zhongguo dianying chubanshe, 1963; 2nd edn, 1981), 2 vols.
8. Andrew Higson, *Waving the Flag: Constructing a National Cinema in Britain* (New York: Oxford University Press, 1995), pp. 16–17, 22.
9. For the latest variations, see 'documentary realism' in Ban Wang, 'In Search of Real-Life Images in China: Realism in the Age of Spectacle', *Journal of Contemporary China* vol. 17 no. 56, August (2008), pp. 497–512; 'post-socialism realism' in Jason McGrath, *Postsocialist Modernity: Chinese Cinema, Literature, and Criticism in the Market Age* (Stanford, CA: Stanford University Press, 2008), pp. 129–64.
10. See Lu Hongshi, *Zhongguo dianying shi 1905–1949: zaoqi Zhongguo dianying de xushu yu jiyi* [Chinese Film History, 1905–1949: Narratives and Reminiscences of Early Chinese Cinema] (Beijing: Wenhua yishu chubanshe, 2005), pp. 61–75; Li Daoxin, *Zhongguo dianying wenhua shi, 1905–2004* [History of Chinese Film Culture, 1905–2004] (Beijing: Peking University Press, 2005), pp. 128–31.
11. After his acclaimed 'leftwing' *The Highway* (Dalu, 1935), Sun Yu was censured by the leftwing critics for his *Back to Nature* (Dao ziran qu, 1936). Similarly, after the left-wing classic *The Goddess* (Shennü, 1934), Wu Yonggang was criticised for his Nationalist-sponsored *Little Angel* (Xiao tianshi, 1935) and his existential *The Desert Island* (Lang taosha, 1936).

12. For the background, see Yingjin Zhang, *Chinese National Cinema* (London: Routledge, 2004), pp. 194–9.

13. Ding Yi and He Jingzhi, 'The White-haired Girl', in Walter Meserve and Ruth Meserve (eds), *Modern Drama from Communist China* (New York: New York University Press, 1970), pp. 105–80.

14. For a discussion of the changing images of Xi'er, see Meng Yue, 'Female Images and National Myth ', in Tani Barlow (ed.), *Gender Politics in Modern China: Writing and Feminism* (Durham, NC: Duke University Press, 1993), pp. 118–36.

15. See these books from Harvard University Press: Denis Hollier (ed.), *A New History of French Literature* (1989); David Wellbery (ed.), *A New History of German Literature* (2004); and Greil Marcus and Werner Sollors (eds), *A New Literary History of America* (2009). They are distinguished by a chronological listing of essays by individual scholars on particular events keyed to specific years, months or even days.

16. Marcel Cornis-Pope and John Neubauer (eds), *History of the Literary Cultures of East-Central Europe: Junctures and Disjunctures in the 19th and 20th Centuries* (Amsterdam: John Benjamins, 2004), vol. 1, p. 18.

17. Linda Hutcheon, Djelal Kadir and Mario J. Valdés, 'Collaborative Historiography: A Comparative Literary History of Latin America' (American Council of Learned Societies Occasional Paper, No. 35, 1996), 2, p. 5.

18. Cornis-Pope and Neubauer (eds), *History of the Literary Cultures of East-Central Europe*, vol. 1, p. xiv.

19. Ibid., pp. 16–18.

20. Hollier (ed.), *A New History of French Literature*, pp. xix–xx.

21. Sacvan Bercovitch (ed.), *The Cambridge History of American Literature, Volume 1, 1590–1820* (New York: Cambridge University Press, 1994), pp. 4–5.

22. I also suggest that comparative film history relies on collaborative work as does comparative literary history; see Hutcheon, Kadir and Valdés, 'Collaborative Historiography'.

23. Liao Jinfeng, *Xiaoshi de yingxiang: Taiyupian de dianying zaixian yu wenhua rentong* [The Faded Images: Cinematic Representation and Cultural Identification in Taiwanese-dialect Films] (Taipei: Yuanliu, 2001), p. 11.

24. The totals come from Lu Feiyi, *Taiwan dianying: zhengzhi, jingji, meixue, 1949–1994* [Taiwan Cinema: Politics, Economy, Aesthetics, 1949–1994] (Taipei: Yuanliu, 1998), Table 11a; Guojia dianying ziliao guan [Chinese Taipei film archive] (ed.), *Taiyu pian shidai* [The Era of Taiwanese-dialect Films] (Taipei: Guojia dianying ziliao guan, 1994), p. 250. See also Huang Ren, *Beiqing Taiyu pian* [Sorrowful Taiwanese-dialect Films] (Taipei: Wanxiang, 1994); Ye Longyan, *Chunhua menglu: zhengzong Taiyu dianying xing shuai lu* [Spring Flowers, Dream Dews: The Ups and Downs of the Authentic Taiwanese-dialect Films] (Taipei: Boyang wenhua, 1999).

25. *Gezaixi*, a regional opera, originated from southern Fujian and was popular in rural Taiwan during the 1950s–60s.

26. Zuo Guifang and Yao Liqun (eds), *Tong Yuejuan huiyilu ji tuwen ziliao huibian* [Tong Yuejuan's Memoire and Collected Materials] (Taipei: Chinese Taipei Film Archive, 2001).

27. Hong Kong Film Archive (ed.), *Hong Kong, Here I Come – Monographs of Hong Kong Film Veterans, 1* (Hong Kong: Hong Kong Film Archive, 2000), pp. 38–43, 69–74, 173–9.

28. Hong Kong Film Archive (ed.), *An Age of Idealism: Great Wall and Feng Huang Days – Monographs of Hong Kong Film Veterans, 2* (Hong Kong: Hong Kong Film Archive, 2001), pp. 290–319.

29. A few memoirs of early film personnel published in the socialist period are usually sanitised; see Wang Hanlun et al., *Gankai hua dangnian* [Reminiscences of Old Times] (Beijing: Zhongguo dianying chubanshe, 1962).

30. Lu Hongshi, *Zhongguo dianying shi 1905–1949*, pp. 153–65, 177–83.

31. Wen-hsin Yeh, 'Between Shanghai and Hong Kong', *American Historical Review* vol. 110 no. 5, December (2005), p. 1501.

32. Laikwan Pang, *Building a New China in Cinema: The Chinese Left-Wing Cinema Movement, 1932–1937* (Lanham, MD: Rowman & Littlefield, 2002), p. 166.

33. See Hong Kong International Film Festival (ed.), *Cinema of Two Cities: Hong Kong – Shanghai* (Hong Kong: Urban Council, 1994), p. 93.

34. Law Kar and Frank Bren, *Kong Kong Cinema: A Cross-Cultural View* (Lanham, MD: Scarecrow, 2004), pp. 74–5.

35. For a list of these people, see Lee Pui-tak, 'To Ban or Counter Ban: Cantonese Cinema Caught Between Shanghai and Hong Kong in the 1930s', in Wong Ain-ling (ed.), *The Hong Kong-Guangdong Film Connection* (Hong Kong: Hong Kong Film Archive, 2005), p. 32.

36. See Yingchi Chu, *Hong Kong Cinema: Colonizer, Motherland and Self* (London: RoutledgeCurzon, 2002), pp. xix–xx, 22–41.

37. For a review of recent Chinese film historiography, see Yingjin Zhang, 'Beyond Binary Imagination: Progress and Problems in Chinese Film Historiography', *Chinese Historical Review* vol. 15 no. 1 (2008), pp. 65–87.

38. See Yu Muyun, *Xianggang dianying shihua* [A Historical Account of Hong Kong Cinema], vol. 2 (Hong Kong: Ciwenhua, 1997), pp. 81–2.

39. See Wu Chufan (Cho-fan Ng), *Wu Chufan zizhuan* [Cho-fan Ng's Autobiography] (Taipei: Longwen chubanshe, 1994).

40. Han Yanli, 'National Defence Cinema: A Window on Early Cantonese Cinema and Political Upheaval in Mainland China', in Wong Ain-ling (ed.), *The Hong Kong-Guangdong Film Connection* (Hong Kong: Hong Kong Film Archive, 2005), p. 69.

41. Paul Fonoroff, *Silver Light: A Pictorial History of Hong Kong Cinema, 1920–1970* (Hong Kong: Joint Publishing, 1997), p. 12; Hong Kong International Film Festival (ed.), *Cantonese Opera Film Retrospective* (Hong Kong: Urban Council, 1987), p. 114.

42. Stephen Greenblatt, 'Racial Memory and Literary History,' in Hutcheon and Valdés (eds), *Rethinking Literary History*, p. 61.

Further Reading in *Chinese Films In Focus II*

On Wu Yonggang, see Chapter 16, '*The Goddess*: Fallen Woman of Shanghai' by Kristine Harris.

On Li Hanxiang, see Chapter 20, '*The Love Eterne*: Almost a (Heterosexual) Love Story' by Tan See-Kam and Annette Aw.

On King Hu, see Chapter 28, '*A Touch of Zen*: Action in Martial Arts Movie' by Mary Farquhar.

On Chen Kaige, see Chapter 13, '*Farewell My Concubine*: National Myth and City Memories' by Yomi Braester, and Chapter 33, '*Yellow Earth*: Hesitant Apprenticeship and Bitter Agency' by Helen Hok-sze Leung.

On Zhang Yimou, see Chapter 17, '*Hero*: The Return of a Traditional Masculine Ideal in China' by Kam Louie; Chapter 21, '*Not One Less*: The Fable of a Migration' by Rey Chow; and Chapter 25, '*Riding Alone for Thousands of Miles*: Redeeming the Father by Way of Japan?' by Faye Hui Xiao.

3 Cinemas of the Chinese Diaspora[1]

Gina Marchetti

In 2006, the National Film Registry of the United States selected Marion Wong's *The Curse of Quon Gwon: When the Far East Mingles with the West* (1916) for inclusion. Although no complete print of the film survives, the fact that film-maker/historian Arthur Dong uncovered several extant reels speaks volumes about the unwritten history of Chinese American film-makers, ethnic Chinese women film-makers and the creative power of overseas Chinese working outside of the commercial Hollywood system. Made shortly after Griffith's *The Birth of a Nation* (1915) and DeMille's *The Cheat* (1915), this Chinese American film must be considered as an equally important achievement within the history of American and world cinema.

Although Wong's efforts in the United States may be somewhat isolated, they are far from unique. In fact, another pioneering ethnic Chinese woman film-maker, Esther Eng/Ng Kam-ha, had a career that spanned decades. Her classics such as *Golden Gate Girl* (1941), made under the auspices of the transnational Grandview Film Company, dramatise life in the Chinese diaspora, appealing to audiences in Hong Kong as well as San Francisco. As a performer, American-born Anna May Wong also had a career that traversed several continents and spanned the silent and sound eras.

This chapter surveys some of the contributions diasporic Chinese film-makers, producers and performers from America, South-East Asia, Europe and elsewhere have made to the history of Chinese cinema. While keeping an eye on past figures such as Marion Wong, Esther Eng and Anna May Wong, the focus shifts to more recent film-makers, including Wayne Wang, Ang Lee, Evans Chan, Mina Shum, Clara Law, Dai Sijie and others who have established reputations outside of Hong Kong, Taiwan and the People's Republic of China. Beyond the United States, Europe and Australia, the continuing importance of ethnic Chinese film-makers in the *Nanyang*/South-East Asia needs to be taken into account, and contributions by Singaporean film-makers Eric Khoo and Royston Tan, as well as the impact of ethnic Chinese talent on the emerging Malaysian New Wave (e.g., Tan Chui Mui, James Lee) must be noted. The flipside of this movement (e.g., of 'overseas' Chinese film-makers like Malaysian-Chinese Tsai Ming-liang 'going back' to China/Taiwan/Hong Kong) will also be considered. This cinematic diaspora, in fact, exposes the existential extremes of the lives of diasporic Chinese – from 'forever foreign',[2] living in an ethnic ghetto, to prosperous 'flexible citizens',[3] with global connections, who have staked a claim to their place in world cinema.

The Diaspora and Nation-Building

At the time *The Curse of Quon Gwon* was made, the Chinese republic was in its infancy. No longer subject to the Qing Empire, the republican Chinese still battled for control of the new nation and continued to suffer the inequities of colonialism and 'extraterritoriality' imposed by Europeans and the Japanese. Ethnic Chinese also made little headway against exclusionary laws in places such as the United States, Canada and Australia. However, commercial trade and the profitability of émigré labour swelled the ranks of the diaspora, and people left the political turmoil and grinding poverty of China to follow the trade routes in

reverse as merchants or cheap 'coolie' (*ku li*) labour.
When the medium of the motion picture appeared, it
circulated with these diasporic populations, and port
cities with ethnic Chinese populations became centres
for film production or the locations for the imagination
of the exotic other. Malaya, Shanghai, Hong Kong
became key points on the Chinese cinema map as
places of exhibition, distribution and production. Films
about Chinatowns in New York and San Francisco,
Limehouse in London, Cholon in Saigon, and elsewhere
offer some of the earliest screen glimpses of life in the
Chinese diaspora.

From the extant bits of *The Curse of Quon Gwon*, it
seems clear that Marion Wong was not only in tune
with life in America's Chinese community but, also,
with the wider ethnic Chinese world. The film takes up,
as part of its plot, supporters of Sun Yat-sen's battle to
overthrow the Qing in conflict with Manchu loyalists.
As the anniversary of the overthrow of the Manchu
regime approaches (2011), this theme remains salient
for diasporic Chinese film-makers. Teddy Chen's
Bodyguards and Assassins (2009) serves as a case in
point. In this film, Donnie Yen (born in Guangdong,
educated in Hong Kong and Boston, MA), who has
worked in China as well as Hollywood with film-
makers such as Zhang Yimou and Guillermo del Toro,
plays a corrupt colonial cop in Hong Kong. With a guilty
conscience, he switches sides to protect Sun Yat-sen –
the founder of the modern Chinese nation, who
emigrated to Hawaii at a young age, was educated in
Hong Kong and the United Kingdom, lived in exile in
Japan, and spent most of his career on the road to raise
money within the overseas Chinese communities
abroad for the building of the modern Chinese nation-
state.

As a transnational production, *Bodyguards and
Assassins* boasts connections to the PRC, ROC/Taiwan,
Macau and Hong Kong, as well as other places
associated with the Chinese diaspora. Mengke Bateer, a
Mongolian born in Beijing, for example, who played for
the NBA in the US before landing a role in the movie,
portrays one of the bodyguards. Macau-born Michelle
Reis, of Portuguese and Chinese descent, has a cameo
role. Peter Chan – who has established perhaps the
most successful 'pan-Asian' cinematic network in
operation today – produced the film on a set in
Shanghai that recreated old Hong Kong.

Film-maker, actor and historical figure all play
prominent roles within the Chinese diaspora. Peter

Bodyguards and Assassins

Chan's career, for example, illustrates the ways in
which various cinemas of the Chinese diaspora
interconnect. Chan spent his early life in Thailand, had
schooling in Hong Kong, went to the United States for
college (where he attended UCLA) and settled back in
Hong Kong to pursue his film-making career. Married to
local comedienne Sandra Ng and co-founder of UFO
Film Company, Chan directs films that tap into the
'structures of feeling'[4] that shape Hong Kong as well as
the Chinese diaspora, including *Comrades, Almost a Love
Story* (1996), which looks at Hong Kong and New York
City as sites of exile and displacement.

Chan founded Applause Pictures (with Teddy Chen
and Allan Fung) in 2000 in order to foster pan-Asian
film production, and the company has produced films
in Thailand, South Korea, Japan, Singapore and the PRC,
as well as Hong Kong. He also has maintained his ties
to Hollywood, where he directed *Love Letter* in 1999.
However, as the PRC market opens for Hong Kong film
productions, Chan also works closely with established
producer-directors there. For *Bodyguards and Assassins*,
for example, he worked with Fifth Generation film-
maker Huang Jianxin, who developed the mammoth
anniversary film *The Founding of a Republic* (2009) at
around the same time. Both films rely on a similar
formula of playing with figures from modern Chinese
history and casting some of the biggest box-office
draws in Chinese-language cinema in cameo roles. Part
of the fun, in each film, is seeing how many illustrious
Chinese celebrities can be spotted and knowing that
the production must have cost a fortune and quite a lot
of the producers' *guan xi* (connections) to get off the
ground. (Many stars appear in both films, including
Donnie Yen, Leon Lai and Hu Jun, and both films take
advantage of their performers' diasporic flexibility.)

Hong Kong, a former colony with a continuing
extraterritorial status under the 'one country two

systems' policy, anchors *Bodyguards and Assassins*. The city provides the story and the home base for the film-makers and many of the actors, as well as being the historical platform for Sun Yat-sen's political manoeuvring. In fact, at least since the Song Dynasty, Hong Kong has been a refuge for Chinese from elsewhere, and, after the establishment of the Crown Colony, it became a piece of Europe in Asia, a link between China and the West, what some have called the 'biggest Chinatown' on earth. Ackbar Abbas, for instance, has provocatively asked, 'Is Hong Kong no more than the world's largest Chinatown?'[5] Hong Kong is a city of immigrants and the children of immigrants, people with multiple passports and global connections. As Chan's film *Comrades, Almost a Love Story* demonstrates, with its fiction's connections to mainland China, England, Hollywood, Thailand and New York City, and *Bodyguards and Assassins* confirms, Hong Kong connects China and its diaspora onscreen and off.

Particularly after the signing of the Joint Accord in 1984 and in the aftermath of the suppression of the demonstrations in Tiananmen Square in 1989, Hong Kong became a port of embarkation for many residents as well as for transients.[6] An ethnic Chinese city connected to the mainland, ruled by the British for over a hundred years, and now part of the PRC, but operating under a separate 'system', Hong Kong continues to be 'home' to Chinese from 'elsewhere' – crossing over from the mainland, but also 'passing through' to North America, Australia, South-East Asia or Europe, returning again, and, perhaps, relocating again to another point within the diaspora. Hong Kong, like Hollywood, has welcomed immigrants with talent from overseas willing to contribute to its own Chinese version of the diasporic 'dream factory'.

Films made in Hong Kong, Taiwan and the People's Republic, in fact, regularly take up stories from the Chinese diaspora – including journeys, homecomings, divided families, displaced people, political exiles, economic migration and all sorts of 'wandering Chinese' throughout history. Within diaspora, identity becomes an issue (sometimes a burden). The same film-maker, performer or fictional character may be, at various points, a Chinese exile, a Hong Kong émigré, an American immigrant, a mainlander, Taiwanese, Cantonese-speaking, Mandarin-speaking, Hokkien-speaking, Hakka or non-Han Chinese, a sojourner, a citizen or naturalised citizen, an overseas Chinese, Chinese American, Asian American, 'majority' Han and 'minority' elsewhere. Ties to China may be strong, weak or broken. Connections to established Chinatowns may be essential to survival or non-existent. Extended families may remain in China or be scattered around South-East Asia or relocated elsewhere on the planet. Within the Chinese diaspora, various dialects of Chinese may or may not be spoken, and films may or may not be in Chinese. Diasporic film-makers may take up ethnic Chinese subject matter or ignore it or do both (e.g., Ang Lee, Wayne Wang).

The focus here is on what Hamid Naficy has termed 'accented cinema' – those films that have been marked by experiences of exile, immigration and diaspora. As Naficy points out, there is a continuum within cinema made by migrant populations ranging from exilic cinema linked to thoughts of the homeland, immigrant ethnic cinema concerned with the new country of residence and diasporic cinema connected to the experiences of others with the same ethnicity living elsewhere.[7] The same film-maker may have a career that spans the entire spectrum; others may be associated with one point or another. Dai Sijie appears to fall on the exilic side of the spectrum. His films, *China, My Sorrow* (1989) – which was shot in the French Pyrenees standing in for the PRC – and *Balzac and the Little Chinese Seamstress* (2002), say next to nothing about his adopted home of France and speak volumes about why he no longer resides in China. As a novelist, Dai works across media, but he does not transverse other borders as freely. Guo Xiaolu, also a novelist/film-maker from the PRC who has settled in Europe, on the

Song of the Exile

一九七三年夏天
Summer 1973

other hand, makes films that bridge China and the United Kingdom (e.g., *She, A Chinese*, 2009).

Ann Hui's semi-autobiographical *Song of the Exile* (1990), as another example, speaks directly to the diaspora as the film's protagonist moves through the United Kingdom, Macau, Hong Kong, the PRC and Japan. Less an 'exile' or 'political' refugee than the child of parents buffeted by post-World War II displacements, the film's heroine has geographic associations too complicated to be contained by the label of 'immigrant'. The term 'diasporic' fits the character as well as the film with its multiple locations, languages and production talents (including Taiwan's Wu Nien-jen as scriptwriter).

Chan – Lost and Found

Wayne Wang began his feature film career with the pioneering *Chan is Missing* (1982). Although many Chinese film-makers had worked in America before,

Chan is Missing represents an important change in orientation – away from an address to the ethnic Chinese community and towards a wider audience. Peter X Feng has described the development of the film's characters, the movement of the narrative, as well as the intervention the film made in Asian American circles as reflecting a shift from 'being Chinese American' to 'becoming Asian American'.[8] However, questions of identity in diaspora extend beyond the political, social, or cultural need for an Asian American sense of community. Wang and the characters in his film move in and out of ethnic groups 'being' and 'becoming' Chinese, Hong Kong Chinese, diasporic Chinese, Asian minorities, American immigrants and 'flexible citizens' of the world in which 'new ethnicities'[9] have replaced older national allegiances. It seems appropriate, then, that Chan should remain missing, and the unsolved mystery at the heart of the film stands as a metaphor for the mercurial nature of identity within diaspora.

Chan is Missing

In addition to the narrative puzzle conjured up by the missing Chan of the title, Wang's film engages with another mystery at the heart of diasporic cinema. Given the pervasiveness of the Chinese throughout the world, the limitation of their screen images to a handful of types begs the question of why Hollywood's Charlie Chan, routinely played by white actors in 'yellow face', should eclipse the ethnic Chinese Chans of the world who always seem to be 'missing' on screen. Racism has haunted ethnic Chinese cinema since the dawn of the medium coincided with the 1900 Boxer Rebellion and film was put in the service of anti-China propaganda.

Chinatown motion pictures, too, justified exclusionary laws by showing hatchet battles, tong wars and opium dens.[10] These images served to legitimise the importance of police surveillance and control in the Chinatown ghettoes, keeping the 'yellow peril' alive and racial hierarchies intact. The Sax Rohmer literary creation, Fu Manchu, the face of this threat, became a commercial film fixture and one of the most enduring figures demonising the Chinese as a venomous, alien force sweeping the planet. More nomadic than diasporic, this Eurasian super-villain still lurks, in various guises, in the dark alleys of the world's cinematic Chinatowns, threatening the white population at every turn.

However, throughout Hollywood history, as Arthur Dong's comprehensive documentary *Hollywood Chinese* (2007) shows, Chinese American performers have been engaged in ongoing negotiations and contestations over their depiction onscreen. A dialectic exists between the ethnic 'insider' and 'outsider' in Hollywood, and many players such as Anna May Wong, Nancy Kwan, Keye Luke and even Jackie Chan, Joan Chen, Lucy Liu and B. D. Wong, struggle with performing an ethnic identity imposed on them while trying to gesture towards resistance.[11] Valued as expert insiders, they still have difficulty not conforming to type and taking up the 'yellow face' offered. Many, such as Bruce Lee, turned back to Asia as a way out of this 'classical mess'. Others, such as Anna May Wong, continued to drift within the diaspora, performing in England and Germany, touring China, and returning to Hollywood during the war years to make films in support of China's struggle against the Japanese. Despite the United States' support for the Chinese cause during World War II, the Asian face, as Chinese American actor Victor Wong points out in Renee Tajima-Pena's film *My America … Or, Honk If You Love Buddha* (1997), represented the 'enemy' for mainstream Hollywood as Chinese triad, Japanese war criminal, Red Chinese spy, North Korean combatant or Vietcong guerrilla fighter.

Diasporic film-makers insist on viewing Hollywood's Chinatown from a different perspective, and Sinophone[12] or multilingual transnational productions probe being Chinese in America from yet another angle. While an occasional film may take place in the heartland, these films, for the most part, are geographically bi-coastal with narratives set in Los Angeles–San Francisco–the American West or located in New York City. As Staci Ford has pointed out in her study of Hong Kong film-makers in the United States, this polarity reflects the divided perception of America as a frontier (the West) open to fantasy (Hollywood) and the United States as the pinnacle of urban modernity (New York).[13]

Wayne Wang, for example, has focused on stories about the Chinese in America. *Chan is Missing*, *Dim Sum: A Little Bit of Heart* (1985), *Eat a Bowl of Tea* (1989) and, to a large extent, *The Joy Luck Club* (1993) are about the Chinatown experience and deal with the consequences of a history of anti-Asian racism within a multigenerational community.[14] Made mainly in English, he casts actors of various ethnicities to portray Chinese Americans, and he has been hailed as a pioneer in Asian American film-making precisely because he has been open to moving outside the Chinese diaspora to tell his tales about ethnicity in America.

In many respects, Wang benefited from a growth spurt of Asian American media activity in the 1970s and 80s. At the crossroads of the Civil Rights Movement and the rise in American independent film production, several Asian American organisations began to scrape together funds to put images of Asians onscreen outside the confines of Hollywood. These included Asian CineVision in New York City, Asian American Arts and Media in Washington, DC, Visual Communications in Los Angeles, National Asian American Telecommunications Association (NAATA) in San Francisco, Foundation for Asian American Independent Media (FAAIM) in Chicago, among others. Other organisations such as Third World Newsreel began to emphasise work done by and about the Asian community in American, including several films about Chinese Americans (notably, Christine Choy's *Mississippi Triangle*, 1984, in collaboration with Allan Siegel and Worth Long). Film festivals dedicated to Asian

American film-making emerged, with Chinese diasporic film-makers, such as Wayne Wang, welcomed. In fact, Wang may have been inspired by the work of other film-makers working in San Francisco's Chinatown, since there appear to be echoes of Curtis Choy's *Dupont Guy: The Schiz of Grant Avenue* (1975) and *The Fall of the I-Hotel* (1983) in his oeuvre.

Wayne Wang, however, also maintains strong ties to Hong Kong, where he grew up. He draws on Hong Kong talent, including his wife actress Cora Miao and fellow film-maker Allen Fong, as well as on Taiwanese American performers like film-maker Peter Wang (dir. *A Great Wall*, 1986; actor *Ah Ying*/dir. Allen Fong, 1983). He operates within and between various identities – Hong Kong, Chinese, Chinese American, Asian American, American independent, diasporic and transnational – as a film-maker. Like Ang Lee, he has made films set in America but completely outside the Asian American community (*Blue in the Face*, 1995; *Smoke*, 1995), and he has also set stories in Hong Kong (*Life is Cheap … But Toilet Paper is Expensive*, 1989; *Chinese Box*, 1997). Although primarily working outside of Hollywood, he has directed films with more substantial budgets for commercial release (*Maid in Manhattan*, 2002; *Because of Winn-Dixie*, 2005; *Last Holiday*, 2006). His career has taken him from Asia to mid-America, from Chinatown to African American New Orleans and Hispanic New York City. He moves freely between ethnic America and the Chinese diaspora, and his career has been built on these transnational connections.

Queer in the Chinese Diaspora

The appearance of Ang Lee's *The Wedding Banquet* (1993) marked a sea change not only for the depiction of the Chinese diaspora onscreen, but for the portrayal of homosexuality and queer desire within Chinese-language cinema. Lee married the 'green card' romantic comedy to the Confucian patriarchal melodrama and placed it within the context of New Queer Cinema. These connections opened a floodgate that highlighted the importance of the Chinese migrant within the queer community as well as spotlighting the sexuality of the diasporic Chinese. While other films explored the diaspora as economic or political and some took up questions of the personal (e.g., emigration as a means of escaping an arranged marriage or some other difficult family situation), *The Wedding Banquet* broached the issue of leaving hearth and home in order to escape from the suffocating consequences of homophobia.

Of course, many Chinese LGBT film-makers had made important contributions to the depiction of Asian queers before 1993. Richard Fung's *Orientations* (1985) and *Chinese Characters* (1986), Ming-yuen S. Ma's *Aura* (1991) and *Toc Storee* (1992), Quentin Lee's *Anxiety of Inexpression and the Otherness Machine* (1992) and Paul Lee's *Thin Lips, Thick Lips* (1994) appeared around the same time as *The Wedding Banquet* or earlier. However, the commercial success of *The Wedding Banquet* encouraged the making of feature films specifically about the queer experience within the Chinese diaspora – from 'coming out' melodramas and queer romantic comedies to meditations on same-sex desire. Alice Wu's *Saving Face* (2004), for example, also set in New York City, looks at lesbian love, in a similar fashion, within the context of the Chinese family and the ethnic community.

Happy Together

Other films took up the queer Chinese diaspora in other parts of the world. Yonfan's *Bugis Street* (1995) explores life on the infamous avenue for transsexual prostitutes in Singapore, and Kenneth Bi's *Rice Rhapsody* (2004) and Glen Goei's *Forever Fever* (1998) also treat LGBT concerns in Singapore. Amir Muhammad's *Pangyau* (2002) narrates a story of queer desire in Kuala Lumpur's Chinatown. Sylvia Chang's *Tempting Heart* (1999), Stanley Kwan's *Hold You Tight* (1998) and Yau Ching's *Ho Yuk: Let's Love Hong Kong* (2002) involve gay and lesbian characters in Hong Kong who have libidinal connections to others in the Chinese diaspora. Wong Kar-wai's *Happy Together* (1997) takes its drifting gay lovers from Hong Kong to Argentina. Hung Wing Kit's *Soundless Wind Chime* (2009) charts a cross-cultural homosexual affair from Hong Kong to Switzerland. Quentin Lee's *Drift* (2001) and Simon Chung's *Innocent* (2005), set in Canada, Ray Yeung's *Cut Sleeve Boys* (2006), set in England, and New York-based film-maker Evans Chan's *Map of Sex and Love* (2001), set mainly in Hong Kong, all probe what it means to drift within intersecting waves of the queer and Chinese diasporas.

These films, in fact, provide a meeting point within what Helen Leung has called the cinematic 'queerscape' for a variety of perspectives on ethnic Chinese as well as queer identities.[15] Song Hwee Lim, referring to the characters in *Happy Together*, has called these queer Chinese diasporic identities 'traveling sexualities'.[16] Moving outside the confines of ethnic cinema, these films speak across genres, genders, generations and sexual orientations to the complexity of living within the Chinese diaspora in ways that Hollywood's Chinatown melodramas never approach. The meeting of the queer and Chinese diasporas, in fact, has brought these screen stories to audiences outside the confines of both the ethnic Chinese and LGBT communities. Being queer and Chinese – multiply marginalised, drifting, shifting and desiring – speaks eloquently, in fact, to many viewers who look beyond the politics of racial, ethnic or sexual identity to the instabilities of all markers of identity within an increasingly global, postmodern frame of reference.[17]

Global Dynamics

Of course, in addition to having a prominent place in American, Canadian and British cinema, Chinese characters regularly appear in a number of other cinemas around the world; for example, Maggie Cheung in Paris in Olivier Assayas' *Irma Vep* (1996) and *Clean*

(2004), Jet Li in Paris in *Kiss of the Dragon* (2001) and in Glasgow in *Danny the Dog* (2005); Jackie Chan in Rotterdam (as well as Africa) in *Who Am I* (1998) and in Paris in *Rush Hour 3* (2007). Tsai Ming-liang, Hou Hsiao Hsien and Johnnie To have all directed films with Parisian connections. Australia, Germany and Hong Kong form the backdrop for Clara Law's *Floating Life* (1996), and Tony Ayres looks at the route from Hong Kong to Australia in *The Home Song Stories* (2007). The Japanese films, *Swallowtail Butterfly* (1996) and *Beijing Watermelon* (1996), deal with Chinese immigrants, and the Jackie Chan-vehicle *Shinjuku Incident* (2009) examines the hardships of being an ethnic Chinese in Tokyo. In Korea, Song Hae-sung's *Failan* (2001) features Hong Kong's Cecilia Cheung as a young woman in search of the Korean side of her family.

South-East Asia has also nurtured indigenous Chinese-language film production over the years, with important ties to Hong Kong, in particular. Hong Kong connections with Thailand (through Peter Chan), the Philippines (through Roger Garcia) and elsewhere remain important, and Chinatowns in other parts of South-East Asia serve as the backdrop for Hong Kong films as well, notably John Woo's *Bullet in the Head* (1990), Ann Hui's *Boat People* (1982) and Tsui Hark's *A Better Tomorrow III* (1989), all set in Vietnam.

Long after the Shaw Brothers and other Chinese film companies abandoned their South-East Asian productions, there has been a particularly dramatic revival of ethnic Chinese film-making in Malaysia and Singapore in the past decade or so. While Eric Khoo brought the predominantly Chinese city-state of Singapore into the global circuit of film festivals with features such as *Mee Pok Man* (1995) and *Twelve Storeys* (1997), Malaysia has emerged, more recently, as a source for cutting-edge fare. Here, too, Hong Kong connections are significant. Patrick Tam's *After This Our Exile* (2006) brings his Hong Kong New Wave sensibility to Malaysia to tell the story of a dysfunctional Chinese family. Hong Kong actress Kara Hui (Wai Ying-Hong) stars as the single mother of an adult son who becomes embroiled in a statutory rape case in Malaysian New Wave film-maker Ho Yuhang's *At the End of Daybreak* (2009). Woo Ming Jin, Liew Seng Tat and James Lee, among others, set their independent features within the Malaysian Chinese community, and the late Yasmin Ahmad explored the issue of an interethnic romance involving a Chinese character in *Sepet* (2004). Even Tsai Ming-liang has drifted back home from Taiwan to make *I Don't Want to Sleep Alone* (2006) in Malaysia.

In fact, as was the case with earlier commercial Chinese Malaysian ventures, the Malaysian New Wave exploits not only its local atmosphere, stories and screen talent, but also its cosmopolitan connections to the global Chinese community. Many of the movement's DV (digital video) features take up Hong Kong New Wave/indie, Taiwan New Cinema and/or the PRC's Sixth Generation aesthetic concerns and subject matter to deal with stories about those alienated and economically disadvantaged by globalisation and the rise of neo-liberalism. These Sinophone Malaysian films circulate at international festivals, are supported by transnational resources and work within an idiom familiar to cineastes around the world. Thus, these very cosmopolitan film-makers can draw on the marginalised working classes living within Malaysia's Chinatown in order to form part of the cutting edge of global Chinese film-making.

Going Back/Facing Forward

As the PRC 'opened' in the late 1970s, diasporic film-makers began to take advantage of increased access to the 'homeland'. Chinese American and Chinese Canadian film-makers made films about their ancestral villages (e.g., Richard Fung's *The Way to My Father's Village*, 1988). Film-makers began to make 'reunion' films such as Peter Wang's *A Great Wall* and Yu Kang-Ping's *Reunion/People between Two Chinas* (1988), and even mainland film-makers picked up on the melodramatic potential of these family get-togethers (e.g., Wang Quan'an's *Apart Together*, 2010). Hong Kong film-makers made several features on returns to the mainland, including Yim Ho's *Homecoming* (1984), Mabel Cheung's *Eight Taels of Gold* (1989) and Ann Hui's *My American Grandson* (1991).

In fact, the ranks of ethnic Chinese film-makers are filled with people who were born in the West, but work in Asia (e.g., from Bruce Lee to Daniel Wu and Michael Wong) or who were born in Asia, educated in Europe or America and established careers in Hong Kong or Taiwan (e.g., the late Edward Yang in Taiwan and virtually all the film-makers associated with Hong Kong's New Wave). Other diasporic film-makers seem to keep their options open (e.g., Evans Chan, Wayne Wang, Clara Law, John Woo, Ang Lee) by moving between Hong Kong or Taiwan and the West. In places such as Malaysia and Singapore, the transnational, the

pan-Asian, the immigrant, the ethnic and the diasporic seem to meet on film screens, and the history of the Chinese in film testifies to the tremendous importance of the Chinese diaspora to the development of not only Asian but also world cinema. The diaspora intrudes and insinuates itself between national cinemas and the transnational, between global film and local productions, as well as between Sinophone movies and various polyglot permutations of ethnic Chinese production – keeping open any absolute definition of what Chinese cinema 'is'.

Notes

1. Film-maker Loni Ding passed away 28 February 2010 and I would like to dedicate this chapter to the memory of her contribution to Asian American and Chinese diasporic cinema.

2. See Mia Tuan, *Forever Foreigners or Honorary Whites: The Asian Ethnic Experience Today* (New Brunswick, NJ: Rutgers University Press, 1998). Also see Lisa Lowe, *Immigrant Acts: On Asian American Cultural Politics* (Durham, NC: Duke University Press, 1996).

3. Aihwa Ong, *Flexible Citizenship: The Cultural Logics of Transnationality* (Durham, NC: Duke University Press, 1999).

4. Raymond Williams, *Marxism and Literature* (Oxford: Oxford University Press, 1977).

5. Ackbar Abbas, 'Building on Disappearance: Hong Kong Architecture and the City', *Public Culture* vol. 6 no. 3 (1994), p. 445.

6. See Sheldon Lu, 'Filming Diaspora and Identity: Hong Kong and 1997', in Fu Poshek and David Desser (eds), *The Cinema of Hong Kong: History, Arts, Identity* (New York: Cambridge University Press, 2000), pp. 273–88. Also see Julian Stringer, 'Cultural Identity and Diaspora in Contemporary Hong Kong Cinema', in Darrell Y. Hamamoto and Sandra Liu (eds), *Countervisions: Asian American Film Criticism* (Philadelphia: Temple University Press, 2000), pp. 298–312.

7. See Hamid Naficy, *An Accented Cinema: Exilic and Diasporic Filmmaking* (Princeton, NJ, and Oxford: Princeton University Press, 2001).

8. Peter X Feng, 'Becoming Asian American: Chinese American Identity, Asian American Subjectivity, and *Chan is Missing*', *Cinema Journal* vol. 35 no. 4 (1996), pp. 88–118.

9. Chen Kuan-Hsing and David Morley (eds), *Stuart Hall: Critical Dialogues in Cultural Studies* (London: Routledge, 1996).

10. Ruth Mayer, 'The Glittering Machine of Modernity: The Chinatown in American Silent Film', *Modernism/Modernity* vol. 16 no. 4 (2009), pp. 661–84. See also Sabine Haenni, 'Filming "Chinatown": Fake Visions, Bodily Transformations', in Peter X Feng (ed.), *Screening Asian Americans* (New Brunswick, NJ: Rutgers University Press, 2002), pp. 21–52.

11. For women, in particular, this has often meant dealing with not only racism but sexism as well in a milieu that makes the expression of their own desires difficult. See Celine Parreñas Shimizu, *The Hypersexuality of Race: Performing Asian/American Women on Screen and Scene* (Durham, NC: Duke University Press, 2007).

12. For more on the definition of the 'Sinophone', see Shu-mei Shih, *Visuality and Identity: Sinophone Articulations across the Pacific* (Berkeley: University of California Press, 2007).

13. Staci Ford, 'Hong Kong Film Goes to America', in Gina Marchetti and Tan See Kam (eds), *Hong Kong Film, Hollywood, and the New Global Cinema* (London: Routledge, 2007), pp. 50–62. For more on Hong Kong/American film connections, see Kwai-Cheung Lo, *Chinese Face/Off: The Transnational Popular Culture of Hong Kong* (Urbana: University of Illinois Press, 2005).

14. Sandra Liu, 'Negotiating the Meaning of Access: Wayne Wang's Contingent Film Practice', in Hamamoto and Liu, *Countervisions Film Criticism* (Philadelphia: Temple University Press, 2000), pp. 90–111.

15. Leung Helen Hok-sze, 'Queerscapes in Contemporary Hong Kong Cinema', *positions: east asia cultures critique* vol. 9 no. 2 (2001), pp. 423–47.

16. Song Hwee Lim, *Celluloid Comrades: Representations of Male Homosexuality in Contemporary Chinese Cinemas* (Honolulu: University of Hawaii Press, 2006), p. 108.

17. See Chris Berry, 'Happy Alone? Sad Young Men in East Asian Gay Cinema', *Journal of Homosexuality* vol. 39 no. 3/4 (June 2000), pp. 187–200.

Further Reading in *Chinese Films in Focus II*

On Ann Hui, see Chapter 5, '*Boat People*: Second Thoughts on Text and Context' by Julian Stringer.

On Ang Lee, see Chapter 30, '*Wedding Banquet*: A Family (Melodrama) Affair' by Chris Berry.

On Singaporean film-making, see Chapter 1, '15: The Singapore Failure Story, "Slanged Up"' by Song Hwee Lim.

4 Six Chinese Cinemas in Search of a Historiography

Song Hwee Lim

A book entitled *The Chinese Cinema Book* presupposes a national cinema model and attempts to construct a historiography of that national cinema. This chapter will delineate the problematic nature and complexity of those two tasks in relation to the concept of Chinese cinema. On the national cinema model, it will map out six different configurations of Chinese cinema that have been presented in English-language scholarship,[1] and highlight the contested meanings of the signifier 'Chinese' within the field of Chinese cultural studies and the challenges to the national cinema model within the discipline of film studies. On historiography, it will argue for the necessity of its multiplicity as a corollary of the multiple configurations of the concept of Chinese cinema, while never losing sight of the issue of power that underlies any historiographic writing. It will, in its conclusion, propose a shift away from the national cinema model altogether in order, to borrow the title of Prasenjit Duara's book, to 'rescue history from the nation'.[2] Instead, taking inspiration from Gilles Deleuze and Felix Guattari,[3] I will argue for a 'minor historiography' in which the (minor) subject of history unsettles the very notion of the (major) Subject of History. It asks, in its final analysis, what does it mean to have a cinema without nation, and to what extent this is conceivable in relation to Chinese cinema.

Chineseness and the National Cinema Model

The term 'Chinese' is ambiguous and contentious for both conceptual and political reasons, and the meaning of Chineseness has been hotly debated within the field of Chinese cultural studies for decades. To begin with, it is often unclear whether the signifier 'Chinese' is 'an ethnic, cultural, linguistic, political or territorial marker'.[4] While some scholars are eager to construct a pan-Chinese identity based on shared values and cultural heritage, others have been quick to highlight dissenting voices and differences that cannot simply be subsumed under or obliterated by such a cultural imaginary.[5] Given that 'few places have a more complex relation to the national than the combination constituted by the People's Republic [of China], Hong Kong, Taiwan, and the Chinese diaspora',[6] it is unsurprising that scholarship on Chinese cinema has been at the forefront in recognising the plurality of the concept of Chinese 'national' cinema by using the plural rather than the singular form when referring to it.[7] However, whether using it in the singular or the plural, the very model of national cinema has been vigorously challenged in the discipline of film studies in recent years, to the extent that any usage of the model almost invariably brings with it an apology. Yingjin Zhang, for instance, begins the introduction to his book, *Chinese National Cinema*, by stating that the publication of another volume on national cinema at the start of the new millennium 'may seem ironic'.[8] Likewise, Chris Berry and Mary Farquhar suggest that the national cinema model is inadequate and propose to approach the 'national as contested and construed in different ways' by reconfiguring 'national cinema' as 'cinema and the national'.[9]

Realising the limitations of the national cinema model, scholarship on Chinese cinema has also led the way in indicating a shift from the national to the transnational with the publication of a volume edited by

Sheldon Hsiao-peng Lu in 1997, entitled *Transnational Chinese Cinemas*.[10] In their introduction to a special issue on transnational cinema in the *Journal of Chinese Cinemas* in 2008, the guest editors Chris Berry and Laikwan Pang note that, with the benefit of hindsight, Lu's 1997 volume was 'a watershed moment in the study of Chinese cinemas' as both the terms 'Chinese cinemas' (in the plural) and 'transnational Chinese cinemas' were rarely used before Lu's book but they now 'name the field that we study and are used routinely'.[11] More recently, Lu has, together with Emilie Yueh-yu Yeh, proposed the concept of 'Chinese-language film' to encompass, like the concept of 'transnational Chinese cinemas', film-making activities that are located in several geographical regions and yet share certain linguistic and cultural traits of 'Chineseness'.[12]

The above account presents four configurations of the concept of Chinese cinema whose historiographies have been constructed in book-length publications in the English language. They can be summarised as follows, with the first three based on a national cinema model and the fourth on a transnational cinema model:

1. Chinese cinema(s), mainly focusing on Mainland China, both before and after the founding of the PRC in 1949, but often also including discussions of films from Taiwan, Hong Kong and the Chinese diaspora;[13]
2. Taiwan cinema, including the colonial period ruled by Japan (1895–1945);[14]
3. Hong Kong cinema, both before and after the handover of Hong Kong to the PRC in 1997;[15]
4. Transnational Chinese cinemas and Chinese-language cinema, which encompass all of the above.

It is noteworthy that, in general surveys of film studies that cover cinemas of the world, the national cinema model has been routinely applied to the three cinemas from China, Taiwan and Hong Kong as if they are distinct 'national' cinemas, reinforcing the first three configurations of Chinese cinema.[16] This raises the question of what the 'national' within the national cinema model is, exactly, given 'the flux of political regimes and the accompanying status of nation-states, the increasingly interconnected global economy, shifting patterns of linguistic innovation and the complications of ethnic and racial identifications' so that the 'very idea of Chinese cinema is always already fractured'.[17] On the other hand, while the first

configuration adopts a national cinema model and the fourth configuration shifts to a transnational mode, they tend to overlap in their all-encompassing coverage of 'Chinese' cinemas. By routinely including cinemas outside of China in its discussion, the first configuration reinforces a China-centrism without necessarily problematising the issue of Chineseness at the very heart of its contention. The fourth configuration, while emphasising border crossing and the global reach of the Chinese language, risks keeping the issue of Chineseness intact by reinstating it in a larger, pan-Chinese, transnational framework.

The four configurations mapped out above, therefore, take the nation (whether contained within a geographical boundary or transcending it) as their organising principle. While the first and the fourth tend to include films produced in the Chinese diasporas in their discussion, the fundamental question concerning the diasporas demands separate treatment precisely because these diasporas have a different relationship to a 'homeland' that is presumed to be China and are located outside of the geopolitical region commonly known as 'greater China'. They form the fifth and sixth configurations of the concept of Chinese cinema as follows:

5. Diasporic cinema, spreading from South-East Asia and Australia to Europe and North America;
6. Sinophone cinema that includes all film production outside of China.

As the final two configurations are, in themselves, complex and controversial and raise further questions for the first four configurations, they deserve dedicated discussion in the following section.

From Diasporic Cinema to Sinophone Cinema

The migration of peoples from China to places across the world has been a historical process dating back centuries. While academic discourse has regarded these migrants as 'overseas Chinese' and, more recently, the 'Chinese diaspora', the critical purchase of these terms is increasingly brought into question by the migrants and their descendents. Because discourses on diaspora and migration tend to assume a host/home binary, this distinction becomes less useful the longer the history of migration. Indeed, how many generations does it take for descendents of Chinese migrants to be regarded not as overseas Chinese or part of the Chinese diaspora but as fully fledged citizens of the countries in which they are born and whereto their forebearers have initially made the journey from China? Depending on the racial mix and ethnic politics in those countries whose Chinese population can range from a majority in Singapore and a substantial minority in Malaysia to a marginal minority in Britain, the Chinese peoples born and bred in each of those locales will have different relationships with the concept of 'Chineseness'. The extent of cultural assimilation/preservation by individuals and communities, among many other socio-political factors, has resulted in these Chinese populations possessing varying degrees of command of Chinese languages and dialects. These individuals and communities also vary in terms of whether they feel compelled to choose between components of hyphenated identities (such as Chinese-American or Chinese-Singaporean, the order of which also differs according to one's politics), or simply identifying themselves as citizens of those countries.

The example of Chinese migration demonstrates the limitations of the discourse of diaspora in its privileging of the home as a cultural imaginary, with its attendant tropes of nostalgia, displacement and longing. Applied to the Chinese case, a diasporic model is essentially China-centric and assumes that Chinese migrants and their descendents necessarily possess a relationship with China, when the reality, in some cases at least, may be that these 'flexible citizens', to borrow Aihwa Ong's phrase,[18] only pledge allegiance to the countries in which they are born and are totally oblivious to the existence of China or the issue of Chineseness. Compared to the long history of Chinese migration, the history of Chinese cinema is a relatively short one. This may be one reason why the fifth configuration that is 'Chinese diasporic cinema' has never gained as much currency in academia, unlike the concept of 'accented cinema' (including diasporic, postcolonial and exilic cinemas by Third World film-makers who have emigrated to the West) formulated by Hamid Naficy.[19] Conventionally, Chinese-language film-making from regions outside China, Taiwan and Hong Kong has been included, if at all, in general discussions of Chinese cinema and transnational Chinese cinema (the first and fourth configurations). While the diasporic model has been applied to recent migrant film-makers to the West (such as Ang Lee in the United

States and Clara Law in Australia) and to production by 'overseas' arms of Hong Kong studios in South-East Asia,[20] it becomes thorny, for reasons laid out above, when dealing with ethnic Chinese film-makers born and bred outside 'greater China' (such as Royston Tan from Singapore or Richard Fung from Trinidad but now resident in Canada).

For Shu-mei Shih, the inability of the Chinese diasporic model to 'see beyond Chineseness as an organising principle' is a 'blindness' that she believes can be overcome by communicating with other scholarly paradigms, leading her to propose what I will list as the sixth configuration of Chinese cinema: Sinophone cinema.[21] Sinophone, in Shih's definition, refers to 'a network of places of cultural production outside China and on the margins of China and Chineseness, where a historical process of heterogenizing and localizing of continental Chinese culture has been taking place for several centuries'.[22] Because the Sinophone recognises that 'speaking fractions of different Sinitic languages associated with China is a matter of choice and other historical determinations', hence, unlike the concept of the Chinese diaspora, it foregrounds 'not the ethnicity or race of the person but the languages he or she speaks in either vibrant or vanishing communities of those languages'.[23] According to Shih, the Sinophone maintains 'a precarious and problematic relation to China, similar to the Francophone's relation to France, the Hispanophone's to Spain, and the Anglophone's to England in its ambiguity and complexity'.[24] The Sinophone is often the site where powerful articulations against China-centrism can be heard,[25] and, in the final sentence of her book, Shih declares, 'When Sinophone expressive cultures become complicit with China-centrism, they lose their articulatory function as the fulcrum of resistant and transformative identities.'[26]

Shih's recent intervention in the conception of Chinese cinema has already generated some debate. In a review of her book, Sheldon Lu insightfully points out several flaws in her arguments. First, the conflation of the Francophone and Anglophone models is problematic as the former does not include French cinema and literature whereas the latter includes cultural production from all English-speaking places and does not exclude Britain.[27] Second, the exclusion of China from the domain of the Sinophone is 'unsound theoretically and inaccurate empirically' as China,

Hong Kong, Taiwan and the Chinese diaspora are 'mutually imbricated in the globalizing world' whose 'ineluctable condition' is transnationality and border crossing.[28] Third, the demand that the only one proper function for the Sinophone is to resist China raises the questions of what China is and what China-centrism is, and also of what the linguistic politics among various speakers of Chinese languages and dialects, and that between them and the Sinophone, are, which cannot possibly be homogeneous or monolithic given the sheer size and population of the subject concerned.[29]

I believe Lu's critique of Shih's conception of the Sinophone is largely valid, and agree with him that, in publishing this 'provocative book', Shih has created an opportunity for a 'fruitful, honest dialogue on a number of important issues'.[30] Shih's critique of the diasporic model is trenchant but her attempt to replace it with the Sinophone does not so much decentre the China-centrism that she challenges; rather, it replaces one form of essentialism with another. For what is the 'Sino' in the Sinophone? In Shih's construction, the Sinophone is defined 'not by the race or nationality of the speaker but by the languages one speaks',[31] but isn't this lingua-centrism itself a form of essentialism that denies access to one's cultural production and cultural identity via a language that is presumably not one's own? While to equate 'nationality, race, and language is to be blind to the existence of multilingualism',[32] for some descendents of diasporic communities, it is precisely because of the reality of multiculturalism and interracial marriages that they may have lost their knowledge of the Chinese language yet somehow identify themselves as Chinese through cultural symbols, rituals and traditions (however unfashionable some of these are).[33] Indeed, some of them even watch Chinese films with the help of subtitles. If the descendents of immigrants are to be expunged from the Sinophone community once they 'no longer speak their ancestors' languages',[34] given the hybridity of identities and the multiplicity and creolisation of languages of these peoples in their countries of residence, how does one judge at which point these languages are no longer spoken? For example, the protagonists in Singaporean film-maker Royston Tan's 15 (2003) speak a combination of Mandarin, Hokkien and Singlish (the colloquial form of English), with a sprinkling of Malay terms, often all in one sentence. As their dialogue will be almost indecipherable to Chinese speakers outside of Singapore and Malaysia, the qualification in Shih's Sinophone model assumes a certain level of linguistic purity whose boundary will be impossible to police when it encounters a film such as 15.[35]

Shih's lingua-centric model also becomes problematic when confronted with the reality of film-making by Chinese-speaking film-makers. For example, would it be possible to examine the careers of Ang Lee and John Woo without taking into account the English-language films they have made in the United States?[36] How do we regard one-off forays into English-language film-making by auteurs such as Wong Kar-wai and Chen Kaige? Can films such as The Joy Luck Club (Wayne Wang, 1993) be considered Sinophone? What about Hou Hsiao-hsien's Japanese-language film, Café Lumière (2003), and French-language film, Flight of the Red Balloon (2007)? Just as the national cinema model has become untenable in a globalised world, it is also unfeasible to insist on organising films based on linguistic criterion alone at a time when translingual film-making is an increasingly commonplace phenomenon. If the national and transnational cinema models adopted by the first four configurations of Chinese cinema have been subject to critical challenge and demand rethinking, the Sinophone model proposed by Shih is not the solution as it does not sufficiently address either the complexity of the diasporas or the reality of translingual film-making.

Rescuing Historiography from the Nation: Towards a Minor Historiography

In his book, Rescuing History from the Nation: Questioning Narratives of Modern China, Prasenjit Duara writes of the need to break with the assumptions underlying most studies of nationalism that privilege the nation as a 'cohesive collective subject'. He suggests that although nationalism and its theory 'seek a privileging position within the representational network as the master identity that subsumes or organizes other identifications, [nationalist consciousness] exists only as one among others and is changeable, interchangeable, conflicted, or harmonious with them'.[37] Rather than seeing nationalism as 'overrid[ing] other identities within a society – such as religious, racial, linguistic, class, gender, or even historical ones – to encompass these differences in a larger identity',[38] Duara proposes that nationalism is best seen as a 'relational identity' as well as a 'historical configuration designed to include certain groups and exclude or marginalize others – often violently'.[39] Finally, as a historian, he charges 'History' for often working to 'secure the mystique of the nation' and its 'dubious claim to an evolving, monistic subjecthood', and sets as his own task to 'expose the repressive teleology of the History of the nation and rescues from this History the ways in which the past is meaningful to the present'.[40]

It is my aim in this chapter to rescue, in the spirit of Duara but departing from it somewhat, Chinese film historiography from the nation. As I have demonstrated above, the first four configurations of Chinese cinema take the (trans)national cinema model either to account for film-making activities within the boundaries of a nation or to emphasise cross-border transnationality. Many of the historiographies based on this model privilege the nation in their discussion of Chinese film as if nationalism and national identities had been the most important and salient features of Chinese film-making throughout its history. While cinema has certainly been mobilised by various agents as part of a nation-building project and has participated in the 'birth of a nation',[41] the obsessive (if not excessive) focus on cinema's role in constructing national identities obscures a similar function that cinema plays in the formation of other, not necessarily subsumable or less important, identities. More importantly, it fails to grant film its own agency so that film historiographies might account, first and foremost, for the formal, aesthetic and generic qualities as well as the industrial, economic and social functions of the medium at local, national, regional and global levels.

On the other hand, proposals to move away from the national cinema model, such as Chinese-language cinema (Lu and Yeh) and Sinophone cinema (Shih), replace a national-ethnic bias with a linguistic one. The lingua-centric model is particularly inadequate in dealing with films made in the so-called Chinese diasporas with their linguistic creolisation and when confronted with translingual film-making by contemporary directors. By using language as a transnational imaginary to account for Chinese film-making across the globe, the models of Sinophone cinema and Chinese-language cinema erect a different kind of essentialism, this time linguistic. In so doing, they lose sight of a very important lesson regarding the diaspora offered by Deleuze and Guattari in their discussion of Kafka, a lesson that is arguably more pertinent now than ever:

> How many people today live in a language that is not their own? Or no longer, or not yet, even know their own and know poorly the major language that they are forced to serve? This is the problem of immigrants, and especially of their children, the problem of minorities, the problem of a minor literature, but also a problem for all of us: how to tear a minor literature away from its own language, allowing it to challenge the language and making it follow a sober revolutionary path? How to become a

Café Lumière

Tsai Ming-liang's *What Time Is It There?*

nomad and an immigrant and a gypsy in relation to one's own language?[42]

Deleuze and Guattari read Kafka as a form of 'minor literature' that does not come from a minor language but rather 'that which a minority constructs within a major language', and whose first characteristic is an affectation of the major language 'with a high coefficient of deterritorialization'.[43] As a Jew in Prague writing in German, Kafka will push the German language towards 'a deterritorialization that will no longer be saved by culture or by myth', bringing it 'slowly and progressively to the desert',[44] so that language 'stops being representative in order to now move toward its extremities or its limits'.[45] To appropriate the model of 'minor literature' to a 'minor Chinese cinema', then, what should concern us is not to exclude from Chinese film historiography those films (whether made within China or beyond) because they are not spoken purely (in both senses of the term) in Chinese languages and dialects, but to include them precisely because their use of these languages and dialects is 'contaminated' and at times indecipherable (as in 15), resulting in a deterritorialisation of the language that brings with it a troubling of its very identity and centrality.

Rather than reinforcing the national cinema model of the first four configurations or reinstating a linguistic hegemony following the sixth configuration of Sinophone cinema, we need to construct a minor Chinese film historiography that can account for films made in any corner of the world that challenge the concept of Chinese-language cinema and that refuses to privilege national identities. By calling for a move towards a minor historiography I am not denying the imagination of the national or the use of Chinese languages and dialects in Chinese film-making but rather argue that they should be reconfigured differently. Hou's *Café Lumière*, set in Tokyo and spoken entirely in Japanese, brings to the fore the (post)colonial relationship between Taiwan and Japan and is arguably a more poignant account of the state of the nation even without using any of Taiwan's national languages. Tsai Ming-liang, a Chinese-Malaysian director whose career has been based in Taiwan, embodies what Kurt Vonnegut calls, in a different context, 'a man without a country'.[46] Tsai's film-making also displaces the centrality of the nation by privileging the cosmopolitan city as the site for the construction of other forms of identity, often in relation to gender and sexuality. Moreover, Tsai's *What Time Is It There?* (2001), with its citation of François Truffaut's *The 400 Blows* (1959), and Hou's *Flight of the Red Balloon*, with its allusion to Albert Lamorisse's *Red Balloon* (1956), illustrate how cross-cultural cinephilia is as valid an inspiration for film-making as any wish to imagine the birth of a nation. *Detours to Paradise* (2008) by Taiwan director Rich Lee features as its protagonists two migrant workers from Thailand and Indonesia whose common language is Mandarin. Lee's film invariably deterritorialises the Chinese language with the protagonists' imperfect pronunciation while highlighting that the dirty work of the nation-building project, from hard labour on the construction site to providing cheap sexual service to the national subject, is increasingly carried out by transnational, migrant subjects in a regional and global economic order that pays scant attention to national borders in its circulation of human and other capital.

These films, therefore, serve to construct a new, minor historiography of Chinese cinema. They represent a different mode of film-making because they do not take the centrality of Chinese languages and dialects as a given or privilege the nation in their narratives. Rather, they seek to give voice to the multilingual polyphony that contemporary subjects increasingly inhabit and to expose the fissures and 'impurities' within the national body politic. They resist participation in the myth of nationalism and push the concept of Chinese cinema to its extremities and limits. Finally, while they may be open to myriad forms of identification, they also reveal themselves first and foremost as artifice made possible by a certain conjunction of economy and capital (*Café Lumière* was commissioned by the Japanese studio Shochiku and *Flight of the Red Balloon* by the Musée d'Orsay in Paris). Rather than seeing cinema as merely providing representations of the nation and its multiple subjects, accepting filmic images as artifice would, as Rey Chow argues, 'liberate us from the constraints of literal, bodily identification, while reminding us of the under-theorized relation between economics, on the one hand, and fantasy and identity, on the other'.[47] Indeed,

in the current context of the rise of China as a global economic giant that has already witnessed the success of blockbuster hits such as *Crouching Tiger, Hidden Dragon* (Ang Lee, 2000) and *Hero* (Zhang Yimou, 2002), films that resuscitate a unification ideology and that interpellate a pan-Chinese identity, it is all the more important to question what form the *investment* in Chinese cinema takes and from whence it comes. As Chinese nationalism surges with the rise of economic prowess, the need for a minor Chinese cinema and its historiography becomes ever more urgent. Gian Piero Brunetta has argued, in the context of Italian cinema, that 'for the film historian, historiographic truth does not consist so much in the ability to produce a *history*, but rather in his [sic.] ability to keep in mind that there are *many histories*, and in knowing how to bring them to light in a net of new, unforeseen relations'.[48] This chapter represents a small step in formulating the multiple possibilities (and questioning the seeming impossibility) in the production of the histories of Chinese cinema. It also insists on this historiographic multiplicity in light of emerging and unforeseen relations both within and beyond the cinematic world.

Notes

1. I emphasise English-language scholarship because it is impossible, given the word limit of this chapter, to also consider the different configurations of the concept of Chinese cinema in Chinese-language scholarship. An insight into the differences in perspectives between scholarships conducted in these two languages can be gleaned in an interview with the film scholar Sheldon Hsiao-peng Lu. See Li Fengliang, 'New Perspectives on "Transnational Chinese Cinemas" Studies: An Interview with Lu Hsiao-peng', *Journal of Chinese Cinemas* vol. 4 no. 3 (2010), pp. 245–60.
2. Prasenjit Duara, *Rescuing History from the Nation: Questioning Narratives of Modern China* (Chicago and London: University of Chicago Press, 1995).
3. Gilles Deleuze and Felix Guattari, *Kafka: Toward a Minor Literature*, trans. Dana Polan (Minneapolis and London: University of Minnesota Press, 1986).
4. Yingjin Zhang, *Chinese National Cinema* (New York and London: Routledge, 2004), p. 4.
5. For a summary of recent debates on the Chinese identity, see Song Hwee Lim, *Celluloid Comrades: Representations of Male Homosexuality in Contemporary Chinese Cinemas* (Honolulu: University of Hawaii Press, 2006), pp. 2–3.

Flight of the Red Balloon

6. Chris Berry and Mary Farquhar, *China on Screen: Cinema and Nation* (New York: Columbia University Press), p. 14.

7. Nick Browne, Paul G. Pickowicz, Vivian Sobchack and Esther Yau (eds), *New Chinese Cinemas: Forms, Identities, Politics* (Cambridge: Cambridge University Press, 1994).

8. Zhang, *Chinese National Cinema*, p. 1.

9. Berry and Farquhar, *China on Screen*, p. 2.

10. Sheldon Hsiao-peng Lu (ed.), *Transnational Chinese Cinemas: Identity, Nationhood, Gender* (Honolulu: University of Hawaii Press, 1997).

11. Chris Berry and Laikwan Pang, 'Introduction, or, What's in an "s"?', *Journal of Chinese Cinemas* vol. 2 no. 1 (2008), pp. 3–8 (3).

12. Sheldon H. Lu and Emilie Yueh-yu Yeh (eds), *Chinese-Language Film: Historiography, Poetics, Politics* (Honolulu: University of Hawaii Press, 2005).

13. For example, Chris Berry (ed.), *Perspectives of Chinese Cinema* (London: BFI, 1991); Browne et al., *New Chinese Cinemas*; Zhang, *Chinese National Cinema*; Berry and Farquhar, *China on Screen*; Chris Berry (ed.), *Chinese Films in Focus II* (London: BFI, 2008).

14. Chris Berry and Feii Lu (eds), *Island on the Edge: Taiwan New Cinema and After* (Hong Kong: Hong Kong University Press, 2005); Darrell William Davis and Robert Ru-shou Chen (eds), *Cinema Taiwan: Politics, Popularity and State of the Arts* (London: Routledge, 2007).

15. Stephen Teo, *Hong Kong Cinema: The Extra Dimension* (London: BFI, 1997); Esther C. M. Yau (ed.), *At Full Speed: Hong Kong Cinema in a Borderless World* (Minneapolis and London: University of Minnesota Press, 2001).

16. For example, in John Hill and Pamela Church Gibson (eds), *The Oxford Guide to Film Studies* (Oxford: Oxford University Press, 1998) and Geoffrey Nowell-Smith (ed.), *The Oxford History of World Cinema* (Oxford: Oxford University Press, 1997).

17. Sean Metzger and Olivia Khoo, 'Introduction', in Olivia Khoo and Sean Metzger (eds), *Futures of Chinese Cinema: Technologies and Temporalities in Chinese Screen Cultures* (Bristol and Chicago: Intellect, 2009), pp. 13–34 (13).

18. Aihwa Ong, *Flexible Citizenship: The Cultural Logics of Transnationality* (Durham, NC, and London: Duke University Press, 1999).

19. Hamid Naficy, *An Accented Cinema: Exilic and Diasporic Filmmaking* (Princeton, NJ, and Oxford: Princeton University Press, 2001).

20. For example, Poshek Fu (ed.), *China Forever: The Shaw Brothers and Diasporic Cinema* (Urbana and Chicago: University of Illinois Press, 2008).

21. Shu-mei Shih, *Visuality and Identity: Sinophone Articulations across the Pacific* (Berkeley: University of California Press, 2007), p. 27.

22. Ibid., p. 4.

23. Ibid., p. 30.

24. Ibid.

25. Ibid., p. 31.

26. Ibid., p. 192.

27. Sheldon Hsiao-peng Lu, 'Review of *Visuality and Identity: Sinophone Articulations across the Pacific* by Shu-mei Shih', *MCLC Resource Center Publication* (January 2008), available online at <mclc.osu.edu/rc/pubs/reviews/lu.htm> (accessed 27 April 2010).

28. Ibid.

29. Ibid.

30. Ibid.

31. Shih, *Visuality and Identity*, p. 185.

32. Ibid., p. 186.

33. See Ien Ang, *On Not Speaking Chinese: Living Between Asia and the West* (London and New York: Routledge, 2001).

34. Shih, *Visuality and Identity*, 185.

35. For a fuller discussion on the linguistic and other issues in 15, see Song Hwee Lim, '15: The Singapore Failure Story, "Slanged Up"', in Berry, *Chinese Films in Focus II*, pp. 9–16.

36. Similarly, does German film historiography exclude the English-language films by Wim Wenders and those of earlier émigré directors to Hollywood? Do we discount from Austrian and Polish cinemas the French-language films made by, respectively, Michael Haneke and Krystof Kieślowski?

37. Duara, *Rescuing History from the Nation*, pp. 7–8.

38. Ibid., p. 10.

39. Ibid., p. 15.

40. Ibid., p. 16.

41. Sheldon H. Lu and Emilie Yueh-yu Yeh, 'Introduction: Mapping the Field of Chinese-Language Cinema', in Lu and Yeh, *Chinese-Language Film*, pp. 1–24 (2).

42. Deleuze and Guattari, *Kafka: Toward a Minor Literature*, p. 19.

43. Ibid., p. 16.

44. Ibid., p. 26.

45. Ibid., p. 23; emphasis in original.

46. Kurt Vonnegut, *A Man Without a Country: A Memoir of Life in George W. Bush's America* (London: Bloomsbury, 2007).

47. Rey Chow, 'A Phantom Discipline', *PMLA* vol. 116 no. 5 (2001), pp. 1386–95 (1393).

48. Gian Piero Brunetta, *Storia del cinema italiano: Dal 1945 agli anni '80* (Rome: Editori Riuniti), p. 13. Quoted in Francesco Casetti, *Theories of Cinema 1945–1995*, trans. Francesca Chiostri and Elizabeth Gard Bartolini-Salimbeni with Thomas Kelso (Austin: University of Texas Press, 1999), p. 311, emphasis in original.

Further Reading in *Chinese Films in Focus II*

On Ang Lee, see Chapter 30, '*Wedding Banquet*: A Family (Melodrama) Affair' by Chris Berry.

On Singaporean film-making, see Chapter 1, '15: The Singapore Failure Story, "Slanged Up"' by Song Hwee Lim.

On Tsai Ming-liang, see Chapter 29, '*Vive L'Amour*: Eloquent Emptiness' by Fran Martin.

PART TWO

Early Cinema to 1949

5 *Shadow Magic* and the Early History of Film Exhibition in China

Xuelei Huang and Zhiwei Xiao

The early history of the motion picture in China follows a drastically different trajectory from that in Europe and the US. In Europe and the US the production, distribution and exhibition of films were closely intertwined from the outset. Major producers, such as Pathé in France and the Edison Company in the US, were simultaneously involved in producing, distributing and exhibiting their products. This pattern would persist well into the World War II era. In China, although the new medium was introduced into the country shortly after it was invented in the West, native film-making did not begin in earnest until decades later. This means that the early history of Chinese cinema is predominantly a history of film screenings, not of production. However, the existing scholarship on pre-1949 Chinese cinema tends to focus on film production while neglecting the other two sectors of the film industry. This chapter is an attempt to call scholarly attention to the henceforth under-studied aspect of film exhibition by taking issue with the feature film *Shadow Magic* (Ann Hu, 2000).

As a joint production by the Beijing Film Studio (China), C & A Productions (USA), Central Motion Picture Corporation (Taiwan) and several Germany film institutions, *Shadow Magic* was released in Australia, Japan and the US as well as in China. Its subject matter (the arrival of motion pictures in China), its easy availability in the West and its deliberate attempt at 'historicism' instead of historical accuracy[1] have made the film a popular choice in university-level courses on Chinese cinema. Therefore, the film deserves serious scholarly assessment. In what follows we will briefly introduce the plot of the film, and then examine the film from a historical perspective. In so doing, we hope to shed some new light on the early history of film exhibition in China and make the film a more effective pedagogical tool in the classroom.

Set in Beijing at the turn of the twentieth century, the film's plot centres on the arrival of motion pictures in China. The opening sequence consists of a series of shots of the old Beijing: the majestic city gate, sitting camels, running rickshaws and peddlers tending their businesses. The focus on the exotic quality of the city smacks of what Edward Said would have called 'the Orientalist gaze'. This sequence is then cut to a close-up of the celebrated Peking Opera star Lord Tan and his daughter riding in a wagon on their way to Fengtai photo studio for a portrait-shooting session.[2] Unbeknownst to Tan, an Englishman named Raymond Wallace has just arrived in town and brought with him some reels of film, the equipment to show them and, most important of all, the dream of starting a film exhibition business in China. The near collision of the wagons of Wallace and Tan on the street foreshadows the conflict between the two men that underlines the rest of the film's narrative.

As Wallace begins showing movies in the city, he has great difficulty convincing the passers-by to step into his makeshift theatre. It is only when Liu Jinglun, Fengtai photo studio's young photographer who is fascinated with all sorts of new gadgets from the West, comes to help him that Wallace's business begins to take off. Liu's collaboration with Wallace jeopardises his career at the photo studio, as well as his romance with Lord Tan's daughter, because Wallace's 'shadow magic' shows are drawing away Tan's audience. On the day of Empress Dowager Cixi's birthday celebration, Lord Tan, Master Ren (boss of the studio) and Wallace are all called in by the authorities to provide their services in the Imperial Palace. In the Imperial Palace, Liu and Wallace try to impress Empress Dowager with their moving pictures, but an unfortunate mechanical malfunction causes an explosion which leads to fire and chaos in the palace. Wallace is accused of attempted assassination and expelled from the country. Liu is badly injured, but granted amnesty, thanks to Lord Tan's plea to Her Majesty on Liu's behalf. Months after the incident, Liu receives a package sent by Wallace from England. In it are several pieces of cinematic apparatus along with the footage of local people and local scenes they shot together before the palace incident. Wallace's gift rekindles Liu's passion for movies and he decides to continue Wallace's 'shadow magic' shows. The film ends with a caption that reads: 'In 1905, the Chinese shot their first motion pictures.'

It is clear that the thematic thrust of the film concerns the tension between 'tradition' and 'modernity'. By dramatising the conflict between Wallace's attempt to start a movie-showing business and the Peking Opera devotees' rejection of the foreign novelty, and by presenting cinema's eventual triumph, the film shows an unambiguous endorsement of the modern 'progress' epitomised by the global expansion of the West. In contrast to the adventurous and inquisitive spirit of the West, as exemplified by the Wallace character, the natives are depicted as ignorant, indifferent and even hostile to foreign inventions. Such a portrayal, however, is too simplistic and ignores the multifaceted historical reality. Admittedly, as a historical drama, *Shadow Magic* may not 'mean to provide literal truths about the past … but metaphoric truths'.[3] However, it is worth noting that the Chinese response to film as presented in this film largely corresponds with the English-language sources published in the 1910s and 1920s while failing to take into account the contemporary Chinese sources. As a result, despite the film's efforts to recreate 'the atmosphere and the stylistic features suggestive of the look or ethos of the past',[4] it presents a skewed picture of the history.

Chinese Reception of the Motion Picture as Described in Contemporary Sources

It is important to note that the linguistic connotation of the film's Chinese title is different from the English translation. The Chinese title *Xiyang jing* means,

literally, 'Western mirror' or 'Western lens', which is suggestive of the initial Chinese perception of this new medium. It emphasises two attributes of the motion picture, namely, its foreign origin and its optical mechanism. In other words, the Chinese title is more cognitive than emotive and implies a rather neutral narrative position. In contrast, the film's English title *Shadow Magic*, emphasises the Chinese bewilderment at the 'magic' power of the western technology and seemingly carries an Orientalist ring. It is not coincidental, but is rather consistent with contemporary English-language journalistic reports regarding film in early-twentieth-century China.

Of the several westerners introducing motion pictures to the Chinese, Benjamin Brodsky (c. 1875–1955) has a special place in Chinese film history. In addition to his role as the founder of the first film-making company in China,[5] he was also one of the few individuals who introduced to the western public the infant Chinese film industry. During his visit to the US in the mid-1910s, he brought with him a documentary film made in China. The exhibition of this film sparked a number of newspaper reports about his career showing motion pictures in China.[6] These reports perfectly illustrate which aspects about the Chinese reception of film earliest western movie showmen wanted to showcase to their fellow countrymen.

As a native of Odessa, Russia, Brodsky gained firsthand knowledge about the Far East during the Russo-Japanese War (1904–5) when he worked as an interpreter. After the war, he moved to San Francisco and lost everything in the devastating earthquake of 1906. The disaster prompted him to try his luck in 'the Orient' again. So he left for China with an old Edison Universal moving-picture machine and forty or fifty reels of junk film. Two years later, he established his first picture theatre in Hong Kong, showing mostly American films to the local audience. During his visit to the US in 1916, he bragged of having been a millionaire and having owned eighty motion-picture theatres throughout China, and two film-producing plants. His stories impressed the reporters, who called him 'film impresario of Orient', 'the most interesting figure in the film world, the David Wark Griffith of the Orient'.[7]

Brodsky's self-aggrandisement aside, those newspaper articles have plenty to say about the Chinese reaction to motion picture shows. For instance, these articles all mention that the Chinese were reluctant to go into the dark auditorium in which Brodsky performed his magic. They called Brodsky's projecting machine a 'magic box' and considered it the white devils' invention. Moreover, Brodsky had to pay 25 cents a head to coax them into his showroom.[8] Once they saw the moving images on the screen, their reaction was nothing short of shock and awe. In some extreme cases, the images of devils or a band of cowboys shooting on the screen even caused panic in the audience.[9] To assure them of their safety, Brodsky invited a few Chinese to examine his film-projecting apparatus and showed them the mechanism of the motion picture projector.[10] Brodsky's stories are echoed in other journalistic accounts. For instance, in a 1914 article published in the *Chicago Daily News*, an American journalist reported that an Englishman had opened a movie theatre in Hong Kong, but the superstitious locals were frightened by the moving images on the screen. To alleviate their anxiety, the Englishman hired audiences to attend his playhouse for three successive weeks, paying each patron a stipulated sum each day until they became used to motion pictures. After a while, his business began to prosper.[11]

While some of these accounts may be credible, others are not. For instance, Brodsky claimed that he had once been jailed in China, but made his escape after getting the whole populace into the jail to view his motion pictures. At another time, he was due to be executed, only to be spared his life after informing his Chinese captors that he could easily put them up on the screen and keep them there forever. Given the extraterritorial rights enjoyed by foreigners in late Qing China and the post-Boxer Rebellion reality in which the powers had dealt the anti-foreign forces in China a crushing defeat, it is highly doubtful that Brodsky would have faced the death penalty in China. The thrust of Brodsky's tall tales is, in the words of Joseph Kraft, to strike 'self adoring poses'.[12] This attitude is typical of travel writing by other westerners in China at the time.

In contrast to the western accounts of Chinese bewilderment at the movies, contemporary Chinese sources suggest a rather different reaction. Several 1897 articles published in Chinese-language Shanghai newspapers contain descriptions of Chinese audiences' initial impression of moving pictures.[13] In one article, the author coined the word 'electric shadowplay' (*dianji yingxi*) for this new medium and viewed it in the same vein as oil painting, western theatre and circus

performance, all of which had been familiar to Shanghai residents. In addition to discussing film's technical innovations and entertainment value, the author also mentions that 'this new spectacle attracted a large number of curious local audiences, despite the high admission price'.[14] There is no mention of the audience panicking at the moving images on the screen. And apparently they had to pay, not *be* paid, to watch the motion picture shows.

In another article, published after its author viewed the Edison Company's *Fifth Avenue* (1896), the author describes that the viewers in the auditorium 'giggled cheerfully as if they themselves were on the street'.[15] He also recalls that he discussed with his friends passionately after watching the film. There is no doubt that they were fairly well informed about the development in motion-picture technology and credited Edison for this new invention.[16] Unfortunately, most early film reviews and advertisements did not mention specific titles of the earliest motion pictures shown in China. For example, one of the earliest advertisements for a movie show simply refers to the programme as 'moving-picture play' (*huodong yinghua xi*).[17] Some evidence suggests that Lumière Brothers' documentary shorts called *les actualités* (actuality films) and Edison Company's early productions, such as *Butterfly Dance* (1894–5), *Fifth Avenue* and *New York* (1896), were among the first moving images that the Chinese audience was exposed to. After the mid-1910s, it became a common practice for film exhibitors to have film titles printed in advertisements. This development coincided with the emergence of serial films.[18] The film serials shown at Shanghai's movie houses usually arrived one or two years after their premiere in the US and Europe, but they met with no less enthusiastic reception and critical acclaim. Titles such as *What Happened to Mary* (Charles Brabin, 1912), *The Perils of Pauline* (Louis J. Gasnier and Donald MacKenzie, 1914), *The Broken Coin* (Francis Ford, 1915), *The Red Circle* (Sherwood MacDonald, 1915) and *The Purple Mask* (Grace Cunard and Francis Ford, 1916) were particularly popular.[19]

From these contemporary Chinese materials we can conclude that cinema was not necessarily perceived as 'shadow magic' when first shown to a Chinese audience. It was looked at also through a 'scientific' lens and was associated with western civilisation. It was not refuted as the devil. Moreover, one source indicates that traditional Chinese opera, French

acrobatic performance and American-made motion
pictures all appeared in the same programme for an
evening of entertainment.[20] The all-inclusive nature of
the programme points to the rather indiscriminate
taste of local patrons. In any event, the supposed
tension between 'traditional' Chinese culture (e.g.,
Peking Opera) and 'modern' cinema, which is at the
heart of the dramatic conflict of Shadow Magic and
Brodsky and his contemporaries' accounts, should be
seriously reconsidered if we take Chinese sources into
account.

Granted, Shanghai was undoubtedly the most
'westernised' city in China and its residents may have
been more cosmopolitan in outlook and more
sophisticated in their cultural consumption than their
country fellows elsewhere. As a result, Shanghai
spectators' reaction to movies probably cannot be
regarded as typical. Nevertheless, the Chinese sources
cited above still remind us of the diversity of Chinese
attitudes towards film and alert us to the potential
inaccuracy of historical details represented in Shadow
Magic. In the next section, we will look at another
aspect of early film showing, namely, the exhibition
venue. In this respect, what is presented in Shadow
Magic does not entirely accord with the historical
reality either.

Early Film Exhibition Venues in China

In Shadow Magic, the Englishman Raymond Wallace
shows motion pictures in a rented warehouse. He
hangs a piece of white cloth on the wall as the screen
and scatters some wooden benches around to seat the
audience. That the condition of film exhibition in the
early days was crude and raw has been discussed in a
number of recent publications.[21] However, such a
cinema house was only one of many film exhibition
venues used in the first two decades of film's arrival in
China. It is a mistake to assume that the early
exhibition of film was invariably substandard. The
popular view that films were initially shown in
teahouses in China is also only partially true. Evidence
suggests that the earliest screenings of films also took
place in upmarket establishments, such as western-
style hotels and theatres.

According to a recent study, motion pictures were
first shown in Shanghai in May 1897 at the Astor House
Hotel (aka Richards Hotel).[22] Built in 1846 and
renovated in 1907, the Astor House was one of the most
luxurious hotels in the city, a handbook for foreign

Astor House Hotel, at the corner of Broadway and Whampoo
Road, Shanghai

travellers published in 1904 stating that 'it caters to
first-class travel only'.[23] The hotel's prestigious status is
also reflected by its prominent guests, including
Bertrand Russell (1920), Albert Einstein (1922) and
Charlie Chaplin (1936). The motion pictures shown at
the hotel in 1897 were claimed to have been taken by
an American photographer named James Ricalton
(1844–1929) who had been dispatched by the Edison
Company.[24] These shows were said to have 'drawn large
crowds' and met with 'unanimous acclaim' from the
audience mainly composed of westerners.[25] The need
to draw an even larger native crowd prompted the
showman to move to a new location, the Arcadia Hall
in the Zhang Garden.

The Zhang Garden was one of the best-known
public entertainment establishments in late Qing
Shanghai. The property, originally owned by a British
company, was bought in 1882 by a Chinese merchant
named Zhang Shuhe who incorporated many western
elements in his renovation, including a stage for
theatrical performance, a ballad theatre, a photo studio,
a billiard room, tennis courts, a dance hall and a
number of restaurants. In 1892, Zhang decided to add
the Arcadia Hall to the building complex. Completed in
1893, the Arcadia Hall was a western-style two-storey
building with elegant and impressive arched ceilings,
beautifully decorated glass windows, and capable of
seating over 1,000 people. As one of the buildings
emblematic of Shanghai's cosmopolitan character, the
Arcadia Hall enjoyed its most radiant years between
1893 and 1909.[26] It is not surprising that it pioneered

Arcadia Hall

the early film shows and introduced the new form of entertainment to the Chinese audience.

In addition to the Astor House Hotel and the Arcadia Hall, a western-style theatre called the Lyceum also screened films in Shanghai in the early years. Located on the Museum Road near the Bund and managed by the Amateur Dramatic Club, the Lyceum's large wooden building regularly hosted concerts, ballet, opera and other theatrical events following its opening in 1867. It is logical that the Lyceum became one of the earliest sites for showing moving pictures. However, the majority of its patrons were 'blue-eyed westerners' and Chinese were only occasionally seen there.[27]

This is probably not because the Chinese wanted to put up a 'cultural resistance' to the foreign influence. More likely, it was the result of economic calculation. The admission prices at the fancy hotels, expensive entertainment centres and exclusive theatres were extremely high and generally beyond the reach of the ordinary Chinese. For instance, the admission at the Astor House Hotel was 1 to 2 Mexican dollars.[28] The Zhang Garden charged 1 dollar for admission. Admission at the Lyceum fluctuated between 1 and 3 dollars, depending on the type of programme. For a comparison, admission for Peking-opera theatres ranged from 5 to 8 cents. Obviously, in financial terms, there was a significant difference between attending the movies and attending traditional Chinese opera performances. For a reference, the average monthly

earnings for a shop clerk in Shanghai at the time ranged from only 1 to 8 dollars. This fact should caution us against interpreting the continuing popularity of traditional opera as a manifestation of Chinese hostility towards the motion picture.[29] Once movies began to be screened at less expensive places, such as the Tianhua Teahouse, and admission price dropped to 10, 20, 40 and 50 cents, Chinese customers began to attend in large numbers.[30]

Until the late 1900s, when purpose-built modern movie houses began to spring up in Shanghai, teahouses were one of the most popular sites for movie exhibitions. The tale of a Spanish businessman named Antonio Ramos starting his movie adventure in China at the Qinglian ge (Green Lotus) Teahouse on Fuzhou Road is a well-known episode in early Chinese film history.[31] For English-speaking people, the word 'teahouse' (*chayuan*) is somewhat misleading because in the Chinese context, the function of a teahouse went beyond serving tea and included staging opera performances. The rise of the teahouse as a centre for performing arts coincided with the growing popularity of the Peking Opera in the late eighteenth century.[32] In Shanghai, teahouses began to appear in the 1860s and 1870s and soon sprung up all over the city. After the 1880s, most teahouses were clustered on Fuzhou Road, which became one of the most vibrant urban centres in Shanghai.[33] The Green Lotus Teahouse, one such establishment, served tea on the first floor and staged opera and variety shows on the ground floor. Qian Huafo, a well-known actor and calligrapher of the time,

Qinglian ge Teahouse, Fuzhou Road, Shanghai

mentioned in his memoirs that this teahouse resembled 'a popular amusement hall'.[34] It made perfect business sense for Ramos to pick this place to show motion pictures to the Chinese crowd.

Another important venue for film exhibition in early days was the amusement resort (youle chang). In many ways, they resembled present-day malls, with multiple storeys housing a variety of businesses, including teahouses, opera theatres, skating rinks, dancing halls, circuses and restaurants.[35] This type of amusement resort emerged in Shanghai in the early 1910s. Most prominent among them were the New World (Xin shijie), which opened in 1915, and the Great World (Da shijie), completed in 1917, which soon became a tourist attraction and one of the bywords for the city's urban splendour, visited by an estimated 15,000–25,000 people daily.[36] This sort of amusement resort, as film critic Jie Fu observed in the early 1920s, should be given full credit for the spread of motion pictures in Shanghai because almost each one, small or large, had one or several rooms for movie showing. In summer, some amusement resorts set up open-air cinemas in their roof gardens, attracting large crowds. Gradually, as Jie Fu observed in 1921, 'the Chinese exposure to motion pictures is increasing, and so does their enthusiasm for this new form of entertainment'.[37]

His remark is corroborated by Bao Tianxiao (1876–1973), one of the most prominent popular writers of the day. Bao mentions in his memoirs that he viewed motion pictures for the first time in a small opera theatre in the Great World. According to his account, the theatre reserved its prime-time show for Peking Opera performances, relegating film shows to the after hours. The film shows normally consisted of detective serials, lasting roughly one and a half hours. The standard admission price was merely 10 or 20 cents. Therefore, the auditorium was usually packed. Much of the audience was made up of ladies from the pleasure quarters of the city.[38] Showing at these already popular amusement venues, film gradually won an audience. Thus, nickelodeon-style theatres that specialised in showing movies appeared. Shadow Magic features exactly this kind of theatre.

The physical conditions at many of the nickelodeons did leave much to be desired. For example, in the early 1900s, a purpose-built nickelodeon called Dream Fairy Theatre (Huanxian xiyuan) opened in Shanghai. It was constructed with nothing more than reed mats and iron plates.[39] A journalist visited the place and wrote an article describing what he saw. The article gives us a vivid glimpse of the crude conditions under which audiences experienced films in the early days:

> There is a movie theatre west of the Mud Creek (Wuni gou), which is no more than a shabby shack standing in a field of wilderness. After sunset, a crowd of men and women swarm in and settle into the wooden chairs, ready to watch the advertised shadow plays. One day, out of curiosity, I went to the theatre by myself. Upon my arrival I saw a dim lighted building packed with people. I was astonished by the chaos and noises in the auditorium. I lifted a curtain made of wretched cloth and was ushered in by a man down the dark aisle. After a good while we finally found an empty seat. The foul smells in the air and the cigarette smoke almost choked me to death.[40]

The experience described here is by no means atypical. Guan Ji'an, a leading film critic of the time, also observed that 'around 1911, film lost its respectability in China and degenerated into an entertainment mostly for the underclass'.[41] His comments point to film's growing appeal to the masses and the shift in film exhibition from highbrow establishments such as luxurious hotels to places where lowbrows congregated.

To be sure, movie showing and attending were not purely Shanghai phenomena. However, generally speaking, until the 1930s film exhibition in China's interior was hampered by many factors. Numerous contemporary sources documented the challenges to bring films to China's hinterland. According to a 1927 report on the Chinese motion picture market compiled by the US Department of Commerce, there were several major obstacles. Chief among them were China's political instability and the constant wars among the different military regimes, inadequate transportation facilities, arbitrary and chaotic interregional taxes, the unavailability of electricity in most rural areas and, finally, the low standard of living of most people. The report gives specific examples to illustrate its points. For instance, the report points out that with China's transportation system at its 1927 level of capacity, it took six months for a film to go the distance of 1,600 miles from Shanghai to Chongqing and back. It took ten days to send a film through the postal service from

Shanghai to Hankou, a distance of about 600 miles. To make the matter worse, taxes were collected at both ends of the route. A film to be sent to Beijing for exhibition would have to pay an export duty before it left Shanghai and then an import duty upon entering Beijing.[42]

For these reasons, film exhibition was largely confined to treaty ports and large cities. When film did reach some provincial towns, its exhibition often resembled a 'road show' in that it was brought to the local people by travelling showmen who made unscheduled stops wherever they saw opportunity for profitability. These early travelling showmen would have to be extremely resourceful and make do with what was available to them. As described in one contemporary source, sometimes the film projector would be set up on the deck of a boat, showing films to audiences on the banks as the boat travelled to various small towns along rivers or canals.[43] On such occasions, film exhibition often functioned in a similar fashion as traditional performing troupes staging opera shows to local people – both were part of local temple fairs, market-day attractions or other celebratory festivities.

To conclude, the arrival of the motion picture in China generated a strong interest and curiosity on the part of the local population across social and cultural divides. The initial Chinese writings about this new medium and other contemporary sources provided ample evidence. Furthermore, the varieties of exhibition venues suggest that during the period of 'cinema as attraction', which lasted well into the 1920s in China, the class character of the audience for motion pictures was not as nearly pronounced as presented in *Shadow Magic*. There is no doubt that the film is based on some real historical events and personalities. A mechanic malfunction during a movie screening for Empress Dowager Cixi did take place in the imperial palace; Fengtai photography studio is credited with making the first Chinese film; and showmen from Europe and America, such as Benjamin Brodsky and Antonio Ramos, were crucial to the early development of cinema in China. However, by building its narrative on an Englishman's adventure and taking liberty with historical facts, *Shadow Magic* projects a problematic picture of film's initial introduction into China. Historical encounters and experiences with this new medium were multifaceted and, beyond doubt, still warrant in-depth enquiries.

Notes

1. Monica Mak, 'East West Movie Magic: *Shadow Magic* as Hybrid Art with Third Space', in *Yishu: Journal of Contemporary Chinese Art* vol. 1 no. 1 (Spring 2002), pp. 68–82.

2. The Lord Tan character is apparently based on the real Peking opera star Tan Xinpei (1847–1917), but the part about his daughter is fictional. See 'Tan pai chuanren tan *Xiyang jing*: "women jia mei zhe zhong shir"', in *Tianjin ribao*, 10 May 2000, <ent.sina.com.cn>. The Fengtai photo studio described in the film is credited by film historians with making the first Chinese film, *Dingjun shan*, which is a recording of Tan's stage performance. See Hong Shi, 'Ren Qingtai yu diyipi guochanpian kaoping' (Ren and the First Wave of Chinese-made Films), *Dianying xinshang* (Film Appreciation) vol. 9 no. 4 (1991), pp. 46–51.

3. Robert A. Rosenstone, *History on Film/Film on History* (Harlow, England; New York: Longman/Pearson, 2006), p. 8.

4. Mak, 'East West Movie Magic', p. 70.

5. Kar Law and Frank Bren, 'The Enigma of Benjamin Brodsky', *Hong Kong Film Archive Newsletter* no. 14 (2000); Xuelei Huang, 'Zhongguo Diyi? Nanfu Nanqi Yu Ta De Jingdian Hua' (China's First Feature? The Canonisation of *The Difficult Couple*), *Dianying xinshang xuekan* (Film Appreciation Academic Section) vol. 27 no. 2 (2009), pp. 161–75.

6. Grace Kingsley, 'Film Impresario of Orient Here to Show Pictures', *Los Angeles Times*, 10 November 1916, III22. Grace Kingsley, 'Too Much Magic. Film Starts Riot: Panic in Chinese Theater Follows Cowboys' Charge in Wild West Photoplay: Strange Experiences of Picture Maker and Exhibitor', *Los Angeles Times*, 12 November 1916, III22. Grace Kingsley, 'Ripples from Reeldom: Orient Takes Queer View of Some of Our Films', *Los Angeles Times*, 17 June 1917, III1.

7. Kingsley, 'Film Impresario of Orient' and 'Too Much Magic'. However, Brodsky's claim is contradicted by a contemporary source which gives the number of movie theatres he owns as eight, not eighty.

8. Ibid.

9. Kingsley, 'Ripples from Reeldom'.

10. Kingsley, 'Too Much Magic'.

11. *Chicago Daily News*, 16 September 1914. Quoted in Jay Leyda, *Dianying/Electric Shadows: An Account of Films and the Film Audience in China* (Cambridge, MA: MIT Press, 1972), pp. 8–9.

12. Quoted in T. Christopher Jespersen, *American Images of China, 1931–1949* (Stanford, CA: Stanford University Press, 1996), p. 188.

13. The three articles are: 'Weichun yuan guan yingxi ji' (Viewing Shadowplays at the *Weichun* Garden), *Xinwenbao*, 11 and 13 June 1897, p. 1; 'Tianhua chayuan guan waiyang xifa guishu suojian' (A Retrospective Account of Viewing Foreign Magical Tricks at the Tianhua Teahouse), *Youxi bao* 54 (16 August 1897); 'Guan meiguo yingxi ji' (Viewing American Shadowplays), *Youxi bao* 74 (5 September 1897).

14. 'Weichun yuan'.

15. 'Guan meiguo yingxi ji'. Also see Leyda, *Dianying/Electric Shadows*, p. 2.

16. 'Weichun yuan'. Film historians are still debating whether motion pictures were first invented in France or America. See Charles Musser, *The Emergence of Cinema: The American Screen to 1907* (New York; Toronto; New York: Macmillan, 1990), introduction and chapter 1.

17. *Shenbao*, 8 June 1897.

18. Cf. Wayne Schutz, *The Motion Picture Serial: An Annotated Bibliography* (New Jersey and London: Scarecrow Press, 1992).

19. Cf. Jianhua Chen, 'Zhongguo Dianying Piping De Xianqu: Zhou Shoujuan "Yingxi Hua" Dujie' (The Pioneer of Chinese Film Criticism: My Readings of Zhou Shoujuan's On Shadowplays), *Xiandai zhongguo* (Modern China) no. 9 (July 2007), pp. 65–7. Advertisements of these serials can be found in *Shenbao*, *North China Daily News* and other local newspapers.

20. 'Weichun yuan'.

21. Zhiwei Xiao, 'Movie House Etiquette Reform in Early-Twentieth Century China', *Modern China* vol. 32 no. 4 (October 2006), pp. 513–36.

22. See Dequan Huang, 'Dianying chudao shanghai kao' (A Historical Examination of Film's Arrival in Shanghai), *Dianying yishu* (Film Art) no. 314 (2007), pp. 102–9. His finding challenges the conventional wisdom that the first film show in China took place at the Xu Garden in Shanghai on 11 August 1896.

23. C. E. Darwent, *Shanghai. A Handbook for Travellers and Residents* (Shanghai [u.a.]: Kelly & Walsh, 1904), pp. viii, 64.

24. See Leyda, *Dianying/Electric Shadows*, pp. 2–3. Leyda did not provide a source to support his claim. This ought to be wrong. James Ricalton is a photographer and explorer who circumnavigated the world several times. He did work for Edison and travelled to China during the Boxer Uprising, but there is no evidence so far to suggest he travelled to Shanghai in 1897. For information about Ricalton, see <www.ricalton.org>. Also see James Ricalton and Christopher J. Lucas, *James Ricalton's Photographs of China During the Boxer Rebellion: His Illustrated Travelogue of 1900* (Lewiston, NY: E. Mellen Press, 1990).

25. *Xinwenbao*, 30 May 1897; 'Weichun yuan'.

26. Yuezhi Xiong, 'Zhang Yuan: Wan Qing Shanghai Yige Gonggong Kongjian Yanjiu' (Zhang Garden: A Study on Public Sphere in Late Qing Shanghai), *Dang'an yu shixue* (Archives and Historical Studies) no. 6 (1996), pp. 31–42.

27. Jie Fu, 'Zhongguo Yingxi Zhi Mengya (1)' (The Birth of Chinese Cinema 1), *Chunsheng ribao* (Spring Voice Daily), 7 May 1921. For the history of Lyceum Cf. Zhen Xi, 'Zhongguo Zuizao De Xishi Juchang: Lanxin Da Xiyuan' (Lyceum Theatre: The First Western-Style Theatre in China), *Dang'an chunqiu* (Memories and Archives) no. 6 (2007), pp. 46–50.

28. The Mexican dollar ($, *yuan* in Chinese) is the most universally used money in Shanghai at the time. There are 100 cents (10 cents = 1 *jiao* in Chinese) to the dollar. Besides, copper coins are also frequently used. 800 coppers (*wen*) are worth about 1 dollar in the early 1900s. See Darwent, *Shanghai*, pp. v–vii. I use 'dollar ($)', 'cent' and 'copper' throughout in this chapter to refer to *yuan*, *jiao*, *wen* in Chinese original texts.

29. For information concerning theatre admission and Shanghai resident income, see *Shenbao*, 3 October 1897; *Xinwenbao*, 2 June 1897; Xi, 'Zhongguo Zuizao De Xishi Juchang', p. 48; Joshua Goldstein, 'From Teahouse to Playhouse: Theaters as Social Texts in Early-Twentieth-Century China', *The Journal of Asian Studies* vol. 62 no. 3 (2003), p. 759.

30 *Shenbao*, 26 July 1897.

31. See Jihua Cheng, Li Shaobai, and Xing Zuwen (eds), *Zhongguo Dianying Fazhanshi* (A History of the Development of Chinese Cinema) (Beijing: Zhongguo dianying chubanshe, 1963), p. 10.

32. Goldstein, 'From Teahouse to Playhouse', p. 758.

33. Yue Meng, *Shanghai and the Edges of Empires* (Minneapolis: University of Minnesota Press, 2006), pp. 86–91.

34. Qian Huafo, *Sanshi nian lai zhi Shanghai* (Shanghai in the Recent Thirty Years); quoted in Peng Zhu, *Shanghai Shi Yange Dili* (The Geographical History of Shanghai) (Shanghai: Xuelin chubanshe, 1989), pp. 297–8.

35. For a careful study of the amusement resorts, cf. Meng, *Shanghai and the Edges of Empires*, pp. 183–209.

36. Hanchao Lu, *Beyond the Neon Lights: Everyday Shanghai in the Early Twentieth Century* (Berkeley: University of California Press, 1999), p. 115.

37. Jie Fu, 'Zhongguo Yingxi Zhi Mengya (2)' (The Birth of
    Chinese Cinema 2), *Chunsheng ribao* (Spring Voice Daily),
    8 May 1921.

38. Tianxiao Bao, *Chuanying Lou Huiyi Lu* (Reminiscences
    from the Studio of Bracelet Shadow) (Taipei: Longwen
    chuban gongsi, 1990), p. 652.

39. See Jianchen Gu, 'Zhongguo Dianying Fadashi' (The
    History of Chinese Cinema), reprint, Dai Xiaolan,
    Zhongguo wusheng dianying (Chinese Silent Cinema)
    (Beijing: Zhongguo dianying chubanshe, 1996), p. 1358.

40. Dungen, 'Yingxi Yuan' (Shadowplay House), *Shenbao*, 29
    April 1912, C3.

41. Ji'an Guan, 'Yingxi Shuru Zhongguo Hou De Bianqian'
    (The Development of Cinema after its Arrival in China),
    Xi zazhi (Theatre Magazine), 1922.

42. C. J. North (ed.), *The Chinese Motion Picture Market (Trade
    Information Bulletin, No. 467)* (United States Department
    of Commerce, Bureau of Foreign and Domestic
    Commerce, 1927), pp. 1–2.

43. Ibid., p. 32.

6 The Making of a National Cinema

Shanghai Films of the 1930s

Laikwan Pang

The 1930s are widely recognised as one of the most exciting periods in Chinese cinematic history. With its distinctive fusion of commercial success, political commitment and artistic experimentation, Shanghai cinema was inimitable and unique to local cultural lives and China's national situation at the time.[1] Prewar film culture in 1930s Shanghai was extraordinarily vibrant – pushed to the limits by many young and enthusiastic film-makers who tried to engage artistically and politically with both pressing social issues and the potentiality of cinema. Intellectuals were for the first time introduced to Chinese film-making circles, despite the film industry's overall commercial orientation. In the absence of a national 'canon', these Chinese film-makers consciously and systematically learned from films produced in other countries – primarily those produced in Hollywood – and foreign film theories were also introduced. Viewers and critics also came to approach films anew, seeing them not only as a means of entertainment but as a cultural form capable of many different kinds of cultural and social signification. Cinema developed as a part of the emerging consumer culture, but the 1930s also saw the formation of a progressive film culture, characterised by an intellectual aura that had previously been foreign to Chinese cinema.

For the first time, we witness the conscious discursive construction of a national cinema in China – film-makers and critics engaged in ferocious debates as to how to depict the new Chinese people and culture and how to construct the best cinema for China at that time. This was a period characterised by the imminence and the anticipation of war, and a yearning for nationalist empowerment was constructed along with a romantic pursuit of individualist liberation reminiscent of the May Fourth Movement. Although different ideological opinions were expressed overtly in the films, artistic concerns and debates were often treated within a framework of national culture, boiled down into the ideological positions film-makers had to take. But film-makers also had to struggle with issues specific to the film medium. Like their international counterparts, Chinese film-makers in the 1930s struggled with the introduction of sound, and they had to reinvent filmic language and acting styles to blend the visual and the aural. Such professional concerns were also inevitably caught up with the current intellectual mêlée, and the use of music and dialects translated into terms of homogeneity and diversity in the making of a national culture. Many new feminine archetypes – ranging from the politically conscious New Woman to the desperate and exploited sing-song girl – appeared onscreen; they also might be seen as representative of various nationalist concerns.

As a summary and an explication of existing scholarship, this chapter is devoted to the various manifestations of this cinema in relation to the national. I seek not to reduce the richness of an epoch into a hackneyed academic category, but I would like to examine what the 'nation' meant to the cinema in 1930s Shanghai. By re-examining discussions related to the national, I hope to draw attention both to the films and to existing scholarship that analyse these films' meanings. I believe that a careful examination of the relationship between cinema and nation, however schematic, can help us understand the intensity of the urgent demand for a national cinema at that time.

Nationalism

It is now generally agreed that nationalism is one of the key defining features of Shanghai cinema of the 1930s. Many scholars have approached this nationalist cinema by analysing the political orientations of the film-makers, who were for the most part politically conscious and forthright about their ideological stances. Two rival groups of film-makers have been identified as dictating the ideological climates of 1930s film circles. Socialist-oriented film-makers advanced a leftwing cinema movement; on the right, a group of film-makers involved themselves in the KMT-initiated Nationalist Film Movement. Critics also dichotomise 1930s Shanghai cinema into hard films and soft films. Hard films (*yingxing dianying*) are those invested with progressive political ideologies; soft films (*ruanxing dianying*) focus on Shanghai's cosmopolitan sensation and consumerist impulse. Although products of the Nationalist Film Movement do not necessarily overlap with soft films, both were considered anathema to leftwing film-makers who were committed to purge their new works of such regressive ideologies as political conservatism, feudalism and consumerism. It is now clear that both dichotomisations are in their own way reductionist, and scholars have observed the remarkably congenial culture of the leftist circle, which was able to construct a united front and gather momentum from a wide range of sympathetic film-makers.[2] It is also very difficult to pin down whether certain film-makers, such as Hong Shen, and certain films, such as *Zimei hua* (*The Sisters*,

1934), belong to the left or the right, as they can be easily placed in both categories. However, it is undeniable that films in the 1930s were to a great extent intertwined with the film-makers' ideological inclinations, and they were not shy to express their political views both in public and in their films. While it is problematic to understand the film community as a simple bi-polar structure, we should not depoliticise the strong ideological elements the film-makers, critics and viewers invested in the films.

Jubin Hu elaborates the ideological split between the two groups by introducing the notion of class; he argues that the leftists spoke for the proletariat, whereas the traditional nationalists represented the interests of the propertied class.[3] But I find it even more difficult to understand the film culture in terms of class – the film *Xiao tianshi* (*Little Angel*, 1935) was sponsored by the KMT government and associated with the Nationalist Film Movement, but the film juxtaposes a rich but corrupt family against a poor but morally dignified one, and the director Wu Yonggang – who made the celebrated leftist film *Shennü* (*The Goddess*) the previous year – clearly sided with the poor, despite the class reconciliation suggested at the film's end. It is clear that after 1932, most films, left or right, were sympathetic to the poor and critical of class exploitation – those that uncritically assumed upper-middle-class perspectives were in the minority.

The impending Japanese invasion further problematised the differentiation between left and

Malu Tianshi (*Street Angels*)

Taoli jie (*Plunder of Peach and Plum*)

Shizi jietou (*Crossroads*)

right. Many film-makers, regardless of political stance, expressed strong patriotic sentiments in their films. As a result, almost all of the 1930s classics – among them *Yuguang qu* (*The Fishermen's Song*, 1934), *Taoli jie* (*Plunder of Peach and Plum*, 1934), *Langshan diexie ji* (*Bloodbath on Wolf Mountain*, 1936), *Malu tianshi* (*Street Angels*, 1937) and *Shizi jietou* (*Crossroads*, 1937) – are oppositional in theme and structure: they spoke for the poor against exploitation, they incited the masses to combat foreign military or financial invasion, and they also treated women's liberation as a battlefield. Direct revolution against the KMT government, however, was rarely featured or even hinted at, largely because of pervasive censorship, but also because such mentalities were not necessarily prominent among film-makers.

The term 'leftwing cinema' was not widely used in the 1930s, and the actual boundary of this film circle cannot be easily demarcated; I use the term to refer to a loosely constructed film movement, which corresponded closely with the overall leftwing cultural movement of that time, and whose film-makers shared a sense of common identity in 'modernising' China's cinema in terms of both ideology and craft. In fact, nationalism permeated the entire film culture, left and right. Nationalist films primarily presented a dichotomy between the national self and the national enemy (the Japanese, in light of that nation's 1931 military invasion and subsequent incorporation of three north-eastern provinces into the puppet state of Manchukuo). But because the KMT government maintained a friendship, however fragile, with the Japanese, overtly anti-Japanese films were not made until 1936, by which time the Japanese drive for empire was transparent to all. Prior to then, any filmic allusions to nationalist sentiments had centred primarily on the condemnations of traditional culture, capitalism and colonialism, and the advancement of China into a modern nation was a common theme found in the majority of the films of the time, regardless of their political orientations. A sense of crisis was always in the background, and discerning critics and viewers were free to associate it with the Japanese invasion.

Nationalism manifested in many forms, and in the following I will analyse them in more detail. But what is striking about Shanghai film culture immediately before the war was the overlap between commerce and politics: simply speaking, nationalism sells. It is very difficult to reconstruct the audience of this cinema, but we can say those interested in these films were primarily middle-class educated or semi-educated urbanites.[4] Melodramatic as they were, films in the 1930s depicted an anxiety of national crisis that transcended class, and it was a common practice to end a film with its protagonist – male or female – leading the people to a better future. Revolution was couched in romantic tones, and the aesthetisation of politics was prominent, although it is problematic to directly apply the Frankfurt School's criticism of fascism to this cinema because of the actual threat of invasion China faced, whereas Germany was to become the invader. No matter how much we might be critical of nationalism as a dominant ideology, we must recognise that nationalism is also a structure of feelings, and it is difficult to differentiate hegemony from populism in the Chinese commercial cinema of the 1930s.[5]

Film Policy

We can also examine the relationship between cinema and nation from the perspective of policy. As Andrew Higson argues, 'national cinema' might be a troublesome concept theoretically, but it is significant at the policy level, because often the focus of film policy is economic development and the promotion of a national image.[6] In the West, cultural policy has been an essential instrument for nation-building and governance, which depend upon a national culture for the legitimisation of sovereignty.[7] Similarly, Chinese film policy in the 1930s was also both nurturing and disciplinary in nature. Materials that were morally harmful and politically destabilising were banned, and in so doing the government also hoped to engineer the development of a new national culture for the right citizenry.

As early as the late 1920s, the Nanjing government was highly aware of the political impact and potentiality of cinema, and a set of policies was developed specifically for cinema.[8] China's first film censorship policy, the Film Inspection Law (*Dianying jiancha fa*), was implemented in November 1930 and updated in January 1931. At that time, film censorship was carried out by a special committee composed of four officials from the Education Department and three officials from the Internal Affairs Department, indicating its pedagogical and cultural orientation. In 1934, this committee was replaced by the Central Film Inspection Committee (*Zhongyang dianying jiancha weiyuan hui*), directly under the control of the Central Propaganda Committee, the KMT's ideological centre.[9] The shift of focus from education to politics was obvious.

But the new censorship policy, as it drove – and was driven by – the increasingly politicised culture of the 1930s, also paved the way for a flourishing leftwing cinema, whose strong nationalist sentiments were in fact legitimised by government attention to cinema. There was a subtle tension between censorship and production, a nuance embodied in the shared and opposing ideologies between the government and film-makers: the harder the government tried to suppress, the more ardently film-makers wanted to express. Patriotism can easily be turned on its head, and people can be agitated, as long as there is room to question the status quo. As Frank Dikötter argues, the Nationalist government was generally more civil and non-military than the Communist government that was to follow it, and rudimentary forms of participatory politics had already developed in Shanghai in the first decade of the twentieth century.[10] It would be wrong to assume a simple dichotomy between government and the people during the 1930s. Similarly, film censorship should also be seen as a site of contestation instead of a simple directional apparatus against the people.

As records show, most of the banned films came not from China but from Hollywood, owing to the Orientalist, derogatory images of China presented in such films as Harold Lloyd's *Welcome Danger* (1929), which allegedly insulted Chinese audiences. In 1934, six of the nine films banned were American films.[11] Then as now, censors and critics cared much about the cinematic representation of the Chinese as a people. However, as Chinese cinema became increasingly politicised, the government grew watchful, and it paid special attention to messages that encouraged revolution. Domestic productions were also under close inspection; some films were released only after extensive editing. The KMT government also struggled to develop a diplomatic relationship with the Japanese, so the expression of anti-Japanese sentiment had to be discouraged until war became inevitable. Soviet films were also politically troublesome; only after China established diplomatic relations with the Soviet Union in 1932 did the Nationalist government accede to the screening of 'Red' cinema in China.

Sound

Shanghai cinema was also affected by the advent of sound. By 1929 the influx of Hollywood sound films forced many theatres to update their equipment in order to screen them. But, for various reasons, Shanghai's studios entered the sound era by steps. Lianhua, for example, did not make its first sound films until 1934, because the films made by the studio were meant for its own theatre chains, most of which were not equipped with sound facilities. On the other hand, Mingxing immediately upgraded their studios, which was a tremendous financial burden for the company. It took almost eight years to turn Shanghai cinema into a speaking one: on the eve of the 1937 Sino-Japanese War, almost all films made in Shanghai were now sound films. In the age of sound, the two main audio sources, film music and film language, became highly alluring to film-makers, who used sound to experiment with a Chinese mode of filmic representation.

Genü hong mudan (Sing-Song Red Peony, 1931), which features the singing of the prominent Peking Opera master Mei Lanfang, is widely considered to be the first Chinese sound film; a wax disc was used to play the synchronised arias. But there had been prior attempts; for example, director Sun Yu used the phonograph to 'lip-synch' the theme song to Yecao xianhua (Wild Flowers, 1930) at each screening.[12] In general, it was the presentation of songs, rather than dialogue, which first fascinated audiences and film-makers. Very soon, sound effects and musical accompaniment were also experimented with, and various western and regional musics were used extensively. Sue Tuohy's pioneer study of film music in the 1930s locates a variety of musical sources and manifestations.[13] Tuohy characterises this infancy period as 'metropolitan', as there was no unified theme or cinematic musical

language at that time. Yueh-yu Yeh follows up on Tuohy's investigations and explores the negotiated practice of 'sinification', a term Yeh uses to refer to the process of translating the foreign film medium into Chinese.[14] Yeh further suggests that leftist film-makers and musicians often made an extra effort to feature both Chinese-style and western music, often in the form of non-diegetic western classical music and diegetic Chinese folk songs.[15] Both Tuohy and Yeh admit that the use of film music was heavily ideological. Andrew Jones also demonstrates that political mobilisation is explicitly staged in music terms in many leftwing films, as most evidently seen in the Nei Er's musical arrangement for Xin nüxing (New Woman, 1935), in which decadent dance-hall music is juxtaposed with patriotic songs, symbolising the different political stances and fates of the two female protagonists, Wei Ming and Li Aying.[16]

Many 1930s film-makers experimented with the use of music and sound as the technology matured – including Cai Chusheng in Yuguang qu, Sun Yu in Dalu (The Highway, 1935), Ouyang Yuqian in Xin taohua shan (The New Peach Blossom Fan, 1935) and Ma Xu Weibang in Yeban gesheng (Song at Midnight, 1937); but, in my view, the most sensitive film-maker in this regard is Yuan Muzhi, whose Dushi fengguang (Scenes of City Life, 1935) and Malu tianshi are both remarkable attempts to integrate music and images in sophisticated film language. Yuan was not interested only in formal experimentations, however, and his use of music also is ideological in nature, providing an additional dimension to his political commentary. For example, Dushi fengguang features songs with nonsense lyrics and comical musical arrangements, meant to poke fun at the urban life of Shanghai. Malu tianshi is the story of a sing-song girl whose miserable life is captured gracefully in the presentation of one song: through music (traditional folk melodies in contrast to the dance-hall music featured elsewhere), lyrics (in which a woman pines for her lover) and in images (documentary war footage at times accompanies her singing). Her songs and her life are in dialogue with the music and lyrics, resulting in a unique and powerful portrayal of national devastation.

Serious debate raged over the use of Mandarin as opposed to other dialects, which directly involved the studios of Shanghai and Hong Kong, two competing Chinese film industries at that time. The promotion of Mandarin as China's only national language was in the interests of the KMT government, and this inclination directly benefited the Shanghai film industry by marginalising Hong Kong's Cantonese cinema.[17] In the name of language unification, in 1935 the KMT government implemented a vague policy barring the screening of all dialect cinemas. But the policy did not reach south to Canton, which had considerable autonomy.[18] The largely ineffective policy was aborted during World War II, but a similar policy was readopted by the KMT government after 1945 – as well as by the CCP government after 1949, attesting to the intimate relationship between language and governance. It took sixty years for Cantonese films to return to major theatres in the mainland.[19]

The New Woman

The most frequently discussed topic in the area of 1930s Chinese culture is probably the depiction of women. Scholars have reminded us how important women figures have been in the pursuit of modernity in the Chinese cultural sphere throughout the twentieth century,[20] and how the nation-building project of the 1930s in particular was engineered through the rich meanings invested in feminine characters. They range from prostitutes to intellectuals, from social butterflies to asexualised blue-collar workers, from juvenile sing-song girls to soul-searching mothers; many of them are chaste lovers, but quite a few give hints that they are sexually active. What we have seen in the 1930s Chinese cinema was not simply a dichotomy between progressive and traditional women, but a wide range of archetypes with different personalities, status and struggles – and who are much more diverse and fascinating, I would say, than their male counterparts.

The film *Xin nüxing*, which depicts the destinies of three women – a working mother, a proletarian worker and a middle-class housewife – is one of the most studied texts in this regard, as it emblematically explores what it meant to be a 'New Woman' in an age of nationalism and anti-imperialism. Using the film as a representative text, Guo-Juin Hong posits that 1930s Chinese cinema had the capacity to review the simultaneous existences and conflicts of the multiple temporalities always at the core of colonial modernity.[21] According to Hong, if *Xin nüxing* can be seen as representative of the new national cinema, it is not a leftist cinema with a clear and present agenda, but 'an insecure cinema representing a nation

in crisis between coloniality and modernity'.[22] Vivian Shen and Yingjin Zhang also provide elaborate analyses of the film that demonstrate how the post-May Fourth New Woman of the 1920s was replaced by the proletarian woman of the 1930s, who has become gender free.[23]

The life and death of Ruan Lingyu, who starred in *Xin nüxing* as the tragic Wei Ming, has received much popular and academic attention. Both Kristine Harris and I have tried to reconstruct the intersection between Ruan's cinematic image and her actual experiences, which culminated in her suicide after intrusive tabloid reportage of a sex scandal involving her.[24] Ruan Lingyu has been seen as an icon of 1930s Shanghai cinema, which was heavily coloured by the talent and the tragedy of this actress. But it would be wrong to take the central position of Ruan in the cinema of the time for granted; in fact, one of the main features of this cinema was the elaborate star system it developed, in which a wide range of female stars were introduced and rose to prominence – among whom are the cultivated Hu Die, the sexually assertive Li Lili, the naive neighbourhood girl Chen Yanyan and also Lan Ping (later Chairman Mao's wife Jiang Qing), who tended to play characters representing the tarnished side of metropolitan Shanghai. The strong patriotic messages blended well with the melodramatic elements, and 1930s Shanghai cinema could be seen as more a feminine than a masculine cinema. However, we must also recognise that there were no female film directors at that time, and the abundant and complex depictions of female characters should be attributed both to the reception by female viewers and the self-pity of the male film-makers.

Alternatives to the National: The Cosmopolitan and Vernacular

Many scholars criticise the focus on ideological matters in studies of 1930s Shanghai film, claiming that it runs the risk of endorsing the canonical film history portrayed by the Chinese Communist Party, which emphasises the ideological split between certain leftwing progressive film-makers and rightwing regressive ones. This overly politicised reading has irritated many contemporary scholars, who find it a hegemonic discourse suppressing other dimensions of the film culture. Some scholars are extremely critical of using concepts of nation-building to define the meanings and significance of Shanghai's cinema at that time, and seek other perspectives and frameworks to understand and theorise this vigorous film culture.

Prewar Shanghai cinema, as described by Leo Lee, is characterised by a pursuit of modernity – in a more pluralistic sense of cosmopolitanism than a homogenising version of nationalism.[25] Shanghai in the 1920s and 30s, as a rising metropolis receptive to new and different ideas, incorporated different lifestyles, values and practices from Japan, the West and different regions within China. Lee characterises the resultant cinema as being more urban than national, and films – both Chinese and imported – were a key source of inspiration for other literary and artistic works. Lee differentiates his work from PRC canonical scholarship that glorifies the politics of leftwing cinema, and so his analysis tends to highlight the consumerist and the depoliticised.

In addition to the discourse of cosmopolitanism there is also that of the vernacular, a notion adopted by a few scholars to describe Shanghai cinema in the 1920s and into the 30s. Miriam Hansen first uses the concept of 'vernacular modernism' to illustrate the promiscuous dimension of the so-called 'classical' Hollywood cinema.[26] Refuting and expanding the earlier understanding of modernism as elitist and pertaining to a repertory of artistic styles, Hansen offers an alternative understanding of modernism along the line of mass-mediated modernity, thereby opening up the discursive space to reimagine Hollywood as modernist. In Hansen's view, modernism should not be understood solely as canonical high art but also as a new mode of organising vision and sensory perception in response to the rise of modernity. In a later article she applies the same concept to Shanghai cinema in the 1920s and 30s to explore the dimension of the quotidian in this cinema.[27]

In her seminal study of pre-1937 Shanghai cinema, Zhen Zhang not only focuses on films and their film-makers, but also introduces the notion of 'amorous economy' to underscore the cinematic experience both on- and offscreen, presenting a comprehensive study of the film culture in its broadest sense.[28] Weihong Bao also picks up on the global dimension of Hollywood's vernacular modernity and demonstrates the intimate relationship between Hollywood and early Chinese cinema in the construction of the seemingly traditional female warrior genre.[29] If Hansen's original use of 'vernacular modernism' was a reaction to David

Bordwell's notion of 'classical Hollywood', and it was meant to connect Hollywood back to everyday life and consumption among the masses, Zhang's and Bao's adoption of the term treads on completely different political ground. The issues they engage with are no longer just the tensions between high and low art; they show us how the study of prewar Shanghai cinema should be alert to and critical of the hegemonic dimension of the national.

Whether scholars highlight politics, in its narrow sense, in their study of prewar Shanghai cinema also depends on the historical periods being emphasised. Zhang and Bao focus more on Shanghai cinema of the 1920s, when film was primarily a form of entertainment; my own scholarship, for example, highlights the periodisation between 1932 and 1937, when Communist Party members began to infiltrate the film industry, and when the imminent Japanese invasion was all the more pressing. I see a clear paradigm shift in 1932, when Xia Yan, Qian Xingchun and Zheng Boqi were recruited by Mingxing Film Company to write film scripts.[30] Films texts and film criticism between 1932 and 1937 attest to the dominant aura of leftist ideologies, and we must admit that 'nation' was clearly the buzzword of the day. But, as the above-mentioned scholars remind us, it is also important to highlight the commercial and the quotidian dimension of Shanghai cinema, even in the 1930s. A combination of different scholarly approaches reveals the richness of this cinema, and also broadens our understanding of the relationship between cinema and politics in the Chinese context.

We must also remember that at that time 'national cinema' was not discursively constructed in the way we understand this term today. There were far fewer discussions of such notions as cinematic tradition or national style than there were of pressing social issues. And the prominent connections and competition between the film industries of Shanghai and Hong Kong also render any simple overlap between Shanghai cinema and Chinese cinema problematic.[31] By tracing the film-makers' concerns and representations of the nation, I do not postulate that 1930s Shanghai cinema was a national cinema, but we must also recognise the allure of the national at that time.

Notes

1. Existing film production in Shanghai came to a dramatic halt in 1937, when the Japanese invaded and

occupied the city, although Japanese-supported productions continued to be made. The 1930s film culture I refer to in this chapter corresponds to that before the war.

2. Jubin Hu, *Projecting a Nation: Chinese National Cinema before 1949* (Hong Kong: Hong Kong University Press, 2003), pp. 82–3; Laikwan Pang, *Building a New China in Cinema: The Chinese Left-wing Cinema Movement, 1932–1937* (Lanham, MD: Rowman & Littlefield, 2002), pp. 41–52.

3. Hu, *Projecting a Nation*, pp. 75–114.

4. For a more elaborate analysis of the spectatorship at that time, see Pang, *Building a New China in Cinema*, pp. 150–60.

5. We might compare the nationalistic sentiments shown in the Chinese commercial cinema at that time to Raymond Williams's dichotomisation of the dominant social character of a period and its structure of feelings, and we would see that Williams's analysis does not easily apply to the Chinese scenario. See Raymond Williams, *The Long Revolution* (Peterborough, ON: Broadview Press, 2001), pp. 77–88.

6. Andrew Higson, 'The Limiting Imagination of National Cinema', in Mette Hjort and Scott MacKenzie (eds), *Cinema and Nation* (New York: Routledge, 2000), pp. 63–74.

7. See Tony Bennett, *The Birth of the Museum: History, Theory, Politics* (London: Routledge, 1995).

8. Zhiwei Xiao, 'Constructing a New National Culture: Film Censorship and the Issues of Cantonese Dialect, Superstition, and Sex in the Nanjing Decade', in Yingjin Zhang (ed.), *Cinema and Urban Culture in Shanghai, 1922–1943* (Stanford, CA: Stanford University Press, 1999), pp. 183–99.

9. Pang, *Building a New China in Cinema*, p. 57.

10. Frank Dikötter, *The Age of Openness: China Before Mao* (Berkeley: University of California Press, 2008), pp. 18–19.

11. 'Dianying jiancha weiyuan hui jiancha yingpian qingxing' (The Censorship of the Film Censoring Committee), in *Zhongguo dianying lianjian* (Chinese Cinema Yearbook) (Nanjing: Zhongguo jiaoyu dianying xiehui, 1934), n.p.

12. Zhang Zhen, *Amorous History of the Silver Screen: Shanghai Cinema, 1896–1937* (Chicago: University of Chicago Press, 2005), p. 314.

13. Sue Tuohy, 'Metropolitan Sounds: Music in Chinese Films of the 1930s', in Yingjin Zhang (ed.), *Cinema and Urban Culture in Shanghai, 1922–1943* (Stanford, CA: Stanford University Press, 1999), pp. 200–21.

14. Yueh-yu Yeh, 'Historiography and Sinification: Music in Chinese Cinema of the 1930s', *Cinema Journal* vol. 41 no. 3 (Spring 2002), pp. 78–98.

15. Ibid., pp. 87–92.

16. Andrew F. Jones, *Yellow Music: Media Culture and Colonial Modernity in the Chinese Jazz Age* (Durham, NC: Duke University Press, 2001), pp. 128–33.

17. Pang, *Building a New China in Cinema*, pp. 179–84.

18. Xiao, 'Constructing a New National Culture', p. 185.

19. See Laikwan Pang, 'Hong Kong Cinema as a Dialect Cinema?', *Cinema Journal* vol. 48 no. 3 (Spring 2010), pp. 140–3.

20. See, for example, Rey Chow, *Woman and Chinese Modernity: The Politics of Reading between West and East* (Minneapolis: University of Minnesota Press, 1991).

21. Guo-Juin Hong, 'Framing Time: New Women and the Cinematic Representation of Colonial Modernity in 1930s Shanghai', *positions: east asian cultural studies* vol. 15 no. 3 (Winter 2007), pp. 553–79.

22. Ibid., p. 577.

23. Vivian Shen, *The Origins of Left-wing Cinema in China, 1932–37* (New York: Routledge, 2005), pp. 101–6; Zhang Yingjin, 'Engendering Chinese Filmic Discourse of the 1930s: Configurations of Modern Women in Shanghai in Three Silent Films', *positions: east asian cultural studies* vol. 2 no. 3 (Winter 1994), pp. 603–28.

24. Kristine Harris, 'The New Woman Incident: Cinema, Scandal, and Spectacle in 1935 Shanghai', in Sheldon Hsiao-peng Lu (ed.), *Transnational Chinese Cinemas: Identity, Nationhood, Gender* (Honolulu: University of Hawaii Press, 1997), pp. 277–302; Pang, *Building a New China in Cinema*, pp. 113–37.

25. Leo Ou-fan Lee, *Shanghai Modern: The Flowering of a New Urban Culture in China 1930–1945* (Cambridge, MA: Harvard University Press, 1999), pp. 82–119.

26. Miriam Bratu Hansen, 'The Mass Production of the Senses: Classical Cinema as Vernacular Modernism', *Modernism/Modernity* vol. 6 no. 2, 1999, pp. 59–77; and 'The Mass Production of the Senses: Classical Cinema as Vernacular Modernism', in Christine Gledhill and Linda Williams (eds), *Reinventing Film Studies* (London: Arnold, 2000), pp. 332–50.

27. Miriam Bratu Hansen, 'Fallen Women, Rising Stars, New Horizons: Shanghai Silent Film as Vernacular Modernism', *Film Quarterly* vol. 54 (2000), pp. 10–22.

28. Zhang Zhen, *Amorous History of the Silver Screen*.

29. Weihong Bao, 'From Pearl White to White Rose Woo: Tracing the Vernacular Body of Nüxia in Chinese Silent

Cinema, 1927–1931', *Camera Lucida* vol. 20 no. 60 (September 2005), pp. 193–231.

30. Pang, *Building a New China in Cinema*, pp. 41–3.
31. Poshek Fu, *Between Shanghai and Hong Kong: The Politics of Chinese Cinemas* (Stanford, CA: Stanford University Press, 2003), p. xii.

Further Reading in *Chinese Films in Focus II*

On Wu Yonggang, see Chapter 16, '*The Goddess*: Fallen Woman of Shanghai' by Kristine Harris.

7 Wartime Cinema

Reconfiguration and Border Navigation

Yiman Wang

The Second Sino-Japanese War (July 1937–August 1945) exerted an indelible impact on Chinese cinema. It reshuffled the previous Shanghai-centred urban cinema, precipitated politicisation and constructed new audience groups both within and without China. Stemming from war, colonisation and forced migration (even diaspora), these new developments fostered a multilocational cinema that effectively negotiated wartime border politics. Put differently, Chinese cinema became deterritorialised just as China's territory, literally, was ruptured and remapped on a massive scale. Yet, the crisis of deterritorialisation offered precisely the opportunity for wartime cinema to develop new strategies of articulating complex relationships between audio-visual mass media and national as well as transnational politics. Indeed, wartime Chinese cinema was so drastically deterritorialised that the very definition of Chinese cinema became destabilised. Some cases of voluntary or coerced co-production, as I shall discuss, not only demonstrate the factual plurality and heterogeneity of Chinese cinema (as has been commonly agreed upon), but, more importantly, underscore the performative and contested nature of 'China' – a concept that became the most powerful rally call precisely as it was hurled into acute crisis and traversed by multiple non-Chinese interventions.

This paradox compels us to conceptualise wartime Chinese cinema as a cinema of emergency, or a cinema emerging from China's emergency situation. This understanding foregrounds the mutual implications between vision(s) of a national identity and the war-torn Chinese cinema. In the following pages, I offer a temporal and spatial mapping of the emerging/emergency cinema in wartime China. During the 1930s and 40s, the Japanese government accelerated its invasion into China. It occupied north-east China in 1931, turning it into the puppet Manchukuo in 1932, and then bombed Shanghai in the same year. This catalysed leftist cinema. When the Second Sino-Japanese War erupted in July 1937, followed by the fall of Shanghai (with the exception of the western concessions) and of Nanking in November and December 1937, 'national defence cinema' (*guofang dianying*) became an important resistance film 'genre' both in Chongqing – the wartime capital of Kuomintang (KMT)'s China, and in Hong Kong – the British colony that offered relative 'freedom' until its fall in December 1941.[1] After December 1941, Japan completely occupied Shanghai, Hong Kong and South-East Asia. Film industries in these areas came under direct control of the Japanese propaganda machine, with variant results.

The sustained period of emergency led to unprecedented decentralisation of Chinese cinema. Following the destruction of most of Shanghai's film companies in the bombing of August 1937,[2] film production was suspended for half a year, and the city lost its position as the centre of Chinese cinema.[3] Many film workers fled or strategically relocated to Hong Kong. Some moved to south-west China along with the military and administrative relocation of the KMT government. A few went to the communist base in Yan'an. The rest remained in the 'orphan island' Shanghai, taking advantage of the protection offered by western concessions that were left unoccupied until December 1941. When the concessions also fell in December 1941, Shanghai film workers had to work in the name of serving the 'Great East Asia War' (*Dai Toa senso*).

Given the massively reshuffled political and filmic cartography, film-making became multilocational, translocational and transnational (by volition or coercion), gearing towards divergent ideologies and agendas, and catering to a wide spectrum of audiences both inside and outside China. In addition, para-cinematic apparatuses proliferated, including new film companies, organisations, societies and film magazines that promoted divergent ideologies and film types, as well as area-specific censorship policies. My mapping below will detail these developments as they unfolded with the expanding war and resistance in the hinterland, Shanghai, north-east China, Hong Kong and Yan'an.[4]

The Hinterland – 'National Defence Cinema' in KMT's China

In KMT-controlled south-west China, film-making was virtually a battle against Japanese invasion. It operated through two main studios: Central Motion Picture Studio (Zhongyang dianying sheying chang or Zhongdian) (relocated from Nanking to Wuhan and Chongqing in 1937–8) and China Motion Picture Corporation (Zhongguo dianying zhipianchang or Zhongzhi) (established in 1937 in Hankou, known as Hankou dianying sheying chang or Hankou Film Studio, then relocated to Chongqing in 1939). Unlike the prewar privately owned Shanghai film studios, these two studios were officially owned by KMT, enabling an important switch from profit-driven commercial cinema to government-supported political cinema, its goal being to educate and mobilise (rather than simply entertain) the rural as well as urban audience.

In the spirit of KMT–CCP (Chinese Communist Party) united front, these studios galvanised Shanghai film workers of different political stripes, including left-leaning figures like Shi Dongshan, Situ Huimin, Sun Yu, Yang Hansheng, Li Lili and Chen Bo'er. Together, they produced national defence cinema, including *Eight Hundred Heroes* (*Ying Yunwei*), newsreels (e.g., *Special Newsreels on Resistance*), animations (e.g., *Resistance Cartoons*) (*Wan Guchan, Wan Laiming, Wan Chaochen*), all made in 1938 by Zhongzhi. They also made feature films, including *Protect Our Home* (*Shi Dongshan*), *Fight to the Last* (*Yuan Congmei*), both made by Zhongzhi in 1938, and *The Sky Rider* (Sun Yu, 1940) produced by Zhongdian. However, the eruption of the Pacific War, which blocked traffic and caused severe shortage of film stock, drastically reduced film-making in hinterland China.[5] Spoken drama, in turn, became an important venue of war mobilisation.

National defence cinema and drama were advocated by para-cinematic apparatuses including political organisations, magazines, newspaper columns and publicity materials. A key organisation was the All China Film Workers' Resistance Society (Zhonghua quanguo dianyingjie kangdi xiehui), founded on 29 January 1938. It launched a magazine, *Resistance Cinema* (*Kangzhan dianying*), in March.[6] In this initial (which also turned out to be the only) issue, film workers collectively stressed the urgency of practising (rather than just theorising) 'national defence cinema'. They also laid out strategies of reaching the broadest possible audience in rural as well as urban China.[7] A recurring rhetoric in the discussion was equating film workers with (silver) soldiers, cameras with machine guns and lighting equipment with search lights.[8] Film-makers were also urged to reduce NG in order to save raw materials for making bullets.[9] Film workers also emphasised domestic and international outreach. For this purpose, they organised mobile projection teams accompanied by narrators to facilitate rural audience's understanding of 'national defence films'.[10] Internationally, they exported films to South-East Asia and the West to win sympathy for China's war against Japan. Furthermore, they adjusted film and documentary styles to better cater to illiterate rural minds. These adjustments included: selecting dramatic, action-oriented, spectacular and

Babai zhuangshi (*Eight Hundred Heroes*)

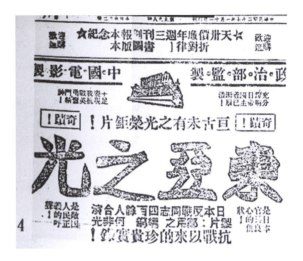

Poster of *Dongya zhiguang* (*Light of East Asia*)

Storm Over Mongolia

emotional materials for newsreels,[11] developing simple and forceful plots, streamlining character psychology and, finally, using slow-tempo acting and detailed narration to avoid confusion.[12]

Wartime cinema in the KMT-controlled south-west hinterland China also strived to find publicity in the West. A 1942 *New York Times* article, for instance, detailed arduous conditions in Chongqing. US raw film had to be smuggled in by camels or elephants; film-drying circular drums were made of rickshaw wheels; and microphone booms were bamboo poles.[13] Films introduced to the American audience (some also screened) included *Fight to the Last* (with English subtitles),[14] *The Light of East Asia* (He Feiguang, 1940, Zhongzhi) (noted for casting Japanese POWs as voluntary actors),[15] *Storm over Mongolia* (Ying Yunwei, 1942, Zhongzhi) (noted for the expensive ten-month

location shooting among Mongolian tribes, budgeted at upwards of $200,000).[16] Additionally, the Movie Education Department of the Science College or the University of Nanking was spotlighted for bringing their documentaries to coolies and other far-off illiterate populations. Some of their ethnographic and educational programmes were circulated in the US by the Rockefeller-endowed American Film Centre.[17]

Nevertheless, despite its importance, national defence cinema was only one of many kinds of movies screened in the hinterland. The wide spectrum encompassed Soviet and Hollywood productions, Hong Kong films, Shanghai silent martial arts series that were banned in the early 1930s by the KMT film censorship, but now revived in new film prints, *and* films made in occupied Shanghai such as the controversial *Mulan Joins the Army* (*Mulan conjun*, 1939,

Bu Wancang) and *Eternal Fame* (Bu Wangcang, Maxu Weibang et al. 1943).[18] The next section deals with film-making in wartime Shanghai.

Shanghai Under Occupation – Double-edged Entertainment

For some hinterland film-makers and viewers, Shanghai cinema under occupation was an intolerable stigma, as amply illustrated in the controversy surrounding *Mulan Joins the Army*. This film, scripted by Ouyang Yuqian, a progressive artist, directed by Bu Wangcang, a veteran Shanghai director, and produced by Zhang Shankun's Xinhua yingye gongsi (New China), successfully ran for over fifty days in Shanghai, and was acclaimed as an allegory of resistance against Japan. Its screening in Chongqing in January 1940, however, was met with an angry crowd that set the reels on fire with the conviction that the film was made by a traitor director with Japanese film stock, produced by a company backed with Japanese funding, and that the narrative defamed Chinese soldiers and harmed China's ethnic harmony. The event was quelled and the screening resumed only with the intervention of KMT's Central Film Censorship that affirmed the film's nationalist message.[19]

The patriotic Chongqing audience's violent act against a Shanghai film crystallised the ideological split between the occupied area and the hinterland. Unlike the explicitly patriotic Chongqing cinema, cinema in

'orphan island' Shanghai (November 1937–December 1941) projected ideological ambivalence that successfully entertained the large influx of war refugees from Shanghai's vicinities.[20] Sandwiched between the conflicting demands from Japanese propaganda, Chinese nationalism and the commercial market, Shanghai's privately owned companies (including Xinhua, Guohua, Yihua, Jinxing and Minhua) veered towards costume dramas. The historical genre could play fast and loose with contemporary politics while proffering the desired star appeal and spectacle effect, which also ensured its popularity with Hong Kong and South-East Asian audiences. Such a fuzzy (albeit potentially allegorical) stance made these films problematic to patriotic minds. The incident of burning *Mulan Joins the Army* stemmed precisely from the ideological split.

In 1940, Wang Jingwei established his collaborationist regime in Nanking and instituted strict censorship on films that detracted from the Great East Asia War.[21] Upon completely falling to Japan on the day of Japan's Pearl Harbor attack, Shanghai's film industry was institutionally folded into Japan's propaganda machine. Kawakita Nagamasa, who had been in charge of film distribution in the occupied central and northern China, was now sent to recruit Shanghai film companies. Partnered with Zhang Shankun, Kawakita consolidated twelve Shanghai studios (including Zhang's Xinhua) into Zhonghua lianhe zhipian gongsi (or Zhonglian) (China United Productions) on 10 April 1942, the professed goal being to produce 'a cinema of the Chinese, by the Chinese, and for the Chinese'.[22]

As a semi-official Sino-Japanese film conglomerate, Zhonglian launched its house magazine, *Xin yingtan* in November 1942, which echoed the Japanese discourse of new East Asian order and Wang Jingwei regime's 'Heping jianguo xuanyan' (Declaration of Peaceful Reconstruction of the Nation) (1942). Interestingly, the hegemonic politics led to similar strategies as those adopted by the hinterland 'national defence cinema'. These strategies included centrally controlled film-making, mobile projection teams[23] and film understood as literal and metaphorical weapon in the war.[24] Their fundamental difference, however, was their diametrically opposite definitions of the enemy. For the nationalists, the enemy was the Japanese aggressors, whereas in the occupied areas, the enemy was British and American colonialists. Echoing Japan's self-legitimisation through media propaganda, Wang

Chen Yongshang crossdressing in *Mulan congjun* (*Mulan Joins the Army*)

Jingwei enlisted Shanghai cinema to promote 'peaceful reconstruction' (*heping jianshe*), as opposed to 'resistance and reconstruction' (*kangzhan jianguo*) in south-west China.

Nevertheless, Zhonglian's actual film production was mainly driven by entertainment. Its staple family dramas were largely adapted from Hollywood, despite the latter's suspension in Shanghai theatres during the Pacific War.[25] Starting from 1943, as Japan intensified its demand for *kokusaku* (national policy) films, Zhonglian made a presumably anti-British–American film, *Eternal Fame*. This mega-production was co-produced with Manchurian Motion Picture Association (or Man'ei, Manzhou yinghua xiehui), and shown in China, Manchukuo and Japan. It dramatises the British–Chinese conflict regarding the opium trade by intertwining it with romantic subplots. It boasted a star-studded cast (including Nancy Chan, Li Xianglan/Yamaguchi Yoshiko, Yuan Meiyu and Wang Yin) and a top-notch directorial collective (including Bu Wancang, Zhu Shilin and Maxu Weibang). The pro-Japan film magazines, *Xin yingtan* and *Huabei yinghua* (Huapei Movie), both extensively covered this film, especially the legendary Man'ei star, Li Xianglan, whose 'Maitang ge' (Candy Song) and 'Jieyan ge' (Song on Abstaining from Opium) became instant hits as the film spread from the occupied China to Chongqing and Yan'an. Despite the discursive fanfare surrounding the making of the film, however, its propaganda value was by no means clear.[26]

Zhonglian's failure to produce explicit and effective propaganda led to further political intervention from both Japanese and Wang Jingwei's regimes. As a result, Zhonglian was replaced by Zhonghua dianying lianhe gufen youxian gongsi (or Huaying) (China Film United) in May 1943.[27] Nevertheless, Huaying ended up mostly following Zhonglian's strategy of making entertaining dramas while battling the aggravated shortage of film stock, rampant inflation and skyrocketing production costs. Its one 'national policy' film was *Remorse in Shanghai* (Hu Xinling and Inagaki Hiroshi, 1944), a period drama that explicitly advocates Japan's goodwill vs the duplicitous Britons who collaborate with the Qing government in crushing the Taiping tianguo uprising. A lavish co-production with Dai Nippon eiga kaisha, the film featured a Sino-Chinese cast, and was singled out as a treason film after the war.

To better understand the controversial nature of wartime Shanghai films, Chinese historians and film scholars have challenged the monolithic nationalist discourse by reinterpreting the few surviving film copies. Poshek Fu, for instance, challenges the binary logic by arguing that Shanghai's occupation cinema was paradoxically 'both within and outside the state apparatus of the occupying power, and both (unwittingly) supported and subverted the occupation'.[28] Paul Pickowicz similarly problematises the proprietary and hegemonic definition of Chinese cinema by reclaiming the stigmatised *Remorse in Shanghai* as an early case of transnational Chinese cinema that prefigures the post-1980s co-production trend.[29]

These timely and inspiring interventions invite us to not only problematise the resistance-or-treason logic, but also to fully understand Japan's expansionism and its impact on Chinese cinema. The fact that occupation cinema has often been perceived as anathema to the 'Chinese' identity and 'Chinese cinema' suggests that Japanese intervention was not just one of many factors, but rather the dominant force in disrupting and/or reorienting Chinese cinema. It instituted and operated all film apparatuses, including facilities of production, distribution and exhibition, print media, but also rigid censorship mechanism. Under such circumstances, the rhetoric of New Asian Order that seemingly promoted transnational harmony inevitably marginalised China (and other Asian colonies). As a result, the occupation cinema inscribed indelible transnational inequity.

This issue can be further illuminated by comparing *Remorse in Shanghai* with *Sons and Daughters of the World* (Fei Mu, 1941), a resistance film made in the 'orphan island' Shanghai in collaboration with Jacob Fleck and Luise Fleck. The Flecks were a Jewish director couple who founded the first Austrian film company and worked for UFA before being interned in German concentration camps. Upon fleeing to Shanghai in 1940, they met with Fei Mu, who decided to work with them for two reasons: 1) their prosecution by German fascism facilitated their sympathy with war-torn China; 2) their film experiences would benefit Chinese cinema.[30] They agreed that the transnational collaboration must address war politics since it was made by two peoples fighting against the fascist enemy.[31] The film was premiered on 4 October 1941 in Shanghai, soon banned upon Japan's complete occupation of Shanghai, but then returned to the screen two years later in Chongqing. It features young men and women leaving the 'orphan island' to join the resistant force. It also conveys the anti-war sentiment through subtle camerawork.[32] This turned out to be Fei's last film during the war, as he shifted to theatre work after December 1941 in order to dodge the Japanese coercion.

Fei's transnational co-production was possible only before the Pacific War. Nevertheless, the comparison of Fei Mu's *Shijie er'nu* with Zhonglian's *Eternal Fame* and Huaying's *Remorse in Shanghai* reveals two different rationales. The first stemmed from an anti-fascist alliance between colonised Chinese film workers and the exiled Jewish couple. The other two resulted from Shanghai film workers' negotiation and coerced collaboration with Japan's fascist ideology. The different rationales highlighted the divergent politics underlying the transnational form, especially at a historical conjuncture when transnational resources and Chinese crises were intertwined. What they did have in common was active engagement with border-crossing alliances/liaisons in order to remap (trans)national border politics in times of crisis. To that extent, Shanghai's wartime cinema exemplified converging logics of war and film-making.

North-east China under Occupation – Man'ei and Li Xianglan

Compared to the Shanghai situation, the occupation cinema in north-east China poses an even greater challenge to the definition of 'Chinese cinema'. Following Japan's occupation of north-east China in September 1931, which resulted in the establishment of the puppet Manchukuo in February 1932, film censorship was instituted in July 1932. Shortly after Man'ei was launched in August 1937 as a joint venture between Manchukuo and Japan's South Manchuria Railway Company, the Manchukuo government issued *Yinghua fa* (The Film Law) in October 1937 and *Yinghua jianyue guize* (Film Censorship Codes) in August 1939. The law and censorship codes dictated positive portrayal of the Japan–Manchukuo relationship, treated Chinese films as foreign films and strictly censored Shanghai-made costume dramas on account of their implicit anti-Japan messages.[33] Set up as Japan's propaganda engine and operated by Amakasu Masahiko, former head of Manchukuo's Ministry of Civil Affairs, Man'ei produced three categories of films: 108 *gomin* (entertainment features), 189 *keimin* (educational documentaries) and *jiji* (newsreels) in both Chinese (*Man'ei jiho*) and Japanese (*Man'ei tsushin*), as

well as children's programmes.[34] To expand its power in the occupied northern China, Man'ei funded Huabei dianying gufen youxian gongsi (Northern Chinese Film Co.) in Beijing in 1939, taking charge of film distribution and production of some propaganda shorts.

Man'ei's feature films were mostly made by Japanese film-makers with mixed casts. A few Chinese graduates from Man'ei's acting school did get promoted. Jiang Xueqian became associate director of the production department; Zhou Xiaobo and Wang Xinzhai served as assistant directors; Wang Qimin worked as a cinematographer; and Zhang Xinshi was recruited as a scriptwriter. Boasting East Asia's best-equipped studio, built in 1939 (modelled upon UFA), Man'ei also attracted well-known Japanese film workers from both left and right. Iwasaki Akira, a leftist critic, for instance, was credited for facilitating the location shooting of a Man'ei–Sochiku co-production, *Sayon no kane* (*Sayon's Bell*, 1943, Shimizu Hiroshi) in Taiwan, and for

Li Xianglan in Taiwan with an indigenous child

producing a Man'ei-Toho musical, *Watakushi no uigosu* (*My Nightingale*, 1944, Shimazu Yasujiro).

Both films feature Li Xianglan (or Yamaguchi Yoshiko) – a Japanese actress born and raised in north-east China. With her bi-cultural, bi-lingual background and formal training in operatic singing, Li was handpicked and promoted as a 'Manchurian star' in her 1938 acting debut. Concealing her Japanese nationality, Man'ei passed her off as a 'local' actress who would appeal to the local audience, thus facilitating Amakasu's vision of 'Making Films for the Manchurians'.[35] Her wartime films, interestingly, all exploited her chameleon metamorphosis – into a Chinese girl in *Eternal Fame*, into a Taiwan aboriginal in *Sayon no kane* and into a Russian-singing adoptee of an exiled Russian musician in *My Nightingale*.[36] Unsurprisingly, Li's participation in the 'national policy films', especially *Shina no yoru* (*China Night*) (Osamu Fushimizu, 1940), led to her postwar trial as a traitor. She was eventually acquitted on account of her Japanese nationality.

If a Japanese national, by logic, could not be a Chinese traitor, could Man'ei films made by Japanese personnel in Manchukuo in multiple languages be counted as Chinese cinema? The answer seems to be yes, since the territory of Manchukuo was forcefully occupied by Japan, and returned to KMT's China upon Japan's surrender in 1945. Man'ei, likewise, was terminated, and became the centre of contention between KMT and CCP. It eventually became Dongbei dianying zhipianchang (North-east Film Studio) in October 1946.[37] Yet, China's long-standing hush over Man'ei productions means that their 'national identity' is by no means clear. Although some of the Man'ei newsreels and feature films (especially those starring Li Xianglan) have been released by Japanese companies (upon their rediscovery in former Soviet archives), the China Film Archive is still locking its copies away. After all, the genie has to be sealed in the bottle due to its abject abnormality. If they were Chinese, how could they look and sound so foreign, and fail to register wartime China's national crisis? If they were not Chinese, how could they be produced in a territory that had always rightfully belonged to China?

Hong Kong – The Crucible of Wartime Cinema

Unlike KMT-controlled south-west China or Japan-occupied Chinese areas, Hong Kong, in spite of having been ceded to Britain in 1842, was linguistically and culturally part of the southern Chinese matrix. Hong Kong's regional affinity, combined with colonial geopolitics, made Hong Kong cinema both nominally part of Chinese cinema and historically marginalised as being lesser Chinese. The 1930s Hong Kong cinema was specifically criticised for 1) using Cantonese, which not only competed with Shanghai-made Mandarin Chinese cinema, but also undermined the KMT government's linguistic nationalism; 2) heavily depending upon South-East Asian market while deviating from China's national politics.

However, Hong Kong's relative freedom from Japan's occupation between 1937 and 25 December 1941 made it an important alternative site for producing and exhibiting Chinese films.[38] Shanghai's Tianyi Film Co. moved to Hong Kong, where it had already set up a branch before the war. Xinhua's boss, Zhang Shankun, also quickly tapped into Hong Kong's human and technical resources. He not only recruited Nancy Chan, the leading actress of *Mulan Joins the Army*, from Hong Kong, but also made her an overnight star in China. He also mobilised Hong Kong resources to finish a costume drama, *Sable Cicada* (Bu Wancang, 1938), which blazed the trail of making Mandarin Chinese films in Hong Kong. Zhang also collaborated with Hong Kong's Nan Yue Film Studio in making dual-language films (in Cantonese and Mandarin Chinese).

Different from Zhang's commercial film activities in Hong Kong during the war, many other film workers and critics sought to regulate and politicise Hong Kong cinema for war mobilisation. Such attempts started with KMT's decree against Cantonese cinema in 1936. Whereas the ban was postponed for three years due to Cantonese film workers' protest, a Guangzhou censorship office was set up in October 1937, screening all Cantonese films before their release in China. In September 1938, Xu Hao, head of the office, convened Hong Kong film workers, urging them to stop making apolitical folklore films. Xu's order was soon aborted with Guangzhou's fall in October 1938.[39] Yet, wartime national politics continued to significantly shape Hong Kong cinema – until December 1941.

As the wartime free zone (despite the colonial government's censorship) and the conduit between China and overseas Chinese communities, Hong Kong screened some Chongqing national defence films (in 16mm subtitled prints), which also travelled to South-East Asia and Euro-America.[40] Furthermore, Hong Kong attracted progressive Shanghai film-makers and KMT government investment that instigated a wave of Hong Kong-made national defence films. Progressive film-makers Cai Chusheng, Situ Huimin and Shen Xiling came to Hong Kong and established Xinshidai yingpian gongsi (New Times Film Studio) in 1938, with the financial support of Yuan Yaohong, a Hong Kong businessman. This company produced two Cantonese national defence films, *Baoshan City Bathed in Blood* (Situ Huimin, 1938) and *March of the Guerrillas* (Situ Huimin, 1938). Whereas the first became an instant hit, the second was banned by the colonial censorship and not screened until June 1941, under a new title, *Zhengqi ge* (*Ode to Justice*), after multiple cuts.

In addition, Chonqing's Zhongzhi sent Luo Jingyu to Hong Kong in 1938 to launch Dadi yingye gongsi (Great Land Film Studio). It funded two Mandarin national defence films. *Orphan Island Paradise* (Cai Chusheng, 1939) ran for twelve days in Hong Kong, followed by enthusiastic reception in Chongqing and South-East Asia. Dadi's second production, *My Motherland* (Situ Huimin, 1940) ran for eighteen days and set Hong Kong's box-office record for that year. Upon Dadi's termination, Cai Chusheng launched Xinsheng yingye gongsi (New Life Film Studio) and made another Cantonese national defence film, *The Boundless Future* (Cai Chusheng, 1941).

Importantly, the production of nationalist films in Hong Kong actually predated mainland China's intervention. Cantonese actor Wu Chufan starred in *Returning from the Battlefield* (Huang Dai, 1934), followed by *The Lifeline* (Moon Kwan, 1935) and *Resistance* (Moon Kwan, 1936). Barely one month after the outbreak of the war, six Hong Kong studios (including Daguan, Nan Yue and Nanyang) collaborated on a high-profile patriotic film, *The Critical Moment* (Chen Pi, Li Zhiqing et al., 1938). The box-office profits were donated to war relief. Another noteworthy documentary was *Scenes of Yan'an*, originally entitled *The Northwest Frontline* (Lin Cang et al., 1941). It was a silent 16mm documentary made by Hong Kong's Lin Cang, Jin Kun and Xu Tianxiang, who spent nine months in Yan'an in the late 1938 in order to make the documentary. Other important Hong Kong-made Cantonese national defence films include *Behind Shanghai's Frontline* (Tang Xiaodan, 1938) and *The Roar of the Nation* (Tang Xiaodan, 1941), both produced by Daguan shengpian youxiang gongsi (Grandview Film Co.). Together, Hong Kong and mainland Chinese film-makers made sixty-one

national defence feature films between 1937 and 1941, among which seventeen were made in 1937, eighteen in 1938, three in Mandarin Chinese and five by progressive Shanghai film workers.[41]

By 1939, the output of national defence films in Hong Kong was reduced by half, compared to 1938. This number again decreased by half in 1940 when they were replaced by Hong Kong's prewar staple genres like folklore drama and horror.[42] Many hybrid films also came into being, mixing patriotic messages with popular genre appeal, as illustrated by the family melodrama, *Twin Sisters from the South* (1939), and 'beauty spy' films.[43] Given Hong Kong's geopolitical position as a British colony on the margins of mainland China and as a transit zone between China, South-East Asia and the West, it is not surprising that Hong Kong cinema was traversed by divergent ideologies and film styles. This became even more pronounced during the war due to the intensified cross-flow of population, resources and political agendas.

On 25 December 1941, however, Hong Kong cinema came to a complete halt upon fall to Japan, after producing over four hundred films. In the next four years, Japan exercised strict censorship and monitored all films shown in Hong Kong. Refusing to work for Japanese propaganda, Hong Kong film-makers either quit or escaped. No films were made during the occupation. Meanwhile, Hong Kong cinema was resumed in a different location – San Francisco, the American immigration hub that witnessed the birth of Joseph Sunn's Daguan (Grandview) in 1933 now hosted its return. During Hong Kong's occupation years, Sunn kept on making Cantonese films for overseas Chinese communities in San Francisco. Some of these films were shot in 16mm colour; and some were shown in Hong Kong after the war.

Yan'an – Burgeoning Documentaries

Wartime decentralisation of Chinese cinema also stimulated documentary-making in Yan'an, the communist base, where it constituted an important form of visual propaganda. With the outbreak of the war, Yuan Muzhi and Wu Yinxian, veteran Shanghai actor-director and cinematographer, went to Yan'an and started the Yan'an Film Team in autumn 1938, supervised by the Political Bureau of the Eighth Route Army. Their initial resources consisted of the camera and film stock donated by Joris Ivens after completing his documentary, *The 400 Million* (1939), about China's resistance war. With these resources, Wu Yinxian made the first documentary, *Yan'an and the Eighth Route Army* (1939). Later documentaries chronicled meetings, campaigns and festivals in Yan'an. Due to lack of sound recording equipment, all documentaries were silent and screened with amplified voice narration.[44]

Shortly after Japan's surrender, Yuan Muzhi, representing CCP, took over Man'ei and transformed it into Dongbei dianying zhipian chang (North-East Film Studio) in 1946, ushering in a new phase of Chinese cinema, to be developed under the communist leadership after 1949.

Conclusion

This chapter has delineated wartime shifts in Chinese cinema, including unprecedented spatial dissemination, resource reallocation, multiplied censorship systems and ideological reconfiguration. These readjustments required that Chinese cinema strategise political propaganda as well as entertainment. This led to four major shifts: diversifying film formats to increase production of documentaries, newsreels and animations; strengthening para-cinematic apparatuses to promote topical films; tapping into rural and overseas audiences by deploying dialects and mobile projection teams; and, finally, strategising border-crossing production and exhibition. Such transformation manifested the centrifugal impetus and centripetal imperative simultaneously. As the centripetal imperative strived to foreground the Chinese identity as a homogeneous agency pitted against Japanese aggressors, the centrifugal impetus deterritorised the prewar Shanghai-centred production, significantly redefining the concept of Chinese cinema. In other words, the intense ideological formulation of a unified Chinese identity unfolded in dialectic tension with actual decentralisation of the identity.

By engaging with the highly volatile and deterritorialised political, economic and cultural cartography, wartime Chinese cinema emerged as a platform where ideological conflicts were staged and realigned, new modes of film-making were theorised and practised, divergent regional and overseas Chinese populations were addressed and constructed. All of these combined to write a critical page in the tortuous history of Chinese cinema, and in the complex wartime reconstruction of the Chinese identity.

Notes

1. 'National defence cinema' was proposed in May 1936 in the spirit of 'national defence literature'. See Zhou Chengren and Li Yizhuang, *History of Early Hong Kong Cinema* (Zaoqi Xianggang dianying shi) (Hong Kong: Joint Publishing, 2005), pp. 224–5.

2. Two major film companies destroyed were Mingxing dianying zhipian chang (Star Film Company) and Lianhua yingye yingshua gongsi (United Photoplay and Publishing Service or UPS). A third major company, Tianyi yingpian gongsi (Unique), moved to Hong Kong, and eventually developed into Shaw Brothers.

3. See Fei Mu's statement in 'Regarding the Establishment of "National Defence Cinema"' (Guanyu guofang dianying zhi jianli), *Kangzhan dianying* (Resistance Cinema), March 1938, p. 5; and Cai Chusheng, 'Today's Paramount Crisis: Privately Run Film Business during the War – An Earnest Appeal to Film Authorities and All Progressive Cultural Critics' (Kangzhan hou de minying dianying, dangqian jueda de weiji – bing yuqing dianying dangju he quanguo jinbu wenhuaren de yanzhong zhuyi), originally published in *Saodang bao*, December 1938, reprinted in Chongqing shi wenhua ju dianying chu (ed.), *Kangri zhanzheng shiqi de Chongqing dianying; 1937–1945* (Chongqing Cinema during the War: 1937–1945) (Chongqing: Chongqing chubanshe, 1991), pp. 266–72 (267). The difference is that Fei Mu saw Hong Kong emerging into a new centre, whereas Cai scathingly criticised Hong Kong's mainstream film workers for their effete and opportunistic approach to 'national defence cinema' as well as their dangerous indulgence in conservative folklore and ghost films.

4. For a brief description of film activities in these areas, see Yingjin Zhang, *Chinese National Cinema* (New York: Routledge, 2004), pp. 83–94.

5. For a historical overview of film-making in south-west China during the war, see Yang Yan and Xu Chengbing, *Minguo shiqi guanying dianying fazhanshi* (History of Government-sponsored Film-making before 1949) (Beijing: Zhongguo chuanmei daxue chubanshe, 2009), chapter 3.

6. Another important magazine that promoted Zhongdian and Zhongzhi's 'national defence cinema' as well as introducing film-making in other parts of China and other countries was *Zhongguo dianying* (Chinese Cinema).

7. See the editor-in-chief, Tang Na's 'Fakan ci' (Opening Statement), *Kangzhan dianying* (Resistant Cinema), March 1938, p. 1; the head of Zhongzhi, Zheng Yongzhi's 'Quanguo de yinse zhanshi men qilai' (Rise, the Silver

Warriors of China), pp. 6–7; and various contributors to 'Guanyu guofang dianying zhi jianli' (Regarding the Establishment of National Defence Cinema), pp. 2–5.

8. Zheng Yongzhi, 'Quanguo de yinse zhanshi men qilai', p. 6.

9. Wang Ruiling, in 'Guanyu guofang dianying zhi jianli', pp. 2–3.

10. Yang Hansheng and Yuan Congmei, in 'Guanyu guofang dianying zhi jianli', pp. 2, 5.

11. Luo Jingyu, 'Tan xinwen jilupina' (On Newsreels), *Kangzhan dianying*, pp. 10–11.

12. Shi Dongshan, 'Guanyu "baowei women de tudi"' (Thoughts on '*Defending Our Home*'), pp. 13–14.

13. Ezra Goodman, 'Keeping Alight the Lamps of China: In the Caves of Chungking the Chinese Film Makers Still Carry on', *The New York Times*, 14 June 1942, X3.

14. *Fight to the Last* advertisement clipping at MoMA.

15. 'Return of Picture Biz in China', *Variety*, 8 January 1941, p. 73.

16. 'Taking Movies among Mongolian Tribes', *China Information*, 25 November 1940.

17. 'Sikang in the Movies', *China Information*, 16 September 1940.

18. The screening of *Eternal Fame* is mentioned by Nancy Chan in Tan Zhongxia, *Yiye huanghou: Cheng Yunshang zhuan* (An Overnight Queen: A Biography of Nancy Chan) (Hong Kong: Dianying shuangzhoukan chuban-she, 1996). For a description of the wide range of films available in wartime Chonqing, see Weihong Bao, 'In Search of a "Cinematic Esperando": Exhibiting Wartime Chongqing Cinema in Global Context', *Journal of Chinese Cinemas* vol. 3 no. 2 (2009), pp. 135–47 (139–40).

19. For a complete account of the incident, see *Dianying shijie* (The Movie World) no. 11 (April 1940), pp. 16, 21.

20. Poshek Fu, 'Projecting Ambivalence: Chinese Cinema in Semi-Occupied Shanghai, 1937–41', in Wen-hsin Yeh (ed.), *Wartime Shanghai* (New York: Routledge, 1998), pp. 86–109.

21. For a detailed historical account of Wang Jingwei's censorship in the occupied east China, including Shanghai, see Wang Chaoguang, 'Kangzhan shiqi lunxianqu de dianying jiancha' (Film Censorship in Occupied Areas during the War), *Kangri zhanzheng yanjiu* (Studies of the Second Sino-Japanese War) no.1 (2002), pp. 28–35.

22. Quoted in Poshek Fu, *Between Shanghai and Hong Kong: The Politics of Chinese Cinemas* (Stanford, CA: Stanford University Press, 2003), p. 97.

23. Huang Tianshi, 'Zhonghua dianying gongsi tuozhan shilue' (The Expansion of China Movie Co.), *Xin yingtan*

no. 1 (November 1942), p. 44. Zhi, 'Jinhou de zhongguo dianying shiye' (Chinese Film in the Future), *Xin yingtan* vol. 2 no. 1 (October 1943), p. 13. Starting from May 1943, *Xin yingtan* became the magazine of Huaying, which succeeded Zhonglian as the leading filming agency in occupied Shanghai (more later).

24. An unidentified film-maker wrote that film stock and bullet were made of the same material, and the scarcity of the material during the war compelled the film-makers to work even harder. See *Xin yingtan*, no. 2 (December 1942), p. 15. For film as a metaphorical weapon that resisted American film propaganda, see Hasumi Tsuneo, 'History of American Filmic Invasion' (Meiguo dianying qinglue shi), trans. by Tao Diya, *Xin yingtan* vol. 2 no. 1 (October 1943), p. 16.

25. Fu, *Between Shanghai and Hong Kong*, p. 102.

26. Ibid., pp. 108–18.

27. An unidentified writer stated that Huaying, integrating production (Zhonglian), distribution (Zhonghua) and exhibition (Shanghai movie theatre company), was poised to work for the 'wounded homeland' (Wang Jingwei's words). See 'Zhonglian chengli yizhounian jinian' (One Year Anniversary of Zhonglian), *Xin yintan* no. 7 (May 1943), n.p.

28. Fu, *Between Shanghai and Hong Kong*, p. 132.

29. Paul Pickowicz, 'Chunjiang yihen de shishi feifei yu lunxian shiqi de zhongguo dianying' (The Conflicts over *Remorse in Shanghai* and the Chinese Cinema in the period of Occupation), trans. by Liu Yuqing, *Wenyi yanjiu*, no. 1 (2008).

30. Fei Mu, 'Jieshao liangwei yiguo de youren: Fulaike fufu' (Introducing Two Foreign Friends – the Fleck Couple), in Wong Ain-ling (ed.), *Shiren daoyan Fei Mu* (The Poet Director Fei Mu) (Hong Kong: Hong Kong Film Critics Society, 1998), pp. 78–80.

31. Sima Yingcai, 'Shijie er'nu de shezhi jingguo' (Shooting Shijie Er'nu), originally published in *Guomin gongbao* vol. 12 (15 December 1943), reprinted in Chongqing shi wen-huaju dianyingchu, 1991, pp. 574–9.

32. Qin Pengzhang, in Wong, *Shiren daoyan Fei Mu*, p. 159.

33. Wang Chaoguang, 'Kangzhan shiqi lunxianqu de diany-ing jiancha', pp. 42–7.

34. Yingjin Zhang, *Chinese National Cinema*, p. 84. For a book-length account of Man'ei, see Hu Chang and Gu Quan, *Manying – guoce dianying mianmian guan* (Man'ei – Perspectives on National Policy Cinema) (Beijing: Zhonghua shuju, 1990).

35. Amakasu Masahiko, 'Manjin no tame ni eiga o tsukuru', *Eiga junpo*, 1 August 1942, p. 3, quoted in Michael

Baskett, *The Attractive Empire: Transnational Film Culture in Imperial Japan* (Honolulu: University of Hawaii Press, 2008), p. 29.

36. For Li Xianglan's performative participation in the New East Asian ideology, see Shelley Stephenson, '"Her Traces are Found Everywhere": Shanghai, Li Xianglan, and the Greater East Asian Film Sphere', in Yingjin Zhang (ed.), *Cinema and Urban Culture in Shanghai, 1922–1943* (Stanford, CA: Stanford University Press, 1999), pp. 222–45.

37. For a description of postwar contention over Man'ei's facilities, see Sun Xiao'ou, 'Cong Manying dao Changying' (From Man'ei to Changchun Film Studio), *Wenshi chunqiu* no. 1 (1996), pp. 51–4.

38. Hong Kong's emergence into a wartime film centre is reflected in the drastically increased film companies and productions. See Chart 1 in Zhou and Li, *History of Early Hong Kong Cinema*, p. 256.

39. Han Yanli, 'Cong guofangpian de zhizuo kan zaoqi yueyu dianying he zhongguo dalu de guanxi' (The Relationship between Early Cantonese Cinema and Mainland China – as Seen from National Defence Cinema), in Wong Ainling (ed.), *Yuegang dianying yinyuan* (The Filmic Connections between Guangdong and Hong Kong) (Hong Kong: Hong Kong Film Archive, 2005), pp. 56–67.

40. Kar Law and Frank Bren, *Hong Kong Cinema: A Cross-Cultural View* (Lanham, MD: Scarecrow Press, 2004), p. 133.

41. See charts in Zhou and Li, *History of Early Hong Kong Cinema*, pp. 256–61.

42. Law and Bren, *Hong Kong Cinema*, p. 136.

43. For two different readings of the nationalist message in *Twin Sisters from the South*, see Poshek Fu, *Between Shanghai and Hong Kong*, chapter 2, and Yingjin Zhang, 'Fandui xiuzheng: Zhanzheng shiqi de xianggang dianying yu diyu zhengzhi' (Against Revisionism: Wartime Hong Kong Cinema and Geopolitics), *Twenty First Century* (Er'shiyi shiji) no. 101 (June 2007), pp. 104–14. For the 'beauty spy' sub-genre, see Han Yanli, 'The Relationship between Early Cantonese Cinema and Mainland China', pp. 62–3. Fei Mu similarly noted the phenomenon of mixture, as suggested by the fact that even a family drama like *Twelve Wives* (Tang Xiaodan, 1937) was advertised for its 'correct ideology'. See Fei in *Kangzhan dianying*, 1938, p. 5.

44. Yuan Muzhi, 'Guanyu jiefangqu de dianying gongzuo' (On Film Work in the Liberated Zone), in Yuan Muzhi, *Yuan Muzhi wenji* (Collected Works of Yuan Muzhi) (Beijing: Zhongguo dianying chubanshe, 1984), p. 590.

Further Reading in *Chinese Films in Focus II*

On Fei Mu, see Chapter 26, '*Spring in a Small Town*: Gazing at Ruins' by Carolyn FitzGerald.

8 Chinese Film-making on the Eve of the Communist Revolution

Paul G. Pickowicz

One of the real bright spots in the history of Chinese film-making was the brief three-year period from mid-1946 to mid-1949. Reflecting now on those tumultuous years, it seems miraculous that any motion pictures were made at all. At the beginning of the period, China was just starting to do the nearly impossible: recover in a timely way from eight bloody years of war with Japanese invaders. Millions had died. The economy was in ruins. China's once-vibrant film industry had ground to a halt by the end of the war. Families had been ripped apart for nearly a decade. Tens of millions of displaced people desperately sought to return home and rebuild shattered lives. To makes matters worse, the conclusion of the war with Japan was followed almost immediately by the outbreak of a full-scale civil war. After eight years of a devastating world war, a massive domestic confrontation that pitted the Nationalist government against its communist foes, a struggle far more deadly than the Russian revolution of 1917 was underway. Once again, millions perished and tens of millions were dislocated. The unravelling of the postwar economy generated one of the world's worst episodes of hyper-inflation and ruined countless lives. As the end of the three-year period approached, demoralised Nationalist forces were looking for ways to flee, while communist peasant armies were preparing to enter major cities. Given all the earth-shaking events unfolding during this brief three-year interval, who had the time or money to make commercial feature films?

The case of the postwar Chinese film industry is fascinating precisely because it did not collapse. Instead, horrendous economic, social and political traumas gave rise to startling cultural productivity, despite harsh conditions and a profoundly unstable work environment. There was a strong demand for fresh pictures, and Chinese film-makers were full of passion when the war ended. Postwar production was underway by mid-1946 and the first films appeared in late 1946.

It is remarkable that in the three-year period under review here slightly more than 150 feature films were produced in mainland China by more than thirty production companies.[1] Most of the movies were made in Shanghai. Many of the studios went out of business after making one or two films. Only seven companies were able to produce more than four films. But these seven compiled a dazzling record. Thirty-eight movies were produced by the three state-owned studios (China Film No. 1 and No. 2 in Shanghai, and China Film No. 3 in Beiping), while an additional sixty-two pictures were produced by the four most important privately owned Shanghai studios, Guotai, Wenhua, Datong and Kunlun. In short, the seven leading studios turned out approximately two-thirds of the feature films made in mainland China from mid-1946 to mid-1949.

But nothing was easy. Some of China's most famous film personalities, popular actresses like Li Lihua and Chen Yanyan, were denounced in the press and by a few in the Nationalist government as 'collaborators' who had worked in the film industry during the Japanese occupation.[2] Some of the film-makers who returned from the inland areas ruled by the Nationalists behaved self-righteously, presenting themselves as patriots who had earned the right to shape the postwar film industry. Some film-makers were pro-government; some were critics. Would it be possible for these groups to cooperate? Government film censors, labouring in a civil war environment, were ordered to be on guard against subversives. The postwar market was flooded with attractive American films. It seemed like unfair competition. Extraordinary inflationary pressures made it extremely difficult for Chinese film-makers to meet production expenses and make a profit. The urban film audience was certainly hungry for new Chinese movies, films that made sense of a world turned upside down for so long, but precisely what sorts of messages about the war and the civil war were film-makers prepared to send?

Of the films made during this short but brilliant era of mainland Chinese cinema, less than half, or approximately sixty-four, survive, and some of these are less than fully intact.[3] Most of the surviving films were made at the seven major studios mentioned above – the state-run China Film studios and the four highly successful private studios. Researchers would like to view all the films, but this is no longer possible. Still, the movies that survive (along with archival materials, late-1940s printed sources and interview data) allow us to see some clear patterns that set this distinctive period of Chinese film-making apart from others.

The Explicitly Political Film

One could hardly blame the urban film audience if it wanted escapist films that allowed people to forget the traumas of war for a couple of hours. What is astonishing about the postwar film scene is that film-makers and audiences alike clearly wanted movies that confronted the war issue directly and tried to measure its short- and long-term impacts on society. Many citizens wanted to know why the 'victory' in the war with Japan felt like 'defeat' in the postwar period. Why was morale so low? Why was there so much postwar domestic strife?

Postwar film-makers approached this challenge in various ways. One of the most important and effective strategies was to make sensational epic films that explored the big picture and told explicit, gut-wrenching stories about the entirety of China's war experience. Many of these epics took the form of 'family melodramas' that functioned as national allegories.

One of the earliest and most successful epics was *Far Away Love* (*Yaoyuan de ai*, January 1947, Chen Liting).[4]

This compelling movie, a work that combines biting satire and tear-jerking melodrama, explodes the myth that all politically critical postwar film-making was carried on by vaguely defined 'leftists' in private-sector film studios. *Far Away Love*, a stunningly polemical film, was made in a government-run studio, China Film No. 2, and was approved by government censorship organs. This production reveals that many in the Nationalist government were deeply concerned about postwar malaise, and were happy to have respected film-makers search for its origins.

Far Away Love concerns the painful story of an uneducated young woman, Yu Zhen, and a well-known professor, Xiao Yuanxi. The film offers a long treatment of wartime traumas, but starts by laying out ten years of essential prewar background. The audience is told that it is impossible to comprehend the complexities of the war years without first grasping the essence of prewar social and cultural dynamics.

Professor Xiao claims to be a champion of women's rights. When he notices that an attractive young servant in his well-appointed home is actually borrowing books from his study, he decides to carry out an 'experiment'. He will prove his fancy theories by personally mentoring the young woman and 'transforming' her into the sort of 'modern' woman China so urgently requires. The experiment appears to be successful, and before long Xiao and Yu Zhen marry. But Xiao's mentoring continues on the grounds that Yu Zhen is not yet the 'ideal' modern woman because she is insufficiently 'independent'. Xiao's notion of 'independence' is never clearly defined.

The relationship seems to be fine until Japan's attack on Shanghai in January 1932. It is at this moment of crisis that the film audience sees clearly that Xiao's definition of the 'modern' woman does not embrace gender equality, despite all his hypocritical rhetoric about 'independence'. Yu Zhen responds to the national crisis by attending more and more public meetings, while Xiao remains 'busy' with his research. Yu Zhen learns leadership skills and even works as a volunteer nurse. Xiao resents her time away from home and her new associations, and is delighted when the crisis blows over and Yu Zhen returns to the domestic sphere.

The dual themes of gender and class divisions are central to *Far Away Love* and resurface in the narrative when total war with Japan breaks out in 1937. By this time the postwar audience can easily predict the course of events. Yu Zhen, a woman from a modest

The wartime reunion of estranged husband and wife goes very badly in *Far Away Love* (*Yaoyuan de ai*) (Courtesy of the Film Archive of China)

social background, expresses strength and patriotic zeal under trying wartime circumstances, while Xiao, the westernised, bourgeois, intellectual snob, exhibits weakness and wavers time and again in the face of cruel enemy assaults.

As Japanese forces advance on Shanghai, Xiao runs away by accepting a comfortable government desk job in the interior of China. He leaves wife and children behind. Yu Zhen freely chooses to stay in Shanghai to do dangerous work at the front. Eventually husband and wife meet up in a Nationalist-controlled city in the interior, but their lives are headed in entirely different directions. Xiao is a cowardly and corrupt minor official, while Yu Zhen is a rank and file soldier in the Nationalist army. Xiao tries to convince Yu Zhen to stay with him and enjoy the good life in safe interior areas, but Yu Zhen departs with her unit for the front.

The war drags on, and the two do not meet until Yu Zhen, still with her heroic unit, spots Xiao in a column of pathetic refugees, mostly women and children, who are fleeing a Japanese air attack in south-west China. The professor begs her to retreat with him to the safety of Chongqing, China's wartime capital, but she rejects the proposal. He asks if she loves another man. She says she loves all 'who have died and all who are still fighting'. Xiao, she states, 'loves only himself'. Xiao then jumps into a truck with women and children and is evacuated from the war zone.

The message sent by this government-run film studio was that wartime social phenomena (positive as

well as negative) were related to prewar patterns. Many of the once humble, including China's women, had sacrificed for the nation; many of the formerly privileged, including prominent men, had behaved selfishly and corruptly during the war. This popular film educated and disturbed postwar audiences.

Another grand epic, *A Spring River Flows East* (*Yi jiang chun shui xiang dong liu*, October 1947, Cai Chusheng and Zheng Junli) was produced at the private Kunlun studio.[5] The film was so popular it continuously played in Shanghai for almost a year. *Spring River* is usually regarded as a leftist work, but it too passed government censorship reviews and, like all postwar epics, built on the solid foundation constructed by *Far Away Love*.

Spring River, a classic family melodrama meant to be read as a national allegory, also features a Shanghai couple, Zhongliang, a handsome night-school teacher, and Sufen, a factory worker. This film also begins with a brief account of responses to an earlier episode of Japanese aggression, the occupation of north-east China in 1931. This time, though, the key male figure, Zhongliang, is seen as a progressive patriot, someone who respects bedrock Chinese values. This time, it is factory bosses who are suspicious of disruptive activities. They do not want to provoke Japan.

When full-scale war breaks out in 1937, Zhongliang fully commits himself to the patriotic cause. His decision to engage in perilous Red Cross work is supported by his adoring, old-style wife, Sufen. He follows government forces to Hankou and Nanchang and is eventually captured by the Japanese and forced to do slave labour. He escapes and shows up penniless in Chongqing, the Nationalist wartime capital. Like many thousands of others, he will be separated from his wife and family for eight years.

Zhongliang experiences hardship, but it is nothing like the misery Sufen confronts every day in occupied Shanghai. A main difference between this film and *Far Away Love* is that *Spring River* offers a gripping portrait of what life was like under the occupation. Postwar film audiences could easily relate to the privation experienced by Sufen, another resilient Chinese woman who rises to the challenges of war and dislocation.

Zhongliang, by contrast, experiences steady and long-term moral decline in China's wartime capital. There appears to be no way for him to give expression to his patriotic instincts. He is willingly seduced by a glamorous, westernised and well-connected young woman – a tough and independent figure in her own

Civil War-era confrontation between morally corrupted husband and upright wife in *A Spring River Flows East* (*Yi jiang chun shui xiang dong liu*) (Courtesy of the Film Archive of China)

right. Zhongliang forgets about his family in occupied Shanghai and gets involved, instead, with war profiteers who live a life of luxury. The theme of wartime corruption in Chongqing dominates the middle portion of the film, and it is painful for the audience to witness Zhongliang's ethical and political decline. He marries the attractive young woman, never revealing that he already has a wife and family.

Spring River goes well beyond *Far Away Love* in thematic terms by continuing the saga into the troubled postwar period. Zhongliang returns to Shanghai after the war to function as a slick operative in the company that engaged so wantonly in wartime profiteering. Like sharks, these businessmen look for opportunities to make a killing in the volatile postwar environment. Zhongliang never thinks of looking for his prewar family members, all of whom are struggling to survive in a dysfunctional economy. Instead, Zhongliang takes up with a third woman, someone who collaborated with the Japanese during the war. Meanwhile, Sufen, the first wife, has been taking excellent care of Zhongliang's mother through eight years of crushing occupation.

The film ends when Sufen, employed as a washerwoman in Zhongliang's postwar house, discovers the truth, confronts Zhongliang and then commits suicide. To be sure, the theme of weak men and strong women is taken up again here, as are class issues and cultural controversies (Who sacrifices for others? Who exploits? Who embodies decent Chinese cultural norms? Who represents corrupt alien values?). But with *Spring River*, the analysis of what plagues postwar China is deepened. True, the film audience is told, prewar modes shaped the ways in which various types of Chinese responded to the wartime holocaust, but it is also clear that toxic social, economic, cultural and political cancers that took root during the war years, especially in the wartime capital of Chongqing, were transported back to the formerly occupied areas after 1945, poisoning the postwar scene. The perception among many citizens was that corrupt people who had lived comfortably in Nationalist-ruled inland areas during the war returned to places like Shanghai after the war to scapegoat and exploit people who had suffered under the occupation and who continued to struggle after the war. There seemed to be no justice.[6]

Why would government censors approve a depressing film of this sort? The short answer is that the problems were real and the government had to point fingers. The Nationalists had great difficulty acknowledging their own wartime and postwar failings, but had no problem shifting the blame to selfish, unpatriotic, bourgeois, westernised, corrupt manipulators of the out-of-control economy.

The Implicitly Political Film

During the Mao years (1949–76) and well into the post-Mao period, the tendency among writers in the People's

Republic (PRC) was to give almost all the credit for critical postwar film-making to a 'progressive' and 'leftwing' camp associated with the privately run Kunlun studio, people said to be connected to underground communist cultural operatives. Explicitly political films like *Far Away Love* and *Heavenly Spring Dream* (Tang Xiaodan, March 1947) made in Nationalist-run state studios were slighted.[7] Another important mode of postwar film-making, what might be called the implicitly political film, was simply ignored or dismissed as apolitical, irrelevant, escapist, or even reactionary.

In fact, many of these allegedly irrelevant works, most of them made at the legendary Wenhua studio, were far from apolitical. They tackled the same sort of postwar issues taken up in explicitly political films, but did so more indirectly and often with greater artistic sensitivity. And they typically went beyond the immediate postwar environment to address longer-term social and cultural issues debated in China both during and after the liberal May Fourth Movement of 1919. Compared to the people who made explicitly political melodramas, the Wenhua group was more intellectual, had closer ties to the theatre world and was comprised mainly of people who had remained in Japanese-occupied Shanghai during the war.

Wenhua films treated postwar problems, but did so in decidedly universalistic and humanistic ways that linked various postwar crises to transnational social currents and to broader themes associated with China's century-old encounter with modernity. True, Wenhua film-makers embraced the family narrative formula, but they usually avoided melodramatic representation, preferring instead to make psychological dramas, comedies and satires. Excellent examples of humanistic, implicitly political film-making are Wenhua's first two postwar features, *Unending Emotions* (Sang Hu, April 1947) and *Fake Bride, Phony Bridegroom* (Huang Zuolin, June 1947).

The war with Japan and related postwar dislocations are nowhere mentioned directly in *Unending Emotions*. Instead, the audience is invited to view an intimate and highly personal moment that seems to have no connection to politics, war, or revolution. The narrative deals with an educated twenty-three-year-old woman, Jiayin, who is a teacher. Nothing is said about her experiences during the war. The story focuses strictly on her complicated postwar relationship with a love interest, a successful

businessman named Xia Zongyu. The two are clearly attracted to each other and are considering a long-term arrangement, but the problem, Jiayin soon discovers, is that Xia is a married man. The dashing Xia relentlessly pursues Jiayin, telling her that he does not really love his sickly wife. Xia feels sorry for his pathetic wife, but he claims she will never agree to a divorce. Jiayin admits to herself that she loves Xia, but agonises about the situation and cannot decide what to do. The story is complicated by the fact that Jiayin's detestable father shows up unannounced and unwelcome. He seeks to manipulate the situation in order to gain access to Xia's considerable resources, suggesting, for example, that Jiayin become Xia's concubine!

Compared to the explicitly political melodramas discussed above, *Unending Emotions* does indeed feel apolitical. And it was dismissed as a petty-bourgeois indulgence by early PRC scholars.[8] But upon closer inspection, the political thrust of this well-received film becomes quite apparent. It is not a shop-worn romance; it is a fascinating anti-romance, a psychological narrative that rejects the logic of melodrama. In fact it is a feminist work, a rare example of a Republican-era screenplay written by a Chinese woman. The screenwriter was Zhang Ailing, China's most famous wartime literary figure, known early in her career for her efforts to rise above the political and to deal with highly intimate and personal subjects. But in the postwar environment, Zhang was very much among those who tackled burning social issues.

Unending Emotions is a feminist work because it regards the pursuit of women's interests as an end in itself. Unlike the admirable figure of Yu Zhen in the epic *Far Away Love*, Jiayin's independence does not have to be justified in terms of her selfless and patriotic dedication to a collective political cause defined and controlled by men. The viewer is caught by surprise at the conclusion of *Unending Emotions* when Jiaying considers all factors and reaches the painful decision to break from Xia because she realises that Xia is really no different from her despicable father. Not only does she break from Xia, she actually leaves Shanghai to take up a teaching post in distant Xiamen.

This long-ignored work is political in two ways. First, the telltale signs of postwar hardship are felt throughout. For example, there are constant references to the economic rigors of the postwar years: Jiaying is unemployed when the film begins, Xia's factory is experiencing difficulties and Jiayin's father is desperate for cash. But the politics of the film do not dwell exclusively on war-related problems. Zhang Ailing's screenplay successfully reconnects to early twentieth-century Chinese (and transnational) debates about women's rights. Modern women, she suggests, want more than the right to choose their own love interest; they want gender equality, jobs and the ability to be independent from men and the various collective political movements launched by men.

Fake Bride, Phony Bridegroom is a hilarious comedy that also appears at first to be apolitical and disconnected from war-related traumas.[9] Like *Unending Emotions*, it seems to centre entirely on the human desire for love. It features the great actor Shi Hui as the lowly barber, San Hao, who decides to find a wife by responding to a personal ad placed in a local newspaper. A wealthy widow, Miss Fan, is looking for a suitable husband. San Hao writes up a pack of lies about his fancy education and vast resources in order to attract the attention of the widow. The 'widow', played nicely by the famous actress Li Lihua, is not wealthy at all, but a panicky single mother struggling to survive. Virtually the entire film involves the elaborate efforts made by these lovable con-artists to deceive the other and to avoid detection of their real circumstances.

Unlike *Unending Emotions*, this is a comedy and thus it ends on a seemingly happy note. Both San Hao and Miss Fan eventually realise that the other is a fraud, but during their long ordeal of discovery they manage to fall in love anyway and will somehow find a way to make a life together and survive. No mention is made whatever of wartime or prewar conditions, and nothing is said directly about the gravity of postwar economic, social and political conditions. Some observers have referred to *Fake Bride, Phony Bridegroom* as a timeless 'screwball comedy' that could just as easily be set in London. It is impossible to deny the universalistic and humanistic appeals of this clever film, but, like *Unending Emotions*, the telltale signs of China's postwar free-fall are visible everywhere and audiences could not have missed them. From beginning to end, decent, likeable people are confronted by overwhelming postwar economic problems. They are denied one of the most basic fruits of victory: the cultural wholeness of a stable family life. Instead, they must learn to survive in a world full of deceit. Day after day they must engage in degrading rituals of deception and fraud. In short, in postwar China, nothing and no one

are what they seem to be. Everything is fake. Viewers no doubt asked: is there any hope at all for decent people?

Glimpses of the Utopian Collective

In late 1946 and early 1947 it was by no means obvious how postwar social and economic problems would be solved and how the revolutionary struggle between the nationalists and communists would turn out. But by mid-1948 and certainly by early 1949 the political situation was becoming increasingly clear. Sooner or later, many believed, the communists would win. Slowly but surely films began to point to a vaguely defined 'better' future, one full of hope for those who felt cheated in the postwar era. As usual, these films focused on family life. But they conceded that family life was in serious disarray and not likely to return to imagined prewar norms of happiness and fulfilment. More importantly, a few films began to hint at a new kind of family, a surrogate collective family, that would embrace and care for those stumbling around in the wreckage of old-style families. The liberal and humanistic Wenhua studio, an artistic enterprise that stressed the psychology and inner preoccupations of individual human actors, tended not to venture into these sorts of futuristic waters. But the more group-oriented Kunlun studio and even the Nationalist state-run studios began to hint at the viability of distinctively collective alternatives to the customary family.

An outstanding example of this tendency is *Streets and Alleys* (*Jietou xiangwei*, November 1948, Pan Jienong), a thoroughly delightful comedy released by the state-run China Film No. 1 studio. Once again, the emphasis is on the consequences of agonising postwar downward social mobility. Li Zhongming, a likeable but unemployed university graduate, has no choice but to take a job as a street-smart pedicab driver. By accident he bumps into an old classmate, Shuqiu, an interesting and talented young woman who works as a school teacher. A romance blossoms, but Shuqiu is soon fired from her teaching post because she is seen in public with the 'lowly' pedicab driver. The two seem to have no future until a collective of working-class friends steps in to help Zhongming buy his own pedicab and assist Shuqiu in setting up a roadside book stall. The audience is told nothing about the blood relatives of either Zhongming or Shuqiu. Instead, they are saved from ruin by a surrogate family of street people who bring meaning back to their lives. The two young college graduates are

Unemployed teacher turned pedicab driver is embraced by a motley but lovable street collective in *Streets and Alleys* (*Jietou xiangwei*) (Courtesy of the Film Archive of China)

proletarianised in the process and successfully integrated into a new-style collective family. Not only does the collective worry about the material needs of the dislocated young people, it is also concerned about their emotional lives. The collective first stages a festive street marriage for Zhongming and Shuqiu. Then, when the masses notice that the shy newlyweds are (on their wedding night!) sleeping on opposite sides of a drawn curtain, they sneak up the stairs to pull down the 'barrier' that blocks the creation of new life.

None of this would seem remarkable were not for the fact that *Streets and Alleys* was made in a Nationalist film studio at the peak of the civil war. Writer and director Pan Jienong was actually a member of the Nationalist Party. But on the eve of revolution he began to express open sympathy for the 'lower classes' and see hopes for the future in what were said to be their life-enhancing collective impulses.

Another excellent example of a popular movie that touted the appeals of the collective alternative is the appropriately named *A Light for Ten Thousand Families* (Shen Fu, July 1948), a nearly subversive film made by Kunlun that was nonetheless approved by Nationalist censors. The screenwriter was Yang Hansheng, a romantic, underground revolutionary who had joined the Communist Party in 1925. This film, like so many other Kunlun works, is a melodrama that introduces a postwar family of three that is full of hope for the future. In this case, husband (Zhiqing), wife (Youlan) and cute young daughter seem to be doing well enough in postwar Shanghai. But things fall apart when Zhiqing's mother and relatives suddenly show up in the big city as penniless refugees who are fleeing rural 'chaos', a code word for civil war rural dislocation. Zhiqing and Youlan try their best by pawning some of their property and building a roof-top shed for the extended family.

Zhiqing tries to borrow money from his boss, but his shady company is collapsing and Zhiqing is left without a job when the head of the firm flees.

A Light for Ten Thousand Families develops the theme of postwar downward social mobility in great detail. In the end, this decent family loses everything and the wife suffers a heartbreaking miscarriage. After the disintegration process has run its course, the husband and wife, whose marital relations have been torn asunder by the stresses and strains of postwar traumas, discover the resilience and viability of a collective community of friends and former colleagues who have also suffered downward mobility. These people are not blood relatives, but they pool their resources and their talents in order to provide a safe haven and a measure of hope for friends whose own nuclear and extended families have failed to take care of their most basic material and emotional needs. In these works, social revolution seems to be the answer to postwar economic, social and cultural disintegration.

Postwar Patterns

It would be ludicrous to suggest that all of the more than 150 feature films made in mainland China from mid-1946 to mid-1949 fit neatly into one of the three modes discussed here. But the patterns are pronounced. A small number of highly memorable films have been highlighted in this chapter, but many others could just as easily have been emphasised. With respect to the first category, the explicitly political epic film, *Eight Thousand Miles of Clouds and Moon* (Shi Dongshan), released by Kunlun in February 1947, is a near perfect fit.[10] When it comes to the implicitly political film, Wenhua's lyrical masterpiece *Spring in a Small Town* (Fei Mu, September 1948) immediately comes to mind. When we think of early glimpses of the future utopian collective, a Kunlun film entitled *Women Side by Side* (Chen Liting, February 1949) is hard to ignore.[11]

The films of the late 1940s played what might be called a performative role in postwar society. Some sought to be helpful by addressing and thus easing postwar dislocations. Some functioned as quasi-protest films. Some sought to locate China's turmoil in the universalistic context of human drama anywhere in the world. Some pointed to the appeals of alternative, even revolutionary, social formations. The films of the late 1940s were popular and made an enormous impact on society. Though revolution was the goal of only a

handful of film-makers, an extraordinary number of films produced in this remarkable period nonetheless aroused passions, destabilised society and questioned the legitimacy of the Nationalist state.

Dramatic expressions of dislocation, alienation and outrage were filmed both outside and inside the party-state cultural apparatus. As director Tang Xiaodan, a state-studio insider, put it, 'Honest and conscientious government employees could barely survive, while crooked, traitorous former collaborators were instantly transformed into "underground workers".'[12] Referring to the down-and-out pedicab driver featured in *Streets and Alleys*, director Pan Jienong, another state-studio insider, wrote, 'The character Li Zhongming is actually myself. I not only shed my scholar's robe, I stripped bare my true nature.'[13]

Notes

1. Cheng Jihua, Li Shaobai, and Xing Zuwen (eds), *Zhongguo dianying fazhan shi* (Beijing: Zhongguo dianying chuban she, 1981), vol. 2, pp. 461–80.

2. Bi Kewei, 'Chunjiang yihen de shishi feifei yu lunxian shiqi de Zhongguo dianying', *Wenyi yanjiu* no. 1 (2007), pp. 105–22.

3. Zhongguo dianying ziliaoguan (ed.), *Zhongguo dianying ziliaoguan guan zang yingpian mulu* (Beijing: Zhongguo dianying ziliaoguan, 1995), pp. 12–16.

4. Paul G. Pickowicz, 'Victory as Defeat: Postwar Visualizations of China's War of Resistance', in Wen-hsin Yeh (ed.), *Becoming Chinese: Passages to Modernity and Beyond* (Berkeley: University of California Press, 2000), pp. 372–6.

5. See Pickowicz, 'Victory as Defeat', pp. 380–4.

6. These themes were also explored in postwar novels. See Paul G. Pickowicz, 'Pa Chin's *Cold Nights* and China's Wartime and Postwar Culture of Disaffection', in Pa Chin, *Cold Nights* (Hong Kong: Chinese University Press, 2002), pp. x–xxxvii.

7. For a discussion of *Heavenly Spring Dream*, see Paul G. Pickowicz, 'Melodramatic Representation and the "May Fourth" Tradition of Chinese Cinema', in Ellen Widmer and David Der-wei Wang (eds), *From May Fourth to June Fourth: Fiction and Film in Twentieth-Century China* (Cambridge, MA: Harvard University Press, 1993), pp. 308–13.

8. See Cheng Jihua et al., *Zhongguo dianying fazhan shi*, vol. 2, p. 269.

9. Paola Iovene, 'Phony Phoenixes: Comedy, Protest, and Marginality in Postwar Shanghai', in Sherman Cochran

and Paul G. Pickowicz (eds), *China on the Margins* (Ithaca: Cornell University East Asia Series, 2010).

10. See Pickowicz, 'Victory as Defeat', pp. 376–80.

11. Paul G. Pickowicz, 'Women and Wartime Shanghai: A Postwar Perspective', in Christian Henriot and Wen-hsin Yeh (eds), *In the Shadow of the Rising Sun: Shanghai under Japanese Occupation* (Cambridge: Cambridge University Press, 2004), pp. 346–61.

12. Tang Xiaodan, 'Jituo yu xiwang: daoyanzhe de hua', quoted in Cheng Jihua et al., *Zhongguo dianying fazhan shi*, vol. 2, p. 184.

13. Pan Jienong, '*Jietou xiangwei* zuotan jilu', quoted in Cheng Jihua et al., *Zhongguo dianying fazhan shi*, vol. 2, p. 204.

Further Reading in *Chinese Films in Focus II*

On Zheng Junli, see Chapter 10, '*Crows and Sparrows*: Allegory on a Historical Threshold' by Yiman Wang.

On Fei Mu, see Chapter 26, '*Spring in a Small Town*: Gazing at Ruins' by Carolyn FitzGerald.

PART THREE

The Forgotten Period: 1949–80

9 The Remodelling of a National Cinema

Chinese Films of the Seventeen Years (1949–66)

Julian Ward

The years following the founding of the People's Republic of China (PRC) in 1949 saw a series of major social and political upheavals, from land reform to the Hundred Flowers campaign, the Great Leap Forward and the ideological split with the Soviet Union. Moreover, having set out on the road to recovery from years of war and natural disasters, China was soon drawn into a major war in Korea. In spite of all these momentous events, the Chinese Communist Party (CCP) paid extremely close attention to the workings of the film industry, quickly establishing control over all matters relating to production and exhibition. Cinema mattered to the new state: leading politicians participated in the debates about how to make films, numerous cinemas were built in the cities and, with the establishment of mobile projection units and regional film studios, film was for the first time taken out to the countryside. The release of new films was carefully orchestrated to coincide, not just with individual campaigns, but with major dates in China's recent history: *Song of Youth* (Cui Wei and Chen Huaikai), *Nie Er* and *Lin Zexu* (both Zheng Junli), for example, to mark the tenth anniversary of the founding of the PRC in 1959, and *The Red Detachment of Women* (Xie Jin) for the fortieth anniversary of the founding of the CCP in 1961.

Although tantalising echoes of a popular cinema with profound aesthetic qualities, evident in such works as *Spring in a Small Town* (Fei Mu, 1948), can be glimpsed in some of the last productions of the private studios in the early 1950s, the style of film-making changed rapidly after 1949, as the CCP sought, in the words of Guo Moruo, speaking in 1950, 'to eliminate the poisonous imperialist films gradually and strengthen the educational nature of the people's film industry'.[1] The central tenets of Mao Zedong's 1942 *Talks at the Yan'an Conference on Literature and Art*, that art should serve politics and be accessible to workers, peasants and soldiers, were enshrined, and film-makers were obliged to adopt Soviet-style Socialist Realism. Until the onset of the Cultural Revolution in 1966, nevertheless, the climate was protean, punctuated by periods of ebb and flow between the severest strictures of Socialist Realism and the Anti-Rightist campaign and the relative relaxation of the late 1950s, and the use of so-called Middle Characters in the early 1960s. All these debates came to an abrupt end in the mid-1960s, by which time production had hit the buffers and Jiang Qing, Mao Zedong's wife who had herself been an actor in Shanghai in the 1930s, was lashing out at the most anodyne films, including *Lei Feng* (Dong Zhaoqi, 1964) and *Red Crag* (Shui Hua, 1965).[2] The Cultural Revolution marks such a decisive moment in the history of modern China that the period from the founding of the PRC in 1949 to 1966 is now known as the Seventeen Years.

The sustained levels of political interference in film-making have ensured that it is all too easy to dismiss the films from the Seventeen Years as mere propaganda fodder, the inevitable result of a film-making community in thrall to its political masters, and a massive let-down after the wonders of the Shanghai film world of the 1930s and the brief but glorious postwar flowering of the late 1940s. Responsibility for the dull style of the new form of cinema, obliged to pay heed at all times to the question of class consciousness, was attributed to those artists who had earned revolutionary credibility through years of hardship in Yan'an, the communist-held area of north-west China, their triumph coming at the expense of more ideologically suspect individuals who had spent the war in either the Nationalist- or Japanese-held areas of China. The new films have been criticised as formulaic in terms of subject matter and of limited artistic quality, suffering from static camerawork, stagey presentation, lack of profound literary content and the avoidance of any potentially confusing features, such as non-linear narratives or unexpected plot twists.[3] The acknowledgment of journeyman director Cheng Yin that he was more concerned with avoiding political errors than achieving artistic excellence, reveals all too clearly the pressures under which the film-makers were operating.[4]

Indeed, the extraordinary level of interference by the organs of state at every stage of the film-making process and the limited artistic quality of the majority of the films from this period are undeniable, a lifeless production like *Inexhaustible Potential* (Xu Ke, 1954), about workers in a steel factory overcoming the conservatism and bureaucratic spirit of certain officials, serving as a prime example. After all, the new organs of state control, including the Central Film Management Bureau and the Film Guidance Committee, were all set up within months of the CCP assuming control. At the same time, however, it is worth remembering that, as was the case with many aspects of life in the early years of communist China, 1949 was not such a stark dividing line between the old and the new: the full impact of the widespread changes in the Chinese film world did not take effect overnight. For example, the censorship regulations issued in 1949, which called for the censorship of films deemed to be anti-communist, anti-Soviet, injurious to world peace, or simply too racy or superstitious, were as vague as those that had been issued by the Nationalists in the early 1930s.[5] Nevertheless, over the course of the 1950s, a highly prescriptive system evolved with a narrow range of subject matter and style, backed up by campaigns of criticism that could arise from a single newspaper article. Whether they compromised, assimilated or rebelled, all Chinese film-makers struggled to come to terms with the demands of their new masters, the new rules creating a climate of fear that became 'ever more deeply ingrained'.[6]

In order to ensure the largest possible audience, mobile projection units were set up, their number rising from a hundred in 1949 to 522 in 1950 and 4,400 by 1956: audiences, bolstered by the fact that batches of tickets were routinely given out to work units and attendance was mandatory, rose from 47 million in 1949 to 146 million in 1950 and 752 million in 1953.[7] In order to ensure that what Tina Chen has called the films' 'Party-sanctioned meaning' was conveyed, local officials would provide commentaries, or even translations in those regions of the country that were unfamiliar with the standard dialect.[8] The early 1950s saw much jockeying for position as conflicts between private and state-organised film-making, and between freedom of expression and state-imposed dogma, were played out. The vexed question of how to deal with the private film studios was speedily resolved. Initially allowed to continue and even loaned money, they soon ran into trouble, their fate sealed by the furore which engulfed the Kunlun production of *The Life of Wu Xun* (Sun Yu, 1950), starring Zhao Dan, one of the great stars of the Shanghai era. Based on the true story of a beggar in nineteenth-century Shandong who amassed enough money to open a charity school, the film was popular with the public, but was accused in an anonymous article, published in the *People's Daily* in May 1951, of spreading feudal culture. This article, later revealed to have been penned by Mao Zedong himself, was followed by forty more on the same theme over the next three months. The film was banned and by 1953 all the private studios had been taken over by the state.

Given the level of interference, the unsurprising result was that few films were made in the opening years of communist rule: nine in 1952 and twelve in 1953.[9] With domestic production low and the staple prewar diet of a mixture of Hollywood movies with a leavening of Shanghai works no longer politically acceptable, the shortfall for a voracious moviegoing public was resolved by the large-scale exhibition of productions from socialist states, around two-thirds of the 1,309 feature films imported into China between 1949 and 1957 coming from Soviet Russia.[10] Here was a ready supply of films whose subject matter and cinematic techniques could be entirely vouchsafed. Kept informed by film magazines full of articles about Soviet stars, Chinese audiences were as familiar with *Lenin in October* (Mikhail Romm, 1937) and *The Gadfly* (Alexander Feinzimmer, 1956) as with any domestic production. The Eastern Bloc wielded a heavy influence not just in terms of the Socialist Realist framework: in such works as *Heroic Driver* (Lü Ban, 1954), Soviet experts were given prominent roles as knowledgeable guides for enthusiastic but ignorant Chinese workers.

Many of those films that were made looked to the recent struggles with Japan (1937–45) or the Nationalists (1945–9), war offering a safe topic, full of potential for guaranteed happy endings, good role models and a prominent guiding role for the CCP. On the domestic front, homilies to life in the PRC were linked to campaigns, such as the anti-bureaucracy or Support Korea/Resist America movements. Unsurprisingly, along with the exponential rise in the number of mobile projection units, came the tackling of a variety of new rural topics, such as land reform and the establishment of communes. A new group of stock characters soon emerged, including the recalcitrant landlord, the granny who recounted the evils of the old society, the youthful idealist and the honest, incorruptible party official whose presence was required to guide the people towards a bright future. Speaking in 1952, Zhou Enlai was clear about the way films should be made: 'our films must have beginning and an ending; plots must be clear; patterns should not be as fast as foreign films. Because we are people from a semi-agriculture society, we can't catch up if it is too fast.'[11]

The template for the new cinema was established with *The White-Haired Girl* (Wang Bin and Shui Hua 1950), based on a local opera performed in Yan'an during the war years, which set standards both for the depiction of heroes and villains and the adaptation of existing works. Operating in similarly safe territory were two biopics of renowned communist martyrs *Zhao Yiman* (Sha Meng, 1950), about a woman executed by the Japanese, and *Liu Hulan* (Feng Bailu, 1950), the tragic tale of a girl of fifteen killed by the Nationalists, which presented the new approved version of the selfless female role model. Elsewhere, with its use of voiceover, intertitles and the explanatory words of onscreen characters to guide the audience towards an understanding of the film's anti-superstition message, *The Spirits are Worthless* (Zhang Bo, 1950) provides a good example of the hortative qualities of Socialist Realism cinema. Throughout the film, the camera barely moves, and only a few brief montages of busy efficient medical staff juxtaposed with the card-playing, mumbo-jumbo-speaking shamans who fleece the innocent villagers, indicate any artistic ambition. *The Urgent Letter* (Shi Hui, 1954), a children's film about a young boy asked by his father to take a letter behind enemy lines during the war against Japan, also uses intertitles and a voiceover to cover areas where the

youthful audience might miss the intended message. *Zhao Xiaolan* (Lin Yang, 1953), a paean to the reformed marriage law, is similarly preachy in its message and uninspired in its execution, its origins in a stage play all too apparent. To a certain extent, any cinematic inadequacies are, and were, irrelevant: what was important was the message and the methods that were adopted to ensure that the audience did not miss this message.

While the staple topics of war and government policies and campaigns were usually trouble free, other subjects proved rather more problematic, moving in and out of favour as the political climate changed: these included spy films, operas, films about China's ethnic minorities, adaptations of tales from traditional Chinese literature or the renowned writers of the literary revolution of the 1920s and 30s, and even a few comedies. The question of how to deal with China's cultural and historical legacy was perhaps the most vexed of all. In the early 1950s, for example, films set in pre-twentieth-century China were generally avoided, but towards the end of the decade films were made about historical figures such as the botanist Li Shizhen and Lin Zexu, Imperial Commissioner during the Opium Wars.

The adaptation of literary texts was another matter altogether. Pre-twentieth-century works naturally paid no attention to class consciousness, and even literary creations from the May Fourth period, although sympathetic to the plight of the ordinary Chinese people, presented their own problems. In adapting Lu Xun's *New Year Sacrifice* (Sang Hu, 1956), Mao Dun's *The Lin Family Shop* (Shui Hua, 1959) and Rou Shi's *Early Spring* (Xie Tieli, 1963), film-makers had to work out precisely how to use stories replete with ideas that accorded all too rarely with the ideological constraints prevailing in the PRC. Xia Yan, a veteran of the prewar Shanghai years, who wrote screenplays for both *New Year Sacrifice* and *The Lin Family Shop*, made subtle changes to each story in an attempt to pre-empt criticism, adding instances of landlord exploitation to the former, while in the latter as he wrote, 'In order to express the inherent obsession with profit of people of Mr Lin's class, and to prevent the audience becoming too sympathetic towards him, I added scenes showing his cruelty to those below him.'[12] Xia, who had been warned of the danger of making a film about a petty capitalist so soon after the Anti-Rightist campaign, was subsequently criticised by Jiang Qing for making a film

The 1956 adaptation of Lu Xun's short story *New Year Sacrifice*

that 'sought to weaken the dictatorship of the proletariat by praising the class enemy'.[13]

Such elaborate feats of self-censorship were all too common for those operating within a system liable to turn against anyone associated with the pre-PRC film industry. Like Xia Yan, the great actor/director Shi Hui made many compromises as he tried to adapt to the new system, including writing an article about actors wanting to be 'good revolutionary workers' who served the people. Shi worked on several of the most artistically successful films made in the dying days of the private film studios: in *This Whole Life of Mine* (1950), which he also directed, he gave a moving performance

Shi Hui (right) in *This Whole Life of Mine*

in the lead role of an honest but naive policeman, while in *Sisters Stand Up* (Chen Xihe, 1951), about the post-liberation reform of Beijing's brothels, he was a convincingly repugnant pimp. Shi directed, and played the role of the eponymous peasant soldier in *Platoon Commander Guan* (1951), but was taken to task for creating a character whose relationship with the soldiers under his command was considered to be insufficiently hierarchical. All these films were made for the Wenhua company which he had helped to set up in 1947. By the time he directed *The Urgent Letter* in 1954, the film industry had been nationalised and he was working for the Shanghai film company. In spite of all his efforts Shi Hui was subjected to heavy criticism and committed suicide in 1957.[14]

This was not an unusual pattern. Zheng Junli, who had made the successful postwar films *The Spring River Flows East* (1947) and *Crows and Sparrows* (1949), went to great lengths to try to make films that would appease the authorities. His *Husband and Wife* (1951), starring Zhao Dan, was praised initially, but soon criticised for the over-sympathetic depiction of an urban intellectual. For *Lin Zexu*, also starring Zhao Dan, Zheng thought he was on safer ground, contriving to turn the ignominy of China's humiliation during the First Opium War into the heroic start of Chinese resistance to imperialist aggression. Once again, the film was warmly received on release but later criticised, on this occasion for supposedly glorifying feudal officials. Zheng died in prison in 1969.[15]

Actors also encountered problems. The state was initially obliged to rely on those who had learned their craft before 1949, but the inevitable links with a Nationalist past could prove troublesome.[16] Although he performed the lead roles in such films as *Lin Zexu* and *Li Shizhen* (Shen Fu, 1956), and was even admitted to the Communist Party in 1957, Zhao Dan was always viewed with suspicion, partly because of his leading role in *The Life Of Wu Xun*, but also because of the films he had made in prewar Shanghai. For his final film role in *Red Crag*, he played a prisoner incarcerated by the Nationalists in a notorious Chongqing prison, reawakening painful memories of the years he had spent in prison during the War of Resistance.[17] Shangguan Yunzhu, the popular star of such prewar films as *Three Women* (Chen Liting, 1947) and *Crows and Sparrows*, appeared in both *Early Spring* and *Stage Sisters* (Xie Jin, 1964), the character she portrayed in each film committing suicide, a fate tragically realised in 1968

Stage Sisters

when, after suffering persecution, she jumped off the roof of a building in Shanghai.

Unlike their Hollywood counterparts, Chinese film stars were lauded not for their unattainability but for their ability to inspire, and be inspired by, the masses. On occasions, actors emerged from an unprivileged background to act out their experiences in film: Wangdui, the leading actor of *Serfs* (Li Jun, 1963), about the humiliations suffered by the Tibetan people during the pre-communist era, had himself been a slave, Huang Baomei, a model worker from a Shanghai cotton mill, was the eponymous star of a 1958 film directed by Xie Jin, while Li Lingyun, the fearsome madam of *Sisters Stand Up*, was a former prostitute. Elsewhere, Zhang Ruifang, who attained fame through her ability to portray an ordinary woman in such films as *Fighting North and South* (Cheng Yin and Tang Xiaodan, 1952), in

which she was a militia leader, and *Nie Er* (as an underground communist), achieved her greatest success as the eponymous heroine of *Li Shuangshuang* (Lu Ren, 1962), a role for which she prepared by living in a commune for several weeks.[18] While Zhang attained popularity though portraying positive role models, other actors were not so fortunate: Xiang Kun, for example, played Nationalist officers in *Fighting North and South*, *After the War was Over* (Cheng Yin, 1962) and *Red Crag*, while Fang Hua, who portrayed a Japanese officer in *Guerrillas on the Plains* (Su Li and Wu Zhaodi, 1955), was obliged to play the same role when the film was remade twenty years later. So desperate was he to avoid being associated with the role, after being accused in public of being a Japanese spy, that he eventually resorted to disguising his features by undergoing plastic surgery.

Fang Hua's actions serve as testimony to the whole-hearted way in which Chinese audiences, many of whom were experiencing cinema for the first time, embraced the cinema. Ban Wang has described the films as having a 'tremendous and indelible emotional impact', suggesting a world far from the image of a bored mass of unwilling individuals dragooned in large numbers into attending compulsory viewings of dour revolutionary epics, while an interviewee in the *Morning Sun* documentary about the Cultural Revolution spoke of his excitement at watching an attractive woman dance a rumba in *Hero in the Bandits' Den* (Yan Jizhou and Hao Guang, 1958).[19] It is all too easy to imagine how enticing the actions and lifestyles of characters in such works as *City Without Night* (Tang Xiaodan, 1957), about Shanghai capitalists before and after 1949, and *Woman Basketball Player No 5* (Xie Jin, 1958), who live in noticeably comfortable surroundings, might have appeared in 1950s China. Indeed, the febrile atmosphere of the Anti-Rightist campaign ensured that *City Without Night* was not released till after the death of Mao Zedong. The difficulty was how to portray decadent characters without presenting them in such a way as to make their lifestyle appear more attractive than that of a poor peasant or an honest party official.

It is worth underlining that many works of enduring artistic value were made during the Seventeen Years, both before and after the demise of the private studios: *Song of Youth* captured the heady days of the student revolutionaries of the 1930s, while the cultural thaw at the start of the 1960s saw *Liu Sanjie* (Su Li, 1960), a musical, set in the Tang dynasty, about a beautiful young woman from the Zhuang minority who outwits an evil landlord, *Early Spring* which depicted small-town life in the 1920s in a refreshingly apolitical way, *Li Shuangshuang*, a popular comedy about the clash between individual and collective aspirations and *Satisfied or Not* (Yan Gong, 1963), also a comedy, about a restaurant worker uncertain about his place in society, this time incorporating humorous cross-talk. During the same period, Xie Jin made *Big Li, Little Li and Old Li* (1962), a humorous take on a group of workers in a meat-processing factory, and *Stage Sisters*, a melodrama about the theatre world in pre- and post-communist China which avoided lazy stereotyping.

The current reappraisal of films from the Seventeen Years, inspired at least in part by nostalgia for the Maoist heyday, has been helped by the advent of the digital age which has seen the repackaging as Red

Classic DVDs of numerous Chinese films of the 1950s and 60s, not just those denounced as 'poisonous weeds' but many titles that had disappeared into obscurity. At the same time, the generally more relaxed atmosphere has led to a more reflective approach from those making films: with *In the Heat of the Sun* (1994) and *Devils on the Doorstep* (1999), for example, Jiang Wen showed the Maoist era could be a source of fun, both works full of playful allusions to films from the Seventeen Years. Along with the growth in the number of accounts written by and about both audience and film-makers has come increased attention being paid to the experiences of individuals rather than the familiar picture of the all-encompassing influence of the CCP.[20]

These studies have looked at actors and directors who were obliged to work under numerous constraints, yet who, by stretching the boundaries of acceptability and taking advantage of moments of relative liberalisation, were able to make films that were artistically challenging and visually stimulating. A particularly interesting and refreshing example is *Before the New Director Arrives* (Lü Ban, 1956), one of a select number of satires made during the Seventeen Years, which recounts the efforts of Section Chief Niu, a self-serving party official, to prepare for the arrival of his new boss. In one telling moment, the hapless Niu, unaware that he is speaking to the new director, boasts of how the two men are old friends who have fought wars and worked in the fields together, when in reality they have never met. How tempting it must have been

The final scene from *Before the New Director Arrives*

for audiences of the time to view this as a sardonic comment on their forced immersion in films championing the unapproachable sanctity of such characters. Lü Ban's film ends with the new director delivering a homily straight to camera about the need for honesty, as Niu, his devious posturing now revealed to all, cowers in the background. Lü's later work, *Unfinished Comedy* (1958), also a satire, included an unflattering portrait of a humourless party official, ran into difficulties and was never shown publicly.[21]

The question of characterisation attracted the attention of the many critics, officials and politicians who participated in the discussions about film-making. In 1953, Chen Huangmei, director of the Film Bureau, acknowledged that creating heroic characters who were credible and at the same time capable of winning the audience's approval was not easy.[22] Zhou Enlai also spoke out in favour of artistic independence when it was expedient to do so, calling in 1961, for example, for a greater range of subject matter and a more democratic atmosphere in the film-making world. Like actors and directors, the fate of critics was also finely balanced, as evidenced by the experience of Zhong Dianfei, a member of the Film Bureau who wrote many articles in the early 1950s. After praising the portrayal of Zhao Yiman, Zhong went on to note failings in the depiction of a party official in *Fighting North and South*, before famously taking advantage of the invitation to criticise the CCP's shortcomings during the Hundred Flowers campaign by lamenting the level of interference in the making of *New Year Sacrifice*. When Mao Zedong responded by accusing Zhong of writing the kind of articles that people on Taiwan liked to read, in which the recent past was held up as a disaster, there could only be one winner: Zhong was expelled from the party and sent off to the countryside.

Conclusion

What has emerged from the accounts written in recent years of cinema made in China during the first seventeen years of communist rule is a clearer vision of the people who populated the film world: the cultural critics and party bureaucrats, who, though capable on occasions of generosity, were frequently vindictive; stars of a new kind, for whom acting skills were all too often of secondary importance to the ability to appear to be a good communist; and directors, who had to be ready at all times to compromise. Despite all the campaigns and all the restrictions, many films do offer a vision of how Chinese film might have developed had directors been able to work without constantly having to look over their shoulders.

From the mid-1960s on, around 400 films were declared to be 'poisonous weeds' and many of the leading figures in the film world, having been accused of peddling 'a hotch-potch of feudalism, capitalism and revisionism', suffered terrible persecution, as Jiang Qing exacted revenge for perceived slights she had endured in Shanghai in the 1930s. Xia Yan, Zhao Dan and Cheng Jihua, author of the first comprehensive history of Chinese film, were all imprisoned, along with many others. *The East is Red* (Wang Ping, 1965), a simplistic panoramic epic depicting the heroes and villains of China's recent history, pointed the way ahead to the Cultural Revolution era Revolutionary Model Operas. While the prime concern of most film-makers during the Seventeen Years was to avoid egregious political error, others sought to avoid the restrictions imposed by the authorities, looking for opportunities for freedom of expression and minor deviations from an approved line that could change at a moment's notice. Initially considered by western scholars almost exclusively in terms of their political content, films from the Seventeen Years are now viewed as much for their aesthetic qualities. The difference today is that it is now possible for some to look back with some fondness, rather than the anger and frustration felt by many of those who lived through the period.

Notes

1. Guo Moruo, quoted in Jay Leyda, *Dianying* (Cambridge, MA: MIT Press, 1972), p. 188.
2. For Mao's Talks see Bonnie McDougall, trans., *Mao Zedong's 'Talks at the Yan'an Conference on Literature and Art': A Translation of the 1943 Text with Commentary* (Ann Arbor: University of Michigan Center for Chinese Studies, 1980). For details of the films attacked by Jiang Qing, see <www.morningsun.org/smash/jq_films.html>.
3. Chris Berry, 'Seeking Truth from Fiction: Feature Films as Historiography in Deng's China', *Film History* vol. 7 (1995), pp. 87–99; Paul Clark, *Chinese Cinema: Culture and Politics since 1949* (Cambridge: Cambridge University Press, 1987), p. 95; Yingjin Zhang, *Chinese National Cinema* (London: Routledge, 2004), p. 212; Meng Liye, *Xin Zhongguo dianying yishu shigao, 1949–1959* (Draft History of the Film of New China 1949–1959) (Beijing: Zhongguo dianying, 2002), pp. 372–8.

4. Cheng Yin, quoted in Li Daoxin, *Zhongguo dianying piping shi, 1897–2000* (History of Chinese Film Criticism 1897–2000) (Beijing: Zhongguo dianying, 2002), p. 234.

5. Xiao Zhiwei, 'The Expulsion of American Films from China, 1949–1950', *Twentieth-Century China* vol. 30 no. 1 (2004), pp. 64–80.

6. Jeremy Brown and Paul Pickowicz, 'Introduction', in Brown and Pickowicz (eds), *Dilemmas of Victory: The Early Years of the People's Republic of China* (Cambridge, MA: Harvard University Press, 2008), p. 10.

7. Clark, *Chinese Cinema*, p. 36.

8. Tina Mai Chen, 'Propagating the Propaganda Film: The Meaning of Film in Chinese Communist Party Writings, 1949–1965', *Modern Chinese Literature and Culture* vol. 15 no. 2 (2003), pp. 154–93.

9. Chinese Film Data Office (eds), *Zhongguo yishu yingpian bianmu (1949–1979)* (Catalogue of Chinese Artistic Films 1949–1979) (Beijing: wenhua yishu, 1982), 2 vols.

10. American films were still shown in China till around the end of 1950, by which time, with the Korean War underway, they had become unacceptable. Xiao Zhiwei, 'The Expulsion of American Films from China', p. 72. Import figures from Chen, 'Propagating the Propaganda Film', p. 183.

11. Zhou Enlai, quoted in Yingchi Chu, *Chinese Documentaries: From Dogma to Polyphony* (London: Routledge, 2007), p. 57.

12. Xia Yan, 'Tan "Linjia puzi" de Gaibian' (Discussion of the Adaptation of 'The Lin Family Shop'), in *Dianying Lunwenji* (Collected Writings on Film), (Beijing: Zhongguo Dianying, 1985), p. 247.

13. Roxanne Witke, *Comrade Qiang Ch'ing* (London: Weidenfeld and Nicolson, 1977), p. 267.

14. See Paul G. Pickowicz, 'Acting Like Revolutionaries: Shi Hui, the Wenhua Studio, and Private-Sector Filmmaking, 1949–1952', in Brown and Pickowicz, *Dilemmas of Victory*, pp. 256–87.

15. Paul G. Pickowicz, 'Zheng Junli, Complicity and the Cultural History of Socialist China, 1949–1976', *The China Quarterly* vol. 188 (December 2006), pp. 1048–69.

16. Greg Lewis, 'The History, Myth, and Memory of Maoist Chinese Cinema, 1949–1976', *Asian Cinema* vol. 16 no. 1 (Spring/Summer 2005), pp. 162–83.

17. See Yingjin Zhang, 'Zhao Dan: Spectrality of Martyrdom and Stardom', *Journal of Chinese Cinemas* vol. 2 no. 2 (July 2008), pp. 103–11.

18. Lu Xiaoning, 'Zhang Ruifang: Modelling the Socialist Red Star', *Journal of Chinese Cinemas* vol. 2 no. 2 (July 2008), pp. 113–22.

19. Ban Wang, *Sublime Figure of History: Aesthetics and Politics in Twentieth-Century China* (Stanford, CA: Stanford University Press, 1997), p. 125.

20. To give some recent examples, films made about the anti-Japanese war are examined in Huang Guozhu et al., *Xunzhao kangzhen jingdian jingpian* (Seeking Out the Classic Films of the War of Resistance) (Beijing: Jiefangjun wenyi, 2006), while Yomi Braester has shown how *Sentinels under the Neon Lights* (Wang Ping, 1964) was part of a campaign to present Shanghai as a symbol of bourgeois decadence rather than a revolutionary centre. See 'A Big Dying Vat: The Vilifying of Shanghai during the Good Eighth Company Campaign', *Modern China* vol. 31 no. 4 (2005), pp. 411–47. In *To The Edge of the Sky* (London: Penguin, 2001), Anhua Gao recalls being shown revolutionary films made in China and the Soviet Union.

21. Ying Bao, 'The Problematics of Comedy: The New China Cinema and the Case of Lu Ban', *Modern Chinese Literature and Culture* vol. 20 no. 2 (Autumn 2008), pp. 185–228.

22. For Chen Huangmei's comment, see Li Daoxin, *Zhongguo dianying piping shi*, p. 295. Ying Bao notes that the party official lampooned in Lü Ban's *Unfinished Comedy* may be a thinly veiled portrait of Chen. Ying Bao, 'The Problematics of Comedy', p. 187.

Further Reading in *Chinese Films in Focus II*

On Fei Mu, see Chapter 26, '*Spring in a Small Town*: Gazing at Ruins' by Carolyn FitzGerald.

On Zheng Junli, see Chapter 10, '*Crows and Sparrows*: Allegory on a Historical Threshold' by Yiman Wang.

On Xie Jin, see Chapter 24, '*The Red Detachment of Women*: Resenting, Regendering, Remembering' by Robert Chi.

10 Healthy Realism in Taiwan, 1964–80

Film Style, Cultural Policies and Mandarin Cinema

Guo-Juin Hong

Taiwan's first domestic colour film was produced in 1964. *Oyster Girls*, co-directed by Lee Hsing and Lee Chia (no relation) was a box-office success and went on to win the Best Film award at the 1965 Asia Film Festival. A landmark for Taiwan cinema's technological advancement, this film marked the beginning of a state-led Mandarin-language film campaign, Healthy Realism. Three decades later, Chiao Hsiung-Ping lamented, because of the emphasis on the 'impoverished peasantry' instead of 'efforts towards modernisation', Healthy Realism could at best be considered a 'glorious failure'. Chiao grouped Healthy Realism with the Yellow Plum Melody costume musicals and romantic melodramas based on Qiong Yao novels, all of which, in her words, are 'lost in nostalgia and escapism'.[1] Her grouping of those different cultural productions into one historical category, films that failed at modernisation, overlooks the muddied history of the structures of production within which those different genres had to operate. While state-run Central Motion Picture Corporation (CMPC) produced most Healthy Realist films and the Yellow Plum Melody musicals had strong affiliations with Hong Kong, the popularity of Qiong Yao melodramas were indebted to both.[2]

This chapter focuses on the influence Taiwan's cultural policies have had on Healthy Realism 1964–80. At a time before a solid industrial infrastructure was established, *culture*, vernacular or state-sanctioned, and *policy*, explicitly political or inherently ideological, generated a highly diverse cinematic imagining of modernisation. Responding to changing political pressures, Taiwan cinema in the 1960s and 70s must be understood as an active agent that partook in the representation and imaginary construction of the nation. Key films by two important film-makers, Lee Hsing (aka Li Xing) and Bai Jingrui (aka Pai Ching-Jui), help demonstrate some salient features of Healthy Realism, ultimately highlighting its politicised aesthetics that anticipate the emergence of the New Cinema of the 1980s and the latter cinema's repoliticisation of aesthetics.

Defining Healthy Realism

Taiwan's Society for Chinese Cinema Studies held a roundtable in 1994, discussing 'The Significance of 1960s Healthy Realism in Taiwan Cinema'.[3] Participants included key practitioners and film scholars. Li Tian-Duo began the discussion by questioning the political, economic, socio-historical context within which Healthy Realism emerged. In response, Huang Ren commented on how many Taiwan's film-makers at that time rejected Hollywood-style film production in favour of Italian neo-realism. He singled out the then director of CMPC, Gong Hong (aka Henry Kung), as the key figure who prioritised Healthy Realism. In Huang's account, Gong believed that 'Italian Neorealist films after World War Two were mostly about the dark side of the society, for example, *Bicycle Thieves*.'[4] The same logic would extend, Huang continued with added emphasis, to another realism: 1930s Shanghai's leftist cinema. Apparently, Gong found that 'the kind of realism flourishing in 1930s Shanghai was a means which the leftist camp employed to incite discontent against the government, posing a threat to the Nationalist government at the time'.[5] Realism remained questionable for the authorities even after the government retreated to Taiwan. As such, realism was not an aesthetic but *political* category.

More importantly, how was realism politicised? Before Healthy Realism became feasible, an acceptable framing of 'realism' had to be in place. If Italian neo-realism was faulted for exposing the darker side of the society, and if 1930s Shanghai leftist cinema was deemed politically suspect, Healthy Realism could only be conceived by what it was *not*: it was not neo-realism, nor was it the Shanghai's leftist cinema. And this *negative* definition of Healthy Realism would inform the conceptualisation of Healthy Realism.

Zhang Yong-Xiang, screenwriter of many important Healthy Realist films, maintained that, 'Healthy Realism derived its meaning from the times we lived in, full of hopes and stories under the sunshine. To tell stories that are healthy, bright and lively means that "healthy" [subject matter] can be realistic, too.'[6] Lee Hsing concurred that, 'under the constricting political circumstances at that time, we decided to produce films that could be made in the sunlight'.[7] In this sense, the political became more than a context or limitation which film-makers created; it imposed itself like an idealist filter through which only selected elements could pass. The much-repeated metaphor of the 'sunlight' attests to the guarded nature of Healthy Realism in its conception.

To define Healthy Realism, film historian Liao Jin-Feng compares it with Italian neo-realism by summarising André Bazin's realist aesthetics. For Laio, Bazinian realism emphasises 'accidental events presented in a meandering narrative structure, non-professional actors, semi-documentary style, black-and-white on-location shooting, natural lighting' and so on. What characterises Healthy Realism, on the other hand, are features including 'plotted narrative structure, studio and on-location shooting, stars casting, artificially created sets' and so forth. While Italian neo-realism is best understood as Bazinian realism, Healthy Realism leans heavily on 'the tradition of formalist aesthetics since Eisenstein and Arnheim'.[8] This comparison follows a conventional realism/formalism dichotomy, which is helpful, but only in a limited way.

Both realism and formalism are sets of aesthetic strategies whose relationship with 'reality' is always representational; whatever means at the film-maker's disposal is always formal. To say this is not to deny the different *tendencies* towards the 'reality effects' between these two traditions. However, any choice tends towards certain desired effects and those effects are always representations of that desire. With such keen understanding of film aesthetics, Bazin famously declares that, '[realism] in art can only be achieved in one way – through artifice'.[9] In the case of Healthy Realism – realist, formalist or otherwise – I focus on the desire to represent, not chasing the elusive 'reality' always in excess of representation. Before engaging more closely with specific film texts, it is crucial to sketch the context of Taiwan's cultural policies, to whose pressures Healthy Realism responds.

Policy in the Middle: The Ambiguous Field between Culture and Propaganda

Cultural policies in Taiwan were never meant, from the beginning, only as state propaganda, nor were they mere forms of censorship. According to Cheng Ming-Lee, the Nationalist's cultural policy began as a reaction to Mao Zedong's 1942 speech in Yan'an, famously declaring that all arts be created from social reality and in the service of class struggle. To counter that claim, top Nationalist propagandist Zhang Dao-Fan published 'The Cultural Policy We Need' later the same year. Expounding on Sun Yat-Sen's *Three Principles of the People*, Zhang claimed the supremacy of nationalism. 'While a private-property [denoting both capitalist and feudalist] society espouses individualism and a communist society class consciousness, a society following the Three Principles of the People produces an ideology that places the nation above all else.'[10] Nationalism is here figured as the Chinese nation's true destiny against other socio-economic systems such as feudalism, capitalism and, most importantly and immediately, communism.

Zhang's politically orthodox notion of national culture may seem naive but its efficacy is derived precisely from that simplicity. For Zhang does not give any rigorous explanation of what distinguishes nationalism from its nemeses besides the empty rhetoric stressing only what his Nationalist agenda will eventually achieve. 'Culture', national or otherwise, becomes a vacant space capable of accommodating all aspects of public life and private thought through a filter of the *positive*. Aside from any of those ostensibly negative qualities attributable to feudalism, capitalism and, especially, communism, everything else can be and, indeed, is made to represent the positive manifestation of the Nationalist ideology. How the promised transformation of all social ills and economic inequality into a utopian nation may be attained eludes specific prescription.

After retreating to Taiwan in 1949, the Nationalist government was quick to establish a cultural policy of militarism (*zhandou wenyi*) with avowed belligerence against the Chinese Communist Party at its core. Penned by none other but Chiang Kai-Shek himself, the single most important document is the 'Two Supplementary Chapters' to Sun Yet-Sen's *Three Principles of the People*. In his discussion of 'National Fecundity, Social Welfare and Education' and 'Health and Happiness', Chiang emphasises that, on the one hand, education is to produce national subjects who 'engage in productive work and dedicate themselves whole-heartedly to the promotion of social progress and national regeneration'[11] and, on the other, the 'literary and artistic policy' is gauged 'with particular reference to the influence which literature and art are likely to exert on the citizen's mental health and happiness'.[12] Chiang goes so far as to name some desired qualities in arts, such as 'intense national feelings' and 'anti-communist and anti-Russian slant'.[13] Such an overt partisan emphasis is, of course, expected and the subsequent waves of pledges of alliance from either Chiang's loyal followers or fearful subordinates also come as no surprise.[14]

In terms of the film industry, however, profit has largely trumped any explicit 'policy' as the commercial cinema remained a battleground for various genres. In the first two decades after Taiwan's return to the Nationalist government, state- or Nationalist Party-owned studios focused mainly on the production of newsreels and educational films, and were no competition against imports from Hollywood, Europe, Japan and Hong Kong, and especially the domestically produced Taiwanese-dialect films to whose eventual demise Healthy Realist Mandarin films greatly contributed. But that would change in 1963 when Gong Hong took the helm of the Central Motion Pictures Corporation and worked hard to conceive a different kind of cinema that would be ideologically compliant as well as commercially viable.

One of the early efforts by the Nationalist government to boost film culture was the establishment of the Golden Horse Awards in 1962. Often regarded as the most important film festival for Chinese-language cinemas, the Awards commenced its annual event under the auspice of the Information Bureau of the Administrative Yuan.[15] The first Best Feature Film winner was a Hong Kong production, *Star, Moon, Sun*. A two-part, near-four-hour epic, the film showcased the robust production conditions of Hong Kong's affluent film industry. Shot with film stock imported from the US and later colour-printed in England, the lavish colour cinematography brilliantly complements the film's sophisticated narrative that spans the entire Sino-Japan War period. In the following year, one of the most successful Yellow Plum Melody films, *The Love Eterne* (1963), another Hong Kong production by the Shaw Brothers Studio, would go on to win several major awards. Both films were crafted by masterful hands, ones that only an established industry could lend. Technical know-how and star power secured the success of these two films and other Hong Kong films like them, rendering the dire conditions of production in Taiwan all the more glaring.

CMPC had been sending technicians to Japan and the US, in fact, to learn colour cinematography. However, a colour production completely independent of foreign, especially Japanese, technical support was not possible until 1963.[16] If CMPC was to invest in colour production and to put forth commercially competitive films that could comply with the state's cultural policy, Gong Hong and his team would have to conceive something different from the two Hong Kong films just mentioned; *Star*'s ambiguous relationship with the communist mainland and *The Love Eterne*'s indulgence in fantasy and melodrama would certainly be inadequate. In other words, when CMPC was finally ready to launch a national cinema campaign in Taiwan, with technology in hand and talents in place, one essential question remained: what kind of film would best present a positive image of the Chinese nation in Taiwan?

Healthy Realism and its Historical (Dis-)Content

Healthy Realism, for historian Liu Xian-Cheng, is a compelling articulation of the political and the economic with the cultural;[17] Lee Hsing came onto the scene at the nexus where those forces intersected. After several productions as actor or assistant director, Lee directed one of the most popular Taiwanese-dialect films in 1958, *Brother Wang and Brother Liu Tour Taiwan*. And after a few years of struggle between directing commercially successful dialect films and making

unsuccessful attempts to join CMPC, Lee Hsing made
an important breakthrough with his 1963 *Head of the
Street, End of the Lane*. Zhang Yingjin praises the film
because it 'conveys not only the bitter pathos
characteristic of Taiwanese-dialect films but is also
reminiscent of the social realism of 1930s Shanghai'.[18]
His revisionist mention of Shanghai's leftist cinema
notwithstanding, Zhang's appraisal may well explain
why CMPC director Gong Hong was convinced that Lee
was the one with whom to collaborate on a cinema
that was 'healthy', 'real' and specific to Taiwan.

What ensued was the first domestically produced
colour film in 1964, *Oyster Girl*. Half way through the
production, however, a new project was conceived and
Lee Hsing was pulled from the Oyster project to direct
Beautiful Duckling (1965). The completion of both films
marked the beginning of a golden age of domestically
produced Mandarin films in Taiwan. *Duckling* is
remarkable because it not only succeeds in employing
realist techniques to tell a compelling family
melodrama, but it also displays distinct film styles and
thematic treatments that would continue to
characterise Healthy Realism – across a wide variety of
genres – in the next decade and a half.

Inspired by Ran In-Ting's watercolours of Taiwan's
rural landscape, particularly duck farming, *Beautiful
Duckling* begins with the camera surveying one such
painting. A female voiceover intones the film's
motivation to present to its audiences the beautiful
agricultural society of Taiwan. When the title appears,
the film cuts abruptly to live footage of flocks of ducks
in the water and, adding to the dramatic effect,
orchestral music swells on cue. Strikingly, the sequence
punctuates each credit with a freeze-frame of the lively
fowl. In other words, the opening scene animates a
static surface with movement – from watercolours to
moving images – and rearticulates that movement with
stills – from moving images to freeze-frames. The film
begins by setting an unambiguous tone that explicitly
foretells, verbosely through its voiceover narration, the
ideological content as its thematic content, aesthetics
in the service of politics. The articulation of plastic
representation (watercolours) with documentary
(cinematic capture of live action) sutures the
constructed with the natural.

What follow are long shots of the idyllic country
landscape, accompanied by music heavily accented by
Taiwanese folk-song motifs. Abundantly clear are the
early efforts of Healthy Realism, focused on imagining

Beautiful Duckling

an agricultural paradise where nature and culture coexist. This co-existence gives off an impression of
timelessness. Indeed, duck farming, like oyster farming
in *Oyster Girl*, represents the age-old ways of livelihoods
pursued by these farmers since time immemorial; this
is a Taiwan that has lived a rural lifestyle of
unchanging tradition and diligent labour.

The notion of *stasis* is not, however, what apparently
characterises Healthy Realist films. For example, a
positive message about the government's investment in
improving the living standards of the fishing villages is
embedded in the tragic-comic romantic drama of *Oyster
Girl*. Similarly in *Beautiful Duckling*, change and, more
importantly, progress through modernisation, is posited
as the main message. However, the central drama of
Beautiful Duckling – the other message concerns the

importance of familial relationships and of social morals and work ethics – evolves around Mr Lin, a duck farmer, and his adopted daughter, Hsiao-Yueh, who does not know about her adopted status. Hsiao-Yueh's biological brother has been blackmailing Mr Lin for money, threatening to disclose the fact to Hsiao-Yueh. *Beautiful Duckling*, essentially, is a moving melodrama about familial bonds, both biological and emotional.

In many ways, Hsiao-Yueh is equated with the ducks – the namesake duckling with untouched innocence and earthy beauty, rurality as such – but something else as well. After the credit sequence, the film proceeds to show Hsiao-Yueh at work with the ducks. Her cheerful movements and playful birdcalls complement the natural landscape, creating a total image of Taiwan's agricultural bliss. After quickly establishing duck farming as an emblem for rural life, the film introduces what changes will occur. The following scene shows Mr Lin conversing with two officials from the Farmers' Association. Lin is commissioned to raise a new hybrid breed of ducks, record their growth in detail and mark each duckling with an identity tag. *Modernising* ducks is thus developed as a parallel line with the film's main narrative of family melodrama, individual/familial development intimately linked with national development.

For Chris Berry and Mary Farquhar, this parallel 'endorses small-scale rural modernisation as the backbone of modern society'. From a fusion of 'Confucian ethics' and 'spirit of capitalism' arises the constructed image of the nation that is the Republic of China on the island of Taiwan.[19] While agreeing with their general assessment of those ideological functions, I want to go further and ask how those functions are performed cinematically before offering a fuller conceptualisation of modernity promoted in this cinematic movement. One way to start is to look closely at how Healthy Realism constructs the cinematic space wherein the heavily burdened ideological themes – Confucian ethics, family values, capitalist entrepreneurship – are staged.

The opening scene introduces one such salient feature of Healthy Realism's spatial construction: realistic sets as counterparts to actual locations. From the outdoor scene of Hsiao-Yueh tending her flock, the film cuts to a close-up of ducklings only slowly to reveal an elaborate set of two adjacent farm houses on a sound stage, furnished with a foot bridge over a tree-lined stream and hundreds of live ducks. The degree of attention to detail and the scale of meticulous construction were unprecedented in domestic production, rivalling the lavish sets associated with Hong Kong-produced costume musicals or martial arts films. Different, of course, from those genre films' spectacle of fantasy is *Beautiful Duckling*'s relentless drive towards realism.

Years after *Duckling*, Lee Hsing reminisced about the conditions of production of the film. Gong Hong's interest in location shooting was so strong that he took the director with him to visit several actual duck farms. When decisions were made to shoot those scenes on a sound stage, no effort was spared to reproduce the actual location as faithfully as possible.[20] The desire to emulate reality would continue to characterise Lee's later films and set a precedent for other productions. It has great ramifications for film aesthetics as well. Unlike earlier domestic films with low budgets, *Beautiful Duckling* opened the door for substantial location shooting as well as realistic set constructions. With these two combined, lengthy montage sequences involving both in- and outdoor shootings are fashioned with such seamlessness that they achieve the Healthy Realist goals to represent the bright side of reality.

One sequence in *Beautiful Duckling* exemplifies this aesthetics. Half way into the film, Mr Lin and Xiao-Yueh embark on their annual trip to bring their ducks to a friend's fields at harvest time. This stunning sequence of the duck parade begins with the father–daughter team herding the flock from their farmhouse across the bridge. The mobile camera smoothly follows their movement until a cut to the next shot effortlessly links the sound stage with the location shots and merging them into a total effect of spatial continuity. Several long shots from various angles capture the beautiful scenery and the farmers' harmonious movement with their ducks across the rural landscape. It is not enough, that is, to suggest the fictional adjacency of those places by continuity editing; realist aesthetics will have also to convince the viewer, visually and stylistically, of such spatial continuum.

It may seem normal at first glance, for it is any realist cinema's goal to create an illusion of spatial and temporal congruity and narrative contiguity through available means. Crucial for Healthy Realism, however, is to place this ability to produce a visual harmony at its ideological core. It is not simply a coincidence that Healthy Realism was conceived and put into practice when CMPC was capable of producing colour films. Inevitably, the new technology increased the effect of realism, but that realism served the ideological mission of representing Taiwan through a beautifying and idealising lens. The abundant beauty of rural Taiwan illuminated in abundance in *Duckling* and other films was deliberately separated from the unclean, even backward, images of actual village life in close-ups. Because the long shots on location capture, in broad strokes and on large canvasses, a serenity of physical beauty at a distance, the camera can then zoom in on the more intimate drama staged on the meticulous sets. The successful cinematic representation of healthy subject matters depends on blurring the boundaries between natural and constructed spaces.

Unparalleled Tracks

Modernisation, ongoing processes of change, is antithetical to stasis; therein lies a fundamental problem of Healthy Realism, especially the notion of *stasis of change* I have been suggesting. In Shanghai's 1930s leftist cinema, the energy is directed towards change and the cinematic means of representation – narrative and framing – are organised to usher in that drive to change. Best represented by Lee Hsing's films discussed so far, Healthy Realism does seem to insist on the notion of stasis – familial relationships, Confucian ethics and so on – but it cannot address how modernisation may bring changes to bear upon those unchanging values. One way to do so, and we see it over and over again in this period, is the repeated affirmation of those thematics that conflate aesthetics with politics; realism becomes a vehicle for how the real can and, indeed, should be represented. To put it differently, Healthy Realism is the successful alternative to Taiwanese-dialect films because it is the epitome of what the dominant politics wishes to see. As exemplified by *Beautiful Duckling*, Healthy Realism shows a utopian space where modernity can be housed in a place of the unchanged. But change turns out to be an unstoppable force even in the site of stasis that Healthy Realism has so painstakingly maintained.

If Taiwan in the mid-1960s could be identified within the unchanged seen in *Beautiful Duckling*, change would come forcefully to the fore in the 70s. The worsening international political climate for Taiwan was bracketed by 1971 when Taiwan was forced out of the United Nations and 1978 when the United States severed its diplomatic relationship with Taiwan in

The Road

recognition of the communist China on the mainland. However, the economy continued to develop rapidly. Even before such turbulent times, films by Lee marked how Healthy Realism already began to reflect these imposing changes as early as the late 1960s. For example, *The Road* (1968) anticipates the entangled relationship between national development and Healthy Realist narrative themes, weaving a compelling melodrama by focusing on individuals, families and village communities. The larger theme of national development remains obscure, much like in *Beautiful Duckling*. A marked difference is, however, that *The Road* devotes much more screen space, if not explicitly narrative significance, to a visualisation of modernisation. For instance, the film opens with a stark sequence of a highway construction crew working heavy equipment. The scene alternates almost mechanically between close-ups and long shots, with deafening noises of machinery on the soundtrack. In other words, there is no music to assign extradiegetic significance as in *Beautiful Duckling*'s opening on Taiwan's rural beauty. It is almost as if road construction were less than desirable. The point was driven home when the crew finishes the day's work to drive home on a truck along a tranquil rural road, puffing exhaust as it passes a goat herder. The rural paradise in previous films is now, quite literally, polluted.

I am not suggesting that Healthy Realism is anti-progress or antithetical to Farquhar and Berry's assessment of this movement, in line with China's Socialist Realism of the same period, as '[conveying] a faith that the present is the road to national utopia through the metaphor of the reconstructed family and rediscovered home'.[21] However, the progress and change in what they call the 'proto-national reunion or *datuanyuan*: "coming home" to Taiwan', plays out only on the narrative level and, even there, with great ambivalence. Although Healthy Realist films do often end with reunions or homecomings, they do so not by a coming together of narrative and aesthetics, content and form, but by conforming to and aligning with the larger ideological, nationalist mandates. The 'homecoming', or, better put, *becoming a nation*, is not possible until a firm sense is established of belonging to the land, for the mainlander and the native Taiwanese alike.

This brings us to another major Healthy Realist film-maker, Bai Jingrui. If Lee's films highlight the unchanging values of family and tradition, Bai's works engage directly with the challenges of modernisation. Bai Jingrui's *Home Sweet Home* (1970), for example, foregrounds precisely the problematic of home/nation in Healthy Realism. Born in China and migrated to Taiwan during the war-torn years of the late 1940s, Bai collaborated with Lee in several theatre productions and worked as high school teacher and journalist, until he left for Italy to study film between 1960 and 1963 and joined CMPC upon his return. In 1964, Bai shot a short film, *A Morning in Taipei*, in the spirit of the city film genre. And in 1967, he made his feature film directorial debut with *Lonely Seventeen* about a teenage girl negotiating between school and family in a vertiginous, fast-changing Taipei City. Compared to Lee Hsing, Bai can be said to have a much keener eye on the urban, even in a broader transnational context.[22]

And it is within this context of Taiwan's state policy in global geopolitics that Bai's representative Healthy Realist work, *Home Sweet Home*, may be appreciated. For James Wicks, *Home Sweet Home* is a 'complex historical document that provides an insight into the official position that the Chinese Nationalist Party (*Guomindang*, KMT) held regarding Taiwan students from Taiwan who studied abroad in the late 1960s and early 1970s'.[23] With the changing international politics mentioned above, the Nationalist government encouraged the return of those study-abroad students and Bai's film contributed to that advocacy, at least on the narrative surface. By depicting several such study-abroad students' homecoming, *Home Sweet Home* negotiates the problematic of home/nation with multiple narrative lines: a filial son and his Chinese American wife, a rich woman and her younger lover

Home Sweet Home

and, finally, an engineer and his estranged/abandoned wife. Each with its own melodramatic intrigue, the three narrative lines ostensibly affirm the state ideology of Taiwan as the national home. Its style tells a different story. Indeed, Bai employs extensively the principle of multiplicity and fragmentation that *formally* fractures the cinematic and, in so doing, undermines the state ideology. Despite the call to represent a positive image of Taiwan through a realist lens, we are here confronted by Healthy Realism's incompatibility or, as Wicks calls it, 'conjunction and disjunction' with the state ideology in the 1970s.[24]

If we look at later Healthy Realist films, we see that the tension between the politicised aesthetics of realism and its representation intensified. Both Bai and Lee Hsing continued to work in different genres throughout the 1970s, including policy films, comedy and, notably, Qiong Yao romantic melodramas, such as *A Curtain of Dreams* (Bai, 1976) and *Heart with a Million Knots* (Lee, 1973). In, arguably, the last Healthy Realist film, *Good Morning, Taipei* (Lee, 1980), the representation wavers between urban and rural spaces and conflates fictional with documentary elements, most explicitly in the opening credit sequence. The use of 'reality' has become impossible to be contained within a 'healthy' frame. A different realism was in order and New Taiwan Cinema would answer that call.

Conclusion

My main argument has been that, under the pressure of state cultural policies, the paradigm of Healthy Realism's politics cuts across generic boundaries and eventually becomes an aesthetic of politics. By imagining a Chinese nation on Taiwan with rigidified styles and generic conventions, however explicitly supportive of the Nationalist ideology, mainstream Taiwan cinema in these two decades ended up obscuring the possible faces of a nation and losing its hold on the real. This left much to be desired for a clear picture of the nation, a new face that would only slowly come into view through New Cinema film-makers' politics of aesthetics starting in the early 1980s.

Notes

1. Chiao Hsiung-Ping, *Shidai xianying: zhongxi dianying lunxu* (Images of Time: Discourses on Chinese and Western Films) (Taipei: Yuanliu, 1998), p. 149. Translations from Chinese sources are mine unless otherwise noted.
2. Yellow Plum Melody refers to a regional operatic style, similar to Beijing Opera in its reworking of familiar historical events and folklores; its filmic form is best known for elaborate sets and costumes and for its male leads normally played by female actors.
3. Transcripts of this event are published in *Film Appreciation* no. 72 (1994), pp. 13–58.
4. Yu Chan-Qu (ed.), 'The Significance of Healthy Realism in 1960s Taiwan', *Film Appreciation* no. 72 (1994), p. 16.
5. Ibid., p. 17.
6. Ibid., p. 19.
7. Ibid., p. 18.
8. Liao, Jin-Feng, 'Towards a Definition of Healthy Realist Films', *Film Appreciation* no. 72 (1994), p. 43.
9. André Bazin, 'An Aesthetic of Reality: Neorealism', *What Is Cinema?*, vol. II (Berkeley: University of California Press, 1971), p. 26.
10. Cheng Ming-Lee (ed.), *Politics and Contemporary Taiwanese Literature* (Taipei: Shibao, 1994), p. 17.
11. Chiang Kai-Shek, 'Two Supplementary Chapters', *The Three Principles of the People* (Taipei: Government Information Office, 1990), p. 266.
12. Ibid., p. 300.
13. Ibid., p. 302.
14. Cheng, *Politics and Contemporary Taiwanese Literature*, pp. 28–33.
15. *Jin-Ma*, meaning 'golden horse', is derived from the two major military off-islands, *Jin-men* and *Ma-zu*, between Taiwan and Fukien Province on the mainland.
16. Huang Ren and Wei Wang (eds), *One Hundred Years of Taiwan Cinema*, vol. 1 (Taipei: Chinese Film Critics Association, 2004), p. 266.
17. See Liu Xian-Cheng, 'Social and Historical Analysis of Taiwan's Healthy Realist Films in 1960s', *Film Appreciation* no. 72 (1994), pp. 48–58.
18. Yingjin Zhang, *Chinese National Cinema* (New York and London: Routledge, 2004), p. 134.
19. Chris Berry and Mary Farquhar, *China on Screen: Cinema and Nation* (New York: Columbia University Press, 2006), p. 98.
20. Huang Ren (ed.), *Xingzhe yingji: Li Xing, dianying, wushi nian* (Tracing a Journeyman's Shadow: Fifty Years of Lee Hsing's Cinema) (Taipei: Shibao, 1999), pp. 48–53.
21. Berry and Farquhar, *China on Screen*, p. 76.
22. Shen Shiao-Ying connects this film to the larger urban film culture in 'A Morning in Taipei: Bai Jingrui's Frustrated Debut', *Journal of Chinese Cinemas* vol. 4 no. 1 (2010), pp. 51–6.
23. James Wicks, 'Projecting a State that Does Not Exist: Bai Jingrui's *Home Sweet Home*', *Journal of Chinese Cinemas* vol. 4 no. 1 (2010), p. 16.
24. Ibid.

Further Reading in *Chinese Films in Focus II*

On Yellow Plum Melody films, see Chapter 20, 'The Love Eterne: Almost a (Heterosexual) Love Story' by Tan See-Kam and Annette Aw.

11 The Hong Kong Cantonese Cinema

Emergence, Development and Decline

Stephen Teo

Introduction

The 'Cantonese cinema' of Hong Kong that most scholars refer to is really the cinema that developed in the post-World War II era, from 1946 to 1969. As far as is known, no Cantonese film produced in the prewar era has survived, and it is thus the Cantonese cinema of the later period that I will be examining in this chapter. It is also my opinion that when Cantonese film production stopped at the end of the 1960s, this cinema effectively came to an end, and that the re-emergence of Cantonese films in the Hong Kong cinema following the success of *House of 72 Tenants* (Chu Yuan, 1973) and the films of Michael Hui and those of the Hong Kong New Wave constituted a quite different kind of 'Cantonese cinema' that did not necessarily continue the legacy, style or substance of the Cantonese cinema that existed before it.

The Cantonese cinema of the 'golden period' (the 1950s and 60s) was much more genuinely Cantonese inasmuch as its audience, spread out transnationally in southern China, Hong Kong and overseas communities in South-East Asia and elsewhere, was still able to see Cantonese films spoken in Cantonese. Audiences at the time also had the choice of Mandarin films which were made in Hong Kong (and increasingly in the 1960s in Taiwan). Such a choice implied that there were not only linguistic but aesthetic differences between Cantonese and Mandarin films. By the 1970s, such a choice had largely vanished. Hong Kong was the only territory where Cantonese films could be shown without being dubbed into Mandarin. Everywhere else (Taiwan, Singapore and Malaysia – the three key countries in the Hong Kong film industry's traditional market), Hong Kong films had to be dubbed into Mandarin.

By the 1980s, it did not really matter whether Hong Kong films were actually spoken in Cantonese or in Mandarin. By then, there was essentially only one Hong Kong cinema and newer generations had grown increasingly distant from the old Cantonese cinema. It is thus all the more imperative for this chapter to delineate the existence of the Cantonese cinema and trace its history from the 1930s onwards in order to remind readers of the heritage of Cantonese films. Hong Kong cinema is distinguished by the fact that it had, from the early period of the production of sound films, produced films spoken in Cantonese. Though the first Cantonese-language feature film, *White Gold Dragon* (Runje Shaw, 1933), was produced in Shanghai and not in Hong Kong, it was the latter that became the centre of Cantonese-movie production in the sound era. The first talkies (though only partly in sound) produced in the colony, *The Idiot's Wedding Night* (Li Beihai, 1933) and *Conscience* (Li Beihai, 1933), were spoken in Cantonese.[1] From then on, Hong Kong was already marking itself out as a Cantonese film production base. The most remarkable fact of Hong Kong cinema as it developed from the 1930s onwards with the introduction of sound was that it was able to survive at all producing dialect movies!

This chapter will present an overview of how the then British colony developed into a base of Cantonese film production and how its particular line of 'dialect film' conflicted with the nationalistic demands of the KMT government in Nanjing in the 1930s. Hong Kong, under British rule, thus developed as a separate Chinese film entity, one that was spoken in a language other than Mandarin. The chapter

Shots from *House of 72 Tenants*, the film that revived the Cantonese language in Hong Kong cinema of the 1970s

will focus on the early period of the development of the Hong Kong Cantonese cinema, discussing the beginnings of Cantonese production, the threats to its existence posed by the KMT (Kuomintang) government in China led by Chiang Kai-shek which decreed a ban on dialect films, and the rise of Cantonese cinema after World War II as the Hong Kong film industry staged a rapid recovery. Cantonese production took off in the 1950s and reached a peak in the early 60s only to dissipate at the end of the decade.

Early Cantonese Production

From the beginning of the sound era, Cantonese talkies proved to be a popular medium of entertainment among Cantonese-speaking audiences, and production of Cantonese features naturally gravitated in those territories where the Cantonese population predominated – in the province of Guangdong and in Hong Kong. The capital of Guangdong, Guangzhou (or Canton as it was then called), was, beside Hong Kong,

the other base of Cantonese film production. It was also a political base for many KMT politicians who gradually went into opposition against Chiang Kai-shek. The KMT rebels, known as the 'Canton faction', declared a separatist regime based in Guangdong in 1931. Politics was never far from the surface of cultural life in Guangdong, and Cantonese cinema eventually became a target for Chiang's retaliatory measures against the KMT rebels. Chiang's government showed itself to be unsympathetic to Cantonese cultural aspirations, and in 1936 announced a ban on Cantonese cinema.

As a British crown colony, Hong Kong was able to keep itself separate from political events on the mainland. However, in terms of the cultural development of the cinema, Hong Kong had always considered itself a part of the national polity of China and was always conscious of supporting nationalistic causes. One such cause was the War of Resistance against Japan in 1937 which aroused patriotic instincts in Hong Kong film-makers who eagerly joined leftwing Shanghai émigrés who had come to Hong Kong to create a cinema of 'national defence' (*guofang pian*). This was a new wartime genre depicting the Chinese populace's awareness of Japan as the enemy of the Chinese people and the people's response to the call of arms. Chinese film historians have regularly invoked the War of Resistance as a watershed moment in the development of Hong Kong Cantonese cinema, pointing, first, to the infusion of mainland progressive talent into the Hong Kong industry and, second, the apparent improvement of content via the patriotic identification with the war effort in China. The war had, in fact, led to the first of the so-called 'clean-up' movements in the Hong Kong film industry in 1939–40, instigated by patriotic organisations and film-makers as well as Chinese government film officials dispatched by Chongqing (the city to which the KMT government had moved in wartime) to supervise and prod Hong Kong film workers into making patriotic films.[2] Political coercion came into play. A 1939 news item in a Hong Kong English-language newspaper *The Sunday Herald* reported that a youth organisation known as the 'Patriotic Association of Chinese Youth' had sent threatening letters to film directors and movie stars, warning them 'not to direct or take part in any "mystery, love-making and other worldly pictures"'. The letter stated that 'effective measures' would be taken against any person who ignored the warning.[3]

The war was, however, a lifesaver for the Hong Kong film industry in another respect. It redirected the energies of the central government towards more important tasks and led it to suspend its edict of banning Cantonese-dialect films announced in 1936.[4] The ban would have been implemented in July 1937 if war had not broken out. Hong Kong producers would not have been issued licences to distribute Cantonese-dialect pictures in the mainland, thus cutting off the southern China market. Hong Kong producers and film-makers had carried on a debate about the ban and its implications for the Hong Kong industry. The Cantonese director Fung Chi-kong put forward this argument:

> If the government takes a hardline attitude, the film circles in the southern China region will be forced to abandon the Chinese interior market. Production companies will concentrate resources in Hong Kong, exporting their films directly to the *nanyang* [the Chinese term for South-East Asia], the Americas and other territories, in order to protect their livelihoods.[5]

A delegation of Hong Kong and Guangdong producers under the banner of the Southern China Motion Picture Association petitioned the Nanjing government to call off the ban, but managed instead to wrest a concession from the government to suspend the ban for three years effective from 1 July 1937.[6] War broke out a week later on 8 July, with the formal declaration of war announced on 17 July. By the time the three-year suspension had run out, the government had had their hands full fighting the war, which would soon expand into a conflict covering the whole expanse of the Pacific Ocean with the entry of the United States into the war. One can only speculate as to what might have happened to the Hong Kong film industry if the war had not intervened and the government had gone ahead with the ban on Cantonese pictures. It is hard to believe that the film industry in Hong Kong would have survived to become what it is today.

To be fair to the national government in China, it had, in fact, frowned upon all dialect pictures ever since sound was introduced into Chinese cinema in 1930. The Film Censorship Committee had issued a circular in 1931 warning all film companies that it would not tolerate dialect pictures.[7] Hong Kong cinema could get away with producing Cantonese features because the Nanjing government had no jurisdiction over Hong Kong, but also because it had totally lost control over the two Cantonese-speaking provinces of Guangdong and Guangxi when the 'Canton faction' within the KMT set up a separatist government in Guangzhou in 1931. Nanjing did not regain control of the two southern provinces until 1936. In the meantime, Cantonese film companies were thriving under the protection of the separatist Canton government, but when Nanjing finally exerted central control, frantic efforts to preserve Cantonese cinema were made by local representatives of the industry through appeals and petitions to the government.[8] Despite these attempts, the Cantonese industry in Guangzhou was comparatively in a much more precarious situation than that of the Hong Kong industry since it now became a direct target for the government. Though protected under British rule, Hong Kong's film-makers were feeling extremely jittery over the ban as it would take away a substantial market in Guangdong and Guangxi, and Hong Kong's film-makers were just as eager to cooperate with the Nanjing authorities and the Central Film Censorship Committee to try to stave off the ban.

When the anti-Japanese war hit Guangzhou in February 1938, Hong Kong was the only place where film production remained active.[9] Thus the Cantonese film industry survived in Hong Kong during the War of Resistance, and it was able to survive after the war because of its separate political cover. That it could do so, however, even under the British, must be attributed, first, to what cultural anthropologist Barbara E. Ward has called the 'colonial paradox'.[10] As Ward explains: 'It was a common paradox of British colonialism that it often permitted (and sometimes actually encouraged) the untrammelled continuance of certain indigenous cultural practices that a native government might have tried to control or even eradicate.'[11] Ward was, in fact, researching the practice of local Chinese opera performances in Hong Kong but her thesis would apply equally to Cantonese cinema. One of the staple genres of the Cantonese cinema would turn out to be the Cantonese Opera film which became so popular in the 1950s that it made up some 34 per cent of total Cantonese production in that decade.[12] Opera stars such as Yam Kim-fai and Pak Suet-sin became icons of the Cantonese cinema.

A second reason for the survival of the Hong Kong film industry was the infusion of talent, capital and equipment from Shanghai. Film producers Runje Shaw

(Shao Zuiweng, the eldest of the fabled Shaw Brothers), Zhu Qingxian and Su Yi had established studios (respectively Tianyi, Nanyue and Quanqiu) in Hong Kong in 1934. These producers recognised early on that Cantonese pictures were commercially viable and that Hong Kong would be an ideal base for developing a market among overseas Chinese communities in the *nanyang*.

Cantonese cinema made a strong comeback after the war. This was achieved despite the odds against the industry being revived. There was a concerted move towards establishing a Mandarin film industry in the colony at the time. A second wave of talent flowed from Shanghai to Hong Kong which was a direct consequence of the lingering resentment targeted at the film-makers who remained behind in the *gudao* (meaning 'Orphan Island', the name given to that part of Shanghai which was unoccupied by the Japanese after the declaration of war between China and Japan in 1937), and in fully occupied Shanghai after 1941 following the outbreak of the Pacific War after the attack on Pearl Harbor. 'In September 1945, one of the hot topics of Shanghai's newspapers was the question of how to mete out punishment to traitors.'[13] Members of the film industry felt vulnerable and they packed their bags for Hong Kong.

The talent that flowed into Hong Kong was a more substantial list than that of the 1937 migration flow. It included the members of practically the whole Shanghai film industry in the *gudao* period. All were fearful of retribution after the war, although most of them were later cleared of suspicions and charges of treason or collaboration. This talent, combined with the capital that also migrated into Hong Kong, caused a speedy recovery of the film industry that had produced not a single feature in the three years and nine months that Hong Kong was occupied by the Japanese. The first Mandarin film company to be set up in Hong Kong after the war was the Da Zhonghua (Great China) Film Company, in 1946. It followed the *gudao* paradigm of a movie company whose interests were to entertain the public. But the company was much more diverse and acted as a kind of microcosm of the Mandarin cinema that had existed in the *gudao* and which would serve as a model for Hong Kong to adopt. The Mandarin cinema that established itself in Hong Kong in 1946 was expected to take off as the major film industry in the territory, but it, in fact, grew as a parallel minor industry to the Cantonese cinema. It was Cantonese cinema that grew in leaps and bounds from 1947 onwards.

The Revival of Cantonese Film-making in Hong Kong

The end of the anti-Japanese war saw the Chinese KMT government revive the ban on the production and distribution of Cantonese pictures on the mainland. This directly affected the production of Cantonese pictures in Hong Kong and it explains why, between 1945 and 1956, 'the production of Cantonese features proceeded in fits and starts'.[14] But, once again, the KMT was thrown off guard in the implementation of the ban on Cantonese films when its uneasy wartime truce with the Chinese Communist Party (CCP) fell apart and the two sides fought a renewed civil war from 1946–9. Shanghai's film producers poured capital into Hong Kong to escape the economic calamity brought about by the civil war, and the political uncertainty further helped to increase the talent pool in Hong Kong with migrations of film-makers. It was at this time that the foundations of Hong Kong's Mandarin cinema were even more firmly established, but a lot of Shanghai film-makers also found work in the Cantonese film industry.

In the immediate period following the end of World War II, the handful of Cantonese films shown in Hong Kong were productions from the Grandview Studio's San Francisco base. In 1947, the first local Cantonese picture to be produced after the war was released. *My Love Comes Too Late* also known as *Never Too Late to Come Home* (Huang Dai, 1947) was an immediate success in the South-East Asian market, which had been starved of Cantonese product in wartime. The picture's success resuscitated the demand for Cantonese pictures in the overseas markets. Producers took the cue to commence Cantonese production using Hong Kong as base. Grandview, a major studio with US interests, moved to the colony. Following on its heels were groups of smaller companies that 'sprang up like bamboo shoots after the rain, while there were countless organizations temporarily putting up office'.[15] Over 70 Cantonese films were released in 1947, and well over a hundred in 1948. Significantly, the film industry was the first industry to recover from the wartime slump and led Hong Kong's booming trade recovery of 1946–9.[16]

Such prolific activity in the Cantonese industry was based on strong demand from the South-East Asian and Hong Kong markets, 'thus the Nationalist

Government's renewed threat to ban Cantonese pictures was not much of a crisis'.[17] However, mainland critics were increasingly drawn back to the old debate about Cantonese cinema and its worthiness, focusing this time on the questions of commerce versus art, and whether cinema should entertain or educate the masses. In 1948, an article published in *Chin Chin Screen*, a Shanghai film magazine, predicted that Hong Kong Cantonese cinema would soon face another crisis of survival as Cantonese pictures were generally of such low quality. 'Even the major studios with better production standards at their disposal wilfully infringe the meaning of art with content that indulges in fantasy and yellow sensationalism' (the term 'yellow' indicating sexual and lewd content).[18]

The Hong Kong Cantonese companies were accused of seeking only profits by catering to the tastes of the vulgar by exposing 'thighs and chests' and indulging in martial arts fantasies that were reworked from the banned genre of *shenguai wuxia* pictures of the old silent days (the term *shenguai* referring to spirits and monsters which formed the aesthetic basis of supernaturalism that authorities in China were guarding against). Since both martial arts fantasies and Cantonese dialect features were banned in China, the criticism against them took on an increasingly harsh tone. Cantonese cinema was described as a 'contagious disease that not only can eradicate the whole film community of the southern Chinese region, but even more abominably, can kill off the "consciences" of the good people of China'.[19] Accordingly, the civilian-representative body of the city of Guangzhou, instigated by the city's KMT branch, moved to prohibit the distribution of Hong Kong's Cantonese films and its genres of 'absurd fantasies'. The Social Affairs Bureau of the police department vowed to implement the ban until Cantonese pictures were completely wiped out in Guangzhou. New and stringent censorship regulations were also proposed by the city government allowing for the banning of all films whose contents were deemed to be 'of no benefit to the people'.[20]

The production of Cantonese features and 'absurd fantasies' of the *shenguai wuxia* variety continued unabated in Hong Kong and a move was underway to 'clean up' the Hong Kong film industry for the second time in its history. To spearhead this second 'clean-up' campaign, Cai Chusheng made a return visit to the territory in 1948 (his first visit was in 1937 following the Japanese occupation of Shanghai, but Cai returned to

the mainland when Hong Kong itself was occupied in 1941). This time, Cai's brief was to set up a branch of the Shanghai Kunlun Studio which had produced critically acclaimed social conscience melodramas such as *The Spring River Flows East* (Cai Chusheng and Zheng Junli, 1947) and *Under Ten Thousand Roofs* (Shen Fu, 1948). He was supposed to make Mandarin films in Hong Kong, but he ended up establishing a different company which he named Nanguo (literally, Southern Kingdom) to make Cantonese pictures instead. Cai and other leftwing émigré film-makers in Hong Kong saw their mission as spreading the gospel of 'new democratic ideas' and reforming the capitalist management structures of film corporations in the colony by raising the status of scriptwriters and directors and instilling a collectivist spirit in creative work and management.[21] The Nanguo Company would take on the task of rearming the Cantonese film industry with a social and moral conscience, cleaning up the whole industry by weaning it away from reliance on the mercurial genres purveying 'absurd fantasies'. One hundred and sixty-four film workers signed a manifesto, declaring: 'We will refuse to participate in productions which are not in our nation's interests or which have a negative influence on society. We will do all we can to bring honour, not shame, to the Cantonese film industry.'[22]

Nanguo produced *Tears of the Pearl River* (Wang Weiyi, 1950), a film now regarded by critics as the first Cantonese picture to achieve the kind of aesthetics displayed by the classic contemporary dramas in the Shanghai cinema circa 1931–7. It portrayed the kind of naturalistic realism that was more the forte of the progressive Mandarin cinema of that golden period, with Cai's own films from that period being representative. The Nanguo Company produced only two more pictures and was wound up after its founders returned to the mainland following the Communist Party's victory in the civil war. Nanguo's line of 'a new wave of energetic and serious filmmaking'[23] was continued by the Union Company (Chung Luen), a film collective set up in 1952 to maintain the realist tendency of the contemporary social conscience melodrama, dealing with problems of poverty, education, housing, unemployment. The Union Company produced some of the most enduring social classics of the Cantonese cinema, including adaptations of Ba Jin's novels *Family* (Ng Wui, 1953), *Spring* (Lee Sun-fung, 1953), *Autumn* (Chun Kim, 1954)

and *Cold Nights* (Lee Sun-fung, 1955), and the social
melodramas *In the Face of Demolition* (Lee Tit, 1953), *The
Guiding Light* (Chun Kim, 1953), *Father and Son* (Ng Wui,
1954) and *Parents' Hearts* (Chun Kim, 1955). Directors
like Chun Kim, Lee Tit, Ng Wui and Lee Sun-fung
established personal styles in such melodramas and
went on to become important and prolific directors in
the Cantonese cinema.

The socialist tendencies of Nanguo and the Union
Company were meant to lift the standards of
Cantonese film-making overall by infusing social
content as an antidote to pure entertainments. The
period dramas, in particular the spectral fantasies of
shenguai wuxia movies, were regarded as 'poison'. In
1950, a writer could still publish articles attacking the
martial arts fantasy genre and invoke the ban in the
early 1930s imposed by the Nanjing government on the
Shanghai film industry as a just cause for the
promotion of quality in the Chinese cinema in general,
reminding one of the Central Film Censorship
Committee's claim that it was banning *shenguai wuxia*
pictures in order to 'lift technical standards'. In an
article entitled 'Cantonese Cinema: Its Past and Future',
a writer using the pseudonym 'Microphone' sounded
like an apologist for the CFCC when he extolled the
virtues of the historic prohibition:

> Since a wave of events that led to the banning of the
> Mingxing Company's *Burning of the Red Lotus Temple*,
> the production of Chinese cinema, under the
> supervision of the government, has raised its level of
> quality and lowered its threshold of quantity. This
> period could be called the period of the rise of the
> artistic (*wenyi*) and conscionable cinema.[24]

According to the writer, certain producers in Shanghai
who put quantity over quality felt hamstrung by the
film censorship law in China and broke through the
cordon of film censorship by coming to Hong Kong, a
libertarian city where they would be free of restrictions.
However, though free in Hong Kong, they did not
produce works of artistic quality, and they were still
unable to produce anything outstanding. Instead, these
companies were simply recycling the types of films or
genres of the old Shanghai cinema in postwar Hong
Kong.[25] Ironically, the *wuxia* films proved to be a
durable genre to this very day, as evidenced by the
success achieved by directors such as Tsui Hark and
Ang Lee.

Kwan Tak-hing (right) as the Cantonese martial arts hero Wong
Fei-hung fighting the villain, perennially played by Sek Kin (left),
in a typical pose from a Wong Fei-hung movie of the 1950s

As Hong Kong developed its film industry into the
late 1950s and 60s the Shanghai connection appeared
to feature as a strong tie in the Mandarin film world,
but they were also operating in the Cantonese film
industry. In the *wuxia* genre, much despised by the
intelligentsia, the Cantonese cinema established a
different line of *wuxia* production in the form of the
Wong Fei-hung series, directed by the Shanghainese Hu
Peng, which would rejuvenate the entire Cantonese
film industry in the 1950s. The Wong Fei-hung films
became recognised as a different strand of *wuxia* film,
and they came to be known as 'kung fu' movies. The
term – a Cantonese expression – is now virtually
synonymous with Hong Kong cinema, and it really
began with Wong Fei-hung. The hero fought with his
fists and legs rather than with the traditional sword,
and 'kung fu' has since come to symbolise a way of
fighting that was different from the Mandarin style of
wuxia. Wong Fei-hung epitomised the Cantonese
cinema for some two decades in the 1950s and 60s, and
it is perhaps in Wong Fei-hung that the Cantonese
cinema found its own unique identity.

Conclusion

While the Shanghai connection in the Hong Kong film
industry underscored a sense of continuity with the
history of the Chinese cinema in the mainland, it was
the ingenuity and distinctiveness of the Cantonese
cinema which distinguished its development in Hong

Kong. In the area of genre, the Cantonese cinema transformed *wuxia* into kung fu, for example. Kung fu best exemplifies how the Cantonese cinema earned its own identity in the Hong Kong film industry while inheriting legacies from the Shanghai cinema that was the centre of Chinese film-making in the 1920s and 30s. The influx of the first generation of Shanghai's film-making community into Hong Kong helped to foster the *wuxia* genre in the Cantonese cinema, which otherwise lacked the talent and the experience to create its own *wuxia* movies, as film historian Yu Mo-wan has claimed.[26]

Other unique Cantonese genres developed: the Cantonese Opera film, the Union-style social melodramas, the comedy (featuring memorable stars such as Yee Chau-shui, Tang Kei-chen, Sunma Si-tsang and Leung Sing-po) and later, in the 1960s, the Cantonese *wuxia* serial of which *Buddha's Palm* (Ling Wan, 1964) is representative. This *was* the golden period of Cantonese cinema, and like all golden periods it would disappear. Indeed, as I have stated in my Introduction above, the Cantonese cinema that is covered by this chapter refers to the cinema that exists no longer, and its cultural or aesthetic legacy was not necessarily the same as the Cantonese cinema that replaced the old one after 1973. Changes in attitudes and lifestyle separated the new Cantonese cinema from its previous incarnation of the golden age. There are clear aesthetic differences as well. The old Cantonese cinema has fortunately not vanished into oblivion. It has lingered as a kind of broken text in the memory and, while much of it may have been lost, that which has been preserved needs to be better known and deserves greater appraisal and appreciation.

Notes

1. See *Hong Kong Filmography, Volume 1, 1913–1941* (Hong Kong: Hong Kong Film Archive, 1997), pp. 20–1.
2. See Li Daoxin, *Zhongguo dianying shi, 1937–1945* (Chinese Film History 1937–1945), (Beijing: Shifan University Press, 2000), p. 221.
3. See *Yilin* (Artland) no. 58 (15 July 1939).
4. See Guan Wenqing, *Zhongguo yintan waishi* (A History of the Chinese Silver Screen) (Hong Kong: Guangjiaojing Chubanshe, 1976), p. 214. See also *Yilin* (Artland) issues 1, 2, 3 (February–April 1937), debating the issue of the ban on Cantonese features.
5. Fung Chi-kong, 'Yueyu yingpian de cunjin wenti' ('The Question of Cantonese Film and its Survival'), *Yilin*

(Artland) no. 3 (1 April 1937). All translations from the original Chinese in this article are by the author.
6. See Chen Zongtong, 'Yue pian guo huan jin yi' (Cantonese Film Ban Suspended'), *Yilin* (Artland) no. 9 (1 July 1937).
7. See Zhiwei Xiao, 'Constructing a New National Culture: Film Censorship and the Issues of Cantonese Dialect, Superstition, and Sex in the Nanjing Decade', in Zhang Yingjin (ed.), *Cinema and Urban Culture in Shanghai, 1922–1943* (Stanford, CA: Stanford University Press, 1999), p. 185.
8. For a full account of the representations made by Cantonese film-makers to the Nanjing government and the Central Film Censorship Committee to save their industry, see Xiao, 'Constructing a New National Culture', pp. 186–90.
9. Ibid., p. 189.
10. See Barbara Ward, 'Regional Operas and Their Audiences: Evidence from Hong Kong', in David Johnson, Andrew J. Nathan and Evelyn S. Rawski (eds), *Popular Culture in Late Imperial China* (Taipei: SMC, 1987), pp. 161–87.
11. Ibid., p. 161.
12. See Yu Mo-wan (Yu Muyun) , 'Xianggang yueju dianying fazhan shihua' ('Anecdotes of the Development of Hong Kong Cantonese Opera Film'), in Li Cheuk-to (Li Zhuotao) (ed.), *Cantonese Opera Film Retrospective* (11th Hong Kong International Film Festival (HKIFF) catalogue) (Hong Kong: Urban Council, 1987), pp. 18–21 (19).
13. Yu Yeying, *Xishuo Li Lihua* (Li Lihua: A Life of Drama) (Taipei: Quanniandai Chubanshe, 1996), p. 130.
14. Law Kar, 'Crisis and Opportunity: Crossing Borders in Hong Kong Cinema, its Development from the 40s to the 70s', in 24th HKIFF catalogue, *Border Crossings in Hong Kong Cinema* (Hong Kong: Leisure and Cultural Services Dept, 2000), p. 116.
15. 'Yueyu pian jiang qu juejing' ('Cantonese Films Soon to be Extinct'), *Qing Qing Dianying* (Chin Chin Screen) no. 32 (6 October 1948).
16. See John Luff, 'Filmmaking in Hong Kong – How it All Started in Shanghai', *South China Morning Post*, 26 January 1970.
17. Law, 'Crisis and Opportunity', p. 117.
18. 'Yueyu pian jiang qu juejing' ('Cantonese Films Soon to be Extinct'), *Qing Qing Dianying* (Chin Chin Screen) no. 32 (6 October 1948).
19. Ibid.
20. Ibid.

21. See Lin Nien-tung, 'Some Trends in the Development of the Post-War Hong Kong Cinema', in 3rd HKIFF catalogue, *Hong Kong Cinema Survey 1946–1968* (Hong Kong: Urban Council, 1979), pp. 15–25.

22. Ibid., p. 19.

23. Shi Yi, 'The Tai Kwong Ming, Nan Kuen and Nam Kwok (Southern) Companies', in 3rd HKIFF catalogue, p. 134.

24. Maige Erfeng (or Microphone), 'Yueyu pian de guoqu weilai' ('Cantonese Cinema: Its Past and Future'), *Dianying Shijie* (Movie World) no. 2 (Hong Kong: 5 August 1950).

25. Ibid.

26. See Yu Mo-wan, 'Swords, Chivalry and Palm Power: A Brief Survey of the Cantonese Martial Arts Cinema 1938–1970', *A Study of the Hong Kong Swordplay Film (1945–1980)* (5th Hong Kong International Film Festival catalogue) (Hong Kong: Urban Council, 1981), pp. 99–106.

Further Reading in *Chinese Films in Focus II*

On Zheng Junli, see Chapter 10, '*Crows and Sparrows*: Allegory on a Historical Threshold' by Yiman Wang.

On the new *wuxia* films, see Chapter 7, '*A Chinese Ghost Story*: Ghostly Counsel and Innocent Man' by John Zou, and Chapter 9, '*Crouching Tiger, Hidden Dragon*: Cultural Migrancy and Translatability' by Felicia Chan.

PART FOUR

The New Waves

12 The Fifth Generation

A Reassessment

Wendy Larson

The term 'Fifth Generation' refers to the fifth class of students graduating from the Beijing Film Academy. Beginning their studies in 1978 and graduating in 1982, the formal education of this cohort was delayed by the policies of the Cultural Revolution (1966–76). Early Fifth Generation films represent an evolution from socialism to a time when commercialisation, urbanisation and capitalism took firmer cultural hold.

This transitional character broadly informs three aspects of Fifth Generation work. First, with large allegorical structures, vast and harsh northern landscapes, and peasant characters evident in many of their films, especially from the early period, the Fifth Generation inherited its moral social framework and focus on the countryside from the socialist period, a tendency that is all the more obvious from the perspective of their successors, the Sixth Generation, who tended to emphasise a decidedly unmoral, mostly urban environment. Second, the Fifth Generation attacked the past as much through aesthetics as through overt theme or plot, bringing in stylistic ambiguity and uncertainty to dislodge the more monolithic messages of the earlier period. In their oft-stunning aesthetic approach, Fifth Generation directors' quest for expression beyond the traditions of socialist realism succeeded, even though they could not completely abandon the old thematic patterns and moral structure. And third, the emergence of the Fifth Generation marked the point when China's film industry made significant inroads into global film distribution and elite film culture, formalising a more pronounced 'star' system and instigating debate on the self-orientalising of Chinese culture.

The most famous of these directors is Zhang Yimou (b. 1950), whose trio of 'red' films – *Red Sorghum* (1987), *Ju Dou* (1990), and *Raise the Red Lantern* (1991) – brought the director lasting fame (as well as lasting criticism) both in China and abroad. The Fifth Generation includes Chen Kaige (b. 1952), Tian Zhuangzhuang (b. 1952), Zhang Junzhao (b. 1952), Peng Xiaolian (b. 1953), Huang Jianxin (b. 1954), Zhou Xiaowen (b. 1954), Hu Mei (b. 1957) and others who for the most part were born in the decade between 1950 and 1960. This chapter will contextualise and interpret the work done by these well-known representatives of the Fifth Generation, analysing their position between socialism and the market, their passionate allegorical aesthetics and the breakthroughs that made their film such a lasting phenomenon in global cinema.

The Socialist Past

It is difficult to overestimate the pervasive presence of the Chinese socialist past in forming the subjectivity of the generation of film-makers who entered the Beijing Film Academy in 1978, only two years after the formal end of the Cultural Revolution. Most of these students were born in the 1950s and grew up at a time when Mao Zedong's theory of 'permanent revolution' was moving into its most radical expression, leading from the Hundred Flowers movement (1956–7) to the Anti-Rightist movement (1957–8), the Great Leap Forward (1959–61) and ultimately the Cultural Revolution. The period now known as the 'Seventeen Years', from the founding of the People's Republic of China in 1949 up to the beginning of the Cultural Revolution, was the golden age of Chinese socialism, when the aesthetic principles and thematic scope of art, literature and film were firmly established and even taken for granted. The revolutionary aesthetic world was comprehensive in its claims on subjectivity, providing an emotionally coherent set of ideas and forms that were expressed idealistically and with exuberance. In films from the 1950s, we can locate the influence of the socialist aesthetic tradition in woodcuts, the fine arts and literature, with bright colours, sharp outlines and striking poses combined with the internal struggles of characters that often journeyed from bourgeois to revolutionary sensibilities. Most of the Fifth Generation film-makers were *zhiqing*, or 'educated youth', asked by Mao Zedong to live and work in the countryside, learn from the peasants and help build socialism.[1]

Chen Kaige's *Yellow Earth* (1984), which featured Zhang Yimou's work as cinematographer, was a good example of an early Fifth Generation film that embraced certain aspects of the socialist perspective while simultaneously distancing itself from easy interpretation along socialist themes. It also was one of the first post-Cultural Revolution films to attract attention to Chinese cinema in the West. *Yellow Earth* was set in the bleak and impoverished northern countryside close to Yan'an, the destination of the Red Army when it was driven out of southern China in the mid-1930s. Yan'an has attained high symbolic status as the site where the Communist Party regrouped in order to fight the Japanese and Chiang Kai-shek's Nationalists, and to regain control of the country; it also is the location most often associated with Mao Zedong's ascent to power. The film begins in 1939, when party cadre Gu Qing is assigned to collect folk songs in the area with the goal of rewriting them with revolutionary lyrics. He stays with a poor family that includes a girl in her early teens, Cui Qiao, her young brother Hanhan and her widowed father. When Gu Qing attempts to talk to the father, most of his efforts are met with stony silence. However, when he describes freedom of choice in marriage and other benefits of life under the communists to Cui Qiao, who is about to be married to an older man, Gu Qing lights a fire in the girl, and she eventually asks him to take her to Yan'an. He tells her he must get permission and leaves, but in order to escape her imminent fate, Cui Qiao sets off across the river herself. The images on Gu Qing's return imply that she has died in her attempt to escape.

Despite the film's clear criticism directed at the Communist Party, whose earnest representative Gu

Qing speaks of liberation but brings catastrophe on the family, *Yellow Earth* carried many elements of socialist cinema. First, as was the case with many early Fifth Generation films, its countryside setting referenced Mao's emphasis on the rural. In Mao's theories, China differed from Russia in its huge peasantry, which he substituted for the urban proletariat that was supposed to lead the revolution. The attitude towards peasants that *Yellow Earth* and many Fifth Generation films expressed echoed Mao's famous comments, made in 1958:

> Apart from their other characteristics, the outstanding thing about China's 600 million people is that they are 'poor and blank'. This may seem a bad thing, but in reality it is a good thing. Poverty gives rise to the desire for changes, the desire for action, and the desire for revolution. On a blank sheet of paper free from any mark, the freshest and most beautiful characters can be written; the freshest and most beautiful pictures can be painted.[2]

Yellow Earth: Cui Qiao, 'Three Obediences and Four Virtues'

Yellow Earth: Gu Qing with Hanhan, Cui Qiao and their father

In choosing the countryside as the site for many films, the Fifth Generation directors reinforced the spiritual depth that Mao Zedong endowed on the rural. They also showcased their unwillingness to directly deal with social life in all of its forms, and their preference for constructing a powerful allegorical setting through which past thematic and aesthetic discourses could be distanced while still lending their existential weight to the new project. The films set in the countryside were not really about the peasants and their lives so much as they were about the directors' abstract concerns with representation, history, language and truth.[3]

Yet *Yellow Earth* also challenged the assumptions behind socialist realism, which would never have depicted a cadre as so fervent to express the party's message about liberation and escape from the oppressive past that he misjudges the effect of his words, and fails to realistically consider the tenacious hold of the traditional network within which a young woman's existence is situated. And while socialist films struggled with the contradiction between 'poor and blank' and the spiritual assets supposedly located in country people and the land they worked, *Yellow Earth* did not shrink from depicting the impoverished peasants as uneducated, superstitious and irrational in the way they cleaved to old habits and ceremonies, such as the frenzied dance to bring rain to the dry, cracked soil. The power of the land, a common early Fifth Generation trope, came through in its emphasis on the dramatic, if barren and stark, landscape of the north, with its bare soil and vast skies. Most important was the film's radical perspective on history, which as opposed to the party narrative appeared unchangeable and permeated all aspects of existence and subjectivity.

The tenets of Socialist Realism – that literature and art be intelligible to workers, realistic, in support of the party and typical – were set in 1932 by Joseph Stalin (1878–1953) in his decree, 'On the Reconstruction of Literary and Art Organisations'. Although socialist realism often failed to live up to these demands, substituting romantic and idealistic for realistic images and characters, the quality of revolutionary optimism, which was so important in Chinese worker models such as Lei Feng (1940–1962), was well expressed through vibrant primary colours. Fifth Generation films combined a striking use of bright colour with the muted brown, yellow and grey of the northern landscape, often producing a spectacular visual experience. Like *Yellow Earth*, Zhang Yimou's *Red Sorghum* featured many long scenic takes, which with his characteristic red and yellow contributed to the lavish display for which Zhang is known.

Eventually becoming the most famous of the Fifth Generation directors, Zhang Yimou began his career as a cinematographer for *One and Eight* (Zhang Junzhao, 1983), *Yellow Earth* and *The Big Parade* (Chen Kaige, 1986). This early work helped train him to focus on the visual effects of film. He joined the Xi'an Film Studio in 1985 at the request of Fourth Generation director Wu Tianming (b. 1939), and ended up playing a major character in Wu's film *Old Well* (1986) about an impoverished village in Shanxi without sufficient water. In 1987, he directed *Red Sorghum*, which was based on two novellas by Mo Yan (b. 1955), a writer who also focused on life in the countryside, emphasising its vital existence as timeless history rather than as any specific or concrete form belonging to a certain era. As did socialist realism in general, *Red Sorghum* used the colour red to indicate passion – here often sexual, if also patriotic and land-based – and struggle, and added lively folk songs to express authenticity. The colour red also predominated in *Ju Dou*, a story about a young woman married to an impotent older man who owned a dye factory. The moral urgency characteristic of the grand conflicts of socialist realism, which often pit individuals against the implacable forces of tradition, also was evident in *Ju Dou*, where the character Ju Dou fought against the impassivity of the village, which would rather allow her husband to beat her to death than risk damage to the patriarchal system by intervening.

Hu Mei, one of a small number of female directors in this cohort, gained fame with her co-directed film *Army Nurse* (1984). Produced by the People's Liberation Army August First Film Studio in Beijing, the film was

Red Sorghum: 'my grandma' and wine vessels

motivated by the conflict between love and revolution, a theme that had played out in numerous pieces of fiction, plays and films since the 1920s. The setting is a rural hospital, where nurse Qiao Xiaoyu falls in love with patient Ding Zhu, but cannot overcome her training and find a way to follow her desires, which are transgressive in that environment. While the outcome of the torturous internal process – expressed not only through acting but also through offscreen narration – around which the film is structured is shown to be negative (i.e., the character does not learn from this experience and correct her desires) rather than positive, as it would have been in a revolutionary film, the moral framework is reminiscent. Like *Song of Youth* (Cui Wei, 1959) and other socialist films, *Army Nurse* organised scenes through a moral conflict informed by a gravity of purpose and an emphasis on subjectivity.

The extent to which the Fifth Generation directors were indebted to the very socialist conceptual and aesthetic traditions from which they ostensibly were trying to escape is all the more obvious when we look at the Sixth Generation, which much more completely demolished this legacy. The new film-makers' choice of the urban setting, their refusal to invest individual struggle with allegorical significance, their eschewing of literary connections and their anti-romantic view of life, space and place brought a new perspective to their often low-budget and visually unspectacular films. Techniques such as the use of a handheld camera and ambient sound dated Zhang Yimou's relatively still camera, and the new group's scorn for the recognition of Chinese traditions or 'Chineseness' implied that the Fifth Generation was a transitional group whose films rely on the techniques, assumptions and themes of the past.[4]

Aesthetic Innovations

Despite the persistent legacy of socialist realism, Fifth Generation film in the immediate post-Cultural Revolution period introduced many innovations. Although like writers and artists of the same period, the Fifth Generation directors marked their departure from the past with new themes, plots and characters, they were most successful in establishing a radically different aesthetic style, which spoke to a new politics and, eventually, a global perspective. So impressive was this new aesthetic direction that it launched Chinese cinema into the world, where it often appeared at international film festivals and garnered important awards, retaining its reputation for craftsmanship and quality to the present time.

Even more importantly, the early Fifth Generation focus on artistic experimentation, with its stylised form of expression, helped it build a new national history that challenged some of the most sacred beliefs of the 1950s and the Cultural Revolution. Much as the modernist Misty poets of the early 1980s befuddled their readers with an unfamiliar ambiguity that rejected the clarity of socialist realism, the Fifth Generation directors partook of a modernist aesthetics of alienation to block the comfort of repetition and create a sense of confusion and unease within viewers. The purpose of this alienation was to disable the monotonous representation of Socialist Realism, create a modern cinematic language and dispense with what socialist realism had designated as real, now thought to be supremely hypocritical, forcing an engagement with a deeper and hidden reality solidly located in history, language and place. The estrangement that writers such as Ah Cheng (b. 1949) and Mo Yan created was grasped by directors who turned their stories into moving images, and expressed through filmic strategies of timing, camera angle and framing.

A good example of aesthetic experimentation is the film that launched the Fifth Generation, *One and Eight*, which presented a striking sense of difference and alienation, using unremarkable images but altering the focus and temporality that gave them meaning in the past. Set in 1939 and centring on prisoners held by Chiang Kai-shek's armies, the plot easily could have unfolded as a paean to the nation, like many of the patriotic films of the 1950s. But the obscure shooting angles and distance shots of cinematographer Zhang Yimou, the use of space as a dramatic element, the profusion of dark shots framed without a centre and the creative use of sound indicate that the film was far from a nationalistic exercise.

Chen Kaige's *King of the Children* (1987), although unsuccessful at the box office, also projected many elements of the new aesthetics, using them to question the commitment of the state to education and the happy image of the countryside. The children who teacher Lao Gan is sent to the countryside to educate are often shot from below, which gives them a lack of cuteness and sentimentality, turning them into living yet undifferentiated critiques of the stultifying combination of traditional and socialist Chinese education. Nonetheless, the emphasis is not on them as much as it is on Lao Gan, whose frenzied attempts to teach students combine with an introspective tendency towards doubt and confusion to foreground his consciousness and self-awareness, which we see reflected in a lengthy gaze into a cracked mirror. By deftly controlling the length of each take, allowing the camera to linger and restricting speech, Chen produced a near-mystical sense of tension that brought together both the possibility invested in the children and their future, and the inevitable shutting down of this hope that eventually drove the dishevelled Lao Gan to a state of near paralysis.

History, language and enduring poverty are the villains of this stark tale, and the film strongly projected the timeless spiritual quest that motivated the Fifth Generation to seek a new aesthetics and to

King of the Children, Lao Gan

reject a focus on contemporary life, which was deemed corrupted by socialist discourse.

Another box-office failure was *The Horse Thief* (1986) in which director Tian Zhuangzhuang also used minimalistic dialogue, overtly to delve into the spiritual life of Norbu, a horse robber, and more generally Tibet, while actually following the same symbolic and allegorical route taken by many other early Fifth Generation films. Directly contradicting the official depiction of cheerful and contented minorities, the civilising state programmes that characterised 1960s films about minorities, and the exoticism attached to minorities in the 1950s, Tian disoriented the viewer by eliminating Han characters and focusing on a mute and brutal reality. Yet eventually the film made it clear that, like Chen Kaige, other Fifth Generation film-makers and many writers of the 1980s, Tian sited his story in minority territory in order to question majority discourse, not to realistically portray the lives of Tibetans. The depiction of minorities as radically different, violent, mysterious and unrepressed was the technique through which Tian and others threw the civilising traditions of Han culture into shocking relief.[5]

Almost a decade later, Jiang Wen's (b. 1963) first film, *In the Heat of the Sun* (1994), so startling and successful in the Chinese market and virtually unknown abroad, thematically bracketed the revolutionary years and shrunk them to background noise, bringing forward the subjective and sensual experiences of a fifteen-year-old boy, Ma Xiaojun. While openly condescending towards socialist ideas and practices, Ma joins his friends in romantically singing Russian folk songs on a roof top as he courts the older Milan. Graduating from the Central Academy of Drama in Beijing in 1984 and working for a decade as an actor, Jiang Wen is not, formally speaking, a Fifth Generation director. Yet his early films continue many of the conflicts and themes characteristic of this group. Jiang Wen based *In the Heat of the Sun* on a story by 'hooligan' writer Wang Shuo (b. 1958), and recreated the sounds, sights and general mood of the late Cultural Revolution period, shoving political ideology to the side. His heightening of sensual experience and displacement of ideology was carried on to a shocking degree, as he showed the cynicism of youth at the end of the high revolutionary period, yet also brought out their innocence and desire to live. Another director who is technically part of the Sixth Generation but because of his age, more accurately thought of as in between generations is He Jianjun (b. 1960). His enigmatic film

The Postman (1995) unfolded a strangely unrealistic urban world devoid of a spiritual centre. Despite the characters' lack of recognition of the depressing environment in which they live, or any overt recollection of the ideals of the past, revolutionary sentiments motivate main character Xiao Dou, who opens letters addressed to other people in order to intervene in their lives, setting right their relationships and motivations. *The Postman*'s awkward exchanges between the near-dysfunctional and inarticulate Xiao Dou and the other characters combine with the camera's slow long takes over the industrial scenes of the city, off-kilter focus on dilapidated doorways and general centring on the grime of the city to present an original aesthetic vision that gestured towards the more substantial revisions of the other members of the Sixth Generation.

Directors such as Jiang Wen and He Jianjun, in their early films positioned stylistically and thematically between the Fifth and Sixth Generations, were joined by some early Fifth Generation directors who also set their films in urban environments and veered away from the allegorical approach. Through their work, we can glimpse the changes that led to the Sixth Generation emphasis on urban discontent, and that pushed the Fifth Generation towards the market. Huang Jianxin, a Fifth Generation director who focused on urban society, used humour to carry out a deconstruction of subjectivity under bureaucracy, an approach that also motivated the writer Can Xue (b. 1953) in her absurdist novella *Yellow Mud Street* (1983). Huang's *The Black Cannon Incident* (1985), a satire on bureaucracy and its guiding emotion of suspicion, shocked not only with its overt thematic critique, but also with its dry humour, circular dialogue and insistence not on clear-cut mistakes or villains but on a set of formalities and procedures, which were part of an ingrained mentality that in turn drove a bizarre and almost predictable logic. Huang's next film, *Dislocation* (1986), concerned a man who developed a robot to take his place at the many boring meetings he must attend. The strategy failed when the robot refused to attend the meetings, demanding the better things of life just like his creator was experiencing. While estrangement is evident in these films, the characters do not feel it as zeal or an anguished agitation, but rather have taken on the trappings of daily life, giving up the feverish missions that characterised the characters in other early Fifth Generation films.[6]

Peng Xiaolian (b. 1953), another well-known female director who like Hu Mei has continued her work in film to the present day, made *Me and My Classmates* (*Wo he wode tongxue*) in 1986, *Women's Story* in 1988 and later six feature films focusing on Shanghai. From the beginning emphasising women's experience, Peng expressed the strongest feminist vision of the Fifth Generation. While her earlier films concentrated on peasant women, who often fled to the cities to improve their lives, her Shanghai films focused on the bias against women in the business world, their problems getting jobs and their familial and career responsibilities. Her emphasis on female subjectivity, brought out by a clear focus on the female characters and their experiences, was for Peng a purposeful act that viewed some Fifth Generation aesthetic approaches, especially the modernist notion of suffering humanity, through a feminist lens.[7]

Global China

After the Tiananmen Incident of 1989 and the firm reassertment of state power, the Fifth Generation seemed to lose their earlier direction, with some turning to television work or emigrating, and others seeking new subject material. It was as if an era that once welcomed their allegorical meditations on tradition, subjectivity, emotion and trauma had gone cold, and suddenly their work appeared dated. The strikingly visual, spiritual and passionate early Fifth Generation films did not have long to capture the public mind before social, cultural and economic changes forced the directors to reconsider the encroaching market and the competition of both younger Chinese directors and foreign films.

It was at this point that the prescient vision of Zhang Yimou, who in Gong Li (b. 1965) cultivated the first Chinese film star to attain global recognition after the Maoist period, set the norm for the development of a Chinese and pan-Asian star system. With her career beginning as an actress in Zhang's *Red Sorghum*, Gong Li went on to star in several of Zhang's films, including *Ju Dou, Raise the Red Lantern, The Story of Qiu Ju* (*Qiuju da guansi*, 1992), and also in Chen Kaige's *Farewell My Concubine* (1993) and *Temptress Moon* (1996), as well as many other films. In the 1990s, the Fifth Generation penetrated the global market and, with Gong Li leading the way, became part of the star and auteur system that characterised the film industry in the United States and Europe.

China's entry into the World Trade Organisation in 2001 rang the death knell of the old system, which had restricted the import of foreign films to twenty a year while DVD and VCD piracy swelled. In 2007, the United States filed a complaint with the WTO with the goal of opening the Chinese market to foreign books, films and music. The WTO ruled in favour of the complaint and rejected a Chinese appeal. Even before this ruling, however, Chinese directors were becoming increasingly global, seeking funding and production abroad and employing foreign technicians and staff. Many films, such as Zhang Yimou's controversial *Hero* (2002), which was nominated for the Best Foreign Language Film Oscar at the 2003 Academy Awards in Hollywood, were funded by various global partners.

Yet the bold entry of Chinese film into global space also augured increased concern for the position and unity of the nation, for within only six years, three historical martial arts epics that combined the mystical abilities of a group of fighters with issues about national unity, ethnic distinctness and struggle came out. The trend began with Zhou Xiaowen (b. 1954), whose first film, *Desperation* (1987), was not a typical Fifth Generation allegory set in rural China, but rather a modern urban thriller. This early nod to the commercial value of entertainment positioned Zhou well to transition into the new mode of flashy historical martial arts films and, in 1996, he came out with *The Emperor's Shadow*, a tale about the king of Qin, who became the first emperor of China, and the founding of the nation. Chen Kaige followed suit with *The Emperor and the Assassin* in 1998, and Zhang Yimou's *Hero* rounded out the triad of foundational stories about the nation, national unification and the forming of a people. Although there was disagreement among critics, many attacked *Hero* and by extension, Zhang Yimou, for condoning authoritarianism when martial arts assassin Nameless backs down from killing the imperialistic king. At the same time, *Hero* was also praised for its complex plot and narrative structure, epic scope, philosophical depth and spectacular fighting scenes.[8]

With these national historical epics, the Fifth Generation film-makers leapt out of their earlier framework and entered the big-budget, globally advertised, star-driven world of cinema. This move resulted in predictable criticism and the claim, voiced earlier but now with greater insistence, that the Fifth Generation had sold out, was on a path of relentless self-Orientalising and had embraced capitalism and consumerism. Along with Ang Lee (b. 1954), a Taiwan director of the same generation whose *Crouching Tiger, Hidden Dragon* (2000) was also an eye-catching martial arts blockbuster, the Fifth Generation used martial arts as their calling card.[9] Martial arts and kung fu turned out to be the perfect vehicle through which to express strength combined with Chinese cultural references, and sensitivity combined with power. Another film along these lines was *Confucius* (2010), directed by Hu Mei, which starred the Hong Kong kung fu expert and globally known actor Chow Yun-Fat (b. 1955) and turned the life of the ancient sage into a romantic action story.

This modernisation and globalisation of a Chinese icon led descendents of the sage, angry at the lack of realism in the film, to bring a suit against the film-makers, who already were stinging from criticism when *Avatar* (James Cameron, 2009) was bumped from theatres by the updated fighting philosopher.

In spring 2010, the online film site dGenerate Films released its list of best Chinese-language films of first decade of the twenty-first century, voted on by a group of some forty-four cultural critics, film directors and academics in Hong Kong, Taiwan, the United States, Europe and China. Directors from the Sixth Generation (Jia Zhangke, b. 1970), from Hong Kong (Wong Kar-wai, b. 1958) and from Taiwan (Tsai Ming-liang, b. 1957; Hou Hsiao-hsien, b. 1947; Ang Lee) dominated, without a single Fifth Generation director appearing in the top ten. The Honourable Mention category included two Fifth Generation directors (Tian Zhuangzhuang and Zhang Yimou) and one in-between director (Jiang Wen).[10]

While not a comprehensive sampling, the list from dGenerate indicated that the influence of the Fifth Generation was finally on the wane, replaced by films that appealed more directly to contemporary sensibilities. The fact that the top ten included directors from Hong Kong and Taiwan who are in the same age cohort as the Fifth Generation indicated, perhaps, that the 1982 Beijing Film Academy graduates, more than others, were constrained by the specific history out of which they emerged and with which they so ardently engaged. The generation that grew up in the golden years of the 1950s and came of age during the high radicalism of the Cultural Revolution, that so fiercely fought to move away from the Socialist Realism that had dominated their consciousness and that of

their peers and that broke Chinese film out of its isolation, moving it towards a global perspective, was giving way to a new vision. The existential romance of the countryside, so heightened under Mao, evolved into a darker and more realistic portrayal under Jia Zhangke, the new global star of the Sixth Generation. While the Fifth Generation made the leap into martial arts blockbusters, it was less successful at so-called art films, where the new group of directors, as well as Chinese directors from outside the mainland, took centre stage.

Nonetheless, the contributions of the Fifth Generation have endured in many ways. Striking scenes have cemented their aesthetic reputation: the mute cowherd urinating into a field in *King of the Children*; the sedan-puller feverishly breaking down the red sorghum as he prepares to rape 'my grandma' in *Red Sorghum*; Hanhan struggling against a sea of peasants running and chanting for rain in *Yellow Earth*; the short but powerful moment when Qiao Xiaoyu touches Ding Zhu's injured shoulder in *Army Nurse*. A group that captured the emotional intensity that revolutionary culture invested into daily life and yet also abused through the excesses of Cultural Revolution, and that turned all aspects of inherited discourse into a fervent query, the Fifth Generation forced a wrenching transformation in Chinese film. The fact that many of this group continue to make films that attract global audiences speaks to their lasting influence.

Notes

1. Zhen Ni, *Memoirs from the Beijing Film Academy: The Genesis of China's Fifth Generation*, trans. Chris Berry (Durham, NC: Duke University Press), 2002.
2. Maurice J. Meisner, *Mao Zedong: A Political and Intellectual Portrait* (New York: John Wiley and Sons, 2006), p. 149.
3. Xudong Zhang, *Chinese Modernism in the Era of Reforms: Cultural Fever, Avant-garde Fiction* (Durham, NC: Duke University Press, 1997).
4. Tian Xiezuo, 'Zhongguo dianying zhi lu – diwu dai daoyan yu diliu dai daoyan zhi bijiao' (The Road of Chinese films – A Comparison between the Fifth and Sixth Generations of directors), *Analyse* (<www.mtime.com/my/analyse/blog/1575087/>), 14 April 2008, accessed 18 May 2010.
5. Dru Gladney, 'Tian Zhuangzhuang, The Fifth Generation & "Minorities Film"', *Public Culture* vol. 8 no. 1 (Autumn, 1995), pp. 161–75.

6. Nick Kaldis, 'Huang Jianxin's *Cuowei* and/as Aesthetic Cognition', *positions: east asia cultures critique* vol. 7 no. 2 (Autumn, 1999), pp. 421–57.

7. 'Interview with Peng Xiaolian', *Camera Obscura: A Journal of Feminist Film Theory* vol. 6 (1988), pp. 26–31.

8. Wendy Larson, 'Zhang Yimou's *Hero*: Dismantling the Myth of Cultural Power', *Journal of Chinese Cinemas* vol. 2 no. 3 (November 2008), pp. 181–96.

9. Zhang Yiwu, 'Yingxiong: xin shijie de yinyu' (*Hero*: A Metaphor of the New Century), *Contemporary Cinema* (Dangdai dianying), February 2002, pp. 11–15.

10. 'Best Chinese Language Films of the 2000s': Ballots, <dgeneratefilms.com/critical-essays/best-chinese-language-films-of-the-2000s-poll-results> (accessed 18 May 2010).

Further Reading in *Chinese Films in Focus II*

On Chen Kaige, see Chapter 13, '*Farewell My Concubine*: National Myth and City Memories' by Yomi Braester, and Chapter 33, '*Yellow Earth*: Hesitant Apprenticeship and Bitter Agency' by Helen Hok-sze Leung.

On Zhang Yimou, see Chapter 17, '*Hero*: The Return of a Traditional Masculine Ideal in China' by Kam Louie; Chapter 21, '*Not One Less*: The Fable of a Migration' by Rey Chow; and Chapter 25, '*Riding Alone for Thousands of Miles*: Redeeming the Father by Way of Japan?' by Faye Hui Xiao.

On films by other Fifth Generation directors, see the following: Chapter 3, '*Black Cannon Incident*: Countering the Counter-espionage Fantasy' by Jason McGrath; Chapter 12, '*Ermo*: (Tele)Visualising Urban/Rural Transformation' by Ping Fu; and Chapter 31, '*Woman, Demon, Human*: The Spectral Journey Home' by Haiyan Lee.

13 Taiwan New Cinema and Its Legacy

Tonglin Lu

In the early 1980s, two films, *In Our Time* (Zhang Yi, Ke Yizheng, Tao Dechen and Edward Yang, 1982) and *The Sandwich Man* (Hou Hsiao-hsien, Wan Ren and Zeng Zhangxiang, 1983), marked a turning point in Taiwan cinema. Both these films, collectively directed by debutant directors (except for Hou Hsiao-hsien), are composed of several episodes. Without exception, these young directors consisted of major forces in the New Cinema Movement for the years to come. Most of them, except for Zhang Yi and Hou Hsiao-hsien, pursued their film studies in the West before returning to Taiwan to join the film and TV industrials as freshmen. Some other directors who went through the local system of the Taiwan film hierarchy like Hou and Zhang, such as Chen Kunhou and Wang Tong, also played important roles in this movement.

This movement lasted for a short period. By February 1987, fifty-three film-makers, artists and critics signed the manifesto penned by Zhan Hongzhi, a film critic, to explain the ideal about film-making in the New Cinema Movement as well as to express their concerns about any real possibility of realising such an ideal due to lack of support from the political institution, from the media and from the system of film critics.[1] In short, the retrospective manifesto already describes the end, but not the beginning, of this movement, as it reveals more doubts than faith about its outcome. By 1986, a number of the New Cinema directors, such as Zhang Yi and Zeng Zhuangxiang, permanently disappeared from the film-making scene, while more, such as Wan Ren, Chen Kunhou and Ke Yizheng, directed films only sporadically, and have gradually sunk into obscurity. Despite its brevity, this movement has left a lasting legacy to the film culture of Chinese-language communities through the works of two great authors: Edward Yang and Hou Hsiao-hsien.

Both Yang and Hou, however, have many more fans in the international art film circle than among their domestic audience. For example, *Yiyi*, which won the best director award at 2000 Cannes Film Festival, was not even publicly shown in Taiwan by the director's choice. Hou Hsiao-hsien, in his turn, stated in an interview that 'the audience for his *Flowers of Shanghai*, his 1998 film based on a Chinese premodern novel, is "twenty thousand in Taipei, two hundred thousand in Paris"'.[2] Twenty thousand spectators in Taiwan would not even have been possible for *Yiyi* (2000); according to my conversation with Wu Nien-jen, as the protagonist of this film and a well-known film-maker, Wu only watched his own performance for the first time through a DVD, which his son, a student in the United States, brought back during his summer vacations.

Ironically, the New Cinema was born out of the dissatisfaction with anti-communist propaganda, commercial genres, such as kung fu and Qiong Yao's type of melodrama (*wenyi pian*), largely because they were disconnected from the local audience.[3] One of the three principles in the New Cinema manifesto is precisely that a film must reflect on local culture,[4] a clear breakdown from the previous dominant trend in the Taiwan film industry, namely, escapism in officially supported propaganda as well as highly commercialised kung fu and *wenyi pian*. In fact, most of Yang's and Hou's works can be considered reflections on contemporary Taiwan culture, although their reflections seem somewhat lost among their local audience. After more than two decades, how should one examine the influences of the New Cinema Movement in Taiwan? What are its impacts on the local and global cultural scenes? How should we explain the apparently self-contradictory nature of the legacy of this movement exemplified by the receptions of works by the two post-New Cinema world-renowned authors: on the one hand, as reflections on contemporary Taiwanese culture and, on the other hand, as the isolated art products of sophisticated moviegoers at the international art-film circle?

In the 1960s and 70s, Taiwan went through rapid expansion economically, transformed from an agricultural, to manufactory industrial and, finally, to a high-tech-oriented society within two decades. Economic prosperity enhanced education and encouraged cultural production. At the same time, a well-educated middle class expected not only greater quantity, but also better quality, of cultural production. In the 1970s, the Taiwan film industry produced one to two hundred mandarin films per year, of which a large number were martial art films.[5] A large quantity of escapist commercial films and anti-communist and military propaganda could no longer satisfy the taste of a growing middle class cultivated by better education and frequent exposure to international film culture through international film festivals and worldwide travel. For example, the Central Motion Pictures Corporation (CMPC) spent 40 million New Taiwan dollars solely on publicity for its big-budget propagandist film *Heroes and Martyrs of the Great Lake* in 1980, while the box-office return was only 5 million, one eighth of its publicity cost.[6] In 1983, after a couple years of decline of box-office values, Qiong Yao, personification of Taiwanese commercially successful melodrama during the 1960s and 70s, had to declare the bankruptcy of her personal company, Super Star Motion Picture Company.[7] Huang Jianye, well-known Taiwan film critic, compares the box-office failures of these two genres to the 'vote of no confident for the Taiwan film industry of several decades … from the moviegoing public'.[8] He describes New Cinema film-makers as 'fortunate':

They were fortunate because the emergence of the Taiwan New Cinema occurred at a moment of crisis in the film industry when the public taste remained undetermined by any preconceived model. During this period, filmmakers, especially directors and

screenwriters, enjoyed such a freedom that we cannot help envying their great fortune. It's hard to believe our eyes if we look at how producers gave complete freedom to the creativeness of the filmmakers in *In Our Time* (1982), *Sandwich Man* (1983), especially *That Day on the Beach* (Edward Yang, 1983). More astonishingly, all these three films were sponsored by CMPC, the studio owned by the Nationalist Party used to produce heavy-handed ideological propagandist pieces.[9]

In other words, the New Cinema Movement started at the CMPC, the cinematic mouthpiece of the Nationalist Party. In 1980, Ming Ji, director of the CMPC, hired two young screenwriters – Xiao Ye and Wu Nien-jen; both had already been well recognised in local film and literary circles – to head, respectively, the planning section and the general editing section. Ming Ji, who had previously promoted propagandist films, including the great box-office failure *Heroes and Martyrs of the Great Lake*, followed the advice of his two young reform-minded employers almost 100 per cent. Both Xiao Ye and Wu Nien-jen contributed to the scripts of a large number of New Cinema works. For a brief period, the two writers played crucial roles in promoting New Cinema by transforming the mouthpiece of the party as the home of young film-makers rebellious against more than three decades of film-making practice, sustained by the same party, partly because certain (enlightened?) party leaders in cultural production, such as Ming Ji and James Soong, director of the Media department, realised the need to open up in order to revive the film market domestically and internationally.

From the point of view of these open-minded governmental leaders in the cultural scene, the New Cinema Movement provided a strategy for them to break away from the dead-end created by the cultural policy that had lasted for several decades: on the one hand, absurd ideological control, for example, the wife of a policeman in a Taiwanese film must be perfectly virtuous;[10] and on the other hand, thoughtless commercialisation in worn-out genres such as Wu Xian and romance. This combination created an overall escapist atmosphere in Taiwan cinema, an atmosphere that had become increasingly tiresome in the eyes of a great number of local moviegoers.

The coincidence between film-makers' artistic aspiration and the strategy chosen by a few cultural officials, however, was based on a misconception: that a more sophisticated film culture would lead to a more commercially successful Taiwan film industry. Not surprisingly, the apparently limitless support the CMPC offered to New Cinema did not last long, while the resistance coming from other official channels concerning censorship and selection for awards often remained powerful. Despite the short-term love affair between the CMPC and the New Cinema Movement, although the movement greatly improved the quality of film-making according to international standards, it was not the right strategy with which to respond to the crisis of the local film industry for the government, whose main concern was marketing domestic cultural products.

Regarding Xiao Ye and Wu Nianjen, the two screenwriters responsible for helping the New Cinema obtain this powerful but short-lived support from the CMPC, their vision was significantly different from, and much more idealistic than, the one that motivated the few officials like Ming Ji. As writers who also participated in the Native Soil Movement in literature, they were more concerned with the development of a local film culture, which, as part of reconfiguration of Taiwanese cultural identity, would become competitive at the international level. In this sense, they helped establish continuity between Native Soil literature and New Cinema in their common concern with contemporary Taiwanese culture, while paying special attention to the cinematographic quality of film as an art.[11]

A great number of scripts selected for New Cinema directors came from Native Soil literature. Huang Chunming, the well-known Native Soil novelist, wrote the three short stories based on which Hou and his colleagues directed *Sandwich Man*. After its box-office success, Huang's works sold like hot cakes during the movement. *A Flower in the Rainy Night* (Wang Tong, 1983), a melodrama about the life of a prostitute, was one of the most successful New Cinema works in terms of box office. Another great box-office hit of New Cinema was the 1983 film directed by Yu Kanping, *Papa, Can You Hear Me Sing?*, a musical and a bitter-sweet melodrama about a deaf soldier from the mainland and his adopted daughter, who became a pop singer in her youth. This film was so popular that it was repeatedly screened in public (eight times within five months), and its box office surpassed 40 million.[12] The songs of Julie Su in this film were so popular in Taiwan during the 1980s that their residual popularity has remained

influential on the mainland. In Jia Zhangke's 2006 award-winning film *Still Life*, for example, a bald pop singer still performs this film's theme song in one of its most memorable scenes.

Despite their box-office successes, few New Cinema film critics paid attention to these two popular melodramas, except mentioning them as somewhat negative examples of the movement, partly because critics believed that they catered to crowd-pleasing generic conventions; their compromises supposedly made their works formalistically less refined. Nevertheless, since both *A Flower* and *Papa* have certain native appeal rooted in local reality, nobody has denied that these two works belonged to New Cinema, despite their supposedly lower qualities. Zhan Hongzhi, the author of the New Cinema manifesto, for example, described *A Flower* as 'mediocre work but a great box office hit'.[13] In his disparaging review of *Papa*, Huang Jianye, another important New Cinema promoter, criticised Yu Kanping's musical as 'catering to cheap sentimentalism of audience'.[14]

If Taiwan New Cinema critics and general audience agreed with the need to produce films rooted in local culture in terms of subject matter, however, they had somewhat opposite views concerning its forms. Many moviegoers, despite their distaste for previous Taiwan films saturated with escapism, were more interested in dramatised stories, a familiar form for them because of their decades of viewing experiences, than in the contemplative display of social reality from an intellectual perspective exemplified by Edward Yang's formalistically impeccable modernist works; while New Cinema critics emphasised 'creativity, artistic quality, and cultural self-awareness' in their manifesto,[15] to a large extent precluding excessive sentimentality in popular melodrama.

Since Taiwan has always been an important market for Hong Kong films, most Taiwanese film-makers grew up watching much more entertaining commercial movies from Hong Kong than the local propagandist pieces.[16] Hong Kong New Wave in the late 1970s, in which often West-trained young local directors started focusing on Hong Kong culture and further professionalising the film industry, had provoked strong reaction from Taiwan cinema film-makers, and motivated them to reform their own film tradition while paying special attention to their local culture. Even though Hong Kong New Wave inspired Taiwan New Cinema, the fate of Taiwan film-makers considerably differed from that of their Hong Kong counterparts in post-New Cinema era. Hong Kong New Wave could never afford to separate itself from commercial film-making as Taiwan New Cinema tried to do at the height of the movement, since Hong Kong film-makers have always relied on the market, their only financial source.

Despite the limited domestic market, a few New Cinema film-makers continued to make popular melodramas rooted in local culture after 1986. This group included Chen Kunhou, director of *Growing Up*, one of the two first New Cinema works released in 1982, and Wang Tong, director of the 1983 box-office hit *A Flower*. The receptions of these films from critics and audience remained subdued. Chen made his last film *Promising Miss Bowie* in 1990; while Wang's 1989 *Banana Paradise* attracted critics' attention partly because it examined the same period, namely the beginning of the Nationalist rule in the late 1940s, as Hou Hsiao-hsien's award-winning *City of Sadness* (1989). None of these films was able to revive the initial interest of domestic audience in New Cinema. It is worthwhile to mention Wu Nien-jen, the screenwriter who, along with Xiao Ye, succeeded in obtaining almost unconditional support from the CMPC for New Cinema briefly in the early 1980s; Wu directed two films in the 1990s: *A Borrowed Life* (1994)[17] and *Buddha Bless America* (1996). Both films can be considered a continuation of the New Cinema Movement, as they combine cultural awareness of Native Soil literature, autobiographical tradition of early New Cinema works and sophisticated cinematography. As an activist disappointed by the limited audience in Taiwan for films like his own, however, Wu withdrew from the film-making scene after his second film to host a popular show in Taiwanese, entitled *Taiwan Nianzhen qing* (Nian-jen's Love for Taiwan). Later, he explained his switch from cinema to TV in an interview: 'these television programs may have a greater influence on society and reach a much larger audience'[18] – a statement that summarises the situation of domestic reception for post-New Cinema works.

Despite the dismal situation of Taiwan cinema, Tsai Ming-liang and Chang Tso-chi, two directors of the younger generation, emerged 'from the ashes of New Taiwan Cinema in the early 1990s' – if we borrow Michael Berry's expression.[19] Although each of them has chosen a highly personal path, both have been visibly influenced by New Taiwan Cinema.

After having directed TV movies for several years, Tsai Ming-liang, a Chinese-Malaysian immigrant, made his debut film, *Rebels of the Neon God* in 1992, a film about adolescent delinquents in Taipei. Upon its release, the film immediately attracted critical attention from the milieu of New Cinema circle, although film-makers such as Wu Nianjen expressed some reservation about its conspicuous debts to Hou Hsiao-hsien's early movies.[20] Tsai, however, demonstrates much more independence in his second feature, *Vive l'amour* (1994), which presents the accidental encounters of three youngsters illegally living in an unoccupied Taipei luxury apartment on different occasions.[21] In this film, almost all the trademark elements of his late works are there – absence of communication, solitude, disintegration of family, impossible sexual relations, environmental disaster – in short, all the existential angst that haunts urban residents in a ultra-modern cosmopolitan city presented in camp style.[22] Like Hou Hsiao-hsien and Edward Yang, Tsai Ming-liang has become an important author for international art-film fans.[23] Nevertheless, Tsai has gone much further in terms of modernist aesthetics in his almost idiosyncratic style; a case in point is his film *I Don't Want Sleep Alone* (Tsai, 2006), focusing on a protagonist who, aphasic and paralysed in an accident, lives in a linguistically and culturally alien world.

Compared with Tsai Ming-liang, Chang Tso-chi has remained relatively unknown in the international art circle, despite a number of awards for his films, which, however, fare better in terms of domestic box office than usual New Cinema works. Having successively worked as an assistant director of two New Taiwan Cinema directors at the opposite ends: Hou Hsiao-hsien and Yu Kanping (director of *Papa, Can You Hear Me Sing?* one of the rare box-office hits of New Taiwan Cinema in 1983), Chang did his New Cinema apprenticeship in art film as well as in commercial melodrama. Like Tsai, after a TV career at the beginning of the 1990s, Chang realised his first feature *Shooting in the Dark* in 1993, a film of which he denies authorship because of a conflict with the Hong Kong producer concerning post-production.[24] Often changing his film scripts on shoot, following the personal development of his non-professional cast (which has included those with special needs, as well as gangsters), Chang has created a hyper-realistic aesthetic in his juvenile delinquency movies to the extent that he even tried to portray the fantasy of his characters realistically.[25] Like most of his TV dramas or documentaries, his features (all together only six) focus on juvenile delinquency, except his 2009 film *How Are You Dad?*, a film composed of ten short episodes of different father figures, a thematic reminiscence of Yu Kanping's famous melodrama, despite their stylistic differences.

The influence of Taiwan New Cinema on their works notwithstanding, it is difficult to group Tsai and Chang as its second generation directors, largely because they have followed completely separate paths in their film-making. Similar to Fruit Chan in relation to Hong Kong New Wave,[26] both can be classified as Taiwan independent film-makers – independent from each other, independent from the New Cinema Movement and independent from the Taiwan film industry in general.

Unlike Hong Kong New Wave, Taiwan New Cinema started with strong support from the official studio, as short-lived as this support was. Unlike Hong Kong New Wave, the Taiwan film industry has never truly been supported by a well-established market. As a result, Hong Kong New Wave directors remained productive after the end of this movement mostly as commercial film-makers until the decline of the local film industry in the 1990s, while Taiwan New Cinema lost most of its initial contributors immediately after the end of the movement, although Hou Hsiao-hsien and Edward Yang have continued their work as great art-film authors in the world. The work of these two film-makers, despite the muted reaction from the local audience, can be considered the most important legacy of Taiwan New Cinema.

In order to illustrate this legacy, I will briefly analyse the latest works on Taiwan by these two authors, namely: Edward Yang's *Yiyi* and Hou Hsiao-hsien's *Three Times* (2005). Yang's film, *A One and a Two* (*Yiyi*) was released in 2000 as his swan song, seven years before his untimely death in 2007. In the meantime, Hou Hsiao-hsien, since his *Three Times*, has not directed a major film on Taiwan, which is the trademark of his important earlier works. Although Hou, commissioned by the Musée d'Orsay, did a loose remake of a 1956 French film, *Le voyage du ballon rouge* (*Flight of the Red Balloon*) in 2007, like his 2003 *Café Lumière* (*Kôhî jikô*) dedicated to the memory of Yasujiro Ozu, this French-sponsored film has nothing to do with Taiwan. In a sense, these two films incorporate different elements of their previous works such that

they can be considered as syntheses of their creative journeys.

From the beginning of his career, Edward Yang remained highly conscientious, constructing narrative with all possible cinematic means. Passionate about Japanese Manga since his childhood and trained in computer programming despite his own artistic inclination, Yang decided to switch his computer engineer career to film-making after having watched a film by Wim Wenders. Closer to European modernist aesthetics, Yang's works from the very beginning have always been favourite topics of discussions in the circle of art-film fans across cultures, largely because his cosmopolitan urban images have no boundary in the world. Although Yang claimed: 'I tried to get everything as average as possible,'[27] art-film and cultural critics consider his works as exemplifying modernism in the era of global modernity.[28] What makes Yang's works stand out is not his rejection of narrative, but rather his perfectionism and originality in cinematic narration, which might be interpreted as 'average' – according to the director's own low-key expression.

Yiyi exemplifies Yang's modernist aesthetics in its maturity while evoking his works in the past. For example, Fatty, a teenage boy, murders the English teacher of Lili, his girlfriend, because he suspects the teacher slept with her. This incident reminds us of *Terrorisers* (1986), in which Yang showed us how easily a bored doctor, a seemingly normal-looking and ordinary individual in the cold and impersonal urban environment, can turn into a murderer at the drop of a hat, as well as of his *A Brighter Summer Day* (1991), in which Xiaosi, a young boy, commits an absurd murder, also because of his desperation in a messy relationship. The relationship between NJ, the protagonist, and Sherry, his childhood sweetheart, is somewhat reminiscence of a childhood romance that can no longer sustain changes brought about by fast-paced urban life as in his *Taipei Story* (1985). At the same time, *Yiyi* presents Taipei with Yang's usual precise and unemotional camera angle. What differs from his preceding works is that, in *Yiyi*, we often gaze at Taipei through the subjective perspective of a precocious young boy, NJ's adorable son Yangyang. This innocent gaze adds warmth and humour to Yang's usually unsentimental portrayal of the city.

Yiyi, a well-constructed melodrama, focuses on a Taipei family headed by a computer engineer father played by Wu Nianjen. In its portrayals of intricate

From time to time, the filmic world in *Yiyi* is filtered through the somewhat innocent camera lens of the observing child Yangyang

personal and work relationships of the family members – the parents, a teenage daughter and a young son, as well as of their relatives: Grandma and the brother-in-law – the film disrupts the established continuous pattern of traditional Hollywood narrative through its neatly original cinematography. Instead of sustaining continuity in the plots, linkages of different scenes often emphasise the contingency of life stories for various characters. Instead of creating a beginning, a development and an ending, Edward Yang's frequent use of parallel shots in this film provides a circulatory narration, as the end often joins the point of departure. Overall, this circulatory narration shows the impasse of human relations. Yang's impeccably constructed cinematography, however, not only neutralises this impasse but also almost makes it enjoyable with a touch of humour – especially from the perspective of the cute little Yangyang. The boy still dreams of being able to make changes through his pictures by telling people's own stories they are not aware of, as he diligently photographs the backs of people's heads.

Another Taiwan New Cinema master, Hou Hsiao-hsien, has completed a different journey. Prior to his first contribution to New Cinema, one episode in *Sandwich Man*, Hou had already made three commercially successful romances in Taiwan in the mood of conventional 'sanitary realism'. Having worked up through the hierarchy of the local film industry, he enjoyed his encounter with other young directors freshly returned from abroad in the early 1980s while feeling somewhat 'anxious' about his own lack of similar professional training and international exposure. Zhu Tianwen, a well-known writer in the literary circle and his screenwriter, gave him Shen Congwen's autobiography. Hou found the best expression of his vision of the world in the book of the first generation Chinese Native Soil writer, as he explained: 'The book used an objective and understated narrative to let the reader feel that even the saddest and most terrible thing can be tolerated by kind-heartedness and love.'[29] This vision, which has dominated his film-making journey since then, has helped Hou distance his works from his initially more conventional aesthetics.

On the one hand, Hou stays close to the Taiwanese (and Chinese) culture and tradition, thus appearing more 'Chinese' in the eyes of international audiences than his cosmopolitan rival Edward Yang. On the other hand, his aesthetics, partly inspired by Shen Congwen's naturalism, goes much further than Yang's impeccably constructed urban melodrama in subverting traditional cinematic narrative structure. The details of his images and sounds are often more revealing than dialogues. Thanks to these details, Hou's films provide personal stories with a sense of historicity and a touch of poetry, as if his works on private lives reveal parts of Taiwan history more intimately, and thus more powerfully, than history books, such as in the case of his 2005 film *Three Times*.

Three Times returns to the form of his first contribution to the New Cinema, *Sandwich Man*. Nevertheless, he made his film of three episodes from the perspective of a single auteur, to the extent that analogical relationships in three periods played by the same two stars remain consistently connected through a vague pattern of repetitions. Further, the three stories in the film can be described as three condensed versions of his previous movies: 'A Time for Love' reminds us of the same historical ambiance and personal touch as in his autobiographical film *A Time to Live, A Time to Die* (1985); 'A Time for Freedom' recreated the sensual atmosphere in the brothels in *Flowers of Shanghai*; the fast-paced third part 'A Time for Youth' stands out from Hou's usual deliberated cinematography as his *Millennium Mambo*

(2001), revealing his hard-to-hide distaste for contemporary lifestyle.

The literal translation of his Chinese title is 'Best Times' (*Zuihao de shiguang*), which means 'not the prettiest or most fun times, but rather, those moments that only exist in our memories, those moments that can be conjured up but never relived or replicated'.[30] In Hou's works, individual memories are intimately linked to a collective past. In order to invoke collective memories, things of the past have become surrogates of personal expressions of emotions to the extent that distinctions between the collective and the personal are blurred, if not erased. The three episodes are marked by important historical moments: first, 'A Time for Love' started with 1966, the beginning of the Cultural Revolution on the mainland; second, 'A Time for Freedom', 1911, the establishment of the first Chinese republic; third, 'A Time for Youth', 2005, the year of release of this film. The structure of three stories is similar amid historical changes: romance between two characters played by Shu Qi and by Zhang Zhen. Despite different paces and historical moments, the narrative patterns are similarly elliptic; the major difference between the three shorts is found in lifestyles, media, clothes and expressions of love determined by historical circumstance and subtly captured by Hou's discerning camera.

Despite their limited popularity at home, Edward Yang and Hou Hsiao-hsien are two great authors in the

Episode on 'A Time for Love' in Hou Hsiao-hsien's *Three Times*

Episodes on 'A Time for Freedom' and 'A Time for Youth' in *Three Times*

cinematic history of Chinese-language communities, largely because they are products of Taiwan's unique cultural and social circumstances: changes in the cultural scene brought about by its political democratisation combined with Taiwan's weak domestic film market. In the 1970s and the 80s, three Chinese communities, Hong Kong, Taiwan and mainland China, followed separate paths in reforming their cinematic cultures. Mainland film-makers, Fifth Generation and later independent film-makers, have been restricted by often-arbitrary censorship as well as by an unevenly developed domestic market; while Hong Kong New Wave directors are easily submerged by the successful Hong Kong global pop cultural market in its single-minded focus on box-office value. In both regions, for different reasons reform-minded film-makers had to compromise themselves so much that most of them lost their initial creative edge.

Like the Fifth Generation, Taiwan New Cinema started with state institutional support; Taiwan directors have also suffered much less from unpredictable state censorship than their mainland counterparts. With the initial institutional support, unlike the Hong Kong New Wave, these film-makers could afford to make claims against commercial trends. This initially privileged position ended up playing against them. As official institutions and the general public withdrew their short-lived support, a dismal domestic film market forced a large number of New Cinema participants to drop out. Edward Yang and Hou Hsiao-hsien, however, had already created a niche in the global market within the short duration of the New Cinema Movement thanks to their international recognition among art-film fans. Further, both of them have chosen uncompromising personal paths, likely because even compromise would not have changed the bleak situation of their domestic market anyway. Relatively independent from box-office value and political restrictions, the two directors have occupied enviable positions because they have been able to concentrate on perfecting their art with the help of international (especially Asian) investors. In this circumstance, Edward Yang, with his globally oriented modernist cinematography, and Hou Hsiao-hsien, with his lyric aesthetics rooted in traditional Chinese culture, firmly established their signatures as authors in the era of global pop culture, where even the expression 'author' seems already out of fashion.

Notes

1. Zhan Hongzhi, '1987 Taiwan Film Manifesto', in Jiao Xiongping (ed.), *Taiwan xin dianying* (Taiwan New Cinema) (Taipei: Shibao chubanshe, 1988), pp. 111–18.

2. Ti Wei, 'How Did Hou Hsiao-hsien Change Taiwan Cinema?: A Critical Reassement', *Inter-Asia Cultural Studies* vol. 9 no. 2 (2008), p. 278.

3. Huang Jianye. '1983 Taiwan Cinema Retrospective', in Jiao, *Taiwan xin dianying*, p. 54.

4. Zhan, '1987 Taiwan Film Manifesto', p. 111.

5. Chen Feibao, *Taiwan dianying shihua* (Narrative History of Taiwan Cinema) (Beijing: Zhongguo dianying chuban-she, 1987), p. 233.

6. Ibid., p. 315.

7. Ibid., p. 159.

8. Huang, '1983 Taiwan Cinema Retrospective', p. 51.

9. Ibid., p. 54.

10. Ibid., p. 52.

11. See my introduction to *Confronting Modernity in the Cinemas of Taiwan and Mainland China* (Cambridge: University of Cambridge Press, 2001), pp. 18–19.

12. Chen, *Taiwan dianying shihua*, p. 333.

13. Zhan, 'The Arrival and the Departure of Taiwan New Cinema', in Jiao, *Taiwan xin dianying*, p. 30.

14. Huang Jianye, '*Papa, Can You Hear me Sing?*', in Jiao, *Taiwan xiu dianying*, p. 373.

15. Zhan, '1987 Taiwan film Manifesto', p. 112.

16. Jiao Xiongping's preface to her *Xianggang dianying feng-mao* (State of Hong Kong Cinema) (Taipei: Shibao weihua chubanshe, 1987), p. 11.

17. See Chen Kuan-hsing, 'A Borrowed life in *Banana Paradise*: De-Cold War/Decolonization, or Modernity and Its Tears', in Chris Berry and Feii Lu (eds), *Island on the Edge: Taiwan New Cinema and After* (Hong Kong: Hong Kong University Press, 2005), pp. 39–53; and also my study of this film: 'A Cinematic Parallax View: Taiwanese Identity and the Japanese Colonial Past', forthcoming in *positions: east asia cultural critique*.

18. Wu Nien-jen, 'Wu Nien-jen: Writing Taiwan in the Shadows of Cultural Colonialism', in Michael Berry, *Speaking in Images: Interviews with Contemporary Chinese Filmmakers* (New York: Columbia University Press, 2005), p. 319.

19. Tsai Ming-liang, 'Trapped in the Past', in Berry, *Speaking in Images*, p. 363.

20. Wu spoke to me about his reservation in a private conversation in Taiwan in summer 1993.

21. Chris Berry, 'Where Is the Love? Hyperbolic Realism and Indulgence in *Vive l'amour*,' in Berry and Lu, *Island on the Edge*, pp. 89–100.

22. See Emilie Yueh-yu Yeh and Darrell William Davis's chapter, 'Camping Out with Tsai Ming-liang', in their book *Taiwan Film Directors: A Treasure Island* (New York: Columbia University Press, 2005), pp. 217–48.

23. See for example, one French monograph on him: Jean-Pierre Rehm et al., *Tsai Ming-liang* (Paris: Dis-Voir, 1999).

24. Chang Tso-chi, 'Shooting from the Margins', Berry, *Speaking in Images*, pp. 404–5.

25. See Chris Berry, 'Haunted Realism: Postcoloniality and the Cinema of Chang Tso-chi', in Darrell Willian Davis and Ru-shou Robert Chen, *Cinema Taiwan: Politics, Popularity and State of the Arts* (London: Routledge, 2007), pp. 33–59.

26. See my article, 'Fruit Chan's *Dumpling* – New "Diary of a Madman" in Post-Mao Global Capitalism', *China Information*, October 2010.

27. John Anderson, *Edward Yang* (Champaign: University of Illinois Press, 2005), p. 4.

28. See, for example, Huang Jianye's book devoted to Yang's films and Jameson's lengthy essay on his *Terrorisers*. Huang Jianye, *Yang Dechang dianying yangju* (Studies on Edward Yang's Films) (Taipei: Yuanliu, 1995), and Fredric Jameson, 'Remapping Taipei', *The Geopolitical Aesthetic: Cinema and Space in the World System* (Bloomington: Indiana University Press, 1992), pp. 114–56.

29. Ti Wei, 'How Did Hou Hsiao-hsien Change Taiwan Cinema?', p. 273, and also see Davis and Chen, *Cinema Taiwan*, pp. 157–61.

30. Hou Hsiao-hsien, 'Cinema and History: Critical Reflections', Petrus Liu, trans., *Inter-Asia Cultural Studies* vol. 9 no. 1 (2008), p. 190.

Further Reading in *Chinese Films in Focus II*

On Hou Hsiao-hsien, see Chapter 14, '*Flowers of Shanghai*: Visualising Ellipses and (Colonial) Absence' by Gary G. Xu, and Chapter 27, '*A Time to Live, A Time to Die*: A Time to Grow' by Corrado Neri.

For Edward Yang, see Chapter 34, '*Yi Yi*: Reflections on Reflexive Modernity in Taiwan' by David Leiwei Li.

On Ang Lee, see Chapter 9, '*Crouching Tiger, Hidden Dragon*: Cultural Migrancy and Translatability' by Felicia Chan, and Chapter 30, '*Wedding Banquet*: A Family (Melodrama) Affair' by Chris Berry.

On Tsai Ming-liang, see Chapter 29, '*Vive L'Amour*: Eloquent Emptiness' by Fran Martin.

On other Taiwan New Cinema and post-TNC films, see Chapter 22, '*The Personals*: Backward Glances, Knowing Looks and the Voyeur Film' by Margaret Hillenbrand, and Chapter 15, '*Formula 17*: Mainstream in the Margins' by Brian Hu.

14 The Hong Kong New Wave

A Critical Reappraisal

Vivian P. Y. Lee

The 'Hong Kong New Wave' commonly refers to a group of directors who began film-making in the late 1970s, a time when the local cinema had become artistically sterile and formulaic, and Cantonese film production had virtually came to a halt. The New Wave films produced between 1979 and 1982 marked 'the most intense period of New Wave output',[1] which was later consolidated when the 'second wave' joined forces with their predecessors in the mid-1980s.[2] Using western cinematic techniques and narrative strategies to address local issues and subject matter, New Wave films reinvigorated the local film industry and became an important arena for the articulation of a local subjectivity in times of social change and political uncertainties. Three decades after its first appearance, the Hong Kong New Wave is seen as a landmark in the history of Hong Kong cinema, signalling a transition from a culturally dependent (China-centred) and stylistically outmoded enterprise into a dynamic creative force embracing both the complexities and sophistication of the cosmopolitan city that Hong Kong had become.

Critics generally agree that the Hong Kong New Wave was not a unified movement and, unlike the French New Wave two decades before, there was no declared oppositional agenda vis-à-vis the mainstream film industry; rather, the 'naming' of this cinematic phenomenon owed as much to the artistic ingenuities of the film-makers as to the intellectual currents and social aspirations of the time.[3] Three interrelated perspectives stand out in the critical reception of the New Wave: the political, social and economic environment that provided the impetus for change within the local film industry in the 1970s and 80s; the symbiotic relations between television and cinema in Hong Kong in the 1970s; and studies on film style, cinematic techniques and subject matter or the 'social relevance' of New Wave films. Western film school training is a credential reflected in the New Wave's visual style. Soon after the release of their first films, the group came to be seen as a champion for a modern cinema situated midway between an 'elite' or auteur cinema in the western sense and a home-grown entity born out of Hong Kong's unique historical and cultural situation.

This chapter is a critical reappraisal of the legacy of the New Wave in light of the imagination of a 'flexible' local cinematic identity[4] in New Wave films vis-à-vis late British colonial culture and a *fin-de-siècle* postcolonial sensibility complicated by ambivalences towards the return to China. A selection of films will be analysed through the prisms of 'migrants and otherness' and 'the city in flux', two recurrent thematic concerns informed by a budding sense of the local as a geocultural hybrid, seen and sought through regional and translocal connections in the cinematic imagination. Some of the films discussed below exhibit a diasporic consciousness that de-essentialises 'Chineseness', while others configure the city as a heteroglossic space, and all tend to problematise, if not resist, normative identity assignations. The influence of the New Wave on later developments will be considered in the last section, 'Afterlife'.

Migrants and the 'Other' Hong Kong Story

Reflecting on the problematic of the 'local' in pre-1997 Hong Kong cinema, Ackbar Abbas comments that 'stories about Hong Kong always turned into stories about somewhere else'.[5] On a similar note, Leo Lee

Ou-fan writes: 'it takes the "other" to understand the self' in the (post)colonial city's cinematic imagination of history.[6] Yingjin Zhang, reflecting on Hong Kong's regional Cantonese culture, remarks that Hong Kong film-makers 'approach Chinese culture … as one consisting of multiple regional cultures characterized by many regional dialects'.[7] This awareness of being 'other', and of the need to seek an 'elsewhere' to locate and articulate its otherness, it seems, both pre-conditions and inspires the visual aesthetics of Hong Kong cinema.

One can trace the genealogy of 'otherness' in Hong Kong's cinematic imagination of the local across a vastly eclectic range of artistic, technical and cultural sources,[8] so much so that the local tends to be an expression, if not epitome, of a heteroglossic amalgam whose 'essence' exists in a state of perpetual flux. In the films examined below, this inherent fluidity underwrites much of the filmic rendition of a transborder geocultural realm in which the local is sought through an ongoing process of 'decentring' or 'othering'. This process inevitably invokes an 'elsewhere' or 'other place' as a site of self-articulation. In addition to irreverent citations and eclectic experimentation with techniques commonly found in Hong Kong cinema, this decentring spatial imagination obtains thematic significance in New Wave films in which multiple social, cultural and linguistic sites are interwoven into the narrative and visual schema, thus putting into question any essentialised claim to 'Chineseness' or 'Hongkongness'.

Migration began to invade the cultural imagination of Hong Kong in the 1980s, not that Hong Kong had not been acquainted with its own history as a colonial settlement and since 1949 a safe haven for émigrés and capital from Shanghai. The 1980s saw the beginning of a massive 'brain drain' to the West in the run-up to 1997 and an unprecedented influx of legal and illegal immigrants from the mainland. Meanwhile, the Hong Kong government was plagued by waves of refugees arriving on its shores from post-liberation Vietnam. Little surprise that migrant figures of all sorts began to appear on local screens big and small. Ann Hui's 'Vietnam Trilogy' consists of one television document drama *The Boy from Vietnam* (1978), and two feature films, *The Story of Woo Viet* (1981) and *Boat People* (1982); Tsui Hark followed up on the success of John Woo's *A Better Tomorrow I* and *II* (1986, 1987) with a third installment (*A Better Tomorrow III*, 1989) set in Vietnam.

The new-found interest in illegal immigrants or the 'mainland other' was not limited to New Wave films. For instance, the so-called 'big circle gang' (*tai huen zai* in Cantonese) abounded in police and gangster films (e.g., Johnny Mak's *The Long Arm of the Law* (1984) and its three sequels). More sympathetic portraits appear in Alfred Cheung's comic-action series, *Her Fatal Ways*, featuring an innocent and upright female police officer on a temporary assignment in Hong Kong.[9] It is fair to say that migrants are a significant demographic on Hong Kong screens in the 1980s, and they are by no means a homogeneous entity.[10]

Given the historical condition of migration in Hong Kong, the social and cultural migrant has appeared in myriad forms in the local cinema. Essentially a figure of movement over space and time, in some Hong Kong films the migrant embodies the dual sense of movement 'beyond' and movement 'within', that is, their diasporic consciousness is both refined and redefined by ambivalence towards movement.

Among the New Wave directors, Ann Hui was among the first to explore the complexity of this ambivalence in her portrayal of migrants in and outside Hong Kong. In her 'Vietnam Trilogy' local sentiments and anxieties are filtered through the experience of an 'other' person/country: Vietnamese coping with the trauma of war and a tyrannical authoritarian regime. The tragic fate befalling these asylum seekers and victims to domestic political violence resonates with the condition of migration and exile of Hong Kong in the latter half of the twentieth century. *Song of the Exile* (1990), a semi-autobiographical film, recasts questions about cultural and national identity in its topography of migration, dispersion and return within a story of generational conflict and reconciliation. Spanning three decades from the end of the Sino-Japanese War to the late 1970s across several historically linked locations (Manchuria, Guangzhou, Macau, Hong Kong and Japan), the story of generational conflicts unfolds in layers of flashback sequences of a young woman, Hueyin (Maggie Cheung) and her Japanese mother Aiko (Lu Hsiao-fen), as mother and daughter struggle to come to terms with the past. The film uses voiceovers and visual motifs – mirrors, point-of-view shots, visual parallels and spatial/temporal overlaps – as transitions to juxtapose Hueyin and Aiko's memories before it funnels their conflicting visions through an intimate journey into Aiko's lesser-known past in Japan, where Hueyin and Aiko are able to articulate, and share, their long-suppressed sense of displacement and alienation. Mirrors, Patricia Erens observes, create a 'split' in the screen composition to highlight the 'illusion of a unified identity'.[11] This split is further complicated by a dialogue mixed with Cantonese, English, Japanese and Mandarin, and the almost universal experience of geocultural and temporal re-/dislocation.

The Japan episode unites the two women in their respective exile and displacement, prompting them – and the audience – to reflect on the nature and meaning of identity. The ending of the film suggests that 'home' is not a given but an active choice. Instead of a fixation on 'homeland' as a geographically and ideologically bounded 'place', to these individuals 'home' is an ongoing act of negotiating one's place in the world. In sharp contrast are the grandfather, to whom '(mainland) China' is forever 'the motherland' (*zuguo*); and Aiko's youngest brother, an ex-Kamikaze fighting a perpetual war within. The crippled figures of the Chinese nationalist and the Japanese militarist embody Hui's critique of a monolithic understanding of nationhood.

Migration is also a recurrent motif in the work of Allen Fong. Blending fact and fiction, *Just Like Weather* (1986) tells the story of a young couple going through a crisis in their relationship. The prospect of emigrating to the US further deepens the tension between the two. Adopting his favourite docu-drama realism, Fong self-reflexively plays the role of a documentary film-maker, setting up interviews with his subjects in both Hong Kong and the US. The US is frequently used as a symbolic reference in Fong's films to allude to the historical and social condition of migration in Hong Kong, the desire for a better life elsewhere, and the need to escape from a present state of impasse. In *Ah Ying* (1983), a US-trained drama teacher inspires a working-class young woman's dream to become an actress. When his 'mission' in the film is accomplished, Cheung, the drama teacher, returns to the US. In Fong's words, Cheung 'functions as a catalyst' in Ah Ying's life.[12] Fong's first film, *Father and Son* (1981), also makes use of the US as a symbolic reference to anchor the tension and contrast between 'home' (a symbol of economic hardship, lack of social mobility, generational conflicts) and 'elsewhere' (a land of opportunity, better education, better future). *Father and Son* embraces the *ethos* of both the older and the younger generations caught in times of social change. In a self-referential manoeuvre, Fong's young male protagonist has a passion for film-making and is offered a job in local television in the end. (In *Ah Ying*, Cheung also has a passion for the cinema, and Ah Ying is invited to a second interview at the local television station.)

Different from *Song of the Exile*, in which the 'diaspora' literally is the origin(s) of the local, the US in Fong's films is an 'elsewhere' through which the aspirations and frustrations at the home front are articulated. Symbolically, the intellectual/artist figure as the catalyst for a budding sense of self-identity, quite prominent in *Ah Ying* but also implicitly present in the other two films, illuminates the complex relationship between 'western' knowledge and local agency. Instead of a unified vision of how this relationship has evolved or will develop, Fong's lens captures the contingency of the present as each story takes on a life of its own.

Migration takes a different turn in Yim Ho's *Homecoming* (1984), which tells the story of the journey of a woman, Shan Shan (Koo Mei-wah) from Hong Kong to her hometown in China to visit her childhood friends, Ah Chun (Siqin Gaowa) and Hao-chong (Tse Wai-hung). Stephen Teo describes this film as 'an homage to China ... tempered by a city-sider's critical perspective'.[13] Among the New Wave directors, Yim has shown a closer cultural affinity to China that underscores many of his films, from *Homecoming* to *Red Dust* (1990) and *King of Chess* (1992, co-directed with Tsui Hark, discussed below). In *Homecoming* the contrast between urban Hong Kong and rural China works to evoke a sense of nostalgic innocence, while the tension and discrepancy between the two places, both in material and psychological terms, are dramatised by the intense emotions in the narrative. This time, the Hongkonger is perceived as the 'other' who takes refuge in the simplicity and tranquility of her home village. Yim's cinematic homecoming is an exceptionally 'serene', and less politicised, rendition of the China–Hong Kong relationship in the pre-handover years. Made not long after his father's death, this film can be seen as 'a mental journey about departing Hong Kong and returning to China'.[14]

The New Wave's relationship with 'imaginary China' is varied and nuanced, and often carries a tinge of scepticism, if not cynicism. This is especially true for Tsui Hark, whose 'new-style martial arts films' (for example the *Once Upon a Time in China* series (1991–4) starring Jet Li as the young kung fu master Huang Feihong/Wong Fei-hung) are famous for their use of 'national allegory' to articulate Hong Kong's political anxiety and identity crisis in the run-up to 1997.[15]

In *King of Chess*, cultural identity and the 'China Syndrome'[16] receive an original treatment combining Tsui's cynical non-conformism and Yim's philosophical contemplation, resulting in a syncretic film text that exemplifies the New Wave's penchant for genre bending and stylistic experimentation. Straddling two distinct historical time-spaces and adapted from two fictional texts (a novel by Chang Hsi-kuo from Taiwan and a novella by A. Cheng from mainland China),[17] *King of Chess* is a border-crossing film at the textual, historical and socio-political levels, and its self-conscious hybridity is a first major attempt to seriously bring in the 'other' Chinese cultural space – Taiwan – into the filmic contemplation of 'China' and 'Chineseness'.

Chang Hsi-guo's novel is set in late 1970s Taipei, a story about a Gobang genius (*wuzi shentong*) who has telepathic power. The juxtaposition between the other-worldly child genius and the worldly and unscrupulous adult characters in the film not only reveals human folly, but also poses the fundamental question about human intent in a largely unknown Universe. A. Cheng's novella recalls the tumultuous years of the Cultural Revolution in the late 1960s. Framed by the memory of an I-narrator, the legendary victory of Wang Yisheng (Tony Leung Ka-fai) over nine players in one single match becomes a vehicle for an exploration into the enduring virtues of the Chinese cultural tradition that the novel suggests has not been completely destroyed by wars and revolutions in recent Chinese history.

The two fictional texts, separate in time and space, become interweaving segments in the film. The alternating mainland and Taipei segments are connected by the central character Cheng Ling (John Shum Kin-fun, aka John Sham). Originally a struggling Taipei artist turned entrepreneur, Cheng is recast as a Hong Kong businessman relocated to Taipei during the 1980s. The China portion of the story is told through Cheng's flashback sequences about his encounters with Wang, the chess genius, in China many years ago. In the film, Cheng Ling acts as a bridge between Taiwan and China, present and past. Although Cheng possesses certain insider knowledge of the two 'Chinas', he remains an outsider to both: in China, he was only a passer-by and observer of events; in Taiwan, he is seen as the opportunistic 'Hongkonger' with no real roots whatsoever. A central and marginal character at the

King of Chess: in between two Chinas

same time, Cheng has links to the two 'Chinas' but remains an outsider – one who seems to be in perpetual motion, unable to settle down in any 'one place', or country.

By transforming Cheng Ling into a Hong Kong observer of Taiwan and China, and someone who feels alienated from both places, the film can be said to have invented its own subject matter. Arguably, Taiwan and China are the primary settings, or screens, onto which Hong Kong's crisis consciousness is projected. Visually, the film frequently cuts between two historical time-spaces: Taiwan, a materialistic capitalist haven, is juxtaposed with its 'mirror opposite', mainland China, a revolutionary dystopia. Between the two 'Chinas', the Hong Kong subject cannot find an easy balance, but remains an in-between character, uprooted and constantly in (need of) motion.

City in Flux

Restless motion is at the core of the New Wave's action aesthetics. Rightly called the New Wave's 'action auteurs',[18] Tsui Hark and John Woo's cinematic connections go deeper than their collaboration in *A Better Tomorrow I* and *II*. (Tsui later directed the third instalment.) Among the New Wave, Tsui and Woo established their positions in the mainstream commercial cinema quite early in their careers, and both were highly innovative and experimental in action aesthetics referencing local and western sources, which soon became a mainstay in Hong Kong cinema. Although national allegory and crisis consciousness are common traits in their films, these thematic preoccupations are channelled through an action aesthetics underscored by a vision of the city where existence is in a perpetual stage of flux.

Tsui's first film in this category is *Dangerous Encounter – 1st Kind* (1980), his third feature.[19] In this film, four youngsters get into trouble with the police and some ex-US soldiers after they find a stack of cheques issued by a Japanese bank. Tsui draws upon his own childhood experience of war in Vietnam and parallels its traumatising effects on the American soldiers with the urban youth's distorted psyche in a repressive society. In this film, Hong Kong appears as a city under siege: international illegal arms deals, random killings and youth crimes are the 'main rhythm' of everyday life. The choice of shooting locations – densely populated public housing units, dilapidated old buildings, barren outskirts and a vast and enfolding cemetery – demarcates the existential wasteland that is Hong Kong where the comfort of home or domesticity is as non-existent as it is irrelevant. As a first attempt to capture the dark undercurrents of the urban city in explosive visual langauge, Tsui's film can be seen as a harbinger of the gunfight-and-bloodbath cinematography he and John Woo later would popularise. Although Tsui did not indulge in violent excess for too long,[20] his urban imagination retains its diabolic allure, which re-emerges in the sci-fi thriller *The Wicked City* (Peter Mak Tai-kit, 1992), which Tsui co-scripted and co-produced.[21]

Tsui's partnership with John Woo was short-lived but its impact on Hong Kong cinema is significant. *A Better Tomorrow* paved the way for Woo's international career that soon followed. Woo's stylistic signatures reveal a hybrid lineage of the Chinese martial arts film, the 'spaghetti' Western and the Hollywood gangster film.[22] In Woo's filmic universe, Hong Kong 'is a city beset by extreme lawlessness and graphic violence', an urban dystopia where '[c]ompeting regimes of justice … merge' without 'a hero on the right side of the law'.[23] *Hard Boiled/Lashou shentan* (1992) begins with a prolonged sequence of stylised gunfighting inside a congested Chinese teahouse and finishes off in an equally elaborated shoot-out scene in a hospital taken hostage by armed gangsters. Echoing Tsui's unrestrained exposition of urban mayhem, Woo's explosive heroics turns the urban space into a minefield of random violence, moral conflicts and existential angst. Amid the endless chaos, Woo's characters would throw in remarks that 'cue' the audience to an allegorical interpretation. An often-quoted dialogue between Tequilla (Chow Yun-Fat) and

his buddy Lung (Bowie Lam) in *Hard Boiled* drives home the shared sentiment of many (would-be) migrants:

> TEQUILLA: Have you ever considered emigrating?
>
> LUNG: No, this is my home. If I'm going to die, I want to be buried here. I wouldn't get used to living abroad. To have early tea time? Impossible.
>
> TEQUILLA: There are Chinese restaurants overseas.
>
> LUNG: But we got the original.

The urban milieu in Yim Ho's *The Happening* (1980), Patrick Tam's *Nomad* (1982) and many action and crime thriller films of this period is also infused by a restless energy and edginess more akin to the kaleidoscopic hotchpotch society of Hong Kong than the nostalgic 'cultural China' in the martial arts films of the previous generation. The city as depicted in the New Wave's action films is less a solid locale than a world adrift, where extreme violence can erupt at any moment. In *The Happening*, a youth gang gets involved in acts of violence along a chain of mishaps on a joyride. Similar to Tsui's *Dangerous Encounter*, deaths and bloodshed are routine 'happenings' in a 'wicked city' where meaning and values are dictated by chance and coincidence rather than reason or any enduring beliefs and values.

I would like to conclude this section with an early 'second wave' film, *Love Unto Waste* (1986), by Stanley Kwan, which I believe is an important transition between his predecessors and later developments. Like *King of Chess*, Kwan's film is among a few that engages Taiwan in Hong Kong's self-narrative in the pre-handover period. As a border-crossing film, *Love* consciously adopts a translocal register in characterisation, setting and plot design: a cast of popular stars of the time from Hong Kong (Tony Leung Chiu Wai, Chow Yun-Fat and Irene Wan Pik Ha) and Taiwan (Elaine Jin and popular singer Tsai Chin), diegetic Canto- and Mandarin pop performances, a detective plot, love triangles and an inchoate bunch of young drifters taking refuge from an aimless existence in short-lived pleasures. Classified as 'drama', *Love* nonetheless has imported a number of generic elements from the crime thriller and melodrama. The diegetic use of Cantonese and Mandarin pop songs in a 'sing-a-lounge' setting[24] readily places the main characters in a certain social type: the young middle class trying to 'make it' in the real world. As the narrative unfolds, their decadent lifestyle is only an

Love Unto Waste: a city of drifters

alibi for a deeply troubling psychological uprootedness. The symbolic lounge setting – an artificial space of transit – captures this sense of ennui and impermanence.

The film's interest in spatial dislocation is manifest in its credit sequence of unconnected spaces in still shots that cannot be precisely located – an office, a hotel room, an interior corridor and a banquet table in a countryside courtyard. This sequence is followed by a close-up on Yuping (Elaine Jin) and Shuling (Tsai Chin) performing Tsai's real-life Mandarin hit in front of a mirror. In the next shot, Billie (Irene Wan), in dark sunglasses, is seen lying on a hotel room bed. She gets up, opens the door and greets her visitor in French. Edited in a piecemeal manner without transitional shots, this opening sequence maps out a larger geocultural realm that alludes to Hong Kong as a site of transit not unlike a transit lounge. In a subsequent scene where a young dandy Tony begins to court Billie, we see a gigantic banner image of Billie hanging outside the Sogo Department Store in Causeway Bay, subtly reminding us of Billie's sojourn in Paris, her connection to the global commodity culture and, more specifically, Japan's cultural presence.

In Kwan's film, visual and verbal references to 'other places' abound. Precisely because of its diasporic awareness, the film's indirect references to China become even more conspicuous: 'It seems Hong Kong still has a future,' says Tony in a casual remark. His statement is visually undermined by the next cut to Shuling's body lying in a pool of blood. The film then enacts a journey to Taiwan that amounts to an encounter with the self: Yuping has an abortion (we know it is Tony's baby), the love triangle dissolves and Yuping decides to stay in her hometown for good. As in

Song of the Exile, in Kwan's film it also takes the other to understand the self, and a sense – and narrative – of 'home' has to be sought elsewhere.

Inherent in *Love* is a budding postmodernist temperament in the visual mapping of the city as a mutating, if not decentring, geocultural realm suffused with foreign signs and images. Seen in the context of the mid-1980s, *Love* is a pioneering attempt to envision the city in a regional and translocal context. In its portrayal of young people adrift in a consumerist haven, the film displaces the popular allegorical link between Hong Kong and China in its topography of dislocation and relocation. China, as a result, becomes an *extrinsic* rather than intrinsic factor. The space of the local, in turn, is constituted by an internalisation of 'other (than China) places'.

Afterlife

Focusing on the decentring vision of the local in New Wave films, this chapter has attempted to outline the hybrid geocultural imagination in the Hong Kong New Wave cinema that de-essentialises the local through multiple inflections – 'China' being only one of many. The New Wave opened up a new terrain for later interventions of which only a few can be gauged here: first, the concern with 'other spaces' was to become a distinctive feature of Hong Kong's brand of postmodernist cinema in arthouse (as in Wong Kar-wai's work) and popular films (e.g., Andrew Lau and Alan Mak's *Infernal Affairs* trilogy, 2002–3).[25] In 'pan-Asian' productions (e.g., the Pang Brothers' horror films, *The Eye* (2002) and *The Eye 2* (2004)),[26] the local is manifest in multiple localities and languages to promote transcultural identification. Second, the diasporic consciousness finds its way into Stanley Kwan's *Full Moon in New York* (1990), Peter Chan's *Comrades, Almost a Love Story* (1996), Mabel Cheung's *An Autumn's Tale* (1987) and Clara Law's *Farewell China* (1990). Different in style and uneven in artistic accomplishments, these films signify a broadening horizon in Hong Kong film-makers' cultural imagination. In the realm of martial arts and action films, Stephen Chow's *Shaolin Soccer* (2001) and *Kung Fu Hustle* (2004) set the standard for hybridising local texts and conventions in a densely digitised, *Matrix*-compatible world of kung fu,[27] while John Woo's action choreography and heroic vision are creatively transformed in Johnnie To's 'neo-noirish' *policiers* and gangster films.[28] Not to be left out is a less glamorous yet quietly surviving strand of Social Realist cinema: Fruit Chan's '1997 Trilogy' (1997–9) raises important questions about Hong Kong's (and China's) cultural psyche in the post-handover period.[29] More recently, Ann Hui's critically acclaimed *The Way We Are* (2008) signals the revival of local-content films in a market dominated by Hollywood and China–Hong Kong co-productions. Hui's success is followed by Mabel Cheung and Alex Law's *Echoes of the Rainbow* (2009), a nostalgic homage to the 1960s. This trajectory, not unforeseen in the New Wave films discussed above, also points to the inherent mobility of the term 'New Wave' itself, for in Hong Kong there exist significant overlaps between art and commercial cinema, and across different generations of film-makers and film stars. This mobility is what makes this cinema a 'Hong Kong' cinema.

Notes

1. Stephen Teo, *Hong Kong Cinema: The Extra Dimension* (London: BFI, 1997), p. 148.
2. Some local critics have claimed the year 1981 marked the 'end' of the New Wave, when its key figure, Tsui Hark, joined Cinema City, a newly formed company specialising in mainstream comedies and action films. This reflects the shared assumptions and expectations of local film critics about 'art film' and its oppositional aesthetics vis-à-vis the commercial cinema. See discussion below.
3. See Law Kar, 'An Overview of Hong Kong's New Wave Cinema', in Esther C. M. Yau (ed.), *At Full Speed: Hong Kong Cinema in a Borderless World* (Minneapolis: University of Minnesota Press, 2001), pp. 38–9; Hector Rodrigues (2001), 'The Emergence of the Hong Kong New Wave', in Yau, *At Full Speed*, pp. 53–67; and Cheuk Pak-tong, *Hong Kong New Wave Cinema (1978–2000)* (Bristol: Intellect, 2007), chapter 1.
4. With reference to Aihwa Ong's notion of 'flexible citizenship', Yau argues that 'flexibility and syncretism are two prevailing modes' that distinguish Hong Kong films in the 1990s, 'which in turn shaped mass audiences' (self-)understanding of Hong Kong identity'. See Yau's introduction to *At Full Speed*, pp. 12–13.
5. Ackbar Abbas (1997), *Hong Kong: Culture and the Politics of Disappearance* (Minneapolis: University of Minnesota Press), p. 25.
6. Leo Ou-fan Lee, *Shanghai Modern: the Flowering of a New Urban Culture in China, 1930–1949* (New York: Harvard University Press, 1999), pp. 323–4.
7. Yingjin Zhang, *Chinese National Cinema* (New York: Routledge, 2004), p. 187.
8. Yau refers to the 'citation and irreverent remaking of cultural materials, mixed locations, and cross-cultural collaborations', resulting in a filmic 'space-time in which Hong Kong appears in many versions'. Yau, Introduction to *At Full Speed*, p. 12.
9. The best-known mainlander figure on the television screen is the 'A Caan' character (played by veteran television comedian Liu Wai-hung) in a TV soap opera, *The Good, the Bad and the Ugly/Wang zhong ren*. This series not only consolidated Chow Yun-fat's local stardom but also popularised 'A Caan' as a nickname for the country bumpkin from mainland China.
10. In his study on Hong Kong's television in the 1980s and 90s, Eric Ma observes how Hong Kong identities are constructed through its mainland other, and how the Hong Kong–mainland identity articulations have become unstable and polysemic in time. See. Ma, *Culture, Politics and Television in Hong Kong* (London: Routledge, 1999), chapters 4 and 5.
11. Patricia Brett Erens, 'Crossing Borders: Time, Memory, and the Construction of Identity in *Song of the Exile*', *Cinema Journal* vol. 39 no. 4 (2000), p. 48.
12. Quoted in Cheuk, *Hong Kong New Wave Cinema*, p. 167.
13. Teo, *Hong Kong Cinema*, p. 154.
14. Cheuk, *Hong Kong New Wave Cinema*, p. 154. Yim's later films about China do not share this optimism but show a deepening interest in more philosophical themes. See Cheuk, *Hong Kong New Wave Cinema*, pp. 155–6.
15. Tony Williams, 'Under Western Eyes: The Personal Odyssey of Wong Fei-Hung in *Once Upon a Time in China*', *Cinema Journal* vol. 40 no. 1 (2000), pp. 3–24; see also Teo, *Hong Kong Cinema*, pp. 168–73.
16. The terms 'China Syndrome', 'China Factor' and 'pre-' and 'post-1997 films' are commonly used in critical writing on Hong Kong films in the last two decades. See the *Hong Kong Cinema Retrospective 2003–2006* (Hong Kong: Hong Kong Film Critics Society, 2007); and *The China Factor in Hong Kong Cinema*, special issue of the 14th Hong Kong International Film Festival (Hong Kong Urban Council, 1990).
17. Set in 1970s Taiwan and 60s China, respectively, the two fictional works coincidentally have the same Chinese title, *Qi Wang* (lit. 'chess king').
18. Teo, *Hong Kong Cinema*, pp. 162–83.
19. Originally named, quite tellingly, *Gang of Four*, the film was banned by the Film Censorship Unit for its

'unhealthy consciousness' and possibly political elements. See Cheuk, *Hong Kong New Wave Cinema*, p. 89.

20. After joining Cinema City, Tsui directed his energy to urban comedies (e.g., *All the Wrong Clues* (1981)) exuding modern middle-class lifestyle and values.

21. The original *Wicked City* (1987) is a Japanese anime directed by Yoshiaki Kawajiri, based on a popular novel of the same name by Hideyuki Kikuchi.

22. See, for example, Williams, 'Space, Place, and Spectacle: The Crisis Cinema of John Woo', *Cinema Journal* vol. 36 no. 2 (1997), pp. 67–84.

23. Chris Berry and Mary Farquhar, *China on Screen: Cinema and Nation* (Hong Kong: Hong Kong University Press, 2006), p. 158.

24. Lounges with live music performances used to be popular hangouts for the young middle class in Hong Kong in the 1980s, before the arrival of karaoke.

25. See Gina Marchetti's discussion on the trilogy's connection to the New Wave and its exploitation of the postmodern 'non-space' in *Andrew Lau and Alan Mak's Infernal Affairs – the Trilogy* (Hong Kong: Hong Kong University Press, 2007), chapters 1 and 2.

26. The films are produced by Peter Chan's Applause Pictures, the first among Hong Kong production companies dedicated to 'pan-Asian cinema'. Applause recently has co-produced big-budget blockbuster films (e.g., *Perhaps Love* (2005) and *The Warlords* (2007)) with Hollywood and mainland partners for the international market.

27. See discussion in Darrell William Davis and Emilie Yueh-yu Yeh, *East Asian Screen Industries* (London: BFI, 2008), pp. 39–43.

28. See, for example, Teo's discussion of To's 'neo-noir' aesthetics in *Director in Action: Johnnie To and the Hong Kong Action Film* (Hong Kong: Hong Kong University Press, 2007), pp. 117–33.

29. See Wendy Gan, *Fruit Chan's Durian Durian* (Hong Kong: Hong Kong University Press, 2005); and Tsung-yi Huang, *Miandui jubian zhong de dongya jingguan: daduhui de ziwo shenfen shuxie* (East Asia in Transformation: Narratives of Self-identity in Metropolitan Cities) (Taipei: Socio, 2008), pp. 43–66.

Further Reading in *Chinese Films in Focus II*

On Ann Hui, see Chapter 5, '*Boat People*: Second Thoughts on Text and Context' by Julian Stringer.

On Stanley Kwan, see Chapter 6, '*Centre Stage*: A Shadow in Reverse' by Bérénice Reynaud.

On Wong Kar-wai, see Chapter 8, '*Chungking Express*: Time and its Displacements' by Janice Tong, and Chapter 18, '*In the Mood for Love*: Intersections of Hong Kong Modernity' by Audrey Yue.

On other Hong Kong New Wave and post-New Wave films, see the following: Chapter 7, '*A Chinese Ghost Story*: Ghostly Counsel and Innocent Man' by John Zou; Chapter 11, '*Durian Durian*: Defamiliarisation of the "Real"' by Esther M. K. Cheung; and Chapter 23, '*PTU*: Re-mapping the Cosmopolitan Crime Zone' by Vivian Lee.

PART FIVE

Stars, Auteurs and Genres

15 Dragons Forever

Chinese Martial Arts Stars

Leon Hunt

From the kung fu heroes of the 1970s to Zhang Ziyi's romantic swordswomen, martial arts stars have been Chinese cinema's most successful and instantly recognisable global export. Cinema studies continues to perpetuate the cult of the director-auteur, but in the popular imaginary, Ang Lee, John Woo and Zhang Yimou will simply never mean as a much as Bruce Lee (aka Li Xiaolong) or Jackie Chan (aka Cheng Long). Lee and Chan have not lacked critical attention, although both are exceptional figures in some ways. Their nearest rival, Jet Li (aka Li Lianjie), is starting to receive more critical attention, while Brigitte Lin (aka Lin Qingxia) has prompted several scholars to interrogate her androgynous and 'transgressive' persona.[1] But there is a long list of important *wuxia* stars who have yet to be studied in depth: Shaw Brothers stars like Wang Yu, David Chiang (aka Jiang Dawei), Di Long, Chen Guantai, Fu Sheng and Gordon Liu, more independent figures like Sammo Hung (aka Hong Jinbao), Yuen Biao (aka Yuan Biao) and Donnie Yen (aka Zhen Zidan), and a multitude of female performers such as Zheng Pei-pei, Xu Feng, Polly Shangguan Lingfeng, Angela Mao Ying, Hui Yinghong and Michelle Yeoh (aka Yáng Ziqióng).

This chapter cannot begin to redress this imbalance; nor is it difficult to understand why figures like Lee and Chan have been allowed to overshadow other stars. Rather, I want to look at these two icons as part of a slightly broader mix, examining six stars in pairs. Bruce Lee and Wang Yu are linked by the shift in popularity from the *wuxia pian* (martial chivalry film) to the kung fu film, the so-called 'remasculinisation' of Chinese martial arts cinema (previously dominated by female stars), by striking articulations of the heroic male body (muscular or mutilated) and by early attempts to put Chinese stars in English-language vehicles (*Enter the Dragon*, Robert Clouse, 1973, and *The Man From Hong Kong*, Brian Trenchard-Smith, 1975, respectively). Fu Sheng and Jackie Chan are linked by the rise of comedy in the genre and by achieving popularity in the role of *xiaozi* ('kid'), a mischievous adolescent – Fu was a Shaws contract player whose 'kid' persona is often linked to tragedy (as Fu himself was by his premature death), while Chan strove for independence and was a key figure in 'modernising' Hong Kong action cinema. Jet Li and Zhang Ziyi are two mainlanders who became perhaps the two most potent icons of transnational *wuxia* cinema – while Li has a longer history in the genre (and all-important martial arts credentials), both have been important to the 'blockbuster' incarnation of the genre that was initiated by *Crouching Tiger, Hidden Dragon* (Ang Lee, 2000). These six stars tell very different stories of martial arts stardom: a Chinese American with a 'real' martial arts reputation, whose early death bestowed on him the status of 'legend' (Lee); two Shaw Brothers stars, one of whom went independent and seemed to 'fall' from *wuxia* idol to 'grindhouse' cult (Wang), the other dying young without ever achieving the posthumous mythology of Lee (Fu); a former stuntman and failed kung fu star whose comic persona and self-endangerment made him Hong Kong's most famous living performer (Chan); a 'national treasure' who dazzled Nixon at the Whitehouse as a boy, whose film debut led to the Shaolin Temple reopening in China, who reinvented a folk legend and other kung fu heroes, who played the 'inscrutable' heavy in his Hollywood debut and then repositioned himself in the new pan-Chinese blockbuster as a hero who dies to 'heal' the nation (Li); a dancer and actress, the 'new Gong Li' and Zhang Yimou's discovery, the desiring, wilful heroine of 'martial arthouse' cinema (Zhang).

Masculinity, Muscles and Mutilation: Bruce Lee and Wang Yu

Bruce Lee and Wang Yu belong to a transitional period for Hong Kong martial arts cinema – female stars were largely giving way to male ones, the *wuxia pian* would be temporarily overshadowed by the 'authentic' action of the kung fu film (which broke onto the international market), and audience expectations of 'martial arts stars' were radically transformed by Lee, to the detriment of performers like Wang. Lee embodied the 'real' in an unprecedented way and this remains central to his mythology – it's rarely mentioned that he was occasionally stunt doubled. What was Wang Yu's qualification for being a *wuxia* star, given that his pre-stardom claim to fame was being a swimming champion? Was it simply because he 'looked "natural" with a sword', as Tony Rayns has suggested?[2] To modern eyes, Wang looks like a 'bad' martial artist – his kicks barely rise above waist-height, he's no more graceful with two arms than he is in the films (of which there are a few) where he is reduced to one. Lee's films may age around him, but he somehow remains vibrant and modern – many of my students (mostly male) are captivated by him and some of them even study Jeet Kune Do, the hybridised fighting style he developed. Wang is an important figure, but could never be mistaken for anything but a martial arts star from an earlier time – not only does he not possess Lee's skills, he doesn't have modern wirework and CGI to help him out either.

While Bruce Lee was still struggling in Hollywood, playing 'Oriental' sidekicks and bad guys, Wang Yu was in the process of becoming the most popular male star in Hong Kong. He supplanted Zheng Pei-pei as Shaw Brothers' top *wuxia* star, signalling the shift from female to male leads – *Golden Swallow* (Zhang Che, 1968) may be named after her character, but it's Wang's brooding, narcissistic and self-destructive Silver Roc who is clearly the centre of the film. Wang's 1960s *wuxia* persona is generally seen to be 'authored' by the director Zhang Che as the first manifestation of Zhang's ongoing preoccupation with *yanggang* (machismo), transcendent death and a homosociality that strikes most modern viewers as nakedly homoerotic. In *The Magnificent Trio* (Zhang Che, 1966)

Wang isn't quite 'Wang Yu' yet. He plays a relatively uncomplicated *xia* (chivalrous hero), noble, compassionate and committed to justice; the only hint of what is to come in later films is when he takes a hundred lashes on behalf of the villagers oppressed by a corrupt district official. The Zhang–Wang protagonist manifests himself in *The One Armed Swordsman* (Zhang Che, 1967), *The Assassin* (Zhang Che, 1967), *Golden Swallow* and *Return of the One-Armed Swordsman* (Zhang Che, 1969). In *The One Armed Swordsman* he's first seen brooding in the snow, a gifted outsider. As if to underline why women must be evacuated from the genre, he loses his arm not to any of the villains but to his master's spoiled daughter in a petulant display of spite. Shaws' house magazine *Southern Screen* described him as a 'lanky daredevil' (July 1967), while later publicity for his English-language debut *The Man from Hong Kong* (1975) characterised him as 'the Asian Steve McQueen' (by that point, Charles Bronson might have been more apt).

Wang's directorial debut at Shaws was *The Chinese Boxer* (Wang Yu, 1970), one of the first Mandarin kung fu films and the start of the wave that would make Bruce Lee the most famous Chinese star in the world. But if Wang helped bring the kung fu film to prominence, the new cycle was crueller in revealing his limitations as a physical performer. Lee's *The Big Boss* (Lo Wei, 1971) raised the bar above the former swimmer's physical talents. At Shaw Brothers, their roster of stars raised their game, helped in no small part by in-house fight choreographer Lau Kar-leung (aka Liu Jialiang.) But Wang, emboldened by Lee's success, left Shaws for Golden Harvest, the company that had signed Lee. What remained of Wang's career might seem like a long, slow journey beyond his sell-by date. His looks had gone, and he possessed neither Lee's physical prowess nor his incandescent charisma. But the picture is slightly more complex than that. Wang was part of the 1970s generation whose films were seen internationally as part of the 'kung fu craze' – he was increasingly billed as 'Jimmy Wang Yu'. He attracted a cult following among kung fu fans in the West, and is still fondly regarded by some (this writer included). In films like *The One Armed Boxer* (Wang Yu, 1971) and *The Master of the Flying Guillotine* (Wang Yu, 1975), he unwittingly relocated to what we might now call 'grindhouse cinema' – the latter film is one of the many referents in Tarantino's *Kill Bill* (Quentin Tarantino, 2003, 2004.) The films are violent, outlandish to the point of being ludicrous, rarely dull, seemingly tailor-made for an international market well disposed to an exotic, blood-soaked cinema of attractions; the English-language print of *The One Armed Boxer* reduces one stretch of exposition to a montage of stills in its rush to get to the next fight. If Lee brought kung fu into the mainstream, Wang took it more into the realm of 'para-cinema' as he fought fanged Japanese fighters, inflatable Tibetans, Indians with extendable arms and blind white-eyebrowed monks with 'flying guillotines'. If Wang's machismo is inherited from Zhang Che, what he takes into his own films is the preoccupation with mutilation and disability. The one-armed *Swordsman* becomes the one-armed *Boxer*, a hero constantly having to transcend loss and physical impairment. Kim Soyoung has observed the trend for impaired action stars in East Asian martial arts cinema such as Japan's

blind Zatoichi, South Korea's 'One-Legged Man' as well as Hong Kong's one-armed heroes; 'East Asian modernity presents itself as marred but as possessing, nonetheless, a hint of promise for a new start.'[3] While Korea's disabled hero seems to negotiate the legacy of Japanese imperialism, Hong Kong's 'new start' might point less to its own colonial history than to its booming economy.

Stephen Teo sees Zhang Che's *yanggang* as a refashioning of Chinese masculinity that rejected not only the 'feminine' Hong Kong cinema of the 1950s and early 60s, but the 'soft' men found in genres like romantic melodrama and *huangmei diao* operas.[4] Teo observes that Zhang's films also paved the way for the muscular hardness of Bruce Lee.[5] Lee's 'hardness' would also resonate with diasporic Chinese audiences who sought a corrective to the emasculated stereotypes

Bruce Lee on the set of *Enter the Dragon*

Jimmy Wang Yu in *The Man from Hong Kong*

perpetuated in western media,[6] and it's commonplace to note that Lee's body constituted an empowering ethnic identity for other groups, too. Moreover, Lee was sufficiently westernised for white audiences, previously resistant to Asian heroes, to be 'colour-blind' towards him. As Teo puts it, 'mutual understanding of Lee remains elusive'[7] – few stars remain so culturally contested, available to diverse and conflicting investments and fantasies. According to Paul Bowman, Lee's legacy rests on a 'multiculturally promiscuous interdisciplinarity'.[8] In his directorial debut *The Way of the Dragon* (Bruce Lee, 1972) his character is a provincial 'bumpkin' in matters of etiquette, a modern *xia* in spirit and an iconoclast and modernist when it comes to martial arts. When he defeats Chuck Norris in the Coliseum, the meaning remains ambiguous – Chinese (but not *simply* Chinese) kung fu triumphs over Americanised karate, but only western martial artists constitute a real challenge for a Chinese hero. Lee is credited with bringing kung fu to the West, but also with 'westernising' it by introducing cross-training, vitamins and health drinks. In a recent English-language documentary, *How Bruce Lee Changed the World* (2009), Lee was even claimed as the 'father' of competitive mixed martial arts. Lee's body, then, eludes definitive closure.

Lee's final completed film *Enter the Dragon* (1973) paved the way for other English-language martial arts films with Chinese stars, although none of them would come close to matching its success. *The Man from Hong Kong*, a Hong Kong–Australian co-production, is the most interesting of these films – it's tempting to suggest that, Lee aside, it's a better film than *Enter the Dragon*. Like *Enter*, it looks to James Bond for a common ground between Chinese and western-genre cinema, except that here 'Bond' is the villain, played by George Lazenby. Wang is an Inspector with Hong Kong Special Branch sent to extradite a Chinese drug dealer from Sydney, Australia, taunted by Lazenby for his colonised status. The film switches between confirming and challenging Asian stereotypes. Wang is a rogue cop given an Orientalist makeover, manifesting the brutal 'East', but at the same time cleaning up the corrupt western city, anticipating Jet Li's Beijing cop let loose in Paris in the later *Kiss of the Dragon* (Chris Nahon, 2001). Almost uniquely for such a vehicle, the film isn't shy about interracial sex – 'Do you often take white girls to bed?' asks one of his two Caucasian conquests. Most interestingly, it situates Wang between two national cinemas that stress 'authenticity' and danger in their action scenes. Two moments capture this converging spectacle – Wang's impressive flying kick that sends stuntman Grant Page (later celebrated for his work on the *Mad Max* films) flying from his speeding motorbike, and the door of an exploding car that narrowly misses the camera. Wang gives one of his most sullen and charmless performances, but he never looked more convincing as an action star. The film has been rediscovered as a part of 'Ozploitation', but its place within Hong Kong cinema needs to be underlined, too – Wang was credited as co-director on the Hong Kong release.[9]

Young Masters: Fu Sheng and Jackie Chan

Jackie Chan has often been seen as debunking the invincible martial arts hero embodied by Bruce Lee and Wang Yu, replacing their 'hardness' (Lee's muscles, Wang's 'Iron Fist') with a pronounced vulnerability.[10] But Chan didn't emerge out of nowhere, simply reacting against Lee. Not only were his peers and periodic collaborators (Sammo Hung, Yuen Biao, choreographer Yuen Wo-ping (aka Yuan Heping)) making similar kinds of films, but he had some predecessors, too.

'Alexander' Fu Sheng was the first graduate of the Southern Drama School, an initiative by Shaw Brothers and TVB (Television Broadcasts, Hong Kong's first free-to-air TV station) to discover new talent. Fu would work extensively with Zhang Che, who had a reputation for shaping male stars and casting them in yin–yang pairings – one muscular (Di Long, Chen Guantai, Qi Guanjun), the other more scholarly or boyish (David Chiang, Fu Sheng). Zhang has been credited with identifying Fu Sheng as a new 'type', the *xiaozi*, a mischievous rascal-hero embodying what Teo calls a 'post-pubescent masculine rebel-without-a-cause figure fated to die young and tragically'.[11] The Chinese title of his best film *Disciples of Shaolin* (Zhang Che, 1975) translates as 'Hung Fist Kid', a title that unites Shaws' focus on the southern *Hung Gar/Hongquan* style (demonstrated by Fu in the credits) and the precocious adolescent hero who will not survive into maturity. Given that Fu's early death (in a car accident) seems to cement the myth, it's surprising that he's been such a comparative absence from critical writing about Hong Kong cinema, largely confined to fan accounts.[12]

Fu's early career coincides with Shaws' cycle of films about the southern Shaolin Temple, and he would play the headstrong, doomed hero Fong Sai-yuk (aka Fang Shiyu) in *Heroes Two* (Zhang Che, 1974), *The Men from the Monastery* (Zhang Che, 1974), *Shaolin Avengers* (Zhang Che, 1976) and *Shaolin Temple* (Zhang Che, 1976). In a couple of these films, Zhang's violent homoeroticism takes a particularly graphic turn – Fu/Fong dies anally penetrated by a sword. *Disciples of Shaolin* stands slightly apart from this cycle, in spite of its English title. He plays a young fighter who arrives barefoot in a town enmeshed in a conflict between two textile mills, the boss of each no better than the other. He first demonstrates his skill by imperceptibly kicking the backside of a pompous foreman, leaving the imprint of his foot on his trousers and giggling to himself. His kung fu skills elevate him to a bodyguard role for one of the bosses and he enjoys some material success that leads to his downfall. Even more than in Lee's *The Big Boss*, there is an emphasis on how martial artists (especially naive ones) can be exploited like any other kind of physical labour by unscrupulous management. The boss he sacrifices himself for is more concerned for his prized cricket (who shares the name of Fu's character) than the young man who has just died in his service. If Fu is unappreciated by his employer, however, the camera positively worships him, fetishising his signature fringe, his feet, his shoes and the gold pocket watch he holds to his ear like a delighted child.

Fu is inserted into master–pupil narratives both onscreen and off – he was 'adopted' as Lau Kar-leung's favourite student. At a studio that generally churned

out stars on a production line, Fu was a 'favourite son' – young, beautiful, talented and likeable. The addition of 'Alexander' to some of his billings suggests that Shaws considered him for international vehicles, and the San Francisco-set *Chinatown Kid* (Zhang Che, 1977) feels like a tentative tryout – in his tight denim outfit, he resembles Chan in *Rumble in the Bronx* (Stanley Tong, 1995). But as David Desser has observed, by the time Fu was Hong Kong's most popular kung fu star, the international market for Hong Kong films was in a post-Lee slump.[13] Fu has links to both Chan and Lee. Seasonal Films had wanted him for *Snake in the Eagle's Shadow* (Yuen Wo-ping, 1978), which would become Chan's breakthrough film, and he was living in Lee's former Kowloon home at the time of his death. The comedy-adventure *The Treasure Hunters* (Lau Kar-wing, 1980) is particularly reminiscent of Chan's later films, mixing kung fu and slapstick and casting Fu as a trickster figure who defeats one superior opponent through the strategic use of glue. He died while making *Eight Diagram Pole Fighter* (Lau Kar-leung, 1983), his character disappearing from the latter half of the film, so that his presence and absence are almost as disquieting as Bruce Lee's in the posthumously completed *Game of Death* (Robert Clouse, 1978). News footage of his funeral cannot help but remind one of Lee's (so widely circulated, often in an exploitative form), but this spectacle of grief would not take on the same mythic force – a local tragedy, not a global one. As a Shaws star, Fu's reputation was undoubtedly affected by the long-time unavailability of the studio's back catalogue. Of the stars discussed here, no one is in more urgent need of reappraisal.

It is well known that Jackie Chan slogged away in unprepossessing kung fu films until *Snake in the Eagle's Shadow*, intended for Fu Sheng, transformed him into a variation on the *xiaozi*. That's not to say that Chan benefited from Fu's premature demise, because their careers overlap and there are some significant differences between them. Fu's 'kids' are also usually masters, but the 'master' is a problematic figure in Chan's kung fu films. He generally plays an everyman figure who triumphs through determination and an essential good-heartedness. In *Snake in the Eagle's Shadow* and *Drunken Master* (Yuen Wo-ping, 1978), his victory still hinges to a certain extent on perfecting a particular technique, an extension of the master–pupil films of the 1970s. *The Young Master* (Jackie Chan, 1980), however, tells a different story. The master who has taken Chan and his brother in as orphans must be taught a lesson about kindness and trust by the younger hero who voluntarily leaves the school to save his wayward brother. The other 'master', Wang In-sik's villainous Master Kim, is a variation on Huang Jang Lee's indomitable kicking machine from Chan's earlier films. This time, the master is not defeated by Chan himself becoming a superior martial artist – he grabs, pinches and pummels Kim while enduring terrible beatings and excruciating joint-locks, fortifying himself with tobacco juice (wood alcohol will serve the same purpose in Chan's later return to kung fu, *Drunken Master 2*, Lau Kar-leung, 1994.) Master Kim is slowly worn down – as David Bordwell puts it, Chan triumphs by 'refusing to lose'[14] – and is reduced literally to a rag doll (we are clearly meant to notice the unconvincing dummy substituted for Wang), thrown around by Chan like a dog shaking a toy.

The Young Master comes towards the end of Chan's kung fu career; martial arts stars would become an anachronism in the more modern Hong Kong cinema of the 1980s and he would refer to himself as an 'action star'. Like Sammo Hung and Yuen Biao, Chan's Chinese Opera training had equipped him with a larger skill set than Fu Sheng, or even Bruce Lee for that matter. Fu had been taken out of action by a career-threatening on-set injury, while injury would be central to the Chan mythology, documented in end-credit outtakes. *The Young Master* is full of Chinese Opera-derived techniques – fights deploying benches, fans and skirts as well as the spins, tumbles and somersaults that have no origin in 'real' martial arts.[15] *Miracles* (Jackie Chan, 1989) is not untypical of Chan's post-kung fu cinema, albeit distinguished by a profligacy that was starting to concern Golden Harvest – if the narrative referent is Capra's *A Pocketful of Miracles* (1961), the visual style is more reminiscent of Coppola's *follies de grandeur* at Zoetrope Studios. The film is indicative of Chan wanting to be seen as a 'proper' film-maker, with its 1930s production design, virtuoso crane shots and on-stage musical numbers. Martial arts are sprinkled throughout the film, in the style that Chan trademarked in the 1980s – the emphasis is on stunts, chases, use of props, uncomplicated punches, kicks and spins, rather than any recognisable techniques. During a fight in a restaurant, he flips across stair balconies, tables and counters; in a rope factory fight, maximum use is made of ropes, ladders and narrow beams, and the choreography moves through space vertically as

well as horizontally. Chan's distinctive approach to negotiating space – perhaps his most unique contribution to cinema – anticipates the later use of *parkour* (or 'free running') in films like *Banlieue 13* (Pierre Morel, 2004) and *Casino Royale* (Martin Campbell, 2006).

Transnational *Yin* and *Yang*: Jet Li and Zhang Ziyi

The careers of Jet Li and Zhang Ziyi belong to an era in which Chinese martial arts cinema – seemingly as obsolete as the Western, but equally prone to periodic revivals and revisions – made two notable comebacks. The first of these was in Hong Kong between 1990 and 1994, a revival credited particularly to the film-maker Tsui Hark and often interpreted (sometimes reductively) as a response to the territory's impending postcoloniality. By the time the boom was fizzling out (as was Hong Kong cinema more generally) Hollywood came calling and Jet Li would follow Jackie Chan, Chow Yun-Fat and others to the US. The second is a much more globally successful cycle of pan-Chinese 'martial arthouse' films starting with *Crouching Tiger, Hidden Dragon*. Only Li is central to both of these developments, while the second turned Zhang Ziyi from Zhang Yimou's latest discovery into arguably the most famous Chinese actress in the world.

Jet Li brought almost as much cultural baggage to his film career as Bruce Lee – many Chinese remembered his performances as China's *wushu* champion and his childhood performance for Nixon at the Whitehouse. No moment in a Jet Li film is ever more breathtaking than the *wushu* forms he performs by himself, a reminder of how he became famous in the first place. His debut film *The Shaolin Temple* (Zhang Xinyan, 1982) was the first to be filmed in the temple itself, but longer-term success eluded him until Tsui Hark cast him as Wong Fei-hung in *Once Upon a Time in China* (Tsui Hark, 1991). Wong had always been played either as an older man (by Kwan Tak-hing in the long-running Cantonese series) or as a younger man who had yet to mature into the Confucian patriarch (Gordon Liu in *Challenge of the Masters*, Lau Kar-leung, 1976, and *The Martial Club*, Lau Kar-leung, 1980, Jackie Chan in *Drunken Master*). Li combined the two, a young man with the grace, dignity and wisdom of a mature 'master'. In Tsui's series of films, Wong interacted with Chinese history – the Treaty of Nanjing, the Boxer Rebellion, Sun Yat-Sen, the Empress Dowager of the declining Qing Dynasty – and negotiated between a progressive Chinese nationalism and western modernity. As Sabrina Yu explains, Li cultivated two star personas – the 'kid' he had played in the *Shaolin Temple* films and would play in two new films about Fong Sai-yuk, and the 'master' embodied by Wong.[16] It's worth saying, however, that Li played more 'masters' than 'kids', reviving a number of the genre's iconic heroes – Hung Hei-kwun/Hong Xiguan, Zhang Sanfeng, both Huo Yuanjia and his semi-fictional student Chen Zhen (the character played by Bruce Lee in *Fist of Fury*, Lo Wei, 1972).

After progressing first to modern-day Hong Kong action films and then to Hollywood (with inevitably mixed results), Li's career entered another phase with *Hero* (Zhang Yimou, 2002) as the nameless assassin who seeks to kill Ying Zheng/Qin Shi Huang, the 'First Emperor' of China – in a bizarre twist Li would later play the Emperor himself as a supernatural villain in the Hollywood film *The Mummy: Tomb of the Dragon Emperor* (Rob Schneider, 2008). Deterred from his mission by the Emperor's apparent philosophical enlightenment, 'Nameless' sacrifices himself to the arrows of the Qin army. If Wong Fei-hung has been constructed as a 'father' to a nation, *Hero* places Li's assassin's sacrifice at 'the birth of a nation-civilisation',[17] and offers an epic spectacle beyond the resources of Hong Kong cinema. *Hero* seemed to add another dimension to Li's persona, that of self-sacrifice. In *Fist of Legend* (Gordon Chan, 1994) his Chen Zhen was

too pragmatic to face the heroic death that Bruce Lee's Chen had in *Fist of Fury* and so lived to fight another day. In *Fearless* (Ronnie Yu, 2006), a kung fu film about renowned northern master Huo Yuanjia, Li dies to heal the 'Sick Man of Asia', a demoralised, self-destructive China that is easy prey for colonial forces, while his more morally ambiguous character in *The Warlords* (Peter Chan Ho-san, 2007) seems to die to maintain the bond of fraternal loyalty that he has otherwise broken. *Fearless* was sold as Li's 'final' martial arts film, although *The Warlords* and his co-starring vehicle with Jackie Chan *The Forbidden Kingdom* (Rob Minkoff, 2008) might make one wonder what that means. It's a satisfying summation of his kung fu career nevertheless, managing to have him play both 'kid' and 'master' – the younger Huo, whose arrogance brings about his downfall, and the Wong-like older Huo who learns that martial arts have a higher purpose than defeating one's opponents and making one's reputation.

As the two key star presences in 'martial arthouse', Jet Li and Zhang Ziyi each represent very different incarnations of the tensions between individual desire and dutiful self-sacrifice, heroic and romantic destiny.[18] Prior to the 1960s, female stars outnumbered males, while subsequently Chinese cinema's engagement with the *nüxia* (female knight-errant) and kung fu heroine has come in fits and starts. When *Crouching Tiger* was released in the West, many observers thought that Zhang Ziyi's character was a new post-feminist figure

Jet Li in *Hero*

Zhang Ziyi in *Crouching Tiger, Hidden Dragon*

or a variation on the 'action babe', rather than part of a long tradition of female stars in the genre. Zhang was less the new 'Gong Li' than the new Zheng Pei-pei, the new Xu Feng or the new Polly Shangguan Lingfeng. Stephen Teo discusses two *wuxia* stars whose personas seem to particularly anticipate Zhang's characters in *Crouching Tiger* and *House of Flying Daggers* (Zhang Yimou, 2004) – Sidney Hung/Suet Nei a 'rebellious, unruly, and finally, pathological figure'[19] and Melinda Chen's 'treacherous ambivalence' in *The Cold Blade* (Chu Yuan, 1970).[20] More commonly, the martial heroine is a dutiful and androgynous figure who seeks to avoid romantic entanglements. Zhang's martial arthouse heroines are wilful, romantic, capricious and fully sexualised. In *Crouching Tiger* her rebellious anti-heroine threatens to disrupt the patrilineal structures of martial learning, while Mei in *House of Flying Daggers* is a warrior, but her fight is explicitly linked to female desire – both sexual desire and a longing for 'freedom' that goes beyond even the idealised mobility of *jianghu*, the abstract martial arts 'world'. In this respect, she is connected to modernity, destabilising traditions, rules and authority, but at the same time too 'selfish' to be entirely heroic. In *Flying Daggers*, *jianghu* has become a female (possibly even matriarchal) world pitted against an explicitly masculine state oppression. Its forest-dwelling amazons, who hurl wooden stakes that evoke *Buffy the Vampire Slayer* (1997–2003), seem to have largely eliminated men from their organisation. And yet Zhang's character betrays this 'sisterhood' for romance

with Takeshi Kaneshiro's undercover government agent. She is first encountered at a brothel, posing as a blind dancer – simultaneously warrior, *femme fatale* and *qingcheng qingguo* (beautiful enough to overrun cities and ruin states).

Postscript: Last *Ip Man* Standing

The success of Thai martial arts film *Ong Bak* (2003) seemed to remind Hong Kong cinema of its own tradition of 'authentic' kung fu stars. Donnie Yen, long denied access to the upper tier of Hong Kong stardom, found himself promoted (belatedly but deservedly) to being its last great martial arts star. Most notable have been his collaborations with director Wilson Yip Wai-shun – in cop dramas *SPL* (Wilson Yip, 2005) and *Flashpoint* (Wilson Yip, 2007), Yen incorporated grappling techniques from mixed martial arts into Hong Kong fight choreography, a fresh twist on 'authenticity'. But Yen's iconic elevation was cemented by his casting as Bruce Lee's teacher, Wing Chun Grandmaster Ip Man. *Ip Man* (Wilson Yip, 2008) and *Ip Man 2* (Wilson Yip, 2010) are unabashed retreads of 1970s kung fu cinema, even down to a nationalist posturing that largely jettisons the more reflective qualities of *Once Upon a Time in China* or *Fearless*. But they are primarily vehicles for Yen's considerable talents. Nevertheless, the clock is ticking – Yen is forty-seven at the time of writing and has no visible successors. But we should know better by now than to count out the Chinese martial arts star too quickly. These Dragons are forever.

Notes

1. See Rolanda Chu, 'Swordsman II and The East is Red: The "Hong Kong", Entertainment and Gender', Bright Lights vol. 13 (1994), pp. 30–5, 36, and Felicia Chan, 'Wuxia Cross-dressing and Transgender Identity: The Roles of Brigitte Lin Ching-hsia from Swordsman II to Ashes of Time', EnterText vol. 6 no.1 (2006), pp. 111–31. Available online at <arts.brunel.ac.uk/gate/entertext/6_1/ET61Wux4FChanEd.doc>.

2. Tony Rayns, 'The Sword as Obstacle', in Lau shing-on (ed.), A Study of the Hong Kong Swordplay Film (Hong Kong: Hong Kong International Film Festival, 1981–96), p. 156.

3. Kim Soyoung, 'Genre as Contact Zone: Hong Kong Action and Korean Halkuk', in Meaghan Morris, Siu Leung Li and Stephen Chan Ching-kiu (eds), Hong Kong Connections: Transnational Imagination in Action Cinema (Hong Kong: Hong Kong University Press, 2005), p. 110.

4. Stephen Teo, Chinese Martial Arts Cinema: The Wuxia Tradition (Edinburgh: Edinburgh University Press 2009), pp. 94–6.

5. Ibid., p. 104.

6. Yuan Shu, 'Reading the Kung Fu Film in an American Context: From Bruce Lee to Jackie Chan', Journal of Popular Film and Television vol. 31 no. 2 (2003), pp. 53–4.

7. Teo, Chinese Martial Arts Cinema, p. 75.

8. Paul Bowman, Theorizing Bruce Lee: Film-Fantasy-Fighting-Philosophy (Amsterdam and New York: Rodopi, 2009), p. 54.

9. For more on The Man from Hong Kong and Wang Yu, see Stephen Teo, 'Australia's Role in the Global Kung Fu Trend: The Man From Hong Kong', Senses of Cinema vol. 16 (2001). Available online at <archive.sensesofcinema.com/contents/cteq/01/16/man_hk.html>, and Leon Hunt, 'One Armed and Extremely Dangerous: Wang Yu's Mutilated Masters', in Xavier Mendik (ed.), Shocking Cinema of the Seventies (Hereford: Noir, 2002), pp. 91–105.

10. For example, Yuan Shu, 'Reading the Kung Fu Film in an American Context', p. 51, and Yvonne Tasker, 'Fists of Fury: Discourses of Race and Masculinity in the Martial Arts Cinema', in Dimitris Eleftheriotis and Gary Needham (eds), Asian Cinemas: A Reader and Guide (Edinburgh: Edinburgh University Press, 2006), p. 453.

11. Teo, Chinese Martial Arts Cinema, p. 105.

12. See, for example, Chris Mercer, 'Alexander Fu Sheng – The Master of Disaster', Eastern Heroes Special Edition vol. 6 (1997), pp. 61–4.

13. David Desser, 'The Kung Fu Craze: Hong Kong Cinema's First American Reception', in David Desser and Poshek Fu (eds), The Cinema of Hong Kong: History, Arts, Identity (Cambridge, New York, Melbourne and Madrid: Cambridge University Press, 2000), p. 37.

14. David Bordwell, Planet Hong Kong: Popular Cinema and the Art of Entertainment (Cambridge, MA, and London: Harvard University Press, 2000), p. 58.

15. For more on Hong Kong cinema's debt to Chinese Opera, see Yung Sai-shing, 'Moving Body: The Interactions Between Chinese Opera and Action Cinema', in Morris et al., Hong Kong Connections, pp. 21–34.

16. Sabrina Yu, 'Can a Wuxia Star Act? Martial Arts, Acting and Critical Responses to Jet Li's Once Upon a Time in China', EnterText vol. 6 no. 1 (2006), p. 143. Available online at <arts.brunel.ac.uk/gate/entertext/6_1/ET61Wux5YuED.doc>.

17. Gilles Deleuze, Cinema 1: The Movement-Image (London: Athlone Press, 1986), p. 148.

18. For more on Jet Li, see Leon Hunt, Kung Fu Cult Masters: From Bruce Lee to Crouching Tiger (London and New York: Wallflower, 2003), pp. 140–56; on Zhang Ziyi, see Leon Hunt, 'Zhang Ziyi, "Martial Arthouse" and the Transnational Nüxia', in Silke Andris and Ursula Frederick (eds), Women Willing to Fight: The Fighting Woman in Film (Newcastle: Cambridge Scholars, 2007), pp. 144–60.

19. Teo, Chinese Martial Arts Cinema, p. 92.

20. Ibid., p. 108.

Further Reading in *Chinese Films In Focus II*

On martial arts and *wuxia* films, see Chapter 28, 'A Touch of Zen: Action in Martial Arts Movie' by Mary Farquhar; Chapter 7, 'A Chinese Ghost Story: Ghostly Counsel and Innocent Man' by John Zou; and Chapter 9, 'Crouching Tiger, Hidden Dragon: Cultural Migrancy and Translatability' by Felicia Chan.

16 The Contemporary *Wuxia* Revival

Genre Remaking and the Hollywood Transnational Factor

Kenneth Chan

The release of *Crouching Tiger, Hidden Dragon* (Ang Lee, 2000) signalled an exciting return of the *wuxia pian* (Chinese swordplay film) to renewed global popularity. Affirming the now iconic status of Ang Lee's film is the growing critical literature canonising it as a classic instance of contemporary transnational Chinese cinema.[1] But what cannot be ignored, of course, is the Hollywood factor in this particular conception of filmic transnationalism. The fact that the film is not only considered a Hollywood product but that it also performed particularly well at box offices in the United States demonstrates an emerging trend: since the late 1990s, mainstream American audiences were beginning to embrace Chinese cinemas, particularly *wuxia* and kung fu films.[2] The undeniable lure of box-office potential had Hollywood studios devising strategies of not just distributing versions of the *wuxia pian* made in Hong Kong and China, but also concocting new ways of appropriating from and remaking the genre themselves. While Chinese martial arts have indeed coloured and transfigured Hollywood action cinema in the past decade since *Crouching Tiger, Hidden Dragon*, the Hollywood–Chinese connection also inflects the aesthetic, cultural and political evolution of the genre outside of Hollywood, attesting again to the latter's hegemonic impact on the production, distribution and consumption patterns of global cinema.

While tracking the manifold permutations that the *wuxia pian* has undergone since finding its place in the Hollywood system, this chapter also mobilises two other registers of critical analysis. It conceptualises the Hollywood remaking of the *wuxia pian* as a formation of genre hybridity, with the Hollywood version exemplifying cross-cultural interfacing, enabled by the dexterity of cinema as genre. At the same time, it counterpoints this dexterity with the rigidities of the genre's historicity, a contradiction demanding a more critically fluid approach to contend with the slippery cultural politics of the new Hollywood *wuxia pian*. I conclude the chapter by deploying this approach in a case-study analysis of *The Forbidden Kingdom* (Rob Minkoff, 2008).

Crouching Tiger, Hidden Dragon and its Transformative Effects

Many American mainstream audiences who are new to the genre come to *Crouching Tiger, Hidden Dragon* without the pleasures, or burdens, of the long, tangled history of the *wuxia pian*. This historically disconnected mode of cinematic consumption is clearly alien to the average ethnic Chinese viewer brought up on a staple *wuxia* diet in both filmic and television forms. The weight of the genre's history on any theoretical approach to the shifting nature of the Hollywood *wuxia*, hence, deserves further comment, a point I will return to in the next section. But, for now, suffice it to say that this historicism has played its role in shaping Ang Lee's film, which in turn directs the new historical trajectory of the genre in the new millennium.

Crouching Tiger, Hidden Dragon is really a fantasy text of personal, cultural, political and cinematic histories. Director Lee's desire to make a *wuxia* film is woven out of the tapestry of these interconnecting histories.[3] While the spatial constraints of this chapter do not allow me to accentuate the continuities and

Crouching Tiger, Hidden Dragon: Michelle Yeoh and Zhang Ziyi fight sequence

contiguities of Lee's film to the genre's vast tradition, it is significant to gesture to the way *Crouching Tiger, Hidden Dragon* obeys *wuxia* conventions while simultaneously subverting them in order to update the genre for a contemporary Chinese and global audience. Therefore, it comes as no surprise that the film has been pegged and labelled in a myriad of ways, including diasporic, feminist and Asian American, while propagating modern themes like individual liberties versus social responsibility and constraints.

But *Crouching Tiger, Hidden Dragon*'s historical importance is also based on the way it has moved the *wuxia pian* from its marginal, subcultural appeal to viewers in American Chinatowns, film festivals and cult followings in the past, to mainstream acceptability today. Chinese-language cinemas from the People's Republic of China, Taiwan and Hong Kong have made their mark at film festivals and in art theatres across Europe and the United States prior to the release of Lee's film. Hollywood was taking note of the incredible energy and creativity emerging out of East Asia, which

it could tap into and appropriate. With the lead-up to the British handover of Hong Kong to the People's Republic of China in 1997, many key players from the Hong Kong film industry found Hollywood welcoming them into its fold: Jackie Chan, John Woo, Yuen Woo-ping, Michelle Yeoh and Chow Yun-Fat, among many others, saw career possibilities in Tinseltown. The arrival of the Hong Kong stalwarts, as they were joined by Chinese stars like Gong Li and Zhang Ziyi, generated a groundswell of interest in Chinese cinematic culture. Taiwanese Ang Lee was thus ready to introduce to America his *wuxia* epic at this critical juncture.

Another key element that critics have latched onto is the representative nature of *Crouching Tiger, Hidden Dragon*'s transnational structure and formation. While most film scholars will readily admit to cinema being inherently transnational in its system of production, distribution, and/or consumption since its inception, the contemporary era of globalisation and transnational capitalism has radically deepened, if not overtly foregrounded, the globalised character of film as a capitalist commodity. Even with the localised cultural specificity of the *wuxia pian*, Lee's film assumed transnational qualities in the form of its creativity, financing and production. While the film is adapted from mainland Chinese Wang Du Lu's novel, American executive producer James Schamus had a crucial role in writing the screenplay. With money flowing in from different parts of the world, Sony Picture Classics, Columbia Pictures and a number of other corporate entities finally helped produce the film, including the China-based China Film Co-Production Corporation. The film features stars and talents from Malaysia, Hong Kong, mainland China and Taiwan.

The transnational nature of *Crouching Tiger, Hidden Dragon* not only imbues the film with an easy mobility in relation to its multisector global audience appeal, it also intensifies a corporate trend that redefines the aesthetic and cultural landscape of the genre's history.[4] Encouraged by the film's success, other Chinese film-makers, who were working presumably outside the Hollywood system[5] sought to ride the wave with their own *wuxia* titles. Hollywood studios also began making plans to incorporate *wuxia* elements and stylistics into their action films, and to produce their own hybrid versions of the genre.

Since *Crouching Tiger, Hidden Dragon*, Chinese and Hong Kong film-makers have taken to the *wuxia* and kung fu genres with gusto: *Hero* (Zhang Yimou, 2002), *House of Flying Daggers* (Zhang Yimou, 2004), *Kung Fu Hustle* (Stephen Chow, 2004), *Seven Swords* (Tsui Hark, 2005), *The Promise* (Chen Kaige, 2005), *The Myth* (Stanley Tong, 2005), *The Banquet* (Feng Xiaogang, 2006), *Fearless* (Ronny Yu, 2006), *The Warlords* (Peter Chan, 2007), *An Empress and the Warriors* (Ching Siu-tung, 2008), *Three Kingdoms: Resurrection of the Dragon* (Daniel Lee, 2008), *Red Cliff* (John Woo, 2008–9), *Mulan* (Jingle Ma, 2009), *Storm Warriors* (Oxide Pang and Danny Pang, 2009), *14 Blades* (Daniel Lee, 2010), *True Legend* (Yuen Woo-ping, 2010) and *Little Big Soldier* (Sheng Ding, 2010). These films were produced with mostly Asian markets in mind, while offering only limited theatrical and subsequent DVD sales in the United States. The titles by Zhang Yimou, Ronny Yu and John Woo were the exceptions so far, as finding wider American theatrical distribution is made easier with the name recognition and star power of Jet Li, Chow Yun-Fat, Gong Li, Zhang Ziyi and John Woo. Two additional observations are worth making here: first, *Crouching Tiger, Hidden Dragon* re-energised global interest in a genre that, throughout

its history, had experienced a cyclical pattern of waning and heightening audience enthusiasm. With the Hong Kong industry suffering a talent haemorrhage to Hollywood, this *wuxia* revivalism is hopefully a shot in the arm to a declining industry, especially as it negotiates coproduction alliances to become part of the larger transnational film effort. Second, this splintering effect from Hollywood's 'cooptation' of the genre also seemingly has an impact on the aesthetic reconfiguration of the new films, as directors innovate by retooling older conventions and presenting fresh modes of visuality to sustain audience interest. A discernable pattern, for example, has emerged in the films *Seven Swords*, *Three Kingdoms: Resurrection of the Dragon* and, especially, *The Warlords*, where a certain earthy and 'gritty' texture in the films' *mise en scène* constructs a hyperbolic realism as a counterpoint to the exotic coloration and visual Disneyfication that Hollywood has too easily latched onto.[6] Whether this aesthetic recalibration has any sustainability remains to be seen; but what is important is that non-Hollywood film-makers, in reacting to and challenging Hollywood's fascination with the *wuxia pian*, are rethinking the genre for a new generation of viewers in Asia.

Before discussing Hollywood's assimilation of the *wuxia pian*, I want to spotlight briefly Zhang Yimou's *Hero*, not simply because it is a visually stunning and politically controversial film, but also that it indirectly highlights Quentin Tarantino as a significant player in facilitating the mainstreaming process of Chinese martial arts cinema in America. In expanding *Hero*'s narrative scope to engage Chinese political and cultural nationalism, Zhang Yimou's *Hero* made its mark in distinguishing itself from *Crouching Tiger, Hidden Dragon*. It is also fair to say that it helped intensify American interest in the genre and cement Zhang's reputation as an auteur par excellence in his ability to construct visually brilliant imagery that caters to mainstream hankering for kung fu exotica and spectacle. Quentin Tarantino's cultural capital played an instrumental part in motivating Miramax Pictures to release the film in the United States two years after its international premiere. Uncertain about *Hero*'s appeal, 'Miramax sought to edit the film but facing resistance from Tarantino, who loved the film, later added his name as a presenter credit to gain greater attention for the release.'[7]

Tarantino's love for the *wuxia pian*, particularly Shaw cinema, has also led him to incorporate elements into

Kill Bill Vol. 1 and *Vol. 2* (Quentin Tarantino, 2003/4), thereby producing a mode of cinematic citationality that represents the film-maker as an 'action film connoisseur'.[8] This form of postmodern cinephilia that Tarantino helped popularise[9] has a profound effect on the morphological transmutations of Hollywood genres in general and, of course, in Hollywood's adoption and remaking of the *wuxia pian*. For a start, it makes cultural, financial and practical sense for corporate Hollywood to either help finance co-productions while leaving the creative expertise to its Asian partners and film-makers, as in the case of *Crouching Tiger, Hidden Dragon*, or to play the role of distributor of foreign-made *wuxia* films, while finding strategic means to brand them with the Hollywood seal of approval – *Hero* through Tarantino is an instance. But with each filmic success, the Hollywood machinery's propensity for saturation and overkill leads to seepage of *wuxia* elements cutting across generic boundaries: science fiction films like *The Matrix* series and the *Star Wars* prequels deploy kung fu and swordplay techniques, borrowed from the *wuxia* and kung fu traditions.[10] Hong Kong actor and director Yuen Woo-ping is now Hollywood's star action choreographer, having worked on *The Matrix* trilogy, *Crouching Tiger, Hidden Dragon*, *Kill Bill* and *The Forbidden Kingdom*. Hybrid versions of the police-detective-crime action flick, like the *Rush Hour* series, *The Tuxedo* (Kevin Donovan, 2002), *The Transporter* series and the *Charlie's Angels* films; the Western, in the form of *Shanghai Noon* (Tom Dey, 2000) and *Shanghai Knights* (David Dobkin, 2003); and the adventure film, such as *The Mummy: Tomb of the Dragon Emperor* (Rob Cohen, 2008) all feature action sequences that tap into the Hollywood-martial arts buzz. To ensure verisimilitude, these films disrupt cultural boundaries and even the laws of space and time to populate *wuxia* or kung fu elements within the films' diegetic worlds. This filmic mechanism of disruption mirrors or parallels the discursive structures of postmodern cinephilia.

Prior to *Crouching Tiger, Hidden Dragon*, Hollywood did not have the cultural fortitude, ability, or desire to produce a clearly identifiable instance of the *wuxia pian* with all its traditional generic trappings. B-movie kung fu-style films of the Bruce Lee ilk were aplenty, especially in the 1970s. More recent titles like *Kung Pow: Enter the Fist* (Steve Oedekerk, 2002) and *Balls of Fury* (Robert Ben Garant, 2007) fall into this category but with a parodic quality that disables the cultural

weightiness of the genre. This comedic mode is probably an easy way to circumvent cultural offence, especially with *wuxia* and kung fu purists, while still imbibing the genre 'authenticity' of films like *Shaolin Soccer* (Stephen Chow, 2001) and *Kung Fu Hustle*. I have in mind particularly DreamWorks Animation's *Kung Fu Panda* (Mark Osborne and John Stevenson, 2008), where Jackie Chan has a supporting voice role to lend the film kung fu 'credibility'. But having animated animal figures assume the roles of human characters again is another strategic mode of circumvention. So, it is within this cinematic context that I wish to situate *The Forbidden Kingdom*, a film I consider to be the closest Hollywood ever got to a moderately convincing attempt at a *wuxia pian* outside Ang Lee's defining film.

The Law of the *Wuxia* Genre

Before embarking on this analysis, I want to return briefly to the question of the *wuxia pian* as genre. The weightiness of *wuxia* historicism presses up against any contemporary attempts to reconfigure the genre, particularly if the agents of these attempts are, or are viewed as, culturally foreign and, hence, intrusive. In his magisterial account of the *wuxia pian*'s connections to Chinese culture, Stephen Teo identifies ties to Beijing Opera, painting, calligraphy, philosophy, religion, ancient and modern literature, political history and, of course, actual martial arts. The cultural gravitas of these interdisciplinary intersections is compounded and complicated by the *wuxia* film's long history, almost as comparably extensive as the history of cinema itself.

What is especially valuable in Teo's narrative of *wuxia pian* history is that he presses back against this weightiness by challenging the cultural purity of the form through confronting its very historicity: 'The genre is unified by its cultural history and its historicism but at the same time is ruptured and torn apart from its historical continuity by history itself, which is far from a smooth process, and by the interruptions of outside forces (chiefly, the influences of foreign genres).'[11] He demonstrates this assertion by showing how the Shanghai versions of the genre in the late 1920s 'were nothing more than imitations of the western, the swashbuckler, or the European medieval romance even though *wuxia* was meant to countervail these genres'.[12] Particularly convincing is Teo's analysis of the 'real kung fu' in the Wong Fei-hung films (of Kwan Tak-hing and the later incarnations of the historic figure by Shaw cinema, Jackie Chan and Jet Li), where he argues that this notion of authenticity is really just '*representations* of the real, involving different forms of resemblance and performance and a high degree of choreography'.[13] This seemingly obvious point is profound in that it throws into relief the cinematic nature of the *wuxia pian*, reinforcing not just its artful constructedness but also its technologised modernity,[14] a comingling of traditional culture, modern practices and capitalist forces that points to the very hybrid nature of cinema and the *wuxia* genre.

As much as one could argue forcefully and convincingly for the generic 'impurity' that is the *wuxia pian*, this theoretical idealism still does not detract from the culturalist insistence of the genre's call, a reality that raises a number of difficult and sometimes visceral questions: as Hollywood assimilates, incorporates, or remakes the *wuxia pian*, how does one critically tend to the fact that corporate Hollywood has the propensity to cannibalise other cinematic traditions for its own capitalist profit? Even if the populist *wuxia pian* should not be treated as some preciously fragile museum cultural artefact, which it should not be, what attitude must one have towards the historical weightiness that the genre brings, especially as Hollywood remixes the form with greater and greater latitude? Will one react in the same way, for instance, to the potential travesty of a Chinese film company remaking a John Ford Western or a treasured classic like *The Wizard of Oz* (Victor Fleming, 1939)? Can the Hollywood *wuxia* remake avoid the Orientalist gaze, particularly when the object of the gaze is a cultural traditionalism and exoticism that the genre already inherently embodies? These ideologically loaded questions are not meant to betray a strident cultural nationalism on my part, an essentialist position that I find problematic, to say the least. Rather, these questions are posed as potential gut reactions from a cultural 'insider' (at the risk of creating a rhetorical straw man) upon which to pivot a series of alternate questions: should one not embrace this remaking as an inevitable part of transnational cinema's postmodern cinephilia, a global trend that can help revitalise the waning industries of the various Chinese cinemas? Should one not celebrate the fact that Chinese cinema through the *wuxia pian* has actually made a successful entry into the American market, which will bode well for the global reception of Chinese culture in the new millennium?[15] Could one not relish the pleasures of a relatively well-made film like *The Forbidden Kingdom* without having to nurse the stigmatisation of consuming its cultural 'inauthenticity'? These competing sets of questions unveil the contradictions that the Hollywood *wuxia* trend portends.

The Forbidden Kingdom: The New Hollywood *Wuxia pian*

Rob Minkoff's *The Forbidden Kingdom* deserves special note in this discussion of Hollywood's remake of the *wuxia pian* for a number of reasons, one of which is that its production circumstance exemplifies the transnational direction Hollywood cinema has taken, especially as it seeks to incorporate the creative cinematic energies of the Asian film industries. Coproduced by a number of American and Chinese film companies and distributed in the United States by Lionsgate and the Weinstein Company, the film was shot on location in China's Gobi Desert, the bamboo forests of Jiangsu and at the Hengdian World Studios.[16] The use of the Hengdian studios marks an important paradigm shift in production philosophy, as Hollywood studios are starting to take advantage of the low-priced rentals of studios in China to make culturally specific films. With China welcoming capital from the West, state-run and private companies like China Film Group and Hengdian World Studios are finding different opportunities of collaborating with Hollywood at various stages of the film production process.[17] While the production circumstance of *The Forbidden Kingdom* is

The Forbidden Kingdom: clash of the kung fu titans. Jet Li and Jackie Chan's screen battle

undoubtedly symptomatic of a transnational capitalist synergistic trend, I also see a production strategy that is culturally pragmatic in its clever short-circuiting of the genre's traditionalism and history by bringing onboard the very best Chinese talent money can buy. Director Minkoff has pulled off a cinematic coup by bringing together two of Chinese kung fu cinema's giants to spar for the very first time: Jackie Chan and Jet Li. With a Chinese cast and crew assisting and advising the production team, a form of representational authenticity is thus enabled. Furthering this meta-narrative of 'authenticity' are biographical details of the director demonstrating how fit he is to take on the genre, thereby revealing a cultural anxiety to forestall, if not counter, the weighty history of the *wuxia pian*:

The Forbidden Kingdom: Liu Yifei's Golden Sparrow pays homage to Cheng Pei-pei's Golden Swallow

> *The Forbidden Kingdom* is the culmination of Minkoff's life-long interest in Chinese culture and tradition. A student of traditional Kung Fu cinema, Minkoff has spent the last ten years since first visiting China living between the US and Beijing. In addition, he and his wife, a 76th generational descendant of Confucius, continue a dedication to the study of Traditional and Pop Chinese Culture.[18]

It is with no personal disrespect to Minkoff, or a need to engage in an essentialist identity politics, that I trace here the subconscious acknowledgment of cultural difference in this discourse of authentication in spite of its assertion of cultural connectedness on a personal level.

While cultural 'authenticity' might play a significant role in the film-maker's considerations of global success, the film needed to distinguish itself from other *wuxia* productions by including American narrative elements that will immediately appeal to mainstream US audiences, thus attenuating the cultural strangeness of its 'faithfulness' to *wuxia* conventions and *mise en scène*. This is achieved through the insertion of South Boston teenage character Jason Tripitikas (Michael Angarano) into the magical *wuxia* world set in a temporally indeterminate ancient China. Transported by the Monkey King's magic staff through a time-warp portal called 'the Gate of No Gate', Jason finds himself joined by Lu Yan the Drunken Scholar (Jackie Chan), the Silent Monk (Jet Li) and Golden Sparrow (Liu Yifei) on the road towards the evil Jade Warlord's mountain hideaway. Therefore, Jason becomes the kung fu-crazed male version of Judy Garland's Dorothy in *The Wizard of Oz*, searching for a way home. The exoticism that is the *wuxia* world parallels the candy-coloured alienation that is the world of Oz; with Jason's companions, aptly characterised by the evil white-haired swordswoman Ni Chang (Li Bingbing) as 'misfits', filling in for the Tin Man, the Scarecrow and the Cowardly Lion. The obviousness of this correlation is intended for American audiences to pick up on. The insertion of contemporary America in the figure of Jason Tripitikas, while symbolically marking Hollywood's entry into the *wuxia pian* market and the mainstream American experience of the genre, also diegetically Americanises the cinematic form enough to produce for the film-maker an additional space for creative and cultural latitude that preempts once more the accusatory force of genre history. Interestingly, the film can also be seen, not unproblematically, as a nominal Asian American text, signalled not only by Jason Tripitikas[19] as a hybrid configuration but also the film's cross-cultural romantic ending where Jason reunites with a reincarnated Golden Sparrow in Asian American guise.

Quentin Tarantino's postmodern cinephilia has had a tremendous influence on how contemporary Hollywood films approach cinematic cultures outside their traditions. *The Forbidden Kingdom* deploys this mode of Tarantinian citationality rather effectively, particularly in the opening sequences where one is introduced to Jason's kung fu preoccupation. As the camera cuts from the Monkey King's battling of the Jade Warlord's military minions on a mountain top to Jason waking up from his dream in his bedroom – implying the possibility that the entire time travel *mise en abyme* to ancient China could conceivably also be a dream sequence bookended by the South Boston narrative – the audience is given a glimpse of what inhabits the psyche of the protagonist. Playing on the television in Jason's bedroom while he is asleep is the Shaw adaptation of *Xiyou ji*, *Monkey Goes West* (Ho Menghua, 1964), a classic instance of *wuxia shenguai*, a hybrid form that infuses supernatural elements into the *wuxia pian*.[20] (*The Forbidden Kingdom* actually belongs to this particular subcategory.) The camera gaze then tilts upwards to capture what is tacked on the wall behind Jason's bed, a collage of posters and images reflecting bits of *wuxia* cinematic history and paraphernalia. These images suddenly spring to life in surrealist fashion, as one is ushered into the opening credit sequence. Painted poster figures from films like *Legendary Weapons of China* (Lau Kar-leung, 1982), *The 36th Chamber of Shaolin* (Lau Kar-leung, 1977), *Come Drink with Me* (King Hu, 1966), *The Flying Guillotine* (Ho Menghua, 1975) and *Return of the One Armed Swordsman* (Chang Cheh, 1969), together with images of Bruce Lee, inundate the screen in rapid succession to build an impressionistic visual archive of classic *wuxia pian* (though mostly taken from the Shaw Brothers collection). The non-diegetic nature of this visual montage provides a tongue-in-cheek homage to the genre's extensive history, reinforcing a deep consciousness of what *The Forbidden Kingdom* will inevitably be compared to. But this tribute also functions as a strategically light-hearted discursive barrier that shields the film from the criticism of never being able to meet up to the cultural standards of the *wuxia* purist on account of its Hollywood status. Thus, it is in this spirit of cinematic homage that the film-maker further includes allusions to *The Bride with White Hair* (Ronny Yu, 1993) in the form of the similarly white-haired Ni Chang; and to Cheng Pei-pei's classic turn as the character Golden Swallow in *Come Drink with Me*, this time in the figure of Golden Sparrow taunting the Jade Warlord with the line 'Come drink with me' as she unsuccessfully attempts to kill the immortal with her jade pin. The effectiveness of this discourse lies in its ability to split itself through humorous self-deprecation as a route towards eventually taking itself seriously, which the shopkeeper Old Hop's jovial response to Jason's DVD queries indicates: 'Leopard style, dragon style, fly though air, fight on water, crouching tiger, spanking monkey. I know you. Another white boy who wants to know kung fu. Kick the ass. Get the girls.' Old Hop's observation is subsequently followed closely by a sequence of scenes that leads to the almost deadly serious affair of ensuring that the mysterious staff in the shop's storeroom is returned to its rightful owner, the basic premise of the film's *wuxia* narrative.

To conclude, I want to turn to Jet Li's and Jackie Chan's response to the making of the film, which serves as an insightful indicator of the fraught cultural politics ethnic Chinese audiences find themselves negotiating. As the film entered into the post-production stage, the level of anticipation of a Jet Li–Jackie Chan match-up was sky high. In order to downplay these expectations, Jackie Chan confesses to the Chinese media that 'the movie I just shot with Jet Li … actually isn't that great … [It] is a movie made for Americans. Chinese viewers may not like it.' Echoing his colleague through his website, Jet Li argues that 'this is an American production, created by an American screenwriter, about an American child's dream of the Journey To The West story. It would be more interesting to approach this film from a different angle.' Clearly, the cultural nationalist slant is meant for their Chinese fans, as is reified by Jackie Chan's intimation of how he 'would rather return to Asia to make … [his] own Asian films'.[21] As the earlier discursive splitting in the film is suggestive of a cultural anxiety on the part of the film-maker, there is a reverse mirroring here at work as Li and Chan seek to straddle both Asia and Hollywood. This splitting effect is again produced in part by the perceived necessity to bow to the historical gravitas of the genre's history, in the articulation that because it 'is an American production', it 'actually isn't that great'; while implicitly acknowledging that taking part in such a production is now a financial and practical necessity borne of the changes engendered by the Hollywood transnational factor. While one empathises and identifies with this sense of conflict, even as one nervously (and maybe contradictorily) relishes the pleasures of the new Hollywood *wuxia pian*, the critical task ahead of us is to track persistently its morphological and political transformations in order to critique incisively the slippery object that is transnational cinema.

Notes

1. See Stephen Teo's discussion of the film and the critical literature he catalogues: Stephen Teo, *Chinese Martial Arts Cinema: The* Wuxia *Tradition* (Edinburgh: Edinburgh University Press, 2009), pp. 172–80.

2. In Teo's extensive definition of the terms, '*wuxia* and kung fu denote respectively the swordplay movie and the fist-fighting movie' and 'can usefully be seen as two distinct but inter-related genres'. Ibid., p. 5.

3. Ang Lee, preface to Linda Sunshine (ed.), Crouching Tiger, Hidden Dragon: *A Portrait of the Ang Lee Film* (New York: Newmarket Press, 2000), p. 7.

4. In arguing that, unlike the kung fu film, the *wuxia pian* has 'been judged by distributors as too esoteric for non-Asian audiences' in the past, Leon Hunt accounts for the film's success by defining it 'as a pan-Asian block-buster' with art film credentials. Leon Hunt, *Kung Fu Cult Masters: From Bruce Lee to* Crouching Tiger (London: Wallflower Press, 2003), pp. 7, 182.

5. With studios creating international production sub-units and participating in co-productions, it is increasingly difficult to delineate what is or isn't Hollywood. Here, I classify Hollywood *wuxia* films as those that have a major Hollywood studio involvement and are given a nationwide US release.

6. Sonia Kolesnikov-Jessop, 'Redefining the Epic', *Newsweek*, 24 December 2007, <www.newsweek.com/id/78119> (accessed 28 November 2009).

7. Eugene Hernandez, 'Better Late Than Never, "Hero" a Hit in US Release', *indieWIRE*, 30 August 2004, <www.indiewire.com/article/better_late_than_never_hero_a_hit_in_u.s._release/> (accessed 28 November 2009).

8. Aaron Anderson, 'Mindful Violence: The Visibility of Power and Inner Life in *Kill Bill*', *Jump Cut: A Review of Contemporary Media* no. 47 (2005), <www.ejumpcut.org/archive/jc47.2005/KillBill/text.html> (accessed 28 November 2009).

9. For Tarantino's cinephilia in his films, see David Desser, 'Global Noir: Genre Film in the Age of Transnationalism', in Barry Keith Grant (ed.), *Film Genre Reader III* (Austin: University of Texas Press, 2003), pp. 526–30.

10. Hunt, *Kung Fu Cult Masters*, pp. 31, 179–81.

11. Teo, *Chinese Martial Arts Cinema*, p. 8.

12. Ibid., p. 10.

13. Ibid., p. 70.

14. Hunt discusses kung fu cinema's negotiation of this technology throughout its history. See especially Hunt, *Kung Fu Cult Masters*, pp. 197–200.

15. Offering an alternative analysis to Hollywood's homogenising impact on Chinese media cultures is Michael Curtin, *Playing to the World's Biggest Audience: The Globalization of Chinese Film and TV* (Berkeley: University of California Press, 2007).

16. The production information comes from <www.imdb.com/title/tt0865556/>

17. Alex S. Dai, 'Made in Asia: China', *The Hollywood Reporter*, 25 September 2008, <www.hollywoodreporter.com/hr/content_display/news/e3ie896e11cd20b3343ec2c8c697252fc85> (accessed 30 November 2009). See also Emilie Yueh-yu Yeh and Darrell William Davis, 'Re-nationalizing China's Film Industry: Case Study on the China Film Group and Film Marketization', *Journal of Chinese Cinemas* vol. 2 no. 1 (2008), pp. 37–51.

18. <www.forbiddenkingdommovie.com/main.html> (accessed 30 November 2009).

19. A figure in Buddhist lore, Tripitaka finds literary incarnation in the sixteenth-century literary classic *Xiyou ji* (Journey to the West).

20. '*Shenguai* denotes gods and spirits (*shen*) and the strange and the bizarre (*guai*: which could also refer to monsters and creatures of legend and the imagination).' Teo, *Chinese Martial Arts Cinema*, p. 11.

21. 'Jackie and Jet's Movie "Isn't Great"', *The Straits Times*, 20 September 2007, Life section, p. 12.

Further Reading in *Chinese Films In Focus II*

17 On the Shoulders of Giants

Tsai Ming-liang, Jia Zhangke, Fruit Chan and the Struggles of Second Generation Auteurism

James Udden

If talent is arguably the most overstated component of auteurism (the director as 'author'), then perhaps the most overlooked is timing, followed by place. Fellini, Bergman, Antonioni and Kurosawa are familiar names in large part because they were all virtual 'firsts' on the burgeoning film festival scene as it was taking shape in postwar Europe; their names came to define postwar 'art cinema' as it was still being institutionalised. There was little need to compare them to predecessors, because in effect there were none. Moreover, they became the standard bearers, the cinematic forefathers, by which subsequent generations of aspiring art cinema auteurs would be compared. In short, Fellini, Bergman et al. were not just a talented group, they happened to be at the right place at the right time.

But what of the second generation auteurs? An ingenious answer is the French New Wave, which had all the advantages of being at the centre of world film culture at the time. These young mavericks largely defined the conceptual parameters of auteurism while writing for *Cahiers du cinéma* in the 1950s. When they began to make films themselves, they strategically acknowledged the film history before them, consciously littering their works with witty homage and loving citations, including exploring the extremes of previous film styles, everything from monstrously long takes to the most fragmentary editing. So successful were Truffaut and Godard in particular that they became the equals of Fellini and Bergman. In this way the French New Wave was also a 'first'. Yet they also created a burden of history for everyone following them, including subsequent new cinemas across the globe. Any film-maker thereafter will invariably be compared to those before, straddled with endless discussions of 'influences', 'reminders', 'similarities', 'cinematic allusions' or 'stylistic derivations'. In some places, such as Japan, the burden can become a straightjacket: for example, Mark Schilling notes that a major obstacle to Shunji Iwai gaining recognition overseas was because he did not emulate the 'golden age' of Japanese cinema embodied in Kurosawa, Ozu and Mizoguchi.[1]

This overall pattern of second generation auteurism has repeated itself in Chinese-language cinema. The Fifth Generation in China, Hou Hsiao-hsien and Edward Yang in Taiwan, and Wong Kar-wai in Hong Kong had a lightened burden of history because they the first directors from their respective 'Chinas' to rise to the top of the well-established festival circuit. Varying degrees of originality notwithstanding, their having no *local* cinematic forebears, coming from 'national' cinemas with no previous festival presence or accolades, played heavily in their favour. Unfortunately, those immediately following are saddled with a daunting challenge: not only must they distinguish themselves from art cinema *en masse*, they face a critical hall of mirrors where their films seemingly cannot be discussed without reference to Hou, Wong, et al.

This becomes evident in the cases of Tsai Ming-liang, Jia Zhangke and Fruit Chan. Hailing from Taiwan, the PRC and Hong Kong respectively, all are present-day, Chinese-language auteurs dependent on the film festivals and articles such as this to perpetuate a discourse concerning their works. More importantly, however, all three are also literally standing on the shoulders of giants, even if they do not always acknowledge them. Of the three, however, only Tsai Ming-liang to date has managed to generate as much critical and academic literature on him as have Wong and Hou. Tsai also has received the most awards at major film festivals around the world. By stark contrast, Fruit Chan has generated the least notice and fewest awards, while Jia Zhangke falls in between. Why this disparity? The primary reason is that of the three second generation auteurs, Tsai Ming-liang had the most stable institutional backing during the crucial early stages of his career. This key advantage has allowed Tsai Ming-liang to most consciously play the requisite 'game' of a second generation auteur within his particular context, and adeptly respond to the welter of cinematic precedence – Chinese and otherwise – he faces. Before explaining these different contexts in detail, we need to first summarise Tsai's standing in the festival and critical community compared to both Jia and Chan.

Despite the significant political and economic differences between Taiwan, mainland China and Hong Kong, all three directors similarly lack both a stable commercial film industry and a reliable domestic audience. Their only viable option remains to make films primarily for foreign audiences at film festivals, making them dependent on the discourses generated by both the critical and academic communities. In this respect, Tsai Ming-liang, Jia Zhangke and Fruit Chan are all successful auteurs, albeit to varying degrees. Their films are accepted at film festival competitions on a regular basis. In both the films and their attendant interviews, all three directors broach issues of philosophical and socio-political import, yet not too clearly or forcefully. This makes their films amenable to a perpetual game of cinematic and non-cinematic intertextuality, most of all between the directors' oeuvres and the not insignificant number of writings about them. Of particular interest are not the

Tsai Ming-liang's *The Wayward Cloud*

Tsai Ming-liang's *The Hole*

convergences in the critical and academic literature, but the divergences and contradictions. If there was unanimous agreement on any of these three directors, then the auteurist games would be over, and the lifeblood discourses sustaining them would cease.

Yet the three are not equal in this regard, mainly due to differing *domestic* conditions. Clearly Tsai Ming-liang has managed to win the largest share of festival awards of the three. With only his second film, *Vive L'amour* (1994), Tsai had already won the top prize at Venice, the Golden Lion. With his next film, *The River* (1997), he won the Silver Bear at Berlin. The controversial *The Wayward Cloud* (2005) not only garnered another Silver Bear for Tsai at Berlin, but also the Alfred Bauer Award, a special jury prize awarded to a film which is deemed to have opened new perspectives in the art of film-making. He has had no less than three films nominated for the Golden Palm at Cannes: *The Hole* (1998), *What Time Is It There?* (2001) and *Visage* (2009). Nothing perhaps better demonstrates Tsai Ming-liang's standing among critics than his winning three special FIPRESCI (International Federation of Film

Critics) awards for *The Hole* (Cannes in 1998), *Goodbye Dragon Inn* (Venice in 2003) and *The Wayward Cloud* (Berlin in 2005).

Jia Zhangke clearly comes in 'second', since he can at least match Tsai with his own Golden Lion at Venice in 2006 for *Still Life*. Moreover, his related documentary, *Dong* (2006) also won two other awards at Venice, including one for best documentary. Two other efforts by Jia – *Platform* (2000) and *The World* (2004) – have been nominated at Venice, while two more have been entered in the competition for the Golden Palm at Cannes: *Unknown Pleasures* (2002) and *24 City* (2008). Two early Jia works, *Xiao Wu* (1997) and *Platform*, won the Golden Montgolfiere, the top prize at the Nantes Film festival.

The highest award that Fruit Chan can claim is arguably his sole Golden Montogolfiere at Nantes for his breakthrough film, *Made in Hong Kong* (1997). This same film also won a special prize that same year at Locarno, where only two years later he would garner the Silver Leopard for *Little Cheung* (1999). Chan has had two films nominated for the Golden Lion at Venice –

Durian, Durian (2000) and *Hollywood Hong Kong* (2001) – and he won a special mention there in 2002 for his short, *Public Toilet* (2002). But unlike Tsai and Jia, Fruit Chan's top prizes to date are all still restricted to the 'gateway' festivals such as Nantes and Locarno and more 'local' festivals in Hong Kong and Taiwan. He has never received a first or second prize at any of the so-call 'big three' festivals of Venice, Cannes and Berlin, nor have any of his films even been even entered in the competitions of the latter two.

An even greater disparity appears in the literature about these three auteurs, at least when using blunt numerical measurements. In November of 2009, the online search engine, *The Film and Television Literature Index*, produced no less than 256 sources for Tsai Ming-liang versus only sixty-two for Fruit Chan. Using both spellings for Jia Zhangke (aka Jia Zhang-ke), produced 206 sources for the mainland director, fifty less than those found for Tsai. The next most thorough search engine was *Academic Search Premier*, and the differences become even more pronounced: Tsai still has 173 references, whereas Jia has eighty-seven and Chan has a mere nineteen. Granted, these are crude measurements and should be taken with a grain of salt. Yet it seems difficult to pretend that these numbers do not tell us something since they conform exactly to their varying degrees of success at top-tiered film festivals.

The reasons for these notable differences can largely be found by looking at the vastly different institutional backing these three directors received early on in their careers. Tsai is not technically Taiwanese, but a Malaysian-born-and-raised Chinese who received his university education in Taiwan, after which he joined the theatre and film worlds on the island. Particularly crucial is that Tsai managed to make his first three films at the KMT (Kuomintang)-run Central Motion Picture Corporation (CMPC) in Taiwan, and received support through the controversial Assistance and Guidance Grant offered by the Taiwanese government. It is no surprise that Tsai Ming-liang chose to remain in Taiwan and pursue the idiosyncratic vein of film-making he is clearly interested in: had he returned to his native Malaysia, he simply would not have found anything like the CMPC or the Assistance and Guidance Grant, not to mention the general openness to certain strong content with which he has peppered his films. More to the point, however, he also would not have had such a clear pipeline to the top film festivals already well established in Taiwan by the time Tsai directed his first film.

In the 1980s, the ROC government in Taiwan first tested the waters of 'upper middle-rank' festivals such as Locarno and Nantes. These festivals were particularly in tune to the economic transformations in East Asia at the time[2] and they served a key role as 'gateway' festivals from which new national cinemas then moved on 'up' to the likes of Cannes and Venice. (Another clear example of this would be Iran.) Due to repeated success at such festivals, by 1986 both Hou Hsiao-hsien and Edward Yang had received awards from the government in recognition of their cultural diplomacy for a 'nation' no longer officially recognised by most other governments in the world.[3]

The biggest changes would be in 1989. Not only was Hou's *City of Sadness* the first Taiwanese film to be entered in the competition of a top-tiered festival (Venice), it also won the top prize. This was the Taiwanese equivalent to Kurosawa's *Rashomon*, which won the same prize in Venice in 1951, thus opening the floodgates for several more Japanese festival victories in the 1950s. Taiwan was already a rising 'hot' cinema, but after 1989 it clearly was the equal of any national cinema in the festival world. During the 1990s Taiwan would have four films nominated for the Golden Palm at Cannes while both Germany and Italy would have none, much to the chagrin of both nations.[4] Meanwhile, 1989 was also the first year of the Assistance and Guidance Grant for cinema in Taiwan, and this provided a key funding base for film-makers, including an aspiring Tsai Ming-liang who made his debut film in 1992, *Rebels of the Neon God*. This is not to say that it has been a piece of cake for Tsai. The Assistance and Guidance Grant has been exceedingly controversial in Taiwan and Tsai Ming-liang proved to be a lightning rod in those controversies since he is from Malaysia.[5] The fact that he was able to contend for a Golden Lion with only his *second* film, *Vive L'amour*, is perhaps more significant than his actually winning that prize. Clearly the trails had already been well blazed for him, just as he made his debut with ample institutional support from a government desperate for any sort of PR, even if it meant funding a film that includes a scene of an accidental hand job between father and son in a gay bathhouse (*The River*). Controversies notwithstanding, by that point Tsai was well established enough that he could thereafter largely rely on international financing. Still, he owes more to Taiwan than he seems to admit.

By stark contrast, Fruit Chan enjoyed no such advantages during the crucial early stage of his career. Hong Kong was long a popular cinema par excellence where stardom and genre trumped any needs for auteurism. The exception to this rule, of course, is Wong Kar-wai. Wong launched his directorial career without government support in 1988, and Fruit Chan would attempt the same in the mid-1990s. Yet when Wong's career began, the Hong Kong film industry was still at its economic peak. Moreover, he started with a genre work, *As Tears Go By* (1988), which capitalised on the 'hero cycle' of the late 1980s with the added benefit of multiple stars. True, Wong nearly ended his career after the box-office disaster of *Days of Being Wild* (1990), yet he managed to make films again in 1994 by riding the coat-tails of the big-budgeted *wuxia* craze in the early 1990s, commencing production on *Ashes of Time* (1994) before it was clearly evident to everyone that the heyday of the Hong Kong film industry had just passed. Wong was also fortuitously obligated by contract to complete a second film in 1994, *Chungking Express*. This was yet another genre film Wong would radically transform, once again with the aid of multiple stars. Thereafter, he was impervious to the industrial decline in Hong Kong since he could depend on international funding and film festivals, even winning Best Director at Cannes in 1997 with *Happy Together*. Fruit Chan, on the other hand, had only one insignificant commercial film under his belt (*Finale in Blood*, 1993) when the Hong Kong film industry took a nosedive as its box office and production numbers halved between 1992 and 1997.[6] He may have had the support of Andy Lau to make his breakthrough work, *Made in Hong Kong*, but he did not have Andy Lau star in the actual film. Moreover, he had to scrounge for leftover film stock over the years, making the film on a shoestring budget of only HK$500,000.[7]

At first glance, Jia Zhangke's beginnings were even more inauspicious. Unlike the Fifth Generation before him, Jia and others of the so-called Sixth Generation did not have the state-run studios (i.e., Xi'an) to support their initial feature-length works. Thus, from the start they were forced to find both funding and audiences from abroad, and without any official government sanction or assistance.[8] Added to this were the political pressures, since Jia's first three films were banned within China itself. This being true, one could still argue that this is the one advantage Jia Zhangke had over Fruit Chan: no doubt both Chan and Jia were

initially 'independent' directors in their respective *economic* contexts, largely because of the circumstances foisted upon them. However, only Jia can claim that he is also *politically* independent, which makes directors of his ilk 'a valued dissident in the eyes of film critics in the West'.[9] Moreover, since the release of *The World*, his films now receive the official sanction of the PRC government, likely because it is to their benefit to appear to be supporting one of their own directors of such international stature, if not also because they now realise that his films represent no immediate political threat. Even if Jia did not have stars to work with much like Fruit Chan, in mainland China it is easier to make a star of your own out of a relative unknown, which Jia has done to some extent with repeated use of actors such as Zhen Tao.

Given these radically differing institutional and industrial contexts, each of these directors has had to play the game of 'second generation' auteur in different ways. Once again, however, Tsai Ming-liang has the most avenues to potentially exploit. Not only has he cleverly infused his films with a diverse array of cinematic and other references, the combined effect of his films, plus his extracinematic commentary, together create an auteurist persona with the clearest set of questions *and* equivocations, most of all with the presence of gay themes, and questions concerning Tsai's national identity and style.

There is no denying that almost every Tsai film features gay themes in conjunction with families not functioning according to societal norms. Tsai Ming-liang, however, complicates the issue when asked about it, as he does here regarding the now infamous bathhouse scene in *The River*: 'I'm sick of people labelling my films as "gay films" or "dysfunctional family films." My films are not about dysfunctional families and they are not about gays, they are about human beings and the difficulties of being human.'[10] Such statements are openings for others to comment. Song Hwee Lim argues 'that despite Tsai's protestations of and self-distancing from such labels, he has constructed a poetics of desire in his works that not only invites but almost demands a reading that is invariably queer'.[11] Emilie Yueh-yu Yeh and Darrell William Davis find a strange hybridity in Tsai that displays 'a peculiar from of camp' (somewhat akin to Jack Smith) which is both highly avant-garde yet in tune with the vitality of working-class street life.[12] In diametrical opposition, Gina Marchetti detects a conservative Confucian undercurrent with the mysterious pain in the neck of the protagonist in *The River*: 'the symptom can be read as the root of the malaise, and the reconstitution of the patriarchy can be seen as a potential cure. From this perspective, Hsiao Kang's homosexuality is his "disease."'[13] It matters not who is 'right' on this issue; what matters for the auteur is that it *remains* an issue, open-ended and irresolvable.

The same applies to Tsai's national identity. Once when asked about which place is home, Tsai jokingly answered, 'I am a Taiwanese director from Malaysia.'[14] Although he goes on to say he does not care about his identities, this is a calculated joke. The films of Hou Hsiao-hsien and Edward Yang are for the most part unthinkable without Taiwan. With Tsai, however, it is debatable whether these films are specifically about Taiwan or not. Certainly the apartments, streets, markets and rivers are all identifiably Taiwanese locales, but they are bleached of the throngs of people who normally inhabit the films of Hou and Yang. Once again, you can go either way. Peter Hitchcock hints at this tension in this statement: 'If Tsai is indeed attempting to distance his work from the messy coordinates of time and space that is Taiwan, then it is remarkable how much of what passes for content in his oeuvre requires precisely this integer of location for the films to work as film.'[15] Others also find Taiwan haunting his films. David Barton says the dead father in *What Time Is It There?* represents 'a fascinating relationship to Taiwan which cannot seem to stop mourning its own dead father, Chiang Kai Shek, because it is undecided if it is dead yet'.[16] Kenneth Chan states that King Hu's film in *Goodbye Dragon Inn* reminds one 'of the wounds of Taiwan's troubled local histories';[17] in particular the Japanese man in the theatre reminds us of 'the Japanese occupation of Taiwan from 1895 to 1945 … just as Japanese culture haunts Taiwanese culture'.[18] Once more one can make viable arguments either way. The real point is the perpetuation of the debate.

Strongly related is the question of style. It may very well be that Tsai's world-view in cinematic terms is dependent on minimal editing and camera movement. Moreover, there is no doubt that his world-view is almost diametrically opposed to that of Hou Hsiao-hsien and Edward Yang. Song Hwee Lim, for example, notes how much these are 'private I' worlds as opposed to the 'historical I' worlds of Hou and Yang.[19] Yet by the time Tsai made his first feature-length film, the long

take coupled with a mostly static camera was already well established as a 'national' style in Taiwan, and was soon to become a pan-Asian style of art cinema. However, Tsai never acknowledges this. When asked about this by Michael Berry, Tsai hints at some lingering resentment at not being welcomed at first by the established directors of the Taiwanese New Cinema from whom he clearly sets himself apart.[20] Elsewhere he speaks openly about Fassbinder, Bresson, Godard and Truffaut as being key influences,[21] but never Hou or Yang. In the films themselves, Tsai makes constant references to the multiple influences on him: Grace Chang (*The Hole*); King Hu (*Goodbye Dragon Inn*); Truffaut's *The 400 Blows* (1959) (*What Time Is It There?*); the modern-day alienation that reminds one of Antonioni; the absurdist humour that reminds one of Tati and Godard. Then there are the constant self-references through repeated motifs (most of all water) or the same roles by the same acting ensemble across several films.[22]

Of all the cinematic influences, Truffaut seems most important – *except at the level of style*. Therefore, while Tsai most violates the 'spirit' of Hou Hsiao-hsien thematically, and in his often starkly depopulated *mise en scène*, he nevertheless follows the literal 'letter' of Hou in at least one major stylistic aspect. Gina Marchetti calls this a 'derivative long take/long shot style',[23] a charge somewhat justified since all of Tsai's films display a strong proclivity towards long, *static* takes. Some attribute this tendency to 'European norms'[24] ignoring how the norm for long-take films both in Europe and elsewhere is not a static camera, but a mobile one. Tsai himself disingenuously attributes this to his own background in experimental theatre.[25] However, since his theatre career predates his cinematic one, why did this static camera/long-take style slowly develop instead of being there from the start? In his earlier films Tsai had some camera movements, while in the later *What Time Is It There?* there is not a single shot in the entire film that is either handheld or even moves for the slightest reframing, even though the average shot length exceeds a minute per shot. (The only exceptions, significantly, are brief inserts from Truffaut's *The 400 Blows*.) Even Hou was never quite this literal about static long takes, but Tsai joins other Asian directors (e.g., Hong Sang-soo from South Korea) in taking a pronounced tendency found in Hou up to *The Puppetmaster* (1993) to its logical conclusion – at least in one or two of their own films.[26]

Once again, this could be an auteurist ploy by Tsai: participating in a distinctive pan-Asian tendency in art cinema that is clearly inspired by Hou, without clear explanation, opens up yet another potential avenue of debate, albeit in this case one not yet fully explored.

It is not surprising, then, that less is written about Fruit Chan and Jia Zhangke. First off, the national and sexual identities of these two directors are not much in dispute. Instead, Chan is discussed mostly in terms of the Hong Kong/China relationship from 1997 to the present, whereas Jia is discussed largely as a cinematic poet/documentarian who, in indelible terms, is recording a period of remarkable and uncertain change in post-Maoist China. Granted, there is much to be discussed in both cases, but still not with the additional questions raised by Tsai Ming-liang. That being the case, there is now clear evidence that Jia Zhangke is subject to a much higher volume of critical/academic discourse than Fruit Chan.

Jia Zhangke does not follow the literal stylistic 'letter' of Hou Hsiao-hsien, but in his exploration of the post-Maoist Chinese experience, he openly acknowledges how much he is following the spiritual path set out by Hou. The seminal influence on Jia was *Yellow Earth* (1984), but he says he parted ways with the Fifth Generation once they pursued 'legend' over present reality.[27] Hou's *The Boys from Fengkuei* (1984), by contrast, inspired Jia to trust his own experiences to cinematically transcribe China's present socio-political landscape.[28] That Hou provides the greatest inspiration makes sense: in his own indelible poetic terms, Hou has recorded an astounding set of socio-political changes in Taiwan, and Jia appears to be doing the same for contemporary China. Both are also masters of quotidian details and landscapes (e.g., the boiling tea kettle at the end of *Platform*; the Three Gorges in *Still Life*).

Yet Jia is careful also to distinguish himself just enough without severing 'familial' ties: he is a consistently long-take director, but he has not taken the track of *literally* imitating Hou's static camera of old.[29] He certainly does not match Hou in terms of the complexity and density of staging and lighting, but would a UFO suddenly fly away in any Hou film as it does in *Still Life*? *The Puppetmaster* may have encouraged Jia to explore the boundaries between fiction and documentaries, but Jia has gone much further with this issue in both *Still Life* and *24 City* than Hou ever has. And perhaps no living director today knows better how

to end a film with images so indelible, from the crowd gathering around in *Xiao Wu*, to the boiling tea kettle in *Platform*, to the suspended tightrope in *Still Life*.

In this way Jia Zhangke has created a stable set of auteurist parameters that artfully begin with Hou, but do not end there. Fruit Chan, by contrast, has no consistent set of parameters, largely because he has to improvise as he goes along given the difficult conditions he now operates under in Hong Kong. It is hard to define what is Fruit Chan's style, or even tone, since both have varied wildly. He is not a long-take director, nor is he a follower of Wong Kar-wai. Even dividing up his career poses challenges: *Made in Hong Kong* and *The Longest Summer* (1998), for example, have been conjoined with *Little Cheung* as a trilogy discussed in relation to Italian neo-realism.[30] Yet only the last of the three, along with its successor, *Durian, Durian*, seem closer to the tone of neo-realism, while the first two seem closer to Chan's own commercial roots in Hong Kong. *Hollywood Hong Kong* is officially the second of the 'prostitute trilogy' that supposedly begins with *Durian, Durian*, yet it seems better to see this as the beginning of a phase of the grotesquery that resembles Takashi Miike. (Thus it should be conjoined instead with both

Fruit Chan's *Hollywood Hong Kong* and *Public Toilet*

Public Toilet and *Dumplings* (2004).) Chan himself is very aware of this, saying he was not trying to copy anyone in *Made in Hong Kong* aside from a montage sequence done in the style of Wong Kar-wai.[31] He has also said that he shifted dramatically in both style and tone with *Hollywood Hong Kong* to avoid critical typecasting after the praise heaped on *Durian, Durian*.[32] Thus, if Fruit Chan resembles anyone at all, it would have to be the stylistic iconoclasm of Nagisa Oshima as discussed by Maureen Turim, who at one point argues that it is harder to define Oshima's auteurism because of how wildly he varied from one film to the next.[33] Chan seemingly pursues his economic and aesthetic independence at all costs. However, one of those costs may be a stable set of auteurist issues to be debated and discussed.

Then again, this is not to suggest that if Fruit Chan only displayed more consistency in his films, then all would be well and he would have as many awards and articles for his work. In many ways the current conditions in Hong Kong, where all focus lies in how to revive a once-thriving commercial film industry, leave him at the biggest disadvantage of the three regardless of what he does personally. Johnnie To is perhaps the sort of auteur one can expect from Hong Kong today, one who displays enough commercial viability along certain generic lines which then allows him to create other films more to his personal liking. Fruit Chan, by contrast, only makes films to his personal liking, and this makes his situation more precarious and less predictable. Like the city itself, Hong Kong cinema is most dictated by the bottom line and has little room for the likes of Chan, Jia or Tsai. (Wong Kar-wai was truly an anomaly.)

To wit, no matter how much Tsai Ming-liang, Jia Zhangke and Fruit Chan share the burden of a second generation auteur, the burdens are not of equal weight due to greatly varying circumstances. Tsai Ming-liang has long enjoyed the most institutional advantages on an island that was already well attuned to how auteurism operates on the global stage. This, along with the additional questions of national and sexual identity, afforded him the luxury of consciously pursuing the auteurist game with almost whimsical glee. Jia Zhangke by contrast began as a marginal figure in China and only recently has found a more stable institutional base. Meanwhile, Fruit Chan remains on the margins of a troubled industry that long has made it difficult for true auteurs to emerge, Wong Kar-wai notwithstanding.

The remaining question is long term. Perhaps a day will come when critics and scholars will place more attention on Jia Zhangke since he best represents a new generation of mainland film-makers who are unconcerned with the cinematic traditions of earlier generations, taking a more unsentimental look at the world around them without blinkers or legendary escapes into a fantastical past. Already there are clear signs that Jia Zhangke is on his way 'up' in the eyes of both film festivals and the academic community: Michael Berry's recent book on Jia's 'Hometown Trilogy' is the first on Chinese cinema in BFI's Film Classics series.[34] Whether this continues will still depend on timing and other extenuating circumstances. No matter which generation – first or second – any auteur lives not on talent alone, but also on a lot of historical luck.

Notes

1. Mark Schilling, *Contemporary Japanese Film* (New York and Tokyo: Weatherhill, 1999), p. 71.
2. Wu Chia-chi, 'Festivals, Criticism and the International Reputation of Taiwan New Cinema', in Darrell William Davis and Robert Ru-shou Chen (eds), *Cinema Taiwan: Politics, Popularity and State of the Arts* (London and New York: Routledge Press, 2007), p. 80.
3. *Cinema in the Republic of China Yearbook 1987* (Taipei: National Film Archive, 1987), p. 4.
4. Kenneth Turan, *Sundance to Sarejevo: Film Festivals and the World They Made* (Berkeley: California University Press, 2002), pp. 26–7.
5. James Udden, 'Taiwan', in Mette Hjort and Duncan Petrie (eds), *The Cinema of Small Nations* (Edinburgh: Edinburgh University Press, 2007), p. 154.
6. Wendy Gan, *Fruit Chan's Durian, Durian* (Hong Kong: Hong Kong University Press, 2005), pp. 16–17.
7. Ibid., p. 20.
8. Cui Shuqin, 'Working from the Margins: Urban Cinema and Independent Directors in Contemporary China', in Sheldon H. Lu and Emilie Yueh-yu Yeh (eds), *Chinese-Language Film: Historiography, Poetics, Politics* (Honolulu: University of Hawaii Press, 2005), pp. 96–7.
9. Ibid., p. 97.
10. Quoted in Michael Berry, *Speaking in Images: Interviews with Contemporary Chinese Filmmakers* (New York: Columbia University Press, 2005), p. 385.
11. Song Hwee Lim, *Celluloid Comrades: Representations of Male Homosexuality in Contemporary Chinese Cinemas* (Honolulu: University of Hawaii Press, 2006), p. 126.

12. Emilie Yeuh-yu Yeh and William Darrell Davis, *Taiwan Film Directors: A Treasure Island* (New York: Columbia University Press, 2005), pp. 240–5.

13. Gina Marchetti, 'On Tsai Ming-liang's *The River*', in Chris Berry and Feii Lu (eds), *Island on the Edge: Taiwan New Cinema and After* (Hong Kong: Hong Kong University Press, 2005), p. 123.

14. Shujen Wang and Chris Fujiwara, '"My Films Reflect My Living Situation": An Interview with Tsai Ming-liang on Film Spaces, Audiences and Distribution', *positions: east asia cultures critique* vol. 14 no. 1 (Spring 2006), p. 224.

15. Peter Hitchcock, 'Taiwan Fever? Tsai Ming-liang and the Everyday Postnation', in Tan See-Kam, Peter X Feng and Gina Marchetti (eds), *Chinese Connections: Critical Perspectives on Film, Identity and Diaspora* (Philadelphia: Temple University Press, 2009), p. 243.

16. David Barton, 'Clepsydra: The Fluid Melancholy of *What Time Is It There*', *Asian Cinema* vol. 19 no. 2 (Autumn/Winter 2008), p. 282.

17. Kenneth Chan, '*Goodbye Dragon Inn*: Tsai Ming-liang's Political Aesthetics of Nostalgia, Place and Lingering', *Journal of Chinese Cinemas* vol. 1 no. 2 (2007), p. 94.

18. Ibid., p. 97.

19. Lim, *Celluloid Comrades*, pp. 127–8.

20. Berry, *Speaking in Images*, p. 371.

21. Wang and Fujiwara, '"My Films Reflect My Living Situation"', p. 232.

22. A better discussion of this than I can possibly undertake here is provided by Song Hwee Lim in 'Positioning Auteur Theory in Chinese Cinema Studies: Intratextuality, Intertextuality and Paratextuality in the Films of Tsai Ming-liang', *Journal of Chinese Cinemas* vol. 1 no. 3 (2007), pp. 223–45.

23. Marchetti, 'On Tsai Ming-liang's *The River*', p. 123.

24. Chris Wood, 'Realism, Intertextuality and Humour in Tsai Ming-liang's *Goodbye, Dragon Inn*', *Journal of Chinese Cinemas* vol. 1 no. 2 (2007), p. 107.

25. Weihong Bao, 'Biomechanics of Love: Reinventing the Avant-garde in Tsai Ming-liang's Wayward "Pornogrpahic Musical"', *Journal of Chinese Cinemas* vol. 1 no. 2 (2007), p. 141.

26. The average shot length (ASL) for *Rebels* is 19.2 seconds per shot, with over 40 per cent of these shots displaying at least some camera movement. In *Vive L'amour*, the figures are 36.0 seconds for the ASL, with 44 per cent of them containing camera movement; *The River* is 55.5 seconds and 43 per cent respectively; *The Hole* is 48.5 and 46 per cent respectively. These are all static works, but not as much as many assume. After the complete stasis in *What Time Is It There?*, camera movements have seemingly returned in Tsai's films, with *Goodbye Dragon Inn* showing movements in 11 per cent of the shots which average 55.1 seconds each, and *The Wayward Cloud* showing movements in nearly one quarter of shots now only averaging 34.2 seconds per shot. (All of these figures are based on analysis by the author.)

27. Berry, *Speaking in Images*, pp. 185, 192.

28. Ibid., p. 201.

29. Even Jia's most static film to date, *Platform*, has camera movements in roughly 50 per cent of its shots which average 68.5 seconds each.

30. Natalia Sui-hung Chan, 'Cinematic Neorealism: Hong Kong Cinema and Fruit Chan's *1997 Trilogy*', in Laura E. Roberto and Kristi M Wilson (eds), *Italian Neorealism and Global Cinema* (Detroit: Wayne State University Press, 2007), pp. 207–25.

31. Berry, *Speaking in Images*, p. 467.

32. Ibid., p. 477.

33. Maureen Turim, *The Films of Oshima Nagisa: Images of a Japanese Iconoclast* (Berkeley: California University Press, 1998), pp. 1–26.

34. Michael Berry, *Xiao Wu, Platform, Unknown Pleasures: Jia Zhangke's 'Hometown Trilogy'* (London: BFI, 2009).

Further Reading in *Chinese Films In Focus II*

On Tsai Ming-liang, see Chapter 29, '*Vive L'Amour*: Eloquent Emptiness' by Fran Martin.

On Jia Zhangke, see Chapter 32, '*Xiao Wu*: Watching Time Go By' by Chris Berry.

On Fruit Chan, see Chapter 11, '*Durian, Durian*: Defamiliarisation of the "Real"' by Esther M. K. Cheung.

18 The Urban Generation

Underground and Independent Films from the PRC

Jason McGrath

The term 'independent cinema' immediately raises the question: independent from what? In English the term generally has been used to indicate independence from Hollywood. However, this definition became questionable after the Hollywood studios largely co-opted their own competition by either buying successful independent production and distribution companies (Disney's purchase of Miramax in 1993, for example) or setting up their own speciality branches to cater to this niche market. Nonetheless, whether defined in terms of actual independent production or in terms of a commoditised 'indie' aesthetic marketed even by Hollywood itself, the term implies a lower-budget alternative to 'mainstream' cinema that is edgier in content and more experimental in form than more commercial genres of film-making.

In China the term 'independent' (*duli* – literally 'standing alone') has a somewhat different valence, in that originally at least it referred to independence from the state-owned film studios and thus to some measure of autonomy from various forms of control and censorship by the Communist government. Particularly when shown in the West, such independent films also have been called 'underground' (*dixia*) to emphasise their apparently subversive nature. Chinese independent film-makers, however, have tended not to embrace the 'underground' label on the rationale that their work is not necessarily meant to antagonise the state but rather to be in the service of the personal vision of the artist. The fact remains, however, that many 'independent' Chinese films are in fact quite dependent on overseas audiences and sources of production funding ('overseas' here including Hong Kong, Taiwan and Japan in addition to the West), so that the often misleading marketing of a film as subversive, underground or 'banned in China' has become a mutually beneficial phenomenon perpetuated by film festivals, art-film distributors, Chinese independent directors and film scholars and critics based in the West.

Despite the generally more politicised connotations of these labels as applied to Chinese film, there has been a general movement 'from underground to independent', as one volume on the subject has put it.[1] That is, as explosive economic growth continues and the Chinese film industry follows the trend of marketisation – including growing exposure to competition from Hollywood – Chinese independent cinema increasingly appears as the same sort of specialised consumer niche that it has become in the West, appealing to a relatively elite audience of educated film buffs at home and abroad and offering an alternative aesthetic to that of mainstream entertainment cinema while frequently being compromised or co-opted by the same.

Going Underground, or 'Leaping into the Sea': The Beginnings of Independent Cinema in China

Independent cinema in the People's Republic of China first emerged during the key transitional period that began around 1989, when massive protests by students and others in Tiananmen Square ended in the bloody crackdown known in China as the June Fourth Incident. Some of the psychological fallout from that event can be observed in Wu Wenguang's pioneering documentary *Bumming in Beijing: The Last*

Dreamers (1990), which was unprecedented for its independent production, its direct-cinema aesthetic of detached observation, and for the lives it depicted as well – artists who had essentially dropped out of mainstream society. In the same year, Zhang Yuan, a recent graduate of the Beijing Film Academy who had eschewed working in the state studio system, released *Mama*, which combined a fictionalised story with documentary interviews and, together with *Bumming in Beijing*, marked the beginning of Chinese independent film-making. *Mama* depicted the problems of the handicapped in China, and Zhang Yuan would go on to make more independent films about marginalised characters, such as rock musicians in *Beijing Bastards* (1993) and gay men in *East Palace, West Palace* (1997). Other young independent directors with similar interests in social outcasts also emerged in the first half of the 1990s, including Wang Xiaoshuai, Guan Hu and He Jianjun.[2]

These directors were among those hailed as the 'Sixth Generation' of Chinese film-makers – an appellation that served to distinguish them from the so-called 'Fifth Generation', the first group of film-makers to train at the Beijing Film Academy after it reopened following the Cultural Revolution. Led by Chen Kaige, Zhang Yimou and Tian Zhuangzhuang among others, that generation had achieved a new global profile for Chinese cinema with its grand historical allegories, lush cinematography and exotic ethnographic portraits of often oppressed yet vital and sensuous peasants. In contrast, the Sixth Generation was said to be interested in the present rather than the past, quotidian life rather than historical melodrama, and gritty urban geography rather than scenic rural settings. Another important distinction, however, was that the Fifth Generation, for all their artistic daring and occasional trouble with the Communist authorities, had made their signature early achievements within the state studio system, while many in the Sixth Generation were making films entirely independent of that institutional structure.

Indeed, the independence of the new underground film movement led to tensions with the state and the occasional banning of films that failed to go through proper official channels before screening at film festivals abroad. Wu Wenguang, Zhang Yuan, He Jianjun, Wang Xiaoshuai and others came into more or less direct conflict with authorities, in some cases being blacklisted from making films for a set period of time (a ban which He Jianjun sidestepped partly by making films under the pseudonym He Yi). These crackdowns only increased the film-makers' cultural capital abroad, as western audiences, critics and festival programmers, primed by Cold War-era ideology, were eager to embrace the image of the dissident artist

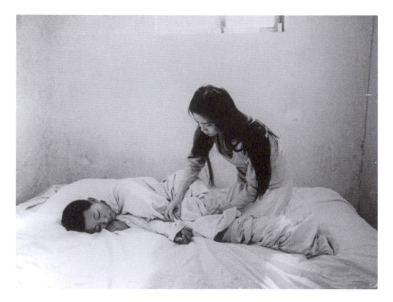

Mama

Beijing Bastards

yearning for freedom under the heel of a totalitarian state.

The real situation for artists in China by the 1990s and particularly after the turn of the century was much more complex than such western liberal fantasies of underground artists would indicate.[3] Not only were no cultural workers thrown into Communist gulags, but in fact many a film-maker – as well as other provocative artists such as the racy Shanghai novelist Wei Hui – achieved international fame and considerable commercial success after, and in large part because of, having a work blacklisted in China. In addition, many of these originally independent film-makers would go on to make films within the state studio system without necessarily sacrificing their artistic integrity in any obvious way. Moreover, the very label 'banned in China' is often quite misleading. For every film that actually raised the ire of authorities in the 1990s–2000s, there were many more that simply were never submitted to the necessary channels for achieving distribution in Chinese theatres; as Chris Berry has put it, 'most of the films described as "banned in Beijing" by foreign journalists have never been near a censor'.[4] These films may not make it to Chinese cinemas and may be advertised in the West as 'banned', but in fact they are readily available from Chinese video stores, pirated DVD vendors and internet file-sharing websites. Those much cheaper venues and formats, not the more expensive movie theatres screening officially sanctioned films, are the primary sources of film viewing for ordinary Chinese people. In short, most of these films are only 'banned in China' in the West, as virtually all of them are readily available for viewing by almost any Chinese person who wants to see them.

From Independent to Market-driven: The Dilution of the State Studio System and the Importance of the Global Art-cinema Circuit

The western fascination with dissident culture under communism partially explains the emphasis, in western critical discussions of Chinese independent cinema, on the so-called Sixth Generation films in the 1990s, particularly those that deal with the sort of marginal subject matter mentioned above. However, such discussions obscure the fact that independent film-making arose in the early 1990s not simply because of the daring of a few artists, but rather in response to new social and economic conditions that reduced the willingness of the state studios to sponsor art films targeted at a narrow audience. These same conditions simultaneously created personal and professional spaces outside the state-run economy, which had previously required that everybody belong to a work unit (*danwei*) that provided not only employment but also housing and all other social benefits in daily life.

Under the new conditions of marketisation, the official film studios, like state cultural institutions everywhere, were expected to make enough profit to be more or less self-sustaining rather than relying on state subsidies to cover their budgets. As a result, for the first time in the PRC, box-office receipts became a primary concern of studio heads alongside artistic merit and political correctness, so that entertainment value for the mass audience emerged as a growing factor in film production. At the same time, the loosening of the bonds of cultural workers to their sponsoring state organisations created the conditions for film-makers to strike out on their own (if sometimes only at weekends with equipment borrowed from official organisations) and make films outside the system if they could secure funding. In some cases, individually produced films were then picked up by a state studio and distributed despite their original status as 'independent'. In this sense many film-makers were joining in the general trend of 'jumping into the sea' (*xiahai*) of the new market economy, abandoning the security of jobs in the state sector in favour of more entrepreneurial activities with potentially higher monetary or artistic rewards.

Examples of this dynamic include not just the Sixth Generation directors but also established older film-makers who, by either choice or necessity, made films with funding from non-state sources. For example, Fifth Generation auteurs Tian Zhuangzhuang and Zhang Yimou made *The Blue Kite* (1993) and *To Live* (1994), respectively, with production money from abroad (Hong Kong and Taiwan) and earned the ire of Chinese officials who cracked down on both directors.[5] Another established director, Zhou Xiaowen, made *Ermo* (1994) independently with help from Hong Kong after no state studios would take up the project, though he later obtained a studio label and successfully distributed it through official channels.

All these instances show not only that the trend of independent fiction film-making went beyond the Sixth Generation directors credited with beginning it, but also that it became increasingly difficult to define independence itself. If a film received production funding from a film company abroad and then was granted a Chinese state studio label for the purposes of distribution, was it truly 'independent'? A further complication arose in the mid- to late 1990s after relaxed restrictions on cultural production in China led to the formation of many quasi-independent production companies that often collaborated with the state studios, providing talent and funding for projects in exchange for an official studio label, which smoothed the way for distribution and profits for all if the film was a hit. By the late 1990s and early 2000s, some of the most commercially successful films in

Chinese theatres had in fact been funded by independent production companies but obtained a state studio backer for distribution.[6] Though rarely called 'independent', these films were part of the overall trend of diversification and decentralisation of the film industry that accompanied deepening market reforms.

Similar complexities applied to the makers of underground art films, who, however independent from the state studio system they may have been, often became highly dependent on both overseas production companies and foreign audiences. A case in point is Jia Zhangke, arguably the most internationally renowned art-film director to have emerged in China since the beginning of the independent film phenomenon. After a student film from his years at the Beijing Film Academy attracted attention at two Hong Kong film festivals, Jia entered a long and fruitful relationship with a Hong Kong producer with whom he made his first three feature films: *Xiao Wu* (1997), *Platform* (2000) and *Unknown Pleasures* (2002).[7] By the end of this streak, Jia had gained fame on the global arthouse circuit, but none of his films had been distributed in China, leading to the perception among many Chinese intellectuals that his films pandered to foreigners – an accusation that had been made about the early Fifth Generation films as well.

Indeed, the question of whether Chinese independent or underground films primarily address overseas spectators rather than Chinese audiences inevitably is raised once 'independent' film-makers

Xiao Wu

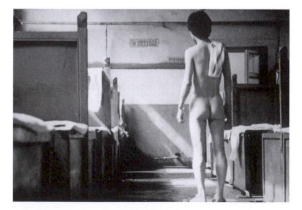

Unknown Pleasures

become dependent on funding from abroad. As Paul G. Pickowicz observes, 'the need for underground artists to chase foreign funding, production, distribution, and discourse networks causes various difficulties, the most obvious of which is the need to make movies about China that one imagines foreign viewers, especially foreign art-house viewers and critics, would like to see'.[8] Given the sometimes cynical 'banned in China' marketing strategy (one producer was directly asked by overseas distributors whether they could use that slogan even if it was not true),[9] it is not surprising that Chinese critics might conclude that 'political factors are generally greater than artistic factors in the reasons these "underground films" win awards' abroad.[10] On the other hand, the influence of the global art-cinema market on the *aesthetics* of Chinese independent films may be just as important as the marketing of their allegedly subversive *politics*. For example, Jia Zhangke's early student films and first feature film employed the sort of documentary realist style that had been evident

in the earlier Sixth Generation underground film-makers, taking many cues from the New Documentary Movement led by Wu Wenguang; however, by his larger-budget second and third features, which received funding from Japan and Europe in addition to Hong Kong, Jia's style had far less of that improvisational, documentary feel and instead fitted into a more contemplative long-take realist aesthetic that was currently in vogue in global art cinema, exemplified by such film-makers as Iran's Abbas Kiarostami or Taiwan's Hou Hsiao-hsien and Tsai Ming-liang.[11]

Partly due to the perception, deserved or not, that independent film-makers were neglecting the domestic audience in favour of kowtowing to foreign tastes – and partly due also to an apparent loosening of censorship by the authorities in an effort to reconcile with underground film-makers – Jia Zhangke along with several of his peers (including Zhang Yuan, Zhu Wen and Liu Hao) eventually dropped his 'independent' or 'underground' status altogether, instead seeking co-production by an official state film studio and thus distribution to Chinese theatres. In an indication of how precarious an artist's 'independence' can be, no sooner had Jia Zhangke and Zhang Yuan countered accusations of pandering to foreigners by securing the domestic legitimacy of state studios than they were then suspected of compromising their integrity by making films within the system.[12] Despite such suspicions, in terms of subject matter and aesthetics, the loss of 'independence' by film-makers who chose to enter the state studio system does not appear to have greatly altered their work. It has, however, shown that when competing with imports from Hollywood as well as blockbuster co-productions between mainland and Hong Kong studios, the domestic audience for Chinese art films with an 'indie' aesthetic is very limited.

The Question of the Audience

Indeed, the ease with which many supposedly independent film-makers have travelled back and forth between insider and outsider status vis-à-vis the state studio system calls into question just how 'underground' their cinema is in the rapidly changing cultural climate of China. As China beat reporter Evan Osnos observes, 'Chinese authorities seem to have concluded that art films, screened at festivals for urbane, like-minded audiences, have limited social impact.'[13] Discussing the discrepancy between the positive reaction of audiences abroad to *Xiao Wu* (also called *Artisan Pickpocket*) compared to the mostly negative reaction at local screenings in China, Yingjin Zhang observes that 'the sharply divided receptions … reveal not so much the politics of censorship in China (an old story repeated over and over by the Western media) as the seemingly unbridgeable gap between the artist's vision and its acceptability by the domestic audience'.[14] In other words, the real scandal may be not so much that Chinese mass audiences are cut off from independent films by the censors but that when exposed to them they often react with indifference or downright hostility.

Thus what market reforms, combined with the loosening of restrictions on film-makers and in many cases their reintegration into the official studio system, have taught both film-makers and authorities is in a sense what has long been evident in the West: that the censorship of the market can be even more restrictive than political censorship, and the audience for potentially subversive underground or art cinema is a niche market that can be catered to without necessarily affecting film culture in general, much less social stability as a whole. As Matthew David Johnson notes, 'It is not so much the existence of domestic and global film markets, but the obvious devolution of new documentary cinema to the position of "just another" commodity *within* those markets that threatens to discredit its producers' self-positioning as subversives, independents, and so on' – an observation that applies equally to independent fiction films.[15] In a classic case of commoditised dissent that is familiar in capitalist democracies, the underground film can be sold to a limited audience of cultural elites without necessarily making its social critique dangerous to the existing dispensation of power in any real sense. On the contrary, 'independent cinema is a consumer product to be marketed', so that '"Indie" is contradictory insofar as it at once serves to oppose the dominant culture but also to produce cultural capital that distinguishes its consumers'.[16]

These considerations necessarily lead to a reconsideration of a central myth, however unspoken, of Chinese underground cinema: namely, that foreign audiences of independent films were getting an unvarnished glimpse of the 'real' China, while the ordinary Chinese people thus depicted were forbidden by censors from seeing their own 'true' cinematic representation.[17] In fact, many of the cinematic techniques that produced such a strong impression of realism in Chinese independent cinema of the 1990s – including on-location shooting, use of non-professional actors, long-shot and long-take cinematography, and a focus on the daily lives of marginal characters such as prostitutes, thieves and migrant workers – by the 2000s had become conventions reproduced in an almost assembly-line fashion for consumption by the global festival audiences that had made such films successful commodities in the first place. However accomplished such independent films as *Orphan of Anyang* (Wang Chao, 2001) and *Blind Shaft* (Li Yang, 2003) might have been, one could not help but notice their similarity in look and theme to earlier Chinese arthouse hits such as *Xiao Wu*, and many other films tried to achieve the same effect without the skill displayed by those; the gritty 'realist' Chinese indie film had become a product designed for the particular audience targeted by film festivals and art-film producers and distributors. By the end of the 2000s, Shelley Kracier noted that although Jia Zhangke himself had struck out in 'new directions',

Jia-ist cinema, through its profound effect on most
younger independent Chinese directors, seems lately
more restrictive than liberating in its influence. Film
language in 'mainstream' indie Chinese films (both
docs and features) seems to have temporarily
congealed into something like formulaic liturgies:
fetishization of the long take, the distant camera, the
objective tone, the unedited minutiae of daily life.[18]

Himself a critic and film festival programmer, Kraicer
was in some sense implicated in the very phenomenon
he described, as were all the scholars and western
journalists who had hailed the Chinese independent
film movement and thus bolstered its
commoditisation, however unintentionally, in the first
place.

A second way in which Chinese underground
cinema's founding myth – that these films showed a
'real' China that the Chinese themselves were not
allowed to see in their own official media – was
gradually undermined was precisely the reaction of
Chinese audiences when they *were* allowed to see such
films. On one hand, there was great scepticism about
whether independent directors were merely making
the films they thought foreigners wanted to see, which,
many felt, often amounted to showing China in the
worst possible light for foreign consumption.[19] On the
other hand, as already noted, to the extent Chinese
indie-style films were screened in China, rather than
attracting the attention of the masses yearning for
truthful representations of themselves, they instead
drew audiences not much different than the self-
selected cultural elites of overseas film festivals and
arthouse theatres. By the end of the 1990s, the
pluralisation of viewing practices and diversification of
film venues had made independent and underground
films – both Chinese and western – widely available at
least to the urban intellectual class. A thriving film club
scene in the major Chinese cities provided spaces for
public screenings even of ostensibly 'banned' films.[20]

Even more significant in terms of viewership, as
mentioned earlier, has been the wide dissemination of
independent films on video compact discs (VCDs) in
the 1990s and on DVDs (often pirated) and computer
file-sharing more recently. The predominance of such
modes of spectatorship in China today makes it
impossible to gauge what Chinese audiences are
actually viewing through box-office statistics from
movie theatres. Instead, home TVs or computers are

the major interfaces with cinema for most people, and
the ready availability of virtually any kind of film or
video – Hollywood and Hong Kong blockbusters, foreign
art films, Chinese independent films, pornography –
makes for a chaotic yet highly democratised or levelled
cinema market in which anything goes and consumer
demand rules. In fact, He Jianjun's independent film
Pirated Copy (2004) depicts precisely the sorts of
cinephilia made possible by the massive outlaw video
culture of China today.[21]

The Urban Generation, Amateur Cinema and the DV Revolution

The independent or underground film movement
(though 'movement' makes it sound more cohesive
than it actually was) certainly has been one of the
major developments in Chinese cinema during the
post-Mao era. Still, as the preceding discussion makes
clear, the very terms 'independent' and 'underground'
are problematic, insofar as the film-makers thus
labelled in fact often have sacrificed their
'independence' to collaborate with the official state
studios and/or to tap sources of foreign capital, which
can then turn 'underground' into an advertising slogan
as much as an actual reality of production.

The broader, alternative label of 'Urban Generation'
is intended to bypass such conundrums by focusing on
a set of characteristics that can include, but is not
limited by, the condition of 'independence' or the
subversive intent implied by 'underground'. The term
'urban generation' was first used by the organisers of a
film series that toured the East Coast of the United
States in 2001. In introducing the volume of essays that
eventually grew out of that series, Zhang Zhen
identified Urban Generation cinema not necessarily as
independent, but more precisely as 'caught in the
dynamic tension between "deterritorialization" by the
state or commercial mainstream (both domestic and
international) and the constant "reterritorialization" by
the same forces that have alienated or marginalized
it'.[22] While marked by certain common themes and
stylistic techniques, the Urban Generation most
importantly emerges as an 'alternative' or 'minor
cinema', positioned in particular against officially
sanctioned mainstream Chinese cinema. In some
aspects of its content (social and economic marginality,
dislocation, urbanisation) and form (the use of
documentary footage in fiction films, a distanced
perspective of 'bearing witness' mixed with occasional

melodrama), Urban Generation cinema draws on the important Chinese precedent of the leftwing cinema movement of the 1930s–40s.

As noted above, however, this cinema also emerges on the cutting edge of changes in media technologies and related informal production and distribution mechanisms in contemporary China. In particular, 'digital video and editing software … have served as the critical catalyst for the conception and dissemination of "amateur cinema" as a democratic form of film practice'.[23] The twenty-first century has brought an explosion of digital film-making in China – particularly documentaries, but also fiction films that occasionally gain some international attention despite their very low budgets and often correspondingly low production values. This digital revolution within the independent film movement stands at the opposite extreme from recent big-budget Chinese blockbusters that indulge in CGI effects to increase their value as spectacle and thus compete with Hollywood products both in China and abroad. In fact, these two poles of Chinese cinema as it transitions, like film-making everywhere, from celluloid to digital video – the low-budget independent work on one end of the spectrum and the commercial special-effects blockbuster on the other – exemplify the cultural and social distinction between a niche audience of mostly intellectual cinephiles seeking 'truth' in art and the mass audience seeking entertainment and escape. The ability of virtually anyone with an idea and a handful of cash to make a digital feature and distribute it online, if not in theatres, promises to give entirely new meaning to the terms 'underground' and 'independent', as the successors to the Urban Generation take post-filmic Chinese cinema in new directions and offer an alternative to both foreign and domestic mainstream cinema.

Notes

1. Paul G. Pickowicz and Yingjin Zhang (eds), *From Underground to Independent: Alternative Film Culture in Contemporary China* (Oxford: Rowman & Littlefield, 2006).

2. Wang Xiaoshuai's *The Days* (1993) was about avant-garde artists in Beijing, He Jianjun's *Red Beads* (1993) was set in a mental hospital, while Guan Hu's *Dirt* (1994), like *Beijing Bastards*, featured the rock counterculture.

3. Many have remarked on the sometimes cynical overuse of the 'banned in China' label. For two discussions, see

Chris Berry, 'Independently Chinese: Duan Jinchuan, Jiang Yue, and Chinese Documentary', in Pickowicz and Zhang, *From Underground to Independent*, pp. 109–22; and Valerie Jaffee, 'Bringing the World to the Nation: Jia Zhangke and the Legitimation of Chinese Underground Film', *Senses of Cinema* no. 32 (July–September 2004), <www.sensesofcinema.com/contents/04/32/chinese_ underground_film.html>.

4. Berry, 'Independently Chinese', p. 115. It is difficult to determine how many films have been actually banned, or even exactly what that would mean. Zhao Xianmin provides an incomplete list of banned films in '90 hou jin pian shi' (History of Banned Films Since 1990), <zmwbbs.com/bbs/thread-52770-1-1.html>; but in fact several films on the list were readily available on DVD even at the state-run Xinhua bookstores at the time of this writing.

5. For details of these cases, see Tony Rayns, 'Censors, Scapegoats and Bargaining Chips', *Index on Censorship* vol. 24 no. 6 (1995), pp. 69–79.

6. One example of this is the 'private' Beijing production company Forbidden City – which in fact had been capitalised partly by public organisations, and which funded several of the very popular 'New Year's films' by the commercial director Feng Xiaogang. The films were then officially released under a state studio label.

7. For a comprehensive discussion of these three films, see Michael Berry, *Xiao Wu, Platform, Unknown Pleasures: Jia Zhangke's 'Hometown Trilogy'* (London: BFI, 2009).

8. Paul G. Pickowicz, 'Social and Political Dynamics of Underground Film-making in China', in Pickowicz and Zhang, *From Underground to Independent*, p. 13.

9. Augusta Palmer, 'BIZ: Taming the Dragon: Part II, Two Approaches to China's Film Market', *indieWIRE*, 8 December 2000, <www.indiewire.com/article/biz_ taming_the_dragon_part_ii_two_approaches_to_chinas_ film_market>; also quoted in Matthew David Johnson, '"A Scene beyond Our Line of Sight": Wu Wenguang and New Documentary Cinema's Politics of Independence', in Pickowicz and Zhang, *From Underground to Independent*, p. 69.

10. Yu Aiyuan, 'Tuwei, taoli, luowang' (Breakthrough, Escape, Ensnarement), *Jinri xianfeng* (Avant-garde Today) vol. 12 (March 2002), p. 39. A similar point is made by prominent Beijing film critic and scholar Dai Jinhua in 'A Scene in the Fog: Reading the Sixth Generation Films', in Jing Wang and Tani E. Barlow (eds), *Cinema and Desire: Feminist Marxism and Cultural Politics in the Work of Dai Jinhua* (London: Verso, 2002), p. 77.

11. Jason McGrath, '"Independent" Cinema: From Postsocialist Realism to a Transnational Aesthetic', in *Postsocialist Modernity: Chinese Cinema, Literature, and Criticism in the Market Age* (Stanford, CA: Stanford University Press, 2008), pp. 129–64; an earlier, shorter version appeared as 'The Independent Cinema of Jia Zhangke: From Postsocialist Realism to an International Aesthetic', in Zhang Zhen (ed.), *The Urban Generation: Chinese Cinema and Society at the Turn of the Twenty-first Century* (Durham, NC: Duke University Press, 2007), pp. 81–114.

12. This phenomenon is discussed in Jaffee, 'Bringing the World to the Nation'.

13. Evan Osnos, 'The Long Shot: Can China's Archly Political Auteur Please the Censors and Himself – and Still Find a Mass Audience?', *The New Yorker*, 11 May 2009, p. 95.

14. Yingjin Zhang, 'My Camera Doesn't Lie? Truth, Subjectivity, and Audience in Chinese Independent Film and Video', in Pickowicz and Zhang, *From Underground to Independent*, p. 38.

15. Johnson, '"A Scene beyond Our Line of Sight"', p. 72.

16. Michael Z. Newman, 'Indie Culture: In Pursuit of the Authentic Autonomous Alternative', *Cinema Journal* vol. 48 no, 3 (Spring 2009), pp. 24, 16.

17. This issue is discussed in detail in Zhang, 'My Camera Doesn't Lie?'.

18. Shelley Kraicer, 'Finding Ways to Fit: Mainland Chinese films at Toronto and Vancouver', dGenerate Films, Wednesday, 18 November 2009, <dgeneratefilms.com/tag/shelly-kraicer>.

19. This suspicion was not without merit; according to one western distributor, only three types of Chinese films could find success with western audiences: (1) 'rural films about very poor Chinese peasants, that make the Westerner feel happy about their own station in life'; (2) 'period films that can dazzle with their costumes and the intrigues of a back-stabbing courtier and his emperor'; and (3) 'films that are banned in China, providing a great promotion and publicity point of attack'. Palmer, 'BIZ: Taming the Dragon: Part II'.

20. For more on film clubs in China, see Seio Nakajima, 'Film Clubs in Beijing: The Cultural Consumption of Chinese Independent Films', in Pickowicz and Zhang, *From Underground to Independent*, pp. 143–87; and Zhang Zhen, 'Bearing Witness: Chinese Urban Cinema in the Era of "Transformation" (*Zhuanxing*)', in Zhang, *The Urban Generation*, esp. pp. 28–33.

21. For a discussion of piracy as 'visual democracy', see Yingjin Zhang, *Cinema, Space, and Polylocality in a Globalizing China* (Honolulu: University of Hawaii Press, 2010), pp. 153–69.

22. Zhang, 'Bearing Witness', p. 1. This paragraph draws on several points in this definitive essay.

23. Ibid., p. 17. 'Amateur cinema' was first used by Jia Zhangke to describe the new independent approach in the 1990s. See his essay 'The Age of Amateur Cinema Will Return', first published in the newspaper *Nanfang zhoumo* in 1999 and translated into English at <dgeneratefilms.com/academia/jia-zhangke-the-age-of-amateur-cinema-will-return>. See also the discussion in Valerie Jaffee, '"Every Man a Star": The Ambivalent Cult of Amateur Art in New Chinese Documentaries', in Pickowicz and Zhang, *From Underground to Independent*, pp. 77–108.

Further Reading in *Chinese Films In Focus II*

On underground and independent film-making from the People's Republic of China, see Chapter 32, '*Xiao Wu*: Watching Time Go By' by Chris Berry; Chapter 4, '*Blind Shaft*: Performing the "Underground" on and beyond the Screen' by Jonathan Noble; and Chapter 19, '*Kekexili: Mountain Patrol*: Moral Dilemma and a Man with a Camera' by Shuqin Cui.

19 Contemporary Mainstream PRC Cinema

Yomi Braester

The critic Dai Jinhua declared in 1999, after the Chinese release of *Titanic* (1997), that 'like *Titanic*, the Chinese film industry is sinking amidst tender feelings and happiness, almost without any measures of resistance'. Similarly, the influential *Southern Weekly* (*Nanfang zhoumo*) declared in 2002 that since *The Fugitive* (1993) was screened in China in 1994, Chinese cinema has itself become a fugitive.[1] These two statements are indicative of many PRC critics' hostility to Hollywood blockbusters and film-makers' anxiety about the future of Chinese cinema in the face of direct competition with foreign films. To a large extent, the story of mainstream PRC cinema since the mid-1990s is that of adaptation to new rules and practices dictated by its increasing integration with the global film market.

This chapter traces the rise of New Year's movies and New Urban Cinema as major trends in mainstream PRC cinema. Also examined are the unique characteristics of the PRC mainstream and the ways in which it differs from the Hollywood model; debates over restructuring the industry and preserving cultural identity; the development of genre film and symbiosis with state-sponsored propaganda; and accommodating transnational production.

The Rise of Mainstream Cinema

The definition of mainstream cinema has itself undergone significant changes during this period. The term would have been meaningless until the mid-1980s, when Fifth Generation directors and the so-called Urban Cinema (*chengshi dianying*) signalled the end of film-making entirely subservient to political agendas. Even as trends diversified during the early 1990s, no approach made a commercial breakthrough. In fact, revenues from domestic productions dropped sharply during that period. A predictable and sustainable following established a commercial mainstream only in the late 1990s, modelled largely after Hollywood – genre films of relatively high production values, financed by private, increasingly transnational investors, and distributed in main venues, with a growing emphasis on multiplexes. PRC mainstream cinema is perhaps best understood as competing with foreign blockbusters by way of emulation (which does not preclude innovation). The commercial trend has also incorporated elements of art film and state propaganda, with the explicit goal of achieving wide distribution and box-office success.

Throughout the 1980s, movie attendance dwindled, from 29.3 billion spectators in 1979 to 10.5 billion in 1992.[2] The decline in spectatorship owed to a variety of factors: the state-controlled film industry was too conservative and complacent to adapt to changing tastes and the disappearance of captive audiences; meanwhile, other leisure activities, such as TV, pirated video and karaoke, replaced moviegoing. In response, the Ministry of Radio, Film and Television (MRFT) opened up the market to ten foreign productions a year, in hope of reviving interest in film and revitalising domestic productions by setting a model for emulation. Film-makers adopted new business models. Some directors sought independence from the state system and created a niche market for independent film. The far larger portion imitated Hollywood by integrating the audiovisual industry, establishing joint ventures, setting up a lobby for

Blush

promoting protective quotas and stimuli, and focusing on churning out genre films. In the short run, however, the measure changed the market dynamics in favour of Hollywood productions and stifled PRC cinema.

Although a systemic response took a few years to formulate, the mid-1990s witnessed the budding of a mainstream cinema. Fifth Generation directors turned to international co-productions and gained popularity in China and abroad with movies combining historical drama and moderately prurient subject matter. Among the most prominent were Chen Kaige (*Farewell My Concubine/Bawang bieji*, 1993; *Temptress Moon/Feng Yue*, 1996), Zhang Yimou (especially following the unbanning of his films with the release of *Shanghai Triad/Yao a yao, yao dao waipo qiao*, 1995) and Li Shaohong (*Bloody Morning/Xuese Qingchen*, 1992; *Family Portrait/Sishi bu huo*, 1992; *Blush/Hong fen*, 1994). Although Chinese critics accused the Fifth Generation, and Chen and Zhang in particular, of elitism and pandering to foreign tastes, those films of the 1990s helped in developing mainstream tastes and production practices.

Another trend turned out to define the coming commercial cinema: the exploits of street-wise urban youth, based on Wang Shuo's witty fiction. Adaptations of Wang's novels had been popular since *Samsara* (*Lunhui*, 1988). The top-grossing film for 1995 was *In the Heat of the Sun* (*Yangguang canlan de rizi*), with revenues exceeding 50 million RMB. In 1996, Beijing Film Studio and Beijing Forbidden City Film Co. looked for a commercial breakthrough and hired Feng Xiaogang, a successful TV director. Feng's subsequent *Dream Factory* (*Jiafang yifang*, 1997) had an immediate appeal. Based on Wang Shuo's 'Ni bushi yige suren' (You're No Ordinary Person), it describes the rise of laid-off workers to successful entrepreneurs. Their company gives common people the chance to play out their heroes for a day; their merrymaking is guided by a genuine interest in doing good, and they eventually give up their profits to help people in need. The movie found a balance between satire and respect for social order. Whereas in 1996 the revenue from domestic productions hit a record low of 800 million RMB, *Dream Factory* showed the way out: it grossed 36 million RMB on an investment of less than 6 million. The people involved in producing *Dream Factory* – including the director, lead actors and producers – followed the patterns set in this film and have risen to prominence. *Dream Factory* not only hit on a winning formula but also established a sustainable business model that has defined PRC mainstream cinema.

Crazy Stone

New Year's Movies

The success of *Dream Factory* owed not only to the comic plot and engaging acting; it was also the first made-in-PRC production to be marketed as a New Year's movie (*hesui pian*). Even before the film was conceived or the director chosen, the producers decided that the New Year's movie label would draw audiences. It was released on 1 February 1997, in time for the lunar New Year vacation. Since *Dream Factory*, many New Year's movies – like Hollywood summer blockbusters – have become milestones of popular culture and shaped mainstream spectators' expectations.

New Year's movies were first produced in Hong Kong, after Michael Hui Koon-Man's *Security Unlimited* (*Modeng baobiao*, 1982). These Hong Kong productions were initially romantic comedies and ribald spoofs, but over the years the trend has included every popular genre. Beginning in 1995 with *Chinese Odyssey* (*Youguang baohe*, 1994) and the Jackie Chan vehicle *Rumble in the Bronx* (*Hongfan qu*, 1995), Hong Kong productions were marketed in the PRC as New Year's movies as part of an attempt to boost filmgoing.

Feng replicated the Hong Kong marketing ploy and aimed for the quotable repartees that made Stephen Chow's films into cult hits. Yet Feng also modified Hong Kong humour to suit postsocialist disenchantment in the PRC and spoofed current cultural trends, producing highly popular comedies such as *Be There or Be Square* (*Bu jian bu san*, 1998), *Sorry Baby* (*Meiwan meiliao*, 1999) and *Big Shot's Funeral* (*Dawan*, 2001). Feng also introduced other genres. *A Sigh* (*Yisheng tanxi*, 2000) and *Cell Phone* (*Shouji*, 2003) broached family drama, and *The Banquet* (*Ye yan*, 2006) was a martial arts film. The practice of releasing promising productions during the holiday season became widespread. Other leading mainstream directors, such as the Fifth Generation veterans Zhang Yimou (*Happy Times/Xingfu shiguang*, 2000) and Chen Kaige (*Together/He ni zai yiqi*, 2002), followed suit in catering for the New Year's movie market.

New Year's movies also indicate the quick transition to genre film. The majority consists of comedies; of these, *Crazy Stone* (*Fengkuang de shitou*, 2006) became another milestone in showing the viability of the business model in the PRC film industry, with a gross exceeding 23 million RMB. Martial arts productions included *Hero* (*Yingxiong*, 2002) and *The Promise* (*Wu ji*, 2005). Horror films, stymied by the interdiction against representing supernatural phenomena, nevertheless garnered growing interest due to J-Horror, the East Asian genre sparked by the success of *Ringu* (1998); *The Door* (*Men*) was among the top-grossing New Year's movies of 2007. War films have also risen to prominence, especially with *Assembly* (*Ji jie hao*, 2007) – modelled after *Saving Private Ryan* (1998), also marketed in the PRC as a New Year's movie. Genre film, the Chinese term for which (*leixing pian*) has become synonymous with commercial film, has consolidated a mainstream cinema focused on the box-office bottom line and precipitated the integration among the film, television and advertisement industries.

The New Urban Cinema

Another test case for the formation of a commercial mainstream is found in the New Urban Cinema. Although post-Maoist films often depicted urban conditions, paving the way for the mainstream's interest in the everyday life of regular citizens, urban films emerged as a commercial genre only in the early 2000s. The so-called Urban Cinema of the mid-1980s through late 1990s – from *Yamaha Fish Stall* (*Yamaha yudang*, 1984) and *Sunshine and Rain* (*Taiyang yu*, 1987), through *Black Snow* (*Benmingnian*, 1990), to *Suzhou River* (*Suzhouhe*, 2000) – was understood as art film, a modernist challenge to Maoist aesthetics and state ideology rather than a commercial alternative. It is emblematic of the rise of mainstream cinema that by

Shower

the turn of the century, Urban Cinema, which opposed the logic of genre film, was taken over by New Urban Cinema, a marketable genre that cashed in on the cutting-edge aura of the earlier trend.

In 1997, the same year in which Feng Xiaogang released *Dream Factory*, Zhang Yang directed the highly profitable *Spicy Love Soup* (*Aiqing mala tang*, 30 million RMB at the box office). The producer IMAR (the first Sino-foreign joint-venture film company) followed with other record-breaking films, including *A Beautiful New World* (*Meili xin shijie*, 1998) and *Shower* (*Xizao*, 1999). Unlike earlier Urban Cinema, these films – set in contemporary Shanghai or Beijing – do not show the seedy social margins. Instead, they depict romance (*Spicy Love Soup*) and family reunion (*Shower*), touching only lightly on sensitive issues, such as real estate speculation (*A Beautiful New World*) and demolition-and-relocation (*Shower*). Other producers released films in a similar vein: Zhang Yimou directed the urban comedies *Keep Cool* (*You hua haohao shuo*, 1997) and *Happy Times*. Audiences welcomed also films such as *A Tree in the House* (*Mei shi touzhe le*, 1999), *The Marriage Certificate* (*Shei shuo wo bu zaihu*, 2001, Huang Jianxin) and *Dazzling* (*Hua yan*, 2002). The commercial trend encompassed also former Urban Cinema rebels such as Wang Xiaoshuai, who directed *Beijing Bicycle* (*Shiqi sui de danche*) in 2001, and Zhang Yuan, who came out with

Green Tea (*Lü cha*) in 2003. With such films, urban subject matter adopted mainstream thematic and visual formulas.

The importance of marketing to the mainstream and fitting within identifiable genres was underlined when these and other films were labelled as New Urban Cinema (*xin chengshi dianying*). The term was probably first used in 2000 in publicity materials by Beijing Forbidden City & Trinity Pictures Co. The news media followed suit, mentioning films such as *Poetic Times* (*Shiyi de niandai*, 1999), *Seventeen Years* (*Guonian huijia*, 1999) and *I Love Beijing* (*Xiari nuanyangyang*, 2000) as New Urban Cinema and commending the contribution of these films to boosting box-office revenues.[3] Notably, Zhang Yibai, the director of *Spring Subway* (*Kai wang chuntian de ditie*, 2002) – a feel-good flick – claimed that his film was an exponent of New Urban Cinema.[4]

As the case of New Urban Cinema demonstrates, by the twenty-first century the mainstream took the edge off the more critical films associated with the early productions of Fifth and Sixth Generation directors. One way to put it is that the division between art film, propaganda and entertainment movies has blurred.[5] Yet it is also possible to see the current state of the Chinese film industry as a continuation of the conditions in the Maoist period, adapted to the market economy. Even when all film production was controlled by the state, efforts were made to imbue propaganda with artistic values and to attract audiences. The mainstream is not only the result of restructuring the film industry to emphasise revenues; equally important, the rise of the mainstream was made possible by – and further precipitated – the collapse of the boundaries between highbrow avant-garde and market-oriented productions. In tandem with the wane of the High Culture fever of the 1980s (a form of elitist modernism) and the rise of Cultural Economy in the mid-1990s (using cultural capital to brand government policies), commercially successful directors became media celebrities and cultural heroes, while risk-taking film-makers were relegated to marginalised fan cults. Critics and audiences alike lionised mainstream cinema as the genuine representative of Chinese screen culture.

Dancing with Wolves

As the examples of New Year's movies and New Urban Cinema demonstrate, Chinese mainstream cinema developed in response to the Hollywood mainstream but did not blindly replicate it. New Year's movies, although similar to the marketing device of the summer blockbuster, are markedly less violent than the Hollywood flicks (the first summer blockbuster was Steven Spielberg's *Jaws*, in 1975). New Year's movies have often emulated the humorous skits at the TV Spring Festival extravaganzas. One of the selling points for Hollywood blockbusters is the huge investment, and spectators go to 'see the money' onscreen; in contrast, New Year's films such as *Dream Factory* and *Crazy Stone* derived prestige from a high investment-to-revenue ratio. It is even harder to find equivalents outside the PRC to New Urban Cinema. With presentation style ranging from comedy to thrillers, from neo-realism to noir, it cannot be easily pinned down – yet, in hyper-urbanising China, it became a recognisable and popular genre. Much can be learned from comparing the Chinese and Hollywood mainstreams and examining the debates that anticipated their encounter.

The Chinese film industry faced the Hollywood business model almost as soon as Deng Xiaoping launched his economic reforms. The Motion Pictures Association of America (MPAA) started pushing for entry into the Chinese market as early as 1980. MPAA's intervention commercialised the industry: instead of flat rates for films subsidised by the state, the new model called for for-profit productions and revenue-sharing distribution. The system overhaul, including opening the market to ten Hollywood blockbusters (*dapian*) every year from 1994 and additional imports from Hong Kong, sparked debates over the wisdom of exposing the domestic market to such fierce competition: would the Chinese industry collapse or undergo long-overdue reform?[6]

Protecting the local industry, thereby allowing the mainstream to form in response to the conditions in the PRC, remained a highly contested issue. China was negotiating entry into the WTO, which stipulated doubling the quota of Hollywood blockbusters and weakening the measures protecting domestic cinema. A month after the PRC joined the WTO in November 2001, a number of prominent film-makers gathered to put their opinion on record and claimed that the potential crisis was in fact a point of departure for a strengthened industry. The director Huang Jianxin summed up the situation: 'The wall has fallen, new convictions have been established. Blind optimism and blind pessimism are useless. Entering the WTO is a good opportunity for realizing the potential of many things. Let us strive to make the potential into reality.'[7] The director and critic Zheng Dongtian explained that two important events took place on 11 November 2001, the day on which China entered the WTO. On that day Prime Minister Zhu Rongji signed into effect new regulations for restructuring the film industry. Zheng welcomed the possibility, introduced by these regulations, that the PRC might follow Japan and Korea, in which ailing film industries turned highly profitable and even resistant to Hollywood's cultural hegemony. Also on that day, Feng Xiaogang premiered *Big Shot's Funeral* (which ended up as the top-grossing film of the year, at over 35 million RMB). For the first time, Feng had collaborated with a foreign producer (Sony/Columbia), bringing in a huge investment (Feng would later describe the experience as unpleasant and vowed to remain independent). Zheng saw in the symbolic confluence of events in 2001 a promise for gradually building up a mighty industry comparable to Hollywood.[8] At the same symposium, the critic Zhang Boqing defied those, like the critic Dai Jinhua, who had compared foreign blockbusters to a pack of wolves. Zhang retorted: 'The "wolves" have come. Let's wrestle with them, welcome them in, dance with them, take on the challenge.'[9] The conference participants seemed to embrace the formation of a commercial mainstream and acknowledged the challenge of shaping it in a manner compatible with the Chinese film industry and culture.

The discourse on Hollywood's influence provides a new, arguably more matter-of-fact perspective on film-makers' role in cultural mediation. Until the mid-1990s, Chinese critics often accused Fifth Generation directors of selling out: the unprecedented social criticism in films such as *Ju Dou* (*Judou*, 1990), combined with their success outside China, brought up charges that these movies were made for foreigners, cashing in on maligning Chinese customs.[10] Others, especially in Taiwan and Hong Kong, detected in these films a different form of complicity, namely the celebration of a PRC-style fascist nationalism; notably, *Farewell My Concubine* was called, in a pun on its Chinese title, 'hegemonic cinema'.[11] Such claims were probably facilitated by the lack of a commercially oriented PRC mainstream at the time. The efforts of Zhang Yimou, Chen Kaige and others met with suspicion since the legitimacy of their business model had not yet been established. These film-makers strove to draw foreign investment, cater to the international film festival circuit, please domestic crowds and negotiate with Communist Party censors. The first steps towards a Chinese mainstream were misidentified as ideological statements. While a debate was raging between proponents and critics of a cinema representative of Chinese national heritage,[12] directors' gestures towards setting up an apolitical and transnational commercial base for film met with disapproval. In contrast, once the winds in China changed in the late 1990s and culture was accepted as a commodity, these directors gained celebrity status. Similarly, Sixth Generation directors were chastised, especially inside China, for manipulating the market through what Geremie Barmé has dubbed 'bankable dissent',[13] yet crossing over to commercial film-making paradoxically voided the charge: those who join the mainstream can be judged by their box-office success alone.

Mainstream Cinema with Chinese Characteristics

The question of commitment to national ideals has also plagued the mainstream through its relation to state-sponsored propaganda. In 1987, MRFT issued a statement encouraging the production of movies 'emphasizing the main melody' to 'invigorate national spirit and national pride'.[14] Insofar as the so-called

'main melody' (*zhuxuanlü*) propaganda films differ from earlier, Maoist propaganda, it is in emulating the commercial mainstream. The many productions released during the first burst of 'main melody' films, from 1989 to 1991, added Hollywood-style special effects to heroic battle scenes. (A notable example is the ten-hour epic *Decisive Engagement/Da juezhan* of 1991, directed by Cai Jiwei, Yang Guangyuan and Wei Lian.) 'Main melody' films are doctrinaire and often wooden; they do not allow for multiple views or inner contradictions, and the communist cause always ends up as the correct and heroic stance. Yet in style, they aspire to the commercial mainstream.

'Main melody' productions operate on a business model opposite to that of the commercial mainstream: rather than relying on box-office revenues, they receive generous government subsidy that regularly makes them even more expensive than commercial productions. In addition, they enjoy free access to government and military facilities and personnel and benefit from preferential media coverage, including recognition by the biased panel of the Golden Rooster Awards.[15] Yet to present effective propaganda, 'main melody' films must also reach wide audiences, and in this capacity they share the mainstream's emphasis on popular reception. Where official productions often fail, incentives to more independent film-makers prove successful. In 1997, the year in which *Dream Factory* and *Spicy Love Soup* were released, 'main melody' drew nearer to the mainstream in *The Opium War* (*Yapian zhanzheng*). Directed and produced by Xie Jin, a prominent director who maintained a semi-independent status from the government, this historical epic provides justification for the 1997 handover of Hong Kong. *The Opium War* signalled a growing symbiosis between 'main melody' and the mainstream.

After the relative failure of 'main melody' productions released for the fiftieth anniversary of the PRC in 1999,[16] in the first decade of the twenty-first century 'main melody' took on even more attributes of commercial cinema. In 2006 *The Knot* (*Yunshui yao*), pushing the PRC's claim to Taiwan, struck a less didactic note and added youthful romance. The PRC/Hong Kong/Taiwan co-production recruited major stars from the Chinese-speaking world and pioneered sophisticated computer-generated imaging. Although it did not become a regional blockbuster as hoped, *The Knot* was a hit in the PRC. A year later, Feng Xiaogang

Assembly

released his *Assembly*, which garners sympathy for People's Liberation Army soldiers killed in battle. This successful New Year's movie was proof that 'main melody' was now being made by mainstream directors and reaching audiences less interested in overt political messages. It also affirmed, and contributed to, the growing nationalist sentiments among the younger moviegoing crowd.

It is in this context that one should understand the background for, and reaction to, the prominent 'main melody' productions of 2009. *City of Life and Death* (*Nanjing! Nanjing!*, 2009) deals with the atrocities known as 'the rape of Nanjing' of 1937. Although it was not chosen as an official selection for celebrating the sixtieth anniversary of the PRC that same year, the film nevertheless toes the 'main melody' line of unmitigated heroism and rewriting history to point to Communist rule as the inevitable outcome of modern Chinese history. At the same time, *City of Life and Death* is much influenced by the blockbuster aesthetics; the critic Shelly Kraicer likens Lu's film to an amalgam of Steven Spielberg's *Saving Private Ryan* and *Schindler's List* (1993) – a Hollywood-like war film and Holocaust film combined. Kraicer detects in *City of Life and Death* – a box-office hit by a commercial director – 'a nascent post-zhuxuanlu cinema', that is, a 'main melody' cinema more attentive to entertainment-seeking audiences.[17]

The commercial tendencies of 'main melody' films are even more starkly illustrated by *The Founding of a Republic* (*Jianguo daye*, 2009). Like many earlier 'main melody' productions, the movie retells the events leading to establishing the People's Republic in October 1949. *The Founding of the Republic* differs in following the casting practices of *The Knot* and pays tribute to mainstream cinema by featuring dozens of star actors, including many Hong Kong martial arts idols. The seemingly incongruous casting is arguably the movie's main attraction – which made it, at over 101 million RMB, the all-time box-office record holder for a Chinese production – yet it is in line with closing the gap between state-sponsored propaganda and entertainment film.[18] The identity of the film's directors is of symbolic significance: Han Sanping, as President of the Beijing Film Studio in 1997, was the initiator of the PRC New Year's movies; later, as the head of China Film Group, he underwrote numerous commercial productions. Huang Jianxin, arguably the first Fifth Generation director to turn to popular genres, has become the key local producer for Hollywood shoots in China. Despite the foreign media hype about the purported innovation of propaganda film turning commercial,[19] *The Founding of the Republic* is no more than the latest culmination of a growing symbiosis between independent and state production.

The Founding of the Republic also demonstrates the difficulty of talking about the unique characteristics of mainstream cinema in the PRC: the national film industry accommodates increasing collaboration with other East Asian countries. The trend is common to many productions, going back to *Big Shot's Funeral*, *Farewell My Concubine* and even earlier. As trade barriers fall, more transnational movies are made after the model of *Crouching Tiger, Hidden Dragon* (*Wohu canglong*, 2000) and *Red Cliff* (*Chi bi*, 2008).

Conclusion

Those involved in making mainstream films have, by dint of their profession, to engage in constant assessment and prediction; this chapter does not have such a mandate. Yet experience since the 1990s shows that the commercial mainstream is growing ever more diverse and viable. It is very vital, as attested by the attendant rise of stars, genres, production patterns and exhibition practices. It also generates critical interest, as an index sensitive to the balance between local identity and globalisation as well as between ideological control and cultural commodification.

Notes

1. Dai Jinhua and *Southern Weekly* are quoted (in translation) in Ting Wang, 'Hollywood's Crusade in China Prior to China's WTO Accession', *Jump Cut: A Review of Contemporary Media* vol. 49 (Spring 2007), <www.ejumpcut.org/archive/jc49.2007/TingWang/index.html> (accessed 1 January 2010). For Dai's original essay, see Dai Jinhua, 'Zhongguo dianying: zai kuaile zhong chenmo ...' ('Chinese Cinema: Sinking in Happiness ...'), *Xiandai chuanbo* (Modern Communications) no. 1 (1999), pp. 21–2 (22). For a reference to the *Southern Weekly* article, see Feng Rui, 'Fengyun jihui dapian dengchang' ('Blockbusters to Debut among Chaos and Confusion'), *Xin Jing bao* (Beijing News), 23 November 2004, <sientechina.china.com.cn/chinese/CU-c/710595.htm>, (accessed 1 January 2010).

2. Wang, 'Hollywood's Crusade in China prior to China's WTO Accession'. Other sources point to an even more dramatic shrinkage in revenue: see, for example, Stanley Rosen, 'The Wolf at the Door: Hollywood and the Film Market in China', in E. J. Heikkila and R. Pizarro (eds), *Southern California and the World* (Westport, CT: Praeger, 2002), pp. 49–77. Box-office data are often unverifiable; throughout this chapter, I have used internet sources such as Wu Jing and Li Huizi, 'Cautiously Optimistic about "Dancing with Wolves": Chinese Cinema Enters the Blockbuster Era', Xinhua News Agency, 14 December 2005, <news.xinhuanet.com/newmedia/2005-12/14/content_3919602.htm> (accessed 1 January 2010); '2008 Zhongguo dianying yishu baogao: Jinkou fenzhang dianying taishi fenxi' ('The 2008 Report on Chinese Film Art: An Analysis of Trends in Split-

Profit Films'), 17 September 2008; 'Zhongguo dianying jinnian yinglai changxian niushi' ('This Year Chinese Cinema Ushers in a Long-term Bullish Market'). Essay published on the Wuhan Municipal Construction Commission: <www.whjs.gov.cn/whty/content/2008-01/04/content_134763.htm> (accessed 1 January 2010); <indus.chinafilm.com/200809/1753365.html> (accessed 1 January 2010).

3. Sun Chen, '"Xin chengshi dianying" miaozhun dushi qingnianren' ('"New Urban Cinema" Aims at Urban Youth'), *Renmin ribao haiwai ban* (People's Daily Overseas Edition), 9 March 2000.

4. 'Zhongguo xinshengdai dianying daoyan: Biaoshu de yuwang' ('China's Newborn Generation of Film Directors: The Desire to Express'), *Qingnian bao* (Youth Daily), 18 April 2002: <news.eastday.com/epublish/gb/paper148/20020418/class014800007/hwz648692.htm> (accessed 1 January 2010).

5. Yingjin Zhang, 'Rebel without a Cause? China's New Urban Generation and Postsocialist Filmmaking', in *The Urban Generation: Chinese Cinema and Society at the Turn of the Twenty-first Century* (ed.), Zhang Zhen (Durham, NC, and London: Duke University Press, 2007), pp. 49–80 (49–50).

6. Wang, 'Hollywood's Crusade in China Prior to China's WTO Accession'. On the reforms in the film industry, see also Ying Zhu, *Chinese Cinema during the Era of Reform: The Ingenuity of the System* (Westport: Praeger, 2003), pp. 72–83.

7. Huang Jianxin, 'Chaiqiang yu xinnian' ('Toppled Walls and Convictions'), in *WTO yu Zhongguo dianying* (WTO and Chinese Cinema), ed., Zhang Zhenqian and Yang Yuanying (Beijing: Zhongguo dianying chubanshe, 2002), pp. 99–104 (104).

8. Zheng Dongtian, 'Zai ziyou de kongjian li jianshou ben minzu wenhua' ('Preserving Our National Culture in the Free Space'), in Zhang Zhenqian and Yang Yuanying, *WTO yu Zhongguo dianying*, pp. 194–7.

9. Zhang Boqing, '"Yu lang gongwu," yingjie tiaozhan – Zhongguo dianying "rushi' ganyan"' ('"Dancing with Wolves," Taking on the Challenge: Reflections on Chinese Cinema "Entering the World"'), in Zhang Zhenqian and Yang Yuanying, *WTO yu Zhongguo dianying*, pp. 217–20.

10. See for example Dai Qing 'Raised Eyebrows for *Raise the Red Lantern*', trans. Jeanne Tai, *Public Culture* vol. 5 no. 2 (Winter 1993), pp. 333–7.

11. Yar See, 'Bawang dianying' ('The Hegemon's Film'), *Sing Tao Evening News*, 11 December 1993; quoted in Jenny

Kwok Wah Lau, ' "Farewell My Concubine": History, Melodrama, and Ideology in Contemporary Pan-Chinese Cinema', *Film Quarterly* vol. 49 no. 1 (1995), pp. 16–27.

12. George S. Semsel et al. (eds), *Chinese Film Theory* (New York: Praeger, 1990), pp. 97–9.

13. Geremie R. Barmé, *In the Red: On Contemporary Chinese Culture* (New York: Columbia University Press, 1999), p. 188.

14. Rui Zhang, *The Cinema of Feng Xiaogang: Commercialization and Censorship in Chinese Cinema after 1989* (Hong Kong: Hong Kong University Press, 2008), p. 35.

15. Zhang, *The Cinema of Feng Xiaogang*, pp. 38–9.

16. Wang, 'Hollywood's Crusade in China prior to China's WTO Accession'.

17. Shelly Kraicer, 'A Matter of Life and Death: Lu Chuan and Post-Zhuxuanlu Cinema', <cinema-scope.com/wordpress/?page_id=1161> (accessed 1 January 2010).

18. Tieming (Iron Name), 'What is the Box Office for *The Founding of the Republic?*', 13 November 2009, <www.woman.org.cn/PublicAsp/daye./html/200911130/2009111363.html> (accessed 1 January 2010).

19. I can attest to this tendency from personal experience. Min Lee of the Associated Press news agency in Hong Kong and François Bougon of Agence France-Presse contacted me separately to illuminate what they found a confusing 'mix between Hollywood and agitprop'.

Further Reading in *Chinese Films In Focus II*

On contemporary mainstream cinema from the People's Republic of China, see Chapter 2, '*Big Shot's Funeral*: Performing a Post-modern Cinema of Attractions' by Yingjin Zhang, and Chapter 17, '*Hero*: The Return of a Traditional Masculine Ideal in China' by Kam Louie.

20 Contemporary Meta-Chinese Film Stardom and Transnational Transmedia Celebrity

Anne Ciecko

The construction of film stardom in Greater China is increasingly reliant on media convergence and local/global negotiations. The post-handover/millennial period marks a new era in Chinese celebrity and fan cultures, with simultaneous trends towards consolidation and disaggregation of nationalism and stardom. In particular, hyper-self-reflexivity, new technologies and national/territorial crossovers have shaped contemporary Chinese transmedia figures. This is exemplified in concatenated transnational systems that leave indelible traces in mega-budgeted Chinese multistarrers, in the legacy of Hong Kong's multipurpose entertainers (the so-called Heavenly Kings), and in the cases of American-born contemporary performers who have worked within the Hong Kong star factory and have found fame and/or infamy across multiple media platforms – including cinema. This chapter aims to expand the dialogue within Chinese cinema and screen studies about film stardom and celebrity in an age of proliferating media.[1] I focus here on the context, impact and implications of star activities that push the boundaries of agency, accent, commodification, sensation and self/public ownership of image.

Heavenly Kings and Multisystem Star Pantheons

I have argued elsewhere that the currency of contemporary male stardom in Asian cinematic contexts is charged by the transdiscursive 'star function' – an adapted version of Foucault's 'author function' demonstrated by a sense of the star as active, self-generating, seemingly ubiquitous, multitalented and resourceful, industrial and industrious.[2] In consumer-oriented Hong Kong popular culture, constant movement between blurred fields of film and popular music and commercial endorsements is especially common and expected, with additional anarchic ruptures and dynamic resistance in the meta-cultural form of star hoaxes or scandals. In the postmodern, post-handover realm of excessive media overload, the discursive servers metaphorically, metonymically, or quite literally, crash and offer at least momentary flashes of an impossibly illusive/elusive referent – the transgressive and/or complicitous 'real' person behind the star image, as if such a thing could ever exist. The contemporary Hong Kong/Chinese/global star cannot be completely owned or controlled, and the transnational public sphere cannot be autocratically orchestrated and manipulated. This is particularly important to note in an era of rising Chinese-language blockbusters, lavishly nostalgic period epics with transnational Chinese and pan-Asian casts and unified China subtexts.

While contemporary ensemble multistarrers (a term I borrow from Bollywood parlance) suggest a celestial pantheon consolidating mainland, Hong Kong and Taiwan (and other Asian) screen talent, these vehicles are primarily 'located' in the imaginary of premodern China, and Mandarin is the privileged, hegemonic dialect of these co-productions that inhabit what Gary G. Wu has called the 'Sinascape', an intersected nexus of transnational production and reception.[3] Shu-Mei Shih identifies this dynamic as 'Sinophone articulations'.[4] Spoken dialogue left undubbed thus reveals traces of accented difference that cannot be fully erased or assimilated. There is unmistakable heterogeneity/heteroglossia, and the stars register as multivalenced because of their performances and personae onscreen and off. Intertextual and extradiegetic factors, including their national/regional/ territorial roots, their career trajectories, their personal lives and their trans-media presence, invite disparate audiences to identify expansively with these Chinese films and dimensions of multisystem stardom. For instance, Feng Xiaogang's star-studded *Hamlet* adaptation set in tenth-century China, *The Banquet* (2006), has mainland headliners joined by American-born Hong Kong star Daniel Wu. Zhang Yimou's box-office record-breaker *Curse of the Golden Flower* (2006) stars Hong Kong's Chow Yun-Fat, Zhang's original muse Gong Li and Taiwanese sensation Jay Chou; the latter's Mandarin pronunciation reveals his Taiwan origins and identity. While the acting role is a non-musical dramatic one, his singer/songwriter status is nevertheless reified, as he also penned and performed songs on the soundtrack, including the theme. His music videos and recorded tracks reference the film. Arguably the most popular Chinese singer in Greater China, Chou represents a new model of broad Chinese pop appeal with fans ready and willing to experience and consume his latest forays into vocal and multi-instrumental music performance, composition and production; film and music video acting, directing and screenwriting; and product endorsements.[5] To cite another example, Hong Kong hero Andy Lau is seemingly omnipresent in the new Chinese prestige blockbusters, but is also extremely well known throughout Asia as a prodigious box-office draw in Hong Kong films for the past two decades, a veteran TV actor (one of the Hong Kong station TVB's Five Tigers) and a top recording artist. As Hong Kong film critic Long Tin asserts in an essay for the 29th Hong Kong International Film Festival honouring Lau's contributions, his 'prolificacy, his star charisma and his close relationship with mainstream film genres' enable his enduring appeal: 'To say that Andy Lau breathes the air of local cinema is not to put it forward as an explanation/rationale of Hong Kong cinematic development, but to serve as a discourse reference, a conceptual arena.'[6]

The Hong Kong entertainment industry's invention of the phenomenon of the 'Heavenly Kings' participates in creating a popular-culture mythology of fragments with a term borrowed from folklore and classical Chinese literature, and the images of the world guardians and evil-fighters of Buddhist religious philosophy – given particular secular embodiment and voice. The 'original' Cantopop Heavenly Kings, Jacky

Cheung, Andy Lau, Leon Lai and Aaron Kwok, solidified the concept of the multitasking star omnipresent in the Hong Kong mediascape. Throughout the 1990s when this term was coined, these deified pop figures especially (but also other prominent male and female Cantopop performers) were constantly visible and audible in films and television (including cable and satellite); music albums, videos and concert performances; advertising campaigns; radio; the Japanese import of karaoke; tabloid publications, and myriad incarnations of fan culture. The Heavenly Kings were firmly rooted in Hong Kong culture but travelled, as already-hybridised Cantonese music and film had done previously, to expanding Asian markets in South-East and East Asia and the global Chinese diaspora. Andy Lau, arguably the most successful of the Heavenly Kings in his film and musical ventures, has performed songs in Cantonese and Mandarin, English, Japanese, Malay and Taiwanese. As Wai-Chung Ho has noted, globalisation is apparent in Cantopop through international stardom, experimentation with different sounds, inter-Asian musical exchange, genres and media, and 'advances in technology speeding the consumption and reception of Hong Kong popular music'.[7] The multiplatform popularity of the Heavenly Kings helped create what he calls, 'Pacific Asia's own version of Hollywood and Bollywood'.[8] Into the 2000s, the internet and mobile communication devices were also inundated with Cantopop images and sounds. Piracy, previously executed via formats of video and audiocassettes and easy-to-be-copied video compact discs (VCDs), was exacerbated by MP3 files and digital duplication. Hong Kong music and film/video sound became ever-more techno-centric with 'employment of synthesizers, sampling, MIDI sequencing, digital recording, digital sound effect processing, audio-visual synchronisation, and digital mixing/mastering for music production, and new technological tools for the transmission and reception of Hong Kong popular music'.[9]

Hong Kong-based media performers are now expected to flexibly function within and across Asian linguistic and media and cultural milieus, with multidialect/multilingual and localised versions of lyrics and dialogue, public performances and endorsements. Outside the Chinese-language nexus, the Korean *hanryu*, or wave of popular culture, swept over Hong Kong with Korean blockbuster movies, K-pop music and television dramas, and challenged Cantopop culture to remain relevant given Korean product's cross-appeal to Hong Kong/Chinese audiences. Youthful Taiwan icons such as the boyband F4 and, especially, Jay Chou, have contributed to further cultural transnationalism with models of non-PRC Chinese pop idols. Chou, in particular, mixes a variety of western/global styles with inserted recognisably Chinese-inflected musical elements and themes, as well as an individualist and outsider 'coolness' factor that Chinese fans have found intoxicating rather than alien.[10] The imagined communities of transnational Chinese fan groups, as well as displays of youth/consumer culture, have expanded with the mediation and access the internet provides. The internet has also served as an alternative forum for star construction and entrepreneurial activity, information and product-sharing, expression of personal and collective opinion and fantasy, and rebellion and resistance. Chinese stars hailing from overseas have been especially catalytic in this regard.

The ABCs: American-born Chinese Stars

Movie and transmedia stars Daniel Wu and Edison Chen represent globalised/westernised/cosmopolitanised images of youthful Chineseness as ethnicity, rather than nationality. Entering the industry in Hong Kong with limited facility with Cantonese and Mandarin dialects of Chinese, each still speak with discernable markers of difference, the accents of non-native speakers; reportedly neither can read Chinese. As 'Chinese' stars in the post-handover era, they are circumscribed by this identity, yet also constantly exceed it. As scholar Ien Ang asserts, 'there can never be a perfect fit between fixed identity label and hybrid personal experience'.[11] The Hong Kong entertainment nexus that Daniel Wu and Edison Chen became part of during the late 1990s has struggled to negotiate its former status as a British crown colony and its position as a Special Administrative Region of the People's Republic of China, cognisant of the apparent need to function within the territory to develop and perpetuate unique localised and profoundly hybridised forms of popular cultural expression, and to operate within China and beyond boundaries for economic survival.

Daniel Wu as shirtless pin-up, and in his parodic directorial debut *The Heavenly Kings* as a boyband member

The trade papers noticed this entertainment-industry trend with headlines like 'Newest Chinese Stars Hail from America', heralding Daniel Wu and Edison Chen as exemplars of the new generation of overseas Chinese finding fame and fortune in Hong Kong.[12] While certainly not the first foreign-born actors in Hong Kong (they were recently preceded by others like New York-born Hong Kong Michael Wong and his brothers, and Montreal native Christy Chung), Wu and Chen were arguably the first ABC mega-stars of the post-handover/millennial age. I contend that stars such as Daniel Wu and Edison Chen can be viewed as 'accented' and 'multi-accentual' in the reverse diasporic trajectory of their respective lives and careers, the multilingual media realms they inhabit, an interstitial 'structure of feeling' that accompanies their star images and the multivalenced and polysemic nature of their celebrity and meta-Chinese identities.[13]

Both stars have similar narratives of 'discovery' while visiting Hong Kong, followed by rapid career expansion. Shortly after graduation from college, Wu, a California native and child of Shanghai immigrants, came to Hong Kong in 1997 to witness the transfer of the colony from the United Kingdom to mainland China. He inadvertently ended up launching a career in modelling when the travel money ran out, which quickly led to film acting. Vancouver native Chen has family roots in southern China (he is also one eighth Macanese/Portuguese) and spent part of his youth studying at the International School in Hong Kong. He was discovered as a teenager on a summer holiday to Hong Kong in 1999, and was subsequently signed with the local talent agency EEG (standing, aptly, for Energy, Exhilaration and Globalisation), known for its creation of teen idols; and he was immediately launched into television commercials, pop music and films.[14]

Both Wu and Chen have played a variety of movie roles (although Wu has, to date, displayed a much wider acting range), underscoring their 'foreignness' and novelty, and others reflexively inscribing them into

Heartthrob Edison Chen as the younger version of Andy Lau's cop/triad mole in the *Infernal Affairs* epic

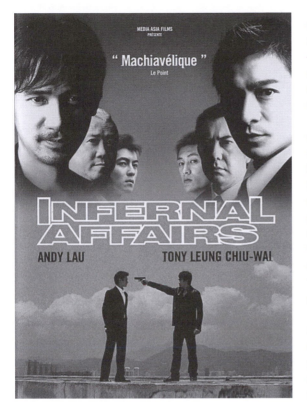

the Hong Kong entertainment nexus. Film critics have also consistently charted their progress with language proficiency and credible inflections, as in the title of the review in Malaysia's *New Straits Times* of Daniel Wu's mainland country bumpkin hitman in *One Night in Mongkok* (Derek Yee, 2004): 'Reluctant Killer with a Strange Accent'.[15] In *Beijing Rocks* (Mabel Cheung, 2001), Wu's culturally confused Hong Kong character, a young Cantopop star come to Beijing, directly addresses the camera to inform the viewer that his Putonghua (standard modern Mandarin Chinese) is not good.

Edison Chen's movie debut was in a Japanese film sequel, *Dead or Alive 2: Birds* (2000), the second instalment in the trilogy by shock auteur Takashi Miike. By the time he made his Hong Kong film debut, in the actioner *Gen Y Cops* (Benny Chan, 2000), the parodic robot-on-a-rampage sequel to the popular *Gen X Cops* (Benny Chan, 1999), he was already a local pop icon. Chen's character in *Gen Y*, reflexively invoking his instant stardom was called, of course, Edison. Early roles offered intertextual reinforcement of the currency of his ABC appeal. He co-starred with Daniel Wu as his older brother in the Taiwan/Hong Kong sci-fi gaming romance *Princess D* (Sylvia Chang and Alan Yuen, 2002) – one of a number of films Chen and Wu have made about erotically charged pleasures, dangers and subversive potential of virtual realities, surveillance, evidence and subjectivities mediated by technology.

Chen's film roles made him seem immediately connected to Hong Kong's entertainment industries; for example, to Cantopop via a supporting role in the Andy Lau/Anita Mui musical *Dance of a Dream* (Andrew Lau, 2001). He was also cast as the younger version of Lau's corrupt cop character Ming in the *Infernal Affairs* trilogy (Andrew Lau and Alan Mak, 2002–3), in the prequel and filmic flashbacks to the pre-handover era. Like Daniel Wu in *Around the World in 80 Days* (Frank Coraci, 2004), Chen was cast in an international Jackie Chan starrer *The Medallion* (Gordon Chan, 2003), albeit in an ill-fitting stereotypical Chinese cameo role.

Chen expanded into high-profile blogging, hip-hop music and limited edition fashion branding with a streetwear company named Clot, aimed especially at a young Chinese market, as well as a store called Juice and eventually a media division for the production of music and movies. By 2005, he had appeared with Jay Chou in the Cantonese version of *Initial D*, the car-racing drama feature film based on the wildly popular Japanese manga series of the same name (directed by *Infernal Affairs*' Andrew Lau and Alan Mak) – a commercial experiment in inter-Asian adaptation and trans-Chinese pop-star casting. He also signed with Schiff and Co., one of Hollywood's biggest talent agencies, and publically announced his widely quoted desire to retire by his early thirties – a prophecy that would (temporarily) come true, for different reasons than expected. Chen's Hollywood debut was in the sequel to its remake of Tashashi Shimizu's *Ju-On* franchise, *The Grudge* 2 (2006), set in Japan and directed by the original's Japanese film-maker. Having established a following throughout East Asia, he also starred in the 2005 Japanese manga-adapted melodrama *Under the Same Moon*, and on the eve of his North American debut, Chen was heralded as 'an impresario for a new Pacific Rim'.[16] His embraced otherness is also demonstrated via cross-ethnic casting; one of his most daring and best-reviewed film roles to date is his central performance in brutally ultra-violent Hong Kong/Japan co-production *Dog Bites Dog* (Pou-Soi Cheang, 2006) as a Cambodian boxer turned hired killer, a feral character unable to speak Cantonese.

Daniel Wu, who has appeared in hyphenate roles such as the French-Chinese chef Michael/Michel in *Drink-Drank-Drunk* (Derek Yee, 2005), has also played marginalised Asian 'others' including a Cambodian character, a Khmer Rouge terrorist in one of his early films, *Purple Storm* (Teddy Chan, 1999). Trained in *wushu* martial arts since childhood, Wu benefited from early mentorship as protégé and sometimes co-star of Hong Kong/global superstar Jackie Chan. He has made multiple films for Media Asia Entertainment, regularly acted in movies directed by local film-makers and frequently alongside Taiwanese top starlet Shu Qi (who, like Wu, earned credibility after a career start with modelling and softcore/violent Category III films). Signed in 1997 with Jackie Chan's management company, Daniel Wu first gained notice in his film debut, the gay-themed *Bishonen* (Yonfan, 1998), where he was first paired with Terence Yin who would become a longtime friend and collaborator. His subsequent breakthrough performance was in Benny Chan's frenetic hit *Gen X Cops*, the Y2K arms-dealer thriller in which he played a character reflexively named Daniel, a Chinese associate of the yakuza villains. Following the model of his mentor Jackie Chan, he did his own stunts in the film and in subsequent actioners. He also expanded his range by serving as producer (as well as star) for the low-budget Category III-rated moody thriller *Night Corridor* (Julian Lee, 2003). A major role in an instalment of the Jackie Chan franchise *New Police Story* (Benny Chan, 2004) garnered significant award recognition, winning the prestigious Golden Horse Award at the Taipei Film Festival for best supporting actor. Wu thus established himself as both a successful pitchman and a power player in films. His chiselled prettiness and image as a metrosexual pin-up was exploited in numerous advertising campaigns, fashion spreads and even a fashion design collection. At the same time, he emerged as one of the most versatile actors of his generation, often compared with another of the territory's biggest stars, the aforementioned Andy Lau, with whom Wu co-stars in the censor-baiting gangster/junkie/narcotics cop drama *Protégé* (Derek Yee, 2007, a PRC/Hong Kong/Singapore co-production – one of the edgiest co-productions with mainland China to date).[17] Unlike Lau, however, Wu has a perceived licence to take extreme risks, and has not shunned nudity and fairly explicit sex scenes. As he states in an interview, the nudity and sex scenes in his film *Cop on a Mission* (Marco Mak, 2001) did not please

his female fans, and invited criticism from the Hong Kong media, but also generated some respect from other directors who subsequently offered roles.[18]

Generic diversification and a sense of self-determination has been instrumental in building Wu's star profile. To date he has appeared in more than forty films, in Cantonese and Mandarin, in arthouse/independent, exploitation and commercial genres including police thrillers, romantic comedies and period epics. Recently, upon the retirement of his manager, Wu asserted the right to shape his own career and create opportunities for others by starting his own talent agency, Revolution Talent Management.

Deconstructed Deities and Fallen Idols

As Wu's career progressed towards firmly established legitimacy, he savvily exploited and sent up his own celebrity with transmedia exploits. Rather than embracing a Heavenly King-type personality, he introduced a kind of postmodern Monkey King trickster figure. He was Creative Producer of MTV Asia's *Chiseen/Whatever Things*, a Jackass/Punk'd-style show hosted by Edison Chen featuring daredevil acts, celebrity pranks, man-on-the street provocateur reportage and 'pure-situational randomness'.[19] Wu himself participated in dangerous physical stunts like shooting firecrackers at a friend and riding a toddler tricycle down a busy Hong Kong street. In 2005, he orchestrated the formation of a faux boyband called Alive as a critique of the Cantopop music industry and as a multimedia vehicle to stimulate the careers of his less successful friends. Together with his collaborators and fellow band members Terence Yin, Andrew Lin and Conroy Chan (and using his star currency as leverage), he launched a website and directed a feature-length mockumentary ironically titled *The Heavenly Kings* about the travails of their group. An advertisement in Hong Kong's Chinese newspaper *Apple Daily*, reportedly sponsored by Daniel Wu's first director Yonfan, read, 'Watch "The Heavenly Kings" to get to know Daniel Wu for the first time.'[20]

The film mixes 'real' interviews with Cantopop artists (including one of the original 'Heavenly Kings' Jackie Chung) and fictionalised scenarios. The band's mentor and producer is Davy Chan (aka DBF, Davy Big Fly), the underground musician, a self-taught drummer and composer, best known for his work with the edgy local hip-hop group LMF (Lazy Muthafucka). Using 'Auto-Tune' technology, Chan barely smoothes out the wretched vocals for Alive's first single 'Adam's Choice', as no one in the group can really sing, with the exception of Terence Yin, whose previous solo career began and ended with an album released in Taiwan. *The Heavenly Kings* frames Yin as Wu's best friend who has all but abandoned his singing.

Frustrated with the shady contract behaviour of record label representatives and the difficulty of getting a deal, Alive launches a multistep process. Playing with the idea of alternative and illegal economies, the group's members upload a song on the internet and pretend it got stolen; after contacting the press, the story appears in the media creating a buzz about the band. A scrolling sequence of images and text from 'news' stories from tabloids reveals its effectiveness. The members give a press conference to reinforce their victimisation, claiming they gave a demo to record companies, and asserting that they are now going to use the internet as a way to share their music with everyone through free downloads on their website, alivenotdead.com. The talking-head subjects/Cantopop informants such as Karen Mok discuss using the media to one's advantage. 'It's a two way street,' Candy Lo asserts. 'Some "artistes" are really clever, mixing work with gossip. Then you'll get publicity.' Singer and actor Nic Tse states that he's learned that in the entertainment business 'lies can become reality' where repeated untruths start to be believed. The Alive band members laughingly describe their trick as a 'marketing strategy'. The group takes on endorsements such as a photo-advertising shoot for a bridal salon to fund the making of their first music video; backstage making-of clips of all these projects are included in the film.

The Heavenly Kings' filmic representation of stardom discourses in Hong Kong underscores the hotness factor, from hiring professional fans (Andrew stealthily requests five pro fans for himself alone) and a stylist (consultation only, as the group ultimately rejects his over-the-top stage costumes) to showcasing pop culture buzz, and looks over talent. Alive is compared throughout the film with the Taiwanese boyband F4, capitalising on Daniel Wu's movie-idol popularity with young audiences. However, Alive is constantly revealed in the film to be more a manufactured concept project by film actors rather than a viable band. The movie dramatises professional conflicts and personality differences as the group does televised concerts in transnational Chinese nodes/hubs, Hong Kong, Taipei and Shanghai. Daniel is depicted as the controlling

workaholic perfectionist, Andrew (presented as the initiator of the project) as the most vain and self-serving member of Alive, Conroy as the lazy jokester ('I'm the fattest boyband member ever!' he asserts in his Australian accent) and Terence as the irresponsible partier – images that are reinforced by two-dimensional cut-out caricatures that appear in animated sequences throughout the film. The parodic coda of the film 'reveals' Andrew's film career revitalised, Terence married to his number-one obsessive fan, Conroy living a life of domestic bliss with his (real-life) more famous wife and Daniel, who suffers a kind of (apparently fictional) breakdown in the film, settling down and making a home in Africa.

The website alivenotdead.com, initially created for the film to perpetuate myth of the band's authenticity with dissemination of information about the group, was relaunched in 2007 by Daniel Wu and his partners (including a fellow Californian and founder of the film criticism website Rotten Tomatoes, Patrick Lee). It now serves as a multifunctional alternative social networking and promotions site for Asian and Asian diasporic creative artists and their fans. The Hong Kong-based site recognises transnational audience/readers with translations into English and simplified Chinese. It features pages for the performers to post blog entries, project updates and videos. While the film *The Heavenly Kings* entertains with its story of manipulation of the discursive tools of celebrity construction and its flow between fact and fiction (differences between them are sometimes quite indiscernible), the website offers another multimedia dialogic forum.

In contrast to Alive's self-generating manifestations, Edison Chen's multitasking career was shaken by a different type of media convergence, participatory fan culture and discursive 'damage control'. Explicit photographs taken by the star in sexual situations with numerous actresses and singers with whom he had collaborated professionally (including Gillian Chung, movie actress and member of the wholesome singing/acting duo The Twins who had previously spoken out again premarital sex, Bobo Chan, Cecilia Cheung and others) were leaked online starting in late January 2008. As the mysterious perpetrator 'Kira' (nicknamed after a taunting vigilante serial killer character in the Japanese manga, anime series and live-action *Death Note* films) incrementally uploaded batches of new photos daily, feeding the drama,

Chinese star gossip on the internet was launched in scandalous new directions. The photos appeared on internet forums, emails and messaging systems.[22]

As the controversy intensified, Chen publically apologised for his indiscretions and declared his intention to (at least temporarily) leave the Hong Kong entertainment industries. He posted written comments and a talking-head video on his own blog, urging people to destroy these images and not to spread them further. He informed the public that the police were handling the situation; and at his press conference several weeks into the crisis, he issued apologies, rhetorically invoking the local and a self-conscious sense of Chinese moral codes (albeit in English). 'Most importantly,' he insisted, ' I would like to say sorry to all the people of Hong Kong. … I know young people in Hong Kong look up to many figures in our society. And in this regard, I have failed. I failed as a role model.'[23] The photographs had apparently been stolen from Chen's laptop computer which he had taken in for repairs, and curious internet and personal technology users throughout Greater China logged on, consumed and circulated the pictures. Tales of triad threats, bounties and a postal-mailed bullet; images of tearful implicated female participants depicted variously as victims, hypocrites, morally tainted, or chastened, permeated the media as if part of a film script. All manner of local and international news outlets picked up on and published versions of the story and images, with front-page presence for weeks on end in Hong Kong. Edison Chen left Hong Kong for exile in North America, lost his Manhattan Titanium credit card endorsement and had his scenes cut from Stephen Fung's hip-hop martial arts film *Jump* (2009, replaced by another interstitial/accented performer, Eurasian Singaporean actor Leon Jay Williams, in a film starring, coincidentally, Daniel Wu). Arrests related to the case regarding the distribution of illegally obtained and variously classified indecent and obscene materials were made in Hong Kong and mainland China. Numerous pundits, bloggers and celebrities weighed in, including Daniel Wu who asserted that the Hong Kong media's focus on sex obfuscated the fact that Chen and the women in the photos were actually victims.[24]

The Edison Chen incident mobilised netizens who helped identify the individuals in the photos, protestors and advocates for privacy and for free speech, government and law enforcement officials, and the press/media in Hong Kong, mainland China and beyond. The cultural ramifications of the phenomenon may never be fully determined. However, as Edison Chen made a tentative return to the Hong Kong entertainment industries approximately one year after his indefinite exit, it was clear that transnational transmedia celebrity – and the public's quest for the 'real' – cannot be fully curtailed or contained. The career vicissitudes of film actors Daniel Wu and Edison Chen thus demonstrate some of the ways the contemporary Chinese star text is fed or bled by ancillary media activities.

Notes

1. See the special issues of *Journal of Chinese Cinemas* on film stars (vol. 2 no. 2, June 2008) and Chinese cinema and/as new media (vol. 3 no. 1, June 2009), including Brett Farmer's fascinating short article, 'Crossing the Line: Reading the Edison Chen Scandal', which discusses the Hong Kong star, moral panic and cyberspace, pp. 71–7. See also Darrell William Davis and Emilie Yueh-yu Yeh, *East Asian Screen Industries* (London: BFI, 2008) and *East Asian Cinemas: Exploring Transnational Connections on Film*, edited by Leon Hunt and Leung Wing-Fai (London: I.B. Taurus & Co., 2008). The pioneering work of Ackbar Abbas (*Hong Kong: Culture and the Politics of Disappearance*, Minneapolis and London: University of Minnesota Press, 1997), Stephen Teo (*Hong Kong Cinema: The Extra Dimensions*, London: BFI, 1997, and elsewhere) and Gina Marchetti (*From Tian'anmen to Times Square: Transnational China and the Chinese Diaspora on Global Screens, 1989–1997*, Philadelphia: Temple University Press, 2006) has been especially useful in analysing developments in the post-handover era of Hong Kong and transnational Chinese cinema.

2. Anne Ciecko, 'Muscle, Market Value, Telegenesis, Cyberpresence: The New Asian Movie Star in the Global Economy of Masculine Images', in Tasha Oren and Patrice Petro (eds), *Global Currents: Media and Technology Now* (New Brunswick, NJ: Rutgers University Press), pp. 186–99.

3. Gary G. Wu, *Sinascape: Contemporary Chinese Cinema* (Plymouth: Rowman & Littlefield, 2007).

4. Shu-Mei Shih, *Visuality and Identity: Sinophone Articulations across the Pacific* (Berkeley: University of California Press, 2007).

5. Anthony Y. H. Fung, 'Fandom, Youth and Consumption in China', *European Journal of Cultural Studies* vol. 12 no. 3 (2009), pp. 285–303.

6. Long Tin, 'Andy Lau Breathes the Air of Local Cinema', *Andy Lau: Actor in Focus*, Hong Kong International Film Society (Series 6, 2005), p. 57.

7. Wai-Chung Ho, 'Between Globalisation and Localisation: A Study of Hong Kong Popular Music', *Popular Music* vol. 22 no. 2 (May 2003), pp. 149–50.

8. Ibid., p. 152.

9. Ibid., p. 153.

10. Fung, 'Fandom, Youth and Consumption in China', p. 288.

11. Ien Ang, *On Not Speaking Chinese: Living Between Asia and the West* (London and New York: Routledge, 2001), p. 11.

12. Wendy Kan, *Variety*, 25–31 March (2002), p. 20.

13. See a relevant discussion of multi-accentuality in the excellent essay 'Articulations of the Dragon: Bruce Lee and Transnational Identity', 12 May 2009, <www.lovehkfilm.com/blog/roninonempty/?p=48>. Hamid Naficy outlines his concepts of accented, exilic and diasporic cinema in *Accented Cinema: Exilic and Diasporic Filmmaking* (Princeton, NJ: Princeton University Press, 2001). The idea of multi-accentuality used here is an amalgamation of the theories of: Stuart Hall, 'On Postmodernism and Articulation', in D. Morley and K.-H. Chen (eds), *Stuart Hall: Critical Dialogues in Cultural Studies* (London: Routledge, 1996); John Storey from *Cultural Consumption and Everyday Life* (New York: Oxford University Press, 1999); and Valentin Volosinov in *Marxism and the Philosophy of Language* (London: Seminar Press, 1973).

14. Jeff Chang, 'Movies, Hip-Hop, Fashion Design–Edison Chen is an Impresario for a New Pacific Rim', 11 October 2006, *SFGate.com*, <www.sfgate.com/cgibin/article.cgi?f=/c/a/2006/10/11/DDGOLLLO541.DTL>

15. Sharon Wong, 'Reluctant Killer with a Strange Accent', *New Straits Times* (Malaysia), 22 May 2004, p. 5.

16. Chang, 'Movies, Hip-Hop, Fashion Design', p. 15.

17. Sonia Kolesikov-Jessop, 'Making the Final Cut: By Working with Government Censors, China's Filmmakers are Stretching the Limits of Acceptability', *Newsweek*, 19 February 2007, p. 3.

18. 'Daniel Wu Interview: Hong Kong Cinema', *Vengeance: The Extreme Movie Magazine*, January 2005, <www.hkcinema.co.uk/Articles/danielwuinterview.htm>.

19. 'Chiseen (aka MTV Whatever Things)', <youngminn.com/blog/2003/08/chiseen-aka-mtv-whatever-things>, 21 August 2003.

20. Alexandra A. Seno, 'Talent is Optional: Hong Kong Actor Daniel Wu Steps Behind the Camera to Direct a Deadpan Satire about Chinese Pop Stars', *Newsweek*, 5 June 2006, <www.newsweek.com/id/52257>

21. Vivienne Chow, 'The Sex Scandal that Rocked HK's Entertainment Industry', *South China Morning Post*, 25 December 2008, p. 4.

22. Edison Chen press conference, Hong Kong, 28 February 2008, <www.youtube.com/watch?v=ewAKWEeC0IU>

23. 'An Interview with Hong Kong Director and Actor Daniel Wu', <www.cinespot.com/einterviews21.html>

Afterword

Liquidity of Being[1]

Rey Chow

In one of the origination myths about the Middle Kingdom, the legendary hero Yu wins the good will of the people by delivering them from catastrophes caused by water. To this day, *Da Yu zhi shui* – 'the great Yu tames the flood' – remains in the Chinese idiom as a reminder of this story about political sovereignty. Rather than a gift from a transcendental source, political sovereignty is conceived in the mythical thinking presented here as the outcome of popular consent. Such consent is conferred on someone only because he has proven himself to be an exceptional governor – not only of the human world but first and foremost of nature, whose capricious excess is brought under control and transformed into a productive resource with which people can coexist in peace and harmony. Subsequent centuries of Chinese history have borne out the truth of these intimate linkages between water, bare life and political power. Even in the twenty-first century, whenever water wreaks havoc on the lives of the people, Chinese political leaders are usually swift to appear on the scene to affirm their concern and compassion. Often amplified nowadays by the contemporary media for so-called public relations purposes, such appearances in fact carry with them a mythical significance. From the latter perspective, what is conjured up and (re)enacted is not so much the immediacy of media appeal as it is the persistence of an implicit socio-political contract.

A specific relation between water and survival, understood not merely naturally but also ideologically, thus constitutes the imaginary accompanying many cultural representations. I propose to address this imaginary with the phrase 'liquidity of being'. Nowhere can this imaginary be better detected than in language, in which fragments assembled from past intelligence and experience offer precious clues to a culture's habits, inclinations and aspirations. In Chinese, the material meanings of water often interfuse with the metaphoric to form part of a collective ambience of routine usages. Between an idiom such as *qishan mo qishui* (better to mess around with a mountain than with water) and *hongyan huoshui* (females, water of ill fortune), there is a strong sense that water is a form of danger, which, when superimposed on sexual divisions, may be attributed to females. Is this straightforward misogyny – or a tacit acknowledgment that women are the sex with the greater power and potential? According to a philosophical text such as the *Dao de jing*, nothing is more submissive and weaker than water, and yet over time it is irresistible and overcomes the hard, the resistant and the strong, reshaping, for instance, the rocks of a stream bed. In common parlance in Cantonese, fate or destiny itself is sometimes referred to as *ming shui*, and water's potency is equated with money: *shui wei cai* (water is money). These are only a few examples of the prominent place occupied by water in Chinese linguistic significations. Not surprisingly, this general chain of associations around liquidity has also informed Chinese cinema in provocative, if seldom observed, ways.

But how may water as such be configured in/as cinema if we are to avoid the facile route of reflectionism? In what ways may liquidity conceptually inform filmic vision and thinking?

Consider the classic *Spring in a Small Town* (1948), directed by Fei Mu. The film could not be more well known, if only because of the tortuous history of its reception, its arousal of suspicion and criticism from the orthodox left, and praise and devotion from film enthusiasts. Narrated by the female protagonist, Zhou

Yuwen, the film tells of the unexpected reunion of Yuwen and her former beloved, Zhang Zhichen, a doctor of western medicine who happens to have known her husband, Dai Liyan, since childhood. During the brief interruption brought by the doctor's visit, amorous feelings are rekindled through memory and physical proximity; emotionally tense situations ensue, including an attempted suicide by Liyan, an invalid. As Yuwen is reawakened by this incident to her obligation to her husband and the doctor departs for his professional responsibilities, the status quo is restored.

Liquidity makes its mark on this film, arguably, as a series of libidinal blockages, as the unfulfilled erotic passion that threatens to overcome but is finally (re)contained within the bounds of propriety. This implicit notion of blockage – of an otherwise uncontrollable liquidity of being – is the common ground shared by those who criticise the film for its political incorrectness and those who adore it for its aesthetic exquisiteness. What unites the polarised receptions is a recognition that the film is the story of an impasse, but whereas for Fei Mu's critics such an impasse suggests the lingering dominance of conservative feudal sentiments (with their investments in the preservation of the kinship family, the hierarchy of class, the self-sacrifice demanded of domestic women and so forth), for his supporters the impasse is rather a crystallisation of restraint, formal as well as emotional, which in turn makes the film a consummate artistic achievement. As the damming of libidinal overflow, the impasse implements the Confucian saying *fa hu qing, zhi hu li* – '[Let things] emanate from the emotions; [let things] stop at propriety.' In Freudian psychoanalytic terms, the hydraulics at work is that of repression, which may be seen as the manifestation on the individual body and mind of a code for socially acceptable conduct.

Were we less hasty with converting blockages and impasses into repression, however, a different kind of question might arise. What exactly does Yuwen want? The film is not only narrated by her voiceover, a voiceover that is, interestingly, both subjective and omniscient, at once preoccupied with its own reflections and seemingly all-knowing, but also begins with her strolling aimlessly along the border of the town, in an undefined open space whose expansiveness stands in contrast to the claustrophobic interiors of her husband's decrepit ancestral home. As

her mute companions in this vast outside, are not the sky, the wind, the water, the trees and the rocks bearing another type of message, one that is other than the telos of heterosexual libidinal gratification? If we are to take Yuwen's desire seriously, does it not seem more rather than less unintelligible as we reflect on her relation to the outside, because such desire does not necessarily inhabit the same plane as the crumbling patriarchal one based on the repressive hydraulic model and the rationale of *fa hu qing, zhi hu li*?

Once the woman's desire is approached as an open question rather than subsumed under a presumptive conclusion, the semiotics of the film begins to unravel, unveiling the possibility of a heterologous, rather than unified, reading. Yuwen's desire, it would seem, is as much about staying still in her condition of *ennui*, in the past, with her husband, as it is about longing for the other man. The repetitive details of her daily routine – embroidery, tending to house plants, putting on different dresses, putting on makeup and waiting around, in addition to going shopping for food and herbal medicine – furnish an environment in which it is precisely the habits, banalities and trivialities inscribed with nuances of caretaking that constitute the etiquette and texture of a lifeworld. (Recall, for instance, how she insists on bringing a hot water bottle, a blanket, a light and so forth to the house guest.) Reiterated performances of social decorum, such details are, nonetheless, not simply signs of being trapped but also detours and byways, in a situation in which communications are indirect and deferred, and human contact 'happens' through objects and objectified, stylised gestures and mannerisms. What appear to be blockages – interruptions, digressions, disappointments, non-meetings – are thus, paradoxically, indicators of the multiplicity of possibilities, a multiplicity that is at once an avoidance and a voiding of the restrictive hydraulic model, which insists on the woman's subordination to the patriarchal text's foregone conclusion about her illicit, adulterous craving. If, as the film's title tells us, this story is one about spring, would it not make sense to shift the meaning of spring from its conventionalised, narrowly eroticised signification in Chinese associations to an ecological one, so that it is the elemental – the seasons, their cycles and the expanse of the outside – that surfaces as the ontological connection the film is establishing through the flux, ambiguity and polymorphism of female desire?

When they brought Chinese cinema to the world's attention in the 1980s, the People's Republic's Fifth Generation directors, too, felt inspired by the immense potential held by the elemental, as they shot the silent, rugged landscape of a poor rural China ravaged by the passage of time. In the hands of Chen Kaige, Zhang Yimou, Tian Zhuangzhuang, Wu Ziniu and their contemporaries, a bold new film language rebels against the plot-driven, melodramatic trappings of Chinese cinema of the previous decades and reinvents itself with a reflexive ethnographic gaze at China through its subaltern groups – hungry and illiterate peasants, uneducated children, women forced into arranged marriages and minority peoples on the fringes of the Han civilisation. In well-known films such as *Yellow Earth* (1984), *Red Sorghum* (1987), *Horse Thief* (1986), *Ju Dou* (1990) and *King of the Children* (1987), the often extreme material deprivation of these subaltern groups is captured compellingly, but such capturing is simultaneously a deterritorialisation: the intervention of the cinematic apparatus means that their stories on Chinese soil, so to speak, now form some of the most spectacular film images to appear – and circulate – on global cinema circuits.

The Fifth Generation directors' preoccupation with subalternity – a preoccupation that ties them to the Communist programme of social justice – also means that their films tend to be marked by a specific occlusion. Left out consistently from the films' conceptual parameters are the affective polyvalences that characterise the more urbane works from the pre-communist and post-socialist periods on the mainland as well as postwar Taiwan and Hong Kong (by directors as diverse as Bu Wancang, Wu Yonggang, Cai Chusheng, Fei Mu, Bai Jingrui, Li Xing, Ang Lee, Edward Yang, Hou Hsiao-hsien, Chen Kuo-fu, Long Gang, Chu Yuan, Stanley Kwan, Wong Kar-wai, Peter Chan, Johnnie To, Wayne Wang, Li Yang, Lou Ye and others). The liquidity of being carries a different kind of import under these circumstances. When it does appear, water often takes the form of a scarcity that makes a landscape inhospitable, an essential nourishment that has been withheld. In *Yellow Earth*, peasants are unable to grow their crops because of a long drought; they live from day to day in uncertainty and fear, with little to eat; they perform a traditional drum dance to the gods to pray for rain. In *Red Sorghum*, under the leadership of a brave married woman, Jiu'er, a group of men is organised into a wine-producing collective; the secret

key to the wine's success is piss, otherwise a waste product, which creates miracles in a dry, scorched land. Water is imagined in these films as an enabler of group survival both physically and spiritually. By making it possible to cultivate food and drink, water endows organised – and organic – meaning on an indistinct mass of men; through hard labour and shared goals, water confers sociality and camaraderie. It follows that, unlike in a chronologically earlier work such as *Spring in a Small Town*, the attention given in these Fifth Generation classics to female desire is considerably more subdued: in *Yellow Earth* the young woman Cuiqiao wishes to join the Red Army but is drowned as she embarks on her journey across the Yellow River in a small boat; in *Red Sorghum*, Jiu'er gains happiness by submitting to the dictates of male sexual desire and social organisation, until she is killed by the Japanese invaders. Though present, female desire in these films is clearly subordinated to (the remnants of) a patriarchal order in which women can and must be sacrificed when the need arises.

Instead of exploring the trajectories of desire, then, the avant-garde film work of the Fifth Generation is culturally redemptive by impulse. The gaze at rural, subaltern figures remains invested in a kind of nativism (or indigenism), which seeks to rescue the 'objects' under the gaze by way of the folk, socialist production, communal purpose and so forth, to which something ineffable like desire, in particular the relatively obscure contours of female desire, must of necessity be subjugated. While the utopian ramifications of redemption are worth contemplating, in the case of contemporary Chinese cinema, the Fifth Generation film-makers' redemptive gestures also, perhaps unbeknown to themselves initially, help inaugurate what, in retrospect, is an unprecedented process of economic-semiotic transfer. Through cinema, investments in Chinese nativism/indigenism are set in motion at a steady pace of deterritorialisation, with the native/indigene – signifying China and Chineseness – henceforth taking on the exchange value of an eminently marketable exhibit. This is perhaps the most remarkable lesson we have learned from Fifth Generation directors: precisely the redemptive efforts to remember the Cultural Revolution and the founding aspirations of Chinese communism – of letting the subalterns speak, of vindicating and empowering the downtrodden classes – lead to the spectacularisation and commodification of subalternity as a type of late-capitalist cinematic sign. To compete for the world's attention, even socialist and utopian visions must now use the same tools as capitalism's; even subalterns must become glamorised screen images.

To this extent, a culmination of the story of contemporary Chinese cinema that began with *Yellow Earth* and *Red Sorghum* is, arguably, the spectacle of the Opening Ceremony of the Beijing Olympics of 2008, under the artistic direction of Zhang Yimou. In orderly massive performances designed for television audiences and tourists from around the world, traditional symbols such as the arts of calligraphy, book learning, music, chess, choreography and so forth showcased Chinese civilisation as an equal if not superior competitor in the arena of transnational sports. With this extravaganza of China's superpower on display, the economic-semiotic transfer as inscribed in contemporary Chinese cinema's ethnographic gaze at the subalterns has come full circle; China, once a subaltern among the world of nations, now talks back fluently and stares back proudly, in languages and images of high-tech, futuristic architecture and finance capital. This economic-semiotic transfer is corroborated in recent years by blockbuster films such as *Crouching Tiger, Hidden Dragon* (2000), *Hero* (2002), *House of Flying Daggers* (2004), *The Promise* (2005), *Curse of the Golden Flower* (2006), *Red Cliff* (2009) and the like, in which a masculinist moral universe (as evidenced in the codes of martial arts) is repackaged for the big-budget cinematic screen with bestselling contemporary ingredients such as naturalised heterosexuality, fetishised female body parts, computer-enhanced cinematography and special effects.

In the context in which the more established directors' film language is solidifying into impeccably orchestrated images of a glorious, imperial past (replete with the thrills of romance, brutality and violence), it is not surprising that the thoughtful works by younger directors such as Jia Zhangke, Yung Chang and Tsai Ming-liang, in which liquidity retains its material-cum-metaphoric resilience, at once destroying and binding human relationships, have commanded such wide-ranging attention.

Jia Zhangke's *Still Life* (2006) may be seen as a unique statement on how China *has arrived* through hydraulic potency. Jia's low-keyed depiction of the discombobulated lives of ordinary citizens as a result of the construction of the Three Gorges Dam along the Yangtze River shows how water not only reorganises energy production but also human relations, as people are forced to abandon their homes, relocate, and work and live far away from loved ones, with whom they may lose touch for years. The quiet disappearance of some histories – literally, in the form of houses sinking below the rising levels of the artificial lake – takes place amid the appearance of technological prowess with its capacity for surveillance and display, as lights on a major bridge along the river can now be turned on in the dark with a mere phone call from the authorities. The English title of Jia's film is suggestive in this regard: it is as though he intends the film at once as a visual portrait (in accordance with the genre of still life) and as a reflection on the probability of stillness at a time when life everywhere has become motion, stream and flow. What does it mean for life to be still – would it be quiet, antiquated, stagnant, unchanging? And how may life be presented as still in the age of unstoppable mobility and information traffic – would it be in the form of a frame, a detachable fragment, a tag? (The linkages among water (as flow), technology and existential angst are perhaps even more pronounced in Jia's other well-known film *The World* (2004), in which the impermanent status of worldly phenomena, from theme park performances parading the costumes of different cultures to kin relations, friendships and sexual partnerships, is intensified by new technologies in daily use such as cell phones and electronic text messages.) Is the stillness of life a thing of the past, for which we can only be nostalgic, or does it remain a potentiality of the future?

As if conceived as a diptych to Jia's film, Chinese Canadian film-maker Yung Chang's documentary *Up the Yangtze* (2007) takes the audience on a cruise along the Yangtze together with American and European tourists, while also pursuing the personal narratives of some Chinese youths who are serving on board as waiters and waitresses. The Three Gorges Dam, Chang demonstrates, forces a specific reflexivity on dwelling – both on those whose lives have been severely disrupted and on those who observe their plight. Reflexivity in this instance is inseparable from the issue of language: how and where to live, in what language and whose language? Is there a dwelling that is mine and ours, that will belong to us in perpetuity? Whether or not posed consciously, these questions cannot but impinge on anyone sailing along the Yangtze in the early twenty-first century. As we notice, the drastic removal of familiar physical sites is far more than physical in effects; what are eliminated are also cultural memories, inscriptions of the classical landscape in centuries of poetry and painting as well as everyday language, even as young Chinese people endeavour, as a new mode of survival, to master English in order to serve the tourists from abroad. Against the official story of progress, so heroically constructed on the recharting of this major waterway, what kinds of subjectivities are generated, and what kinds of subjectivities are erased? 'Don't bother to come to China; we've gone through this reorganisation of the classical landscape and are paying a high price for modernisation; it's not worth it …' – is this the message Chang's film embodies for those watching it from abroad? How should the myth of Great Yu taming the flood be retold at this juncture, as water has become such a glamorous spectacle of energy governance, while the sovereignty it bestows on those in power has become ever more challengeable, as, for instance, by the millions of former dwellers along the Yangtze who see their homes irrevocably liquidated and sunk, who find themselves reduced to what may be called 'bare life'?

To this extent, perhaps no Chinese-speaking director has offered a more far-reaching series of contemplations on the liquidity of being and dwelling than Tsai Ming-liang, in whose works the spectres of ontology and phenomenology are handled in philosophically as well as cinematically innovative forms of non-transcendence. Water is everywhere in Tsai's work, as an indispensable resource that also, frequently, turns into a crisis, a source of problems giving rise to more problems. Consider *The River* (1997), which begins with Xiao Kang, the young male character, being approached by a film director, Ann Hui, to play a corpse floating on a polluted river. Xiao Kang's performance satisfies the director but also results (or so we are led to believe) in the mysterious illness of a pain in the neck, which defies all attempts of healing. Xiao Kang's father is plagued with another kind of water problem: in the form of a not-so-subtle index to the old man's closeted homosexuality, the ceiling in his bedroom leaks. Instead of informing his wife and son of the worsening situation, however, the old man devises an absurd hydraulic 'solution' made up of basins, buckets, bathtub and toilet to catch the overflow, to no avail. He finally resorts to picking up a large piece of plastic from a junk yard to channel the water from the ceiling out on to the verandah into a

potted plant, but sure enough, this ingenious diversion collapses when it pours one night. These non-solutions, disguised as solutions – note the link to water in the word 'solution'! – are part and parcel of what may be called a water dialectic, one that, in Tsai's work, oscillates epistemologically between form and formlessness, containment and deluge, government and anarchy, and that generates assemblages of resistant objects, chance happenings, accidental encounters and unexpected illuminations that often lead not to coherent endings but rather to fissures, disjunctions and apertures.

Such *evacuation* of false syntheses and finalities is also a key to Tsai's manner of coming to terms with loneliness, a theme that permeates his stories. Instead of exploring loneliness through the more familiar route of subjectivity formed through repression, Tsai depicts this human condition through the most ordinary circumstances, including unflattering, awkward- or embarrassing-looking physical positions such as urination and orgasmic release. Tsai's fairly recent film *I Don't Want to Sleep Alone* (2006), set in Kuala Lumpur, the capital of Malaysia, his home country, is a notable example of his method. The film begins with the camera pausing at length at the bedside of a paralysed man who has been lying in a coma and is kept alive with the hands-on care provided by his family. This opening serves as a striking statement on objects, not merely in the sense of the plenitude of inanimate things that surround humans, but also in the sense of a person whose existence has become a burden to those around him because he has lost all subjective human qualities. Such is the way human bodies often come across in Tsai's work – not only as means of momentary physical pleasure (through masturbation, copulation, food, or sleep) but also as perilous sites of sickness, siege and vulnerability, which plunge their occupants into tragi-comical situations of neediness. As an object, the human body in Tsai is seldom the conventionally eroticised fetish that it is in the hands of other film directors; it is rather a locus of fragility, dysfunction and humiliation, often with no possible lines of escape. Both the paralysed man and his caretakers – such as the man's mother and the young woman servant who tends to his cleanliness and feeding – are stuck in a hopeless situation in which things may remain unchanged for months or years.

At the same time, as if to prevent this bleak scenario from becoming exclusive, Tsai offers us another object: an old mattress, which a group of poor construction workers pick up from a junk heap on a back street one night. On their way home, they run into a young Chinese man (played by Li Kang-sheng, who is also playing the role of the paralysed guy), who has been seriously wounded by thugs and fainted. After they bring the Chinese man home, Rawang, one of the workers, starts taking care of him, keeping him fed, dressed and cleaned, helping him get up and urinate, and so forth, even though the latter, who does not speak Malay, remains silent. In a parallel manner, Rawang tends to the old mattress by washing, scrubbing and airing it, turning it into a temporary comfort zone for his guest and himself.

This gathering of the guest and the mattress is evocative not least because the guest, too, is in fact a found object, while the mattress may be analogised to an unexpected guest. This imaginative juxtaposition of guest and object finds a felicitous expression in the Chinese term for object, *keti*, which literally means 'guest body' (as opposed to *zhuti*, the subject or, literally, one's own body). In the context of this film, the notion of *keti* offers an electrifying way of staging the consistent thematic in Tsai's work of the mutuality between physical bodies (which are foreign, estranged, desperate and obtrusive), on the one hand, and on the other, human existence itself as a floating object, whose ultimate truth lies, as Zen Buddhism teaches us, in its transience, its non-containability within the secure boundaries of possession and permanence, including those of the most intimate commitments. Rather than being the occasion for melancholy, however, this apprehension of life as something adrift

becomes for Tsai the very inspiration of creativity, as we watch the mattress go through its various incarnations – from being a piece of junk, a hindrance to lug around and a pain in the butt to clean and disinfect, to being a makeshift shelter and resting place for host and guest, and, finally, by the end of the film, a magic island on which a new kind of community keeps afloat together in a dark, wide sea.

Indeed, by placing Rawang, the homeless guy and the young woman servant on the mattress – which, I contend, is really a fourth character – Tsai is providing an example of a Deleuzian groupuscule, one that goes beyond the twosomeness of conventional heterosexual and homosexual couplings. This final, luminescent image of the three (four) characters descending from the top of the frame, accompanied by Tan Soo Suan's resonant voice singing the old love song 'Xin qu', signifies at once a renovated arrangement of the human *socius* in an environmentally precarious time and a space of an as-yet unknown emergence. As much as its sensuous beauty, the conceptual power of this dreamlike emergence makes it an unforgettable occurrence. Human existence itself as a kind of flotsam, drifting, shimmering, breaking up and submerging again in water: this philosophical reflection is now a cinematic vision; the liquidity of being, a moving image.

Note

1. I am indebted to Michael Silverman for innumerable inspiring discussions, including many on Chinese cinema. For reasons of space stipulated by the publishing agreement, my references to various films in this chapter are brief and without endnotes.

Appendix 1

Book-length Studies of Chinese Cinema in the English Language

Wan-Jui Wang, Louise Williams and Song Hwee Lim

Pre-1990

Chen, Kaige, and Tony Rayns, King of the Children & The New Chinese Cinema (London: Faber & Faber, 1989).

Clark, Paul, Chinese Cinema: Culture and Politics Since 1949 (Cambridge: Cambridge University Press, 1987).

Jarvie, Ian, Window on Hong Kong: A Sociological Study of the Hong Kong Film Industry (Hong Kong: Centre of Asian Studies, University of Hong Kong, 1977).

Leyda, Jay, Dianying: An Account of Films and the Film Audience in China (Cambridge, MA: MIT Press, 1972).

Liu, Alan P. L., The Film Industry in Communist China (Cambridge, MA: MIT Press, 1965).

Semsel, George S. (ed.), Chinese Film: The State of the Art in the People's Republic (New York: Praeger, 1987).

1990s

Berry, Chris (ed.), Perspectives on Chinese Cinema (London: BFI, 1991).

Browne, Nick, Paul Pickowicz, Vivian Sobchack and Esther Yau (eds), New Chinese Cinemas: Forms, Identities, Politics (Cambridge: Cambridge University Press, 1994).

Chow, Rey, Primitive Passions: Visuality, Sexuality, Ethnography and Contemporary Chinese Cinema (New York: Columbia University Press, 1995).

Ehrlich, Linda and David Desser (eds), Cinematic Landscapes: Observations on the Visual Arts and Cinema of China and Japan (Austin: University of Texas Press, 1994).

Kuoshu, Harry H., Lightness of Being in China: Adaptation and Discursive Figuration in Cinema and Theater (New York: Peter Lang, 1999).

Lalanne, Jean-Marc, David Martinez, Ackbar Abbas, Jimmy Ngai and Wong Kar-wai, Wong Kar-Wai (Paris: Dis Voir, 1997).

Lu, Sheldon Hsiao-peng (ed.), Transnational Chinese Cinemas: Identity, Nationhood, Gender (Honolulu: University of Hawaii Press, 1997).

Rehm, Jean Pierre, Olivier Joyard and Danièle Rivière, Tsai Ming-liang (Paris: Dis Voir, 1999).

Semsel, George S., Xia Hong and Hou Jianping (eds), Chinese Film Theory: A Guide to the New Era (New York: Praeger, 1990).

Semsel, George S., Xia Hong and Hou Jianping (eds), Film in Contemporary China: Critical Debates, 1979–1989 (Westport: Praeger, 1993).

Silbergeld, Jerome, China into Film: Frames of Reference in Contemporary Chinese Cinema (London: Reaktion, 1999).

Stokes, Lisa Odham and Michael Hoover, City on Fire: Hong Kong Cinema (London: Verso, 1999).

Tam, Kwok-kan and Wimal Dissanayake, New Chinese Cinema (Hong Kong: Oxford University Press, 1998).

Teo, Stephen, Hong Kong Cinema: The Extra Dimensions (London: BFI, 1997).

Zhang, Xudong, Chinese Modernism in the Era of Reforms: Cultural Fever, Avant-Garde Fiction and the New Chinese Cinema (Durham, NC: Duke University Press, 1997).

Zhang, Yingjin, The City in Chinese Literature and Film (Stanford, CA: Stanford University Press, 1996).

Zhang, Yingjin and Zhiwei Xiao, Encyclopedia of Chinese Film (New York: Routledge, 1998).

Zhang, Yingjin (ed.), Cinema and Urban Culture in Shanghai, 1922–43 (Stanford, CA: Stanford University Press, 1999).

2000

Bordwell, David, Planet Hong Kong: Popular Cinema and the Art of Entertainment (Cambridge, MA: Harvard University Press, 2000).

Donald, Stephanie Hemelryk, *Public Secrets, Public Spaces: Cinema and Civility in China* (Lanham, MD: Rowman & Littlefield, 2000).

2001

Gateward, Frances (ed.), *Zhang Yimou: Interviews* (Jackson: University Press of Mississippi, 2001).

Morton, Lisa, *The Cinema of Tsui Hark* (Jefferson: McFarland, 2001).

Yau, Esther C. M. (ed.), *At Full Speed: Hong Kong Cinema in a Borderless World* (Minneapolis: University of Minnesota Press, 2001).

2002

Chu, Yingchi, *Hong Kong Cinema: Coloniser, Motherland and Self* (London: Routledge, 2002).

Cornelius, Shelia, with Ian Hadyn Smith, *New Chinese Cinema: Challenging Representations* (London: Wallflower, 2002).

Dai Jinhua, *Cinema and Desire: Feminist Marxism and Cultural Politics in the Work of Dai Jinhua*, ed. Jing Wang and Tani S. Barlow (London: Verso, 2002).

Fu, Poshek and David Desser (eds), *The Cinema of Hong Kong: History, Arts, Identity* (Cambridge: Cambridge University Press, 2002).

Hu, Jubin, *Projecting a Nation: Chinese National Cinema Before 1949* (Hong Kong: Hong Kong University Press, 2002).

Kuoshu, Harry, *Celluloid China: Cinematic Encounters with Culture and Society* (Carbondale and Edwardsville: Southern Illinois University Press, 2002).

Lu, Tonglin, *Confronting Modernity in the Cinemas of Taiwan and Mainland China* (Cambridge: Cambridge University Press, 2002).

Ni, Zhen, *Memoirs from the Beijing Film Academy: The Genesis of China's Fifth Generation*, trans. Chris Berry (Durham, NC: Duke University Press, 2002).

Pang, Laikwan, *Building a New China in Cinema: The Chinese Left-wing Cinema Movement 1932–1937* (Oxford: Rowman & Littlefield, 2002).

Reynaud, Bérénice, *A City of Sadness* (London: BFI, 2002).

Zhang, Yingjin, *Screening China: Critical Interventions, Cinematic Reconfigurations, and the Transnational Imaginary in Contemporary Chinese Cinema* (Ann Arbor, MI: Center for Chinese Studies, 2002).

2003

Berry, Chris (ed.), *Chinese Films in Focus: 25 New Takes* (London: BFI, 2003).

Braester, Yomi, *Witness Against History: Literature, Film and Public Discourse in Twentieth Century China* (Stanford, CA: Stanford University Press, 2003).

Cui, Shuqin, *Women Through the Lens: Gender and Nation in a Century of Chinese Cinema* (Honolulu: University of Hawaii Press, 2003).

Fu, Poshek, *Between Shanghai and Hong Kong: The Politics of Chinese Cinemas* (Stanford, CA: Stanford University Press, 2003).

Hunt, Leon, *Kung Fu Cult Masters: From Bruce Lee to Crouching Tiger* (London: Wallflower, 2003).

Wang, Shujen, *Framing Piracy: Globalisation and Film Distribution in Greater China* (Oxford: Rowman & Littlefield, 2003).

Zhu, Ying, *Chinese Cinema During the Era of Reform: The Ingenuity of the System* (London: Praeger, 2003).

2004

Berry, Chris, *Postsocialist Cinema in Post-Mao China: The Cultural Revolution after the Cultural Revolution* (London: Routledge, 2004).

Law, Kar and Frank Bren, *Hong Kong Cinema: A Cross-Cultural View* (Lanham, MD: Scarecrow, 2004).

Schroeder, Andrew, *Tsui Hark's 'Zu: Warriors from the Magic Mountain'* (Hong Kong: Hong Kong University Press, 2004).

Silbergeld, Jerome, *Hitchcock with a Chinese Face: Cinematic Doubles, Oedipal Triangles and China's Moral Voice* (Seattle: University of Washington Press, 2004).

Yip, June, *Envisioning Taiwan: Fiction, Cinema and the Nation in the Cultural Imaginary* (Durham, NC: Duke University Press, 2004).

Zhang, Yingjin, *Chinese National Cinema* (London: Routledge, 2004).

2005

Berry, Chris and Lu Feii (eds), *Island on the Edge: Taiwan New Cinema and After* (Hong Kong: Hong Kong University Press, 2005).

Brunette, Peter, *Wong Kar-wai* (Illinois: University of Illinois Press, 2005).

Clark, Paul, *Re-inventing China: A Generation and its Films* (Hong Kong: Chinese University Press, 2005).

Davis, Darrell William and Emilie Yueh-yu Yeh, *Taiwan Film Directors: A Treasure Island* (New York: Columbia University Press, 2005).

Donald, Stephanie Hemelryk, *Little Friends: Children's Film and Media Culture in China* (Lanham, MD: Rowman & Littlefield, 2005).

Elder, Robert (ed.), *John Woo: Interviews* (Jackson: University Press of Mississippi, 2005).

Kong, Haili and John Lent (eds), *One Hundred Years of Chinese Cinema: A Generational Dialogue* (Norwalk: EastBridge, 2005).

Lu, Sheldon H. and Emilie Yueh-yu Yeh (eds), *Chinese-Language Film: Historiography, Poetics, Politics* (Honolulu: University of Hawaii Press, 2005).

Meyer, Richard J., *Ruan Ling-yu: The Goddess of Shanghai* (Hong Kong: Hong Kong University Press, 2005).

Pang, Lai-kwan and Day Wong (eds), *Masculinities and Hong Kong Cinema* (Hong Kong: Hong Kong University Press, 2005).

Shen, Vivian, *The Origins of Leftwing Cinema in China: 1932–37* (London: Routledge, 2005).

Teo, Stephen, *Wong Kar-wai* (London: BFI, 2005).

2006

Berry, Chris and Mary Farquhar, *China on Screen: Cinema and Nation* (New York: Columbia University Press, 2006).

Berry, Michael, *Speaking in Images: Interviews with Contemporary Chinese Filmmakers* (New York: Columbia University Press, 2006).

Lim, Song Hwee, *Celluloid Comrades: Representations of Male Homosexuality in Contemporary Chinese Cinemas* (Honolulu: University of Hawaii Press, 2006).

Marchetti, Gina, *From Tian'anmen to Times Square: Transnational China and the Chinese Diaspora on Global Screens, 1989–1997* (Philadelphia: Temple University Press, 2006).

Morris, Meaghan, Siu Leung Li and Stephen Chan Ching-kiu (eds), *Hong Kong Connections: Transnational Imagination in Action Cinema* (Durham, NC: Duke University Press and Hong Kong: Hong Kong University Press, 2006).

Pickowicz, Paul and Yingjin Zhang (eds), *From Underground to Independent: Alternative Film Culture in Contemporary China* (Lanham, MD: Rowman & Littlefield, 2006).

Zhang, Zhen, *An Amorous History of the Silver Screen: Shanghai Cinema, 1896–1937* (Chicago: University of Chicago Press, 2006).

2007

Chen, Ming-May Jessie and Mazharul Haque, *Representation of the Cultural Revolution in Chinese Films by the Fifth Generation Filmmakers: Zhang Yimou, Chen Kaige, and Tian Zhuangzhuang* (New York: Edwin Mellen Press, 2007).

Chow, Rey, *Sentimental Fabulations, Contemporary Chinese Films: Attachment in the Age of Global Visibility* (New York: Columbia University Press, 2007).

Curtin, Michael, *Playing to the World's Biggest Audience: The Globalization of Chinese Film and TV* (Berkeley: University of California Press, 2007).

Davis, Darrell William and Ru-Shou Robert Chen (eds), *Cinema Taiwan: Politics, Popularity and State of the Arts* (London: Routledge, 2007).

Dilley, Whitney Crothers, *The Cinema of Ang Lee: The Other Side of the Screen* (London: Wallflower, 2007).

Khoo, Olivia, *The Chinese Exotic: Modern Diasporic Femininity* (Hong Kong: Hong Kong University Press, 2007).

Lin, Sylvia Li-Chun, *Representing Atrocity in Taiwan: The 2/28 Incident and White Terror in Fiction and Film* (New York: Columbia University Press, 2007).

Lu, Sheldon Hsiao-Peng, *Chinese Modernity and Global Biopolitics: Studies in Literature and Visual Culture* (Honolulu: University of Hawaii Press, 2007).

Marchetti, Gina, *Andrew Lau and Alan Mak's 'Infernal Affairs – The Trilogy'* (Hong Kong: Hong Kong University Press, 2007).

Marchetti, Gina and Tan See Kam (eds), *Hong Kong Film, Hollywood and the New Global Cinema: No Film is an Island* (London: Routledge, 2007).

Shih, Shu-mei, *Visuality and Identity: Sinophone Articulations Across the Pacific* (Berkeley: University of California Press, 2007).

Teo, Stephen, *Johnnie To and the Hong Kong Action Film* (Hong Kong: Hong Kong University Press, 2007).

Xu, Gary G., *Sinascape: Contemporary Chinese Cinema* (Lanham, MD: Rowman & Littlefield, 2007).

Zhang, Zhen (ed.), *The Urban Generation: Chinese Cinema and Society at the Turn of the Twenty-First Century* (Durham, NC: Duke University Press, 2007).

Zhou, Xuelin, *Young Rebels in Contemporary Chinese cinema* (Hong Kong: Hong Kong University Press, 2007).

2008

Berry, Chris (ed.), *Chinese Films in Focus II* (London: BFI, 2008).

Berry, Michael, *A History of Pain: Trauma in Modern Chinese Literature and Film* (New York: Columbia University Press, 2008).

Cheuk, Pak Tong, *Hong Kong New Wave Cinema (1978–2000)* (Bristol: Intellect, 2008).

Fu, Poshek (ed.), *China Forever: The Shaw Brothers and Diasporic Cinema* (Urbana and Chicago: University of Illinois Press, 2008).

Ford, Stacilee, *Mabel Cheung Yuen-Ting's An Autumn's Tale* (Hong Kong: Hong Kong University Press, 2008).

McGrath, Jason, *Postsocialist Modernity: Chinese Cinema, Literature, and Criticism in the Market Age* (Stanford, CA: Stanford University Press, 2008).

Sibergeld, Jerome, *Body in Question: Image and Illusion in Two Chinese Films by Director Jiang Wen* (Princeton, NJ: Princeton University Press, 2008).

Tan, Kenneth Paul, *Cinema and Television in Singapore: Resistance in One Dimension* (Leiden and Boston: Brill, 2008).

Zhang, Rui, *The Cinema of Feng Xiaogang: Commercialization and Censorship in Chinese Cinema after 1989* (Hong Kong: Hong Kong University Press, 2008).

2009

Berry, Michael, *Xiao Wu, Platform, Unknown Pleasures: Jia Zhangke's 'Hometown Trilogy'* (London: BFI, 2009).

Chan, Kenneth, *Remade in Hollywood: The Global Chinese Presence in Post-1997 Transnational Cinemas* (Hong Kong: Hong Kong University Press, 2009).

Cheung, Esther M. K., *Fruit Chan's Made in Hong Kong* (Hong Kong: Hong Kong University Press, 2009).

Hall, Kenneth E., *John Woo's The Killer* (Hong Kong: Hong Kong University Press, 2009).

Ingham, Michael, *Johnnie To Kei-Fung's PTU* (Hong Kong: Hong Kong University Press, 2009).

Khoo, Olivia and Sean Metzger (eds), *Futures of Chinese Cinema: Technologies and Temporalities in Chinese Screen Cultures* (Bristol: Intellect, 2009).

Lee, Vivian P. Y., *Hong Kong Cinema Since 1997: The Post-Nostalgic Imagination* (Basingstoke, Hampshire: Palgrave Macmillan, 2009).

Lu, Sheldon H. and Jiayan Mi (eds), *Chinese Ecocinema: In the Age of Environmental Challenge* (Hong Kong: Hong Kong University Press, 2009).

Stokes, Lisa Odham, *Peter Ho-Sun Chan's He's a Woman, She's a Man* (Hong Kong: Hong Kong University Press, 2009).

Tan, See-Kam, Peter X Feng and Gina Marchetti (eds), *Chinese Connections: Critical Perspectives on Film, Identity, and Diaspora* (Philadelphia: Temple University Press, 2009).

Teo, Stephen, *Chinese Martial Arts Cinema: The Wuxia Tradition* (Edinburgh: Edinburgh University Press, 2009).

Udden, James, *No Man an Island: The Cinema of Hou Hsiao-Hsien* (Hong Kong: Hong Kong University Press, 2009).

Vojkovic, Sasha, *Yuen Woo Ping's Wing Chun* (Hong Kong: Hong Kong University Press, 2009).

Williams, Tony, *John Woo's Bullet in the Head* (Hong Kong: Hong Kong University Press, 2009).

2010

Berry, Chris, Lu Xinyu and Lisa Rofel (eds), *The New Chinese Documentary Film Movement: For the Public Record* (Hong Kong: Hong Kong University Press, 2010).

Braester, Yomi, *Painting the City Red: Chinese City and the Urban Contract* (Durham, NC: Duke University Press, 2010).

Braester, Yomi and James Tweedie (eds), *Cinema at the City's Edge: Film and Urban Networks in East Asia* (Hong Kong: Hong Kong University Press, 2010).

Deppman, Hsiu-Chuang, *Adapted for the Screen: The Cultural Politics of Modern Chinese Fiction and Film* (Honolulu: University Hawaii Press, 2010).

Farquhar, Mary, and Yingjin Zhang (eds), *Chinese Film Stars* (New York and London: Routledge, 2010).

Lin, Xiaoping, *Children of Marx and Coca-Cola: Chinese Avant-garde Art and Independent Cinema* (Honolulu: University of Hawaii Press, 2010).

Ma, Jean, *Melancholy Drift: Making Time in Chinese Cinema* (Hong Kong: Hong Kong University Press, 2010).

Martin, Fran, *Backward Glances: Contemporary Chinese Cultures and the Female Homoerotic Imaginary* (Durham, NC: Duke University Press, 2010).

Rawnsley, Gary D. and Ming-Yeh T. Rawnsley (eds), *Global Chinese Cinema: The Culture and Politics of 'Hero'* (New York and London: Routledge, 2010).

Rosen, Stanley and Ying Zhu (eds), *Art, Politics, and Commerce in Chinese Cinema* (Hong Kong: Hong Kong University Press, 2010).

Voci, Paolo, *China on Video: Smaller-screen Realities* (Abingdon, Oxon: Routledge, 2010).

Zhang, Yingjin, *Cinema, Space, and Polylocality in a Globalizing China* (Honolulu: University of Hawaii Press, 2010).

Appendix 2

Chinese Names

Zou Yijie

This list includes characters for Chinese names of film-makers, actors and characters that appear in the chapters in this volume. It is organised alphabetically according to family name. For example, 'Jackie Chan' is listed under 'C' for 'Chan'. In the interest of consistency, all Chinese characters use now standard simplified forms. However, as there is no standard romanisation for Chinese names, they are given as they appear in the chapters. Different versions of the same name may appear in different chapters. In these cases, each translation receives a separate entry.

Bai Jingrui 白景瑞
Bao Tianxiao 包天笑
Kenneth Bi 毕国智
Bu Wancang 卜万苍

Cai Chusheng 蔡楚生
Bobo Chan 陈文媛
Benny Chan 陈木胜
Conroy Chan 陈子聪
Davy Chan (aka DBF 大飞) 陈匡荣
Evans Chan 陈耀成
Fruit Chan 陈果
Jackie Chan 成龙
Peter Chan 陈可辛
Philip Chan 陈欣健
Teddy Chan 陈德森
Chang Che 张彻
Grace Chang 葛兰
Sylvia Chang 张艾嘉
Yung Chang 张侨勇
Winston Chao 赵文瑄
Pou-Soi Cheang 郑保瑞
Chen Bo'er 陈波儿
Chen Guantai 陈观泰
Chen Huaikai 陈怀皑
Chen Huangmei 陈荒煤

Chen Kaige 陈凯歌
Chen Kuo-fu 陈国富
Chen Liting 陈鲤庭
Chen Pi 陈皮
Tina Chen 陈婷
Chen Xihe 陈西禾
Chen Yanyan 陈燕燕
Chen Yunshang/Nancy Chan
    陈云赏
Edison Chen 陈冠希
Joan Chen 陈冲
Teddy Chen 陈德森
Cheng Jihua 程季华
Cheng Pei-pei 郑佩佩
Cheng Yin 成荫
Alfred Cheung 张坚庭
Cecilia Cheung 张柏芝
Jacky Cheung 张学友
Mabel Cheung 张婉婷
Maggie Cheung 张曼玉
David Chiang 姜大卫
May Chin 金素梅
Ching Siu-tung 程小东
Jay Chou 周杰伦
Chow Yun-fat 周润发
Stephen Chow 周星驰

Christine Choy 崔明慧
Chu Yuan 楚原
Cuiqiao 翠巧
Cui Wei 崔巍
Christy Chung 钟丽缇
Gillian Chung 钟欣桐
Simon Chung 钟德胜

Datong 大同
Dai Jinhua 戴锦华
Dai Sijie 戴思杰
Deng Xiaoping 邓小平
Di Long 狄龙
Ding Sheng 丁晟
Dong Zhaoqi 董兆其
Arthur Dong 曾亦田

Esther Eng/Ng Kam-ha 伍锦霞

Fang Hua 方化
Fei Mu 费穆
Feng Bailu 冯白鲁
Feng Xiaogang 冯小刚
Allen Fong 方育平
Fu Sheng 傅声
Allan Fung 冯意清

Stephen Fung 冯德伦

Glen Goei 魏铭耀
Gong Hong 龔弘
Gong Li 巩俐
Guan Hu 管虎
Guo Moruo 郭沫若
Guo Xiaolu 郭小橹

Han Sanping 韩三平
Hao Guang 郝光
He Feiguang 何非光
He Jianjun (He Yi) 何建军（何一）
Ho Menghua 何梦华
Ho Yuhang 何宇恒
Sammo Hong 洪金宝
Hou Hsiao-hsien 侯孝贤
Hu Die 胡蝶
Hu Jun 胡军
Huang Baomei 黄宝美
Huang Jianxin 黄建新
Huang Zuolin 黄左临
Hui Yinghong 惠英红
Kara Hui (Wai Ying-Hong) 惠英红
Michael Hui Koon 许冠文
Hung Wing Kit 洪荣杰
Ann Hui 许鞍华
Sammo Hung 洪金宝

Jia Zhangke 贾樟柯
Jiang Qing 江青
Jiang Wen 姜文
Jiang Xueqian 姜学潜
Jie Fu 絜父
Jin Kun 金昆

Eric Khoo 邱金海
King Hu 金铨
Moon Kwan (Guan Wenqing)
    关文清
Nancy Kwan 关南施
Stanley Kwan 关锦鹏
Kwan Tak-hing 关德兴
Aaron Kwok 郭富城

Leon Lai 黎明
Ringo Lam 林岭东
Lan Ping (Jiang Qing) 蓝萍（江青）
Lau Kar-leung 刘家良

Lau Kar-wing 刘家荣
Andrew Lau 刘伟强
Andy Lau 刘德华
Alex Law 罗启锐
Clara Law 罗卓瑶
Ang Lee 李安
Bruce Lee 李小龙
Daniel Lee 李仁港
Lee Hsing 李行
James Lee 李添与
Julian Lee 李志超
Quentin Lee 李孟熙
Rich Lee 李奇
Li Bingbing 李冰冰
Li Hanxiang 李翰祥
Li Jun 李俊
Li Kang-sheng 李康生
Li Lihua 李丽华
Li Lili 黎莉莉
Li Lingyun 李凌云
Li Pingqian 李萍倩
Li Quanxin 李全新
Li Shaohong 李少红
Li Xianglan/Yamaguchi Yoshiko
    李香兰/山口淑子
Li Yang 李杨
Li Zhiqing 李芝清
Jet Li 李连杰
Liang Zhefu 梁哲夫
Liao Gene-fon (Liao Jinfeng)
    廖金凤
Liew Seng Tat 刘城达
Lin Cang 林苍
Lin Yang 林扬
Andrew Lin 连凯
Brigitte Lin 林青霞
Lin Dai 林黛
Justin Lin 林诣彬
Liu Hao 刘浩
Liu Jinglun 刘经纶
Liu Yifei 刘亦菲
Gordon Liu 刘家辉
Lucy Liu 刘玉玲
Liu Qiong 刘琼
Lo Wei 罗维
Candy Lo 卢巧音
Lou Ye 娄烨
Lu Hongshi 陆红实
Lu Ren 鲁韧

Lu Xun 鲁迅
Lü Ban 吕班
Keye Luke 陆锡麒
Luo Jingyu 罗静予

Mao Dun 茅盾
Mao Zedong 毛泽东
Maxu Weibang 马徐维邦
Jingle Ma 马楚成
Alan Mak 麦兆辉
Johnny Mak 麦当雄
Marco Mak 麦子善
Angela Mao-ying 茅瑛
Mei Lanfang 梅兰芳
Cora Miao 缪骞人
Ming Ji 明骥
Karen Mok 莫文蔚
Anita Mui 梅艳芳

Cho-fan Ng 吴楚帆
Sandra Ng 吴君如
Ng Wui 吴回

Ouyang Yuqian 欧阳予倩

Pan Jienong 潘孑农
Danny Pang 彭发
Oxide Pang 彭顺

Qi Guanjun 戚冠军
Qian Huafo 钱化佛

Ran In-Ting 蓝荫鼎
Michelle Reis 李嘉欣
Rou Shi 柔石
Ruan Lingyu 阮玲玉

Sang Hu 桑弧
Sha Meng 沙蒙
Shangguan Yunzhu 上官云珠
Polly Shangguan Lingfeng
    上官灵凤
Shen Fu 沈浮
Shen Xiling 沈西苓
Shi Hui 石挥
Shi Dongshan 史东山
Shu Qi 舒淇
Shu Shi 舒适
Shui Hua 水华

Mina Shum　沈小艾
Sit Kok-seen　薛觉先
Situ Huimin　司徒慧敏
Su Li　苏里
Sun Yat-sen　孙中山
Sun Yu　孙瑜

Patrick Tam　谭家明
Tan Xinpei　谭鑫培
Royston Tan　陈子谦
Tang Xiaodan　汤晓丹
Tian Zhuangzhuang　田壮壮
Johnnie To　杜琪峰
Stanley Tong　唐季礼
Tong Yuejuan　童月娟
Tsai Ming-liang　蔡明亮
Nicholas Tse　谢霆锋
Tsui Hark　徐克

Wan Chaochen　万超尘
Wan Guchan　万古蟾
Wan Laiming　万籁鸣
Wang Bin　王滨
Wang Chao　王超
Wang Danfeng　王丹凤
Wang Du Lu　王度卢
Wang Dui　旺堆
Wang Jingwei　汪精卫
Wang Ping　王萍
Wang Qimin　王启民
Wang Quan'an　王全安
Wang Shuo　王朔
Wang Xiaoshuai　王小帅
Wang Xinzhai　王心斋
Wang Yin　王引
Wang Yu　王羽
Peter Wang　王正方
Wayne Wang　王颖
Wenhua　文华
Wong Fei-hung　黄飞鸿

Wong Kar-wai　王家卫
Anna May Wong　黄柳霜
B.D. Wong　黄荣亮
Michael Wong　王敏德
Victor Wong　黄自强
James Wong Howe　黄宗霑
Woo Ming Jin　吴明金
John Woo　吴宇森
Wu Chufan　吴楚帆
Wu Nien-jen　吴念真
Wu Wenguang　吴文光
Wu Yinxian　吴印咸
Wu Yonggang　吴勇刚
Wu Zhaodi　武兆堤
Wu Ziniu　吴子牛
Alice Wu　伍思薇
Daniel Wu　吴彦祖

Xia Yan　夏衍
Xiang Kun　项堃
Xie Jin　谢晋
Xie Tieli　谢铁骊
Xu Feng　徐枫
Xu Ke　许珂
Xu Tianxiang　徐天翔

Yan Gong　严恭
Yan Jizhou　严寄洲
Yang Hansheng　阳翰笙
Edward Yang　杨德昌
Yau Ching　游静
Derek Yee　尔冬升
Donnie Yen　甄子丹
Michelle Yeoh　杨紫琼
Ray Yeung　杨曜恺
Yim Ho　严浩
Terence Yin　尹子维
Ying Yunwei　应云卫
Yonfan　杨凡
Yu Kang-Ping　虞戡平

Jessica Yu　虞琳敏
Ronny Yu　于仁泰
Alan Yuen　袁锦麟
Yuan Congmei　袁丛美
Yuan Meiyu　袁美云
Yuan Muzhi　袁牧之
Yuan Yang-an　袁仰安
Yuan Yaohong　袁耀鸿
Yuen Biao　元彪
Yuen Woo-ping　袁和平

Zhang Ailing　张爱玲
Zhang Bo　张波
Zhang Boqing　章柏青
Zhang Che　张彻
Zhang Ruifang　张瑞芳
Zhang Shankun　张善琨
Zhang Shuhe　张叔和
Zhang Xinshi　张辛实
Zhang Yang　张杨
Zhang Yibai　张一白
Zhang Yimou　张艺谋
Zhang Yuan　张元
Zhang Ziyi　章子怡
Zhao Dan　赵丹
Zhao Shucan/Joseph Sunn　赵树燊
Zhao Tao　赵涛
Zhao Xiaolan　赵小兰
Zhao Yiman　赵一曼
Zheng Dongtian　郑洞天
Zheng Junli　郑君里
Zheng Pei-pei　郑佩佩
Zhong Dianfei　钟惦棐
Zhou Enlai　周恩来
Zhou Xiaowen　周晓文
Zhu Rongji　朱镕基
Zhu Shilin　朱石麟
Zhu Wen　朱文

Appendix 3

Chinese Film Titles

Zou Yijie

This list includes characters for the titles of Chinese films that appear in the chapters in this volume. It is organised alphabetically according to the English translations of the titles. For example, *A Beautiful New World* is listed under 'B' for 'Beautiful'. In the interest of consistency, all Chinese characters use now standard simplified forms. However, as there are no standard English translations for film titles, they are given as they appear in the chapters. Different translations of the same title may appear in different chapters. In these cases, each translation receives a separate entry.

14 Blades 锦衣卫
15 十五
24 City 二十四城记
The 36th Chamber of Shaolin
　　少林三十六房

After the War was Over
　　停战以后
After This Our Exile 父子
Ah Ying 半边人
An Autumn's Tale
　　秋天的童话
Apart Together 团圆
Army Nurse 女儿楼
As Tears Go By 旺角卡门
The Assassin 大刺客
Assembly 集结号
Ashes of Time 东邪西毒
At the End of Daybreak 心魔
Autumn 秋

Balzac and the Little
　　Chinese Seamstress
　　巴尔扎克与小裁缝
Banana Paradise 香蕉天堂
The Banquet 夜宴

Baoshan City Bathed in Blood
　　血溅宝山城
Be There or Be Square
　　不见不散
Beautiful Duckling 养鸭人家
A Beautiful New World
　　美丽新世界
Before the New Director Arrives
　　新局长到来之前
Behind Shanghai's Frontline
　　上海火线后
Beijing Bastards 北京杂种
Beijing Bicycle 十七岁的单车
Beijing Rocks 北京乐兴路
A Better Tomorrow III
　　英雄本色3
A Better Tomorrow (1, 2 & 3)
　　英雄本色 (1, 2 & 3)
The Big Boss 唐山大兄
Big Li, Little Li and Old Li
　　大李，小李和老李
The Big Parade 大阅兵
Big Shot's Funeral 大腕
Bishonen 美少年之恋
The Black Cannon Incident
　　黑炮事件

Black Snow 本命年
Blind Shaft 盲井
Bloodbath on Wolf Mountain
　　狼山喋血记
Bloody Morning 血色清晨
The Blue Kite 蓝风筝
Blush 红粉
Boat People 投奔怒海
Bodyguards and Assassins
　　十月围城
A Borrowed Life 多桑
The Boundless Future
　　前程万里
The Boy from Vietnam
　　狮子山下：来客
The Boys from Fengkuei
　　风柜来的人
The Bride with White Hair
　　白发魔女传
A Brighter Summer Day
　　牯岭街少年杀人事件
Brother Wang and Brother Liu
Tour Taiwan
　　王哥柳哥游台湾
Buddha Bless America
　　太平天国

Buddha's Palm 如来神掌
Bugis Street 妖街皇后
Bullet in the Head 喋血街头
Bumming in Beijing:
    The Last Dreamers
    流浪北京：最后的梦想者

Café Lumière 咖啡时光
Cell Phone 手机
Challenge of the Masters
    陆阿采与黄飞鸿
Chan is Missing 寻人
China, My Sorrow 牛棚
Chinatown Kid 唐山街小子
The Chinese Boxer 龙虎斗
Chinese Odyssey 月光宝盒
Chungking Express 重庆森林
City of Life and Death
    南京！南京！
City of Sadness 悲情城市
City Without Night 不夜城
The Cold Blade 龙沐香
Cold Nights 寒夜
Come Drink with Me 大醉侠
Comrades, Almost a Love
    Story 甜蜜蜜
Confucius 孔子
Conscience 良心
Cop on a Mission 知法犯法
Crazy Stone 疯狂的石头
The Critical Moment
    最后关头
Crossings 错爱
Crossroads 十字街头
Crouching Tiger, Hidden
    Dragon 卧虎藏龙
Crows and Sparrows
    乌鸦与麻雀
Curse of the Golden Flower
    满城尽带黄金甲
The Curse of Quon Gwon:
    When the Far East Mingles with
    the West 关公的咒语
A Curtain of Dreams
    一帘幽梦
Cut Sleeve Boys 我爱断臂衫

Dalu (The Highway) 大路
Dance of a Dream 爱君如梦

Dangerous Encounter –
    1st Kind 第一类型危险
The Days 冬春的日子
Days of Being Wild 阿飞正传
Dazzling 花眼
Delamu 德拉姆
Desperation 最后的疯狂
Detours to Paradise
    歧路天堂
Devils at the Doorstep
    鬼子来了
Dim Sum: A Little Bit
    of Heart 点心
Dirt 头发乱了
Disciples of Shaolin 洪拳小子
Dislocation 错位
Dog Bites Dog 狗咬狗
Dong 东
Double Happiness 双喜
Dream Factory 甲方乙方
Drink Drank Drunk 千杯不醉
Drunken Master 醉拳
Drunken Master 2 醉拳2
Dumplings 饺子
Durian, Durian 榴莲飘飘

Early Spring 早春二月
The East is Red 东方红
East Palace, West Palace
    东宫西宫
Eat a Bowl of Tea 一碗茶
Eat Drink Man Woman
    饮食男女
Echoes of the Rainbow
    岁月神偷
Eight Diagram Pole Fighter
    五郎八卦棍
Eight Hundred Heroes
    八百壮士
Eight Taels of Gold 八两金
Eight Thousand Miles of
    Clouds and Moon
    八千里路云和月
The Emperor and the
    Assassin 荆轲刺秦王
The Emperor's Shadow 秦颂
An Empress and the
    Warriors 江山美人
Enter the Dragon 龙争虎斗

Ermo 二嫫
Eternal Fame 万世流芳
The Eye/The Eye (2)
    见鬼/见鬼2

Fake Bride, Phony Bridegroom
    假凤虚凰
Family 家
Family Portrait 四十不惑
Far Away Love 遥远的爱
Farewell China
    爱在别乡的季节
Farewell My Concubine
    霸王别姬
Father and Son (1954)
    父与子
Father and Son (1981)
    父子情
Fearless 霍元甲
Fight to the Last 热血忠魂
Fighting North and South
    南征北战
Finale in Blood 大闹广昌隆
The Fishermen's Song
    渔光曲
Fist of Fury 精武门
Fist of Legend 精武英雄
Flight of the Red Balloon
    红气球的旅行
Floating Life 浮生
A Flower in the Rainy Night
    看海的日子
Flowers of Shanghai 海上花
The Flying Guillotine 血滴子
The Founding of the Republic
    建国大业
Full Moon in New York
    人在纽约

Game of Death 死亡游戏
Gen X Cops 特警新人类
Gen Y Cops 特警新人类2
The Goddess 神女
Golden Gate Girl 金门女
Golden Swallow 金燕子
Goodbye Dragon Inn 不散
Good Morning, Taipei
    早安台北
A Great Wall 北京故事

Green Tea 绿茶
Growing Up 小毕的故事
Guerrillas on the Plains
　　平原游击队
The Guiding Light 苦海明灯

The Happening 夜车
Happy Times 幸福时光
Happy Together 春光乍洩
Hardboiled 辣手神探
Head of the Street, End of
　　the Lane 街头巷尾
Heart with a Million Knots
　　心有千千结
The Heavenly Kings 四大天王
Heavenly Spring Dream
　　天堂春梦
Her Fatal Ways
　　表姐,你好野!
Hero 英雄
Hero in the Bandits' Den
　　英雄虎胆
Heroes and Martyrs of the
　　Great Lake 大湖英烈
Heroes Two 方世玉与洪熙官
Heroic Driver 英雄司机
The Highway 大路
Ho Yuk: Let's Love Hong
　　Kong 好郁
Hold You Tight 愈快乐愈堕落
The Hole 洞
Hollywood Hong Kong
　　香港有个荷里活
Home Sweet Home 家在台北
Homecoming 似水流年
Hong Kong Hollywood
　　香港有个荷里活
The Horse Thief 盗马贼
House of 72 Tenants
　　七十二家房客
House of Flying Daggers
　　十面埋伏
How Are You Dad?
　　爸你好吗?
Husband and Wife
　　我们夫妇之间

I Don't Want Sleep Alone
　　黑眼圈

I Love Beijing 夏日暖洋洋
The Idiot's Wedding Night
　　傻仔洞房
Illegal Immigrant 非法移民
In the Face of Demolition
　　危楼春晓
In the Heat of the Sun
　　阳光灿烂的日子
In Our Time 光阴的故事
Inexhaustible Potential
　　无穷的潜力
Infernal Affairs 无间道
Infernal Affairs II 无间道II
Infernal Affairs III
　　无间道III: 终极无间
Initial D 头文字D
Innocent 只爱陌生人

Ju Dou 菊豆
Jump 跳出去
Just Like Weather 美国心

Keep Cool 有话好好说
King of Chess 棋王
King of the Children 孩子王
The Knot 云水谣
Kung Fu Hustle 功夫

The Last Aristocrats
　　最后的贵族
Legendary Weapons of China
　　十八般武艺
Lei Feng 雷锋
Li Shizhen 李时珍
Li Shuangshuang 李双双
The Lifeline 生命线
The Life of Wu Xun 武训传
The Light of East Asia
　　东亚之光
The Lin Family Shop
　　林家铺子
Lin Zexu 林则徐
Little Angel 小天使
Little Big Soldier 大兵小将
Little Cheung 细路祥
Liu Hulan 刘胡兰
Liu Sanjie 刘三姐
The Long Arm of the Law
　　省港旗兵

The Longest Summer
　　去年烟花特别多
Love Unto Waste 地下情
Lust, Caution 色戒

Made in Hong Kong 香港制造
The Magnificent Trio
　　边城三侠
Mama 妈妈
The Man From Hong Kong
　　直捣黄龙
Map of Sex and Love
　　情色地图
March of the Guerrillas/
　　Ode to Justice
　　游击进行曲/正气歌
The Marriage Certificate
　　谁说我不在乎
The Martial Club 武馆
Martial Law 过江龙
The Master of the Flying Guillotine
　　独臂拳王大破血滴子
Me and My Classmates
　　我和我的同学
The Medallion 飞龙再生
The Men from the Monastery
　　少林子弟
Millennium Mambo
　　千禧曼波
Miracles 奇迹
Monkey Goes West 西游记
Mulan 花木兰
Mulan Joins the Army
　　木兰从军
My American Grandson
　　上海假期
My Love Comes Too Late
　　郎归晚
My Motherland 白云故乡
Myriad of Lights 万家灯火
The Myth 神话

The New Peach Blossom Fan
　　新桃花扇
New Police Story 新警察故事
New Woman 新女性
New Year Sacrifice 祝福
Nie Er 聂耳
Night Corridor 妖夜回廊

Nomad 烈火青春
The Northwest Frontline
　　西北线上

Old Well 老井
One and Eight 一个和八个
The One Armed Boxer
　　独臂拳王
The One Armed Swordsman
　　独臂刀
One Night in Mongkok
　　旺角黑夜
Once Upon a Time in China
　　黄飞鸿
Once Upon a Time in China 2
　　黄飞鸿之二男儿当自强
Once Upon a Time in China 3
　　黄飞鸿之三狮王争霸
Once Upon a Time In China 4
　　黄飞鸿之四王者之风
Once Upon a Time In China 5
　　黄飞鸿之五龙城歼八霸
The Opium War 鸦片战争
Orphan of Anyang
　　安阳的孤儿
Orphan Island Paradise
　　孤岛天堂
Oyster Girls 蚵女

Papa, Can You Hear Me Sing?
　　搭错车
Parents' Hearts 父母心
Perhaps Love 如果爱
Ping Pong Playa 乒乓小子
Pirated Copy 蔓延
Platform 站台
Platoon Commander Guan
　　关连长
Plunder of Peach and Plum
　　桃李劫
Poetic Times 失意的年代
The Postman 邮差
Princess D 想飞
The Promise 无极
Promising Miss Bowie 祝福
Protect Our Home
　　保卫我们的土地
Protégé 门徒
Public Toilet 人民公厕

The Puppetmaster 戏梦人生
Purple Storm 紫雨风暴
Pushing Hands 推手

Raise the Red Lantern
　　大红灯笼高高挂
Rebels of the Neon God
　　青少年哪吒
Red Beads 悬恋
Red Cliff 赤壁
Red Crag 烈火中永生
The Red Detachment of
　　Women 红色娘子军
Red Dust 滚滚红尘
Remorse in Shanghai
　　春江遗恨
Resistance 抵抗
Resistance Cartoons
　　抗战标语卡通
Return of the One Armed
　　Swordsman 独臂刀王
Returning from the
　　Battlefield 战地归来
Reunion/People Between Two
　　Chinas 海峡两岸
Rice Rhapsody 海南鸡饭
The River 河流
The Roar of the Nation
　　民族的怒吼
Rumble in the Bronx 红番区

Sable Cicada 貂蝉
Samsara 轮回
The Sandwich Man
　　儿子的大玩偶
Satisfied or Not 满意不满意
Saving Face 面子
Scenes of City Life 都市风光
Scenes of Yan'an 延安内貌
Security Unlimited 摩登保镖
Sentinels under the Neon Lights
　　霓虹灯下的哨兵
Seven Swords 七剑
Seventeen Years 过年回家
Serfs 农奴
Shanghai Triad
　　摇啊摇,摇到外婆桥
Shaolin Avengers
　　方世玉与胡惠乾

Shaolin Soccer 少林足球
Shaolin Temple 少林寺
Shinjuku Incident 新宿事件
Shooting in the Dark
　　暗夜枪声
Shower 洗澡
Siao Yu 少女小渔
A Sight 一声叹息
Sing-Song Red Peony
　　歌女红牡丹
The Sisters 姊妹花
Sisters Stand Up
　　姐姐妹妹站起来
The Sky Rider 长空万里
Snake in the Eagle's Shadow
　　蛇形刁手
Song at Midnight 夜半歌声
Song of the Exile 客途秋恨
Song of Youth 青春之歌
Sons and Daughters of the
　　World 世界儿女
Sorry Baby 没完没了
Soundless Wind Chime
　　无声风铃
Special Newsreel on Resistance
　　抗战特辑
Spicy Love Soup 爱情麻辣烫
The Spirits are Worthless
　　神鬼不灵
Spring 春
Spring in a Small Town
　　小城之春
A Spring River Flows East
　　一江春水向东流
Spring Subway
　　开往春天的地铁
Stage Sisters 舞台姐妹
Still Life 三峡好人
Storm over Mongolia
　　塞上风云
Storm Warriors 风云 Ⅱ
The Story of Woo Viet
　　胡越的故事
Streets and Alleys 街头巷尾
Street Angels 马路天使
Sunshine and Rain 太阳雨
Suzhou River 苏州河

Taipei Story 青梅竹马

Tears of the Pearl River
  珠江泪
Tempting Heart 心动
Temptress Moon 风月
Terrorisers 恐怖分子
This Whole Life of Mine
  我这一的辈子
Three Kingdoms: Resurrection of
  the Dragon 三国之见龙卸甲
Three Times 最好的时光
Three Women 丽人行
Time to Live, Time to Die
  童年往事
To Live 活着
Together 和你在一起
Tongs, A Chinatown Story
  堂口故事
The Treasure Hunters 刺陵
A Tree in House 没事偷着乐
True Legend 苏乞儿

The True Story of Ah Q 阿Q正传
Twelve Wives 金屋十二钗
Twin Sisters from the South
  南国姊妹花

Unending Emotions 不了情
Unfinished Comedy
  未完成的喜剧
Unknown Pleasures 任逍遥
The Urgent Letter 鸡毛信

Vive l'amour 爱情万岁

The Warlords 投名状
The Way of the Dragon
  猛龙过江
The Way We Are
  天水围的日与夜
The Wayward Cloud
  天边一朵云

The Wedding Banquet 喜宴
What Time Is It There?
  你那边几点?
White Gold Dragon 白金龙
The White Haired Girl
  白毛女
The Wicked City 妖兽都市
Wild Flowers 野草闲花
Woman Basketball Player
  No 5 女篮五号
Women Side by Side 丽人行
The World 世界
Xiao Wu 小武

Yamaha Fish Stall
  雅马哈鱼档
Yan'an and the Eighth Route
  Army 延安与八路军
Yellow Earth 黄土地
The Young Master 师弟出马

Index

List of Illustrations

Hero, © Elite Group Enterprises; *Still Life*, © Xstream Pictures Limited; *The Life of Wu Xun*, Kunlun Film Company; *The White-Haired Girl*, North-East Film Studio; *Bodyguards and Assassins*, Cinema Popular/We Pictures; *Song of the Exile*, Cos Films Company/Central Motion Picture Corporation; *Chan is Missing*, Wayne Wang Productions; *Happy Together*, Jet Tone Production/Block 2 Pictures/Prenom H Co. Ltd/Seawoo Film Co. Ltd; *Café Lumière*, © Shochiku Co. Ltd/© Asahi Shimbun Company/© Sumitomo Corporation/© Eisei Gekijo/© Imagica; *What Time Is It There?*, © Aréna Films/Arte France Cinéma; *Flight of the Red Balloon*, © 3H Productions/© Margofilms/© Films du Lendemain; *Plunder of Peach and Plum*, Diantong Film Company; *Street Angels*, Mingxing Film Company; *Crossroads*, Mingxing Film Company; *Eight Hundred Heroes*, Central Motion Pictures Corporation; *Light of East Asia*, China Motion Pictures Corporation; *Storm Over Mongolia*, China Motion Pictures Corporation; *Mulan Joins the Army*, Huacheng Film Company; *Far Away Love*, Xi'an Film Studio; *A Spring River Flows East*, Lianhua Film Company/Kunlun Film Company/Peak Film Industries Corporation; *Streets and Alleys*, Independence; *New Year Sacrifice*, Beijing Film Studio; *This Whole Life of Mine*, Wenhua Film Company; *Stage Sisters*, Tianma Film Studio; *Before the New Director Arrives*, Changchun Film Studio; *Beautiful Duckling*, Central Motion Pictures Corporation; *Home Sweet Home*, Central Motion Pictures Corporation; *House of 72 Tenants*, Shaw Brothers; *Yellow Earth*, Guangxi Film Studio; *Red Sorghum*, Xi'an Film Studio; *King of the Children*, Xi'an Film Studio; *Yi Yi*, © 1+2 Seisaku Iinkai; *Three Times*, SinoMovie.com/Paradis Films/Orly Films; *King of Chess*, Golden Princess Film Productions/Film Workshop Co. Ltd; *Love Unto Waste*, Pearl City; *Enter the Dragon*, Warner Bros./Concord Productions; *The Man from Hong Kong*, Movie Comany/Golden Harvest; *Crouching Tiger, Hidden Dragon*, © United China Vision Incorporated/UCV LLC; *The Forbidden Kingdom*, © J&J Project LLC; *The Wayward Cloud*, © Aréna Films/Homegreen Films/Arte France Cinéma; *The Hole*, Haut et Court/Arc Light Films; *Hollywood Hong Kong*, Movement Pictures/Media Suits/Nicetop Independent; *Public Toilet*, Nicetop Independent; *Mama*, Xi'an Film Studio; *Beijing Bastards*, Beijing Bastards Group; *Xiao Wu*, © Radiant Advertising Company/Hu Tong Communications; *Unknown Pleasures*, © Office Kitano/© Lumen Film/© E-Pictures; *Blush*, Beijing Film Studio; *Crazy Stone*, Beijing Frontline Productions/Concord Creation International/Warner China Film/Focus Films; *Shower*, Xi'an Film Studio; *Assembly*, © Huayi Brothers Media & Co. Ltd/© Media Asia Films (BVI) Ltd.